Globalization and Catholic Social Thought

Globalization and Catholic Social Thought

Present Crisis, Future Hope

Edited by John A. Coleman, S.J.
and William F. Ryan, S.J.

Maryknoll, New York 10545

Cover design: Christiane Lemire
Cover image: Ingram
Layout: Caroline Galhidi

Business Office:
Novalis
49 Front Street East, 2nd Floor
Toronto, Ontario, Canada
M5E 1B3
Phone: 1-800-387-7164
Fax: 1-800-204-4140
E-mail: cservice@novalis-inc.com
www.novalis.ca

Library and Archives Canada Cataloguing in Publication
BX1753.G56 2005 261.8'088'282 C2005-904690-2
ISBN 2-89507-602-2

First published in the United States by Orbis Books, Maryknoll, New York 10545-0308.
Phone: 1-800-258-5838
Fax: 1-914-941-7005
E-mail: orbisbooks@maryknoll.org
www.maryknoll.org

Library of Congress Cataloging-in-Publication Data
BX1753.G54 2005 261.7--dc22 2005021943
ISBN: 1-57075-608-2 (pbk.)

Printed in Canada.

We acknowledge the financial support of the Government of Canada through the Book Publishing Industry Development Program (BPIDP) for our publishing activities.

5 4 3 2 1 09 08 07 06 05

Contents

Preface

This volume stems, in most part, from an initiative by my co-editor, Bill Ryan S.J. He saw the need to bring together a group of academicians and social advocates that would probe the resources of Catholic Social Thought (CST) to understand, reform, and guide globalization. On the one hand, Ryan feared the new caution that is showing up in episcopal social pronouncements. This turn to a focus on interior church issues – which eclipses the need for a bold, credible, and consistent ecclesial call for justice in an emerging world order (or disorder, as it may become) – contains both promise and peril and lacks sufficient Catholic reflection. Moreover, CST needed a new injection to help it penetrate more effectively into the pews and the hearts and minds of the laity. Thus a seminar was co-planned by Ryan and me, and the we agreed to co-edit the volume that would result from the seminar.

Bill Ryan was able to raise funds, in part through the Canadian Jesuit province's Jesuit Centre for Social Faith and Justice, to bring together an international group of 27 scholars at Guelph, Ontario, in September 2003. We are also grateful to the Jesuit General Superior, Hans Kolvenbach S.J., and to Canadian Bishops John Sherlock, Fred Henry, and Ronald Fabbro CSB for their support and generous financial help for the seminar and this book. With the exception of Peter Henriot's chapter on Africa and globalization, those who attended the seminar wrote all of the essays in this volume.[1]

The seminar was rich, stimulating, and exciting far beyond our initial expectations and hopes. I am aware, however, that trying to convey the collective effervescence of a meeting to those who were not there may not be worthwhile. Some experiences cannot be duplicated for those who were absent. I must note, at least, that the success of the seminar turned largely on the fact that maximum participation of all around the table was facilitated by the hour or more given to discussion after the brief presentation of each draft paper.

A number of participants at the seminar deeply enriched the conversation but they did not write essays for this volume. A French Canadian, Jean-Marc Biron S.J., the director of the Jesuit review *Relations,* brought a perspective from French-speaking Canada. Yvon Elenga S.J., a West African, now studying for his doctorate at the Weston School of Theology in Boston, engaged knowingly on issues of regionalization and globalization in Africa. Bishop Fred Henry, the Bishop of

Calgary, Alberta, and Joe Gunn, Director of the Social Affairs Department of the Canadian Conference of Catholic Bishops (CCCB), anchored for us the process and perspective of more official Catholic teaching (its value and limits). Heather Eaton, who advises the CCCB's Social Affairs Department, brought a feminist and ecological perspective. Many of us have read with profit her recent book, *Ecofeminism and Globalization: Exploring Culture, Context and Religion* (Rowman and Littlefield, 2003). Eaton and Gunn had just finished preparing a Canadian bishops' document on ecology for release on the feast of St. Francis of Assisi and reminded us of the pressing need for communication with people in the pews.

Other important participants included Jim Profit S.J., coordinator of the Guelph office of the Jesuit Centre for Social Faith and Justice and director of the Guelph organic farm, who served as a host and a resource on how globalization has affected agriculture. Peggy Steinfels, the editor of *Commonweal*; Gordon Rixon S.J., a theologian at Regis College, Toronto; James Stormes S.J., the Director of the Secretariat for Social and International Ministries of the United States Jesuit Conference; and long-time writer and journalist Bernard Daly[2] all took vigorous part in the dialogue. Peter Bisson S.J. – a theologian from Campion College, the University of Saskatchewan in Regina – served us well as recorder and gave continuing feedback to us on the themes that were emerging, converging, or in tension. Brother Art White S.J. served as secretary to the seminar meetings and also cared for our material needs.

We came away from Guelph convinced that our conversation needed to bear richer fruit in the form of a book, and from that experience this volume has been written. We are also most grateful to Father Jack Costello S.J., director of the Jesuit Centre for Social Faith and Justice in Canada; besides being an active participant, he helped to raise the funds needed to finance the seminar.

John A. Coleman S.J.

1

Making the Connections: Globalization and Catholic Social Thought

John A. Coleman S.J.

The preface to this book describes the larger seminar that led to this volume. The originating idea was to get a conversation going that was enriched by both male and female voices. This is important because of the key role feminism plays in ecological movements and as a global movement in its own right; additionally, in some places Catholic Social Thought (CST) seems in tension with elements of feminism. Also important were the participants from a number of cultures and language groups; they provided input on the different emphases of globalization in Africa, Asia, and Latin America, as well as in Europe and North America. Another important aspect of this conference was the conversation across different disciplines of theology, philosophy, sociology, political science, economics, and history. The common denominator was a keen sense that globalization represents both peril and promise to our world and that CST has resources to engage the hopes and fears brought forth by globalization. We are convinced that the conversation we begin in this book, making connections between globalization and CST, needs to continue, to be refined and put into action in many venues. These venues include the pews of our parishes, study groups, student advocacy circles, and Catholic peace and justice networks.

This introductory chapter deals with four major themes: (1) a delineation of globalization, (2) a brief introduction and review of the resources of CST, (3) a look at the effect of globalization on Roman Catholicism itself and on its capacities to respond, and (4) a presentation of the outline for the book.

I. Globalization Delineated and Situated

In his 1999 Director's Lectures on globalization at the London School of Economics, sociologist Anthony Giddens remarked, trenchantly, that in his view, no one could be a practising social scientist of any minimal sophistication if they did not grasp the globalization debate. For Giddens, this debate is by far the most significant and disputatious discourse now occurring in our world. It confronts us with a world not firmly under our control, says Giddens, but one which seems "to be an erratic, dislocated world, if you like, a runaway world."[1] For the authors of this volume, globalization – that much vaunted if variously defined term – names a phenomenon that is real, urgent, and in many respects new and unsettling. Further, CST, if it is to serve as a resource of some sophistication and wisdom, must use its rich intellectual tradition of root metaphors about human life and ethical principles to position itself, effectively and humanely, in the debates and advocacy about the direction of globalization.

Yet it becomes exceedingly difficult to take a neutral stance about a process that is still contested in a world that, in the words of Harvard International Relations expert Robert Keohane, remains only "a partially globalized world."[2] I have recently spent six months at the University of California, Santa Barbara, whose Center for Global Studies speaks easily about globalizations – using the plural! There are fiercely competing hopes and fears about our global society. Globalization seems to divide as much as it unites. In the short run, there are both winners and losers. Losers in this global gamble can experience the loss of security about the most basic human needs, undergo identity dislocation, suffer humiliation and loss of dignity, face uncompensated mass resettlement to make way for a new dam, or find their job suddenly and irretrievably outsourced.

Sociologist Roland Robertson has famously insisted that the essence of globalization lies in its simultaneous compound effect of producing both differentiation and homogenization, which is a universalizing trend, and also in attempts to reinvent and reassert the local. Robertson coins the inelegant word "glocal" to indicate that the advancing process of globalization will likely foment the resistance of more nationalistic and ethnic groups. It may also bring the repressive suppression (by governments, intergovernmental organizations such as the International Monetary Fund [IMF], or overreaching multinational corporations) of vibrant varieties of localism. So-called anti-globalization movements may, paradoxically, eagerly anticipate an alternative form of globalization. "Another world is possible" runs the slogan.[3] Globalization involves perilous risks. Even now our society is increasingly interdependent. The spillover effects from weapons of mass destruction, genetically modified crops, terrorism, global crime, climate changes, and new diseases such as SARS affect us all. Additionally, the loss of forests, water pollution, the depletion of the fishing stock in the global commons of the ocean, and the Asian financial crisis all leave residues on and in our own terrain. Yet globalization also presents immense opportunities: the vision of a global commons, a shared sense of the *humanum*, and promises of improved economics and health.

Starkly differing projects of globalization exist. David Korten paints the neo-liberal project for us in his anti–neo-liberal book *When Corporations Rule the World*. He sees it as an attempt "to integrate the world's national economies into a single borderless global economy in which the world's mega-corporations are free to move goods and money anywhere in the world that affords an opportunity for profit, without governmental interference. In the name of increased efficiency, the alliance seeks to privatize public services."[4] British sociologist Zygmunt Bauman echoes Korten's unmasking of certain crass elements in the rhetoric of globalization: "Robbing whole nations of their resources is called promotion of 'free trade'; robbing whole families and communities of their livelihood is called 'downsizing' or just 'rationalization'."[5]

Quite different, and in exact opposition, is the project of the World Social Forum that convenes popular movements and non-governmental organizations (NGOs) (including representatives from Brazilian Catholic agencies) with the hope of meeting basic human needs, reducing poverty, and guaranteeing the rights of indigenous people. It also strives to encourage citizen involvement in government and champions a program of disclosure, transparency, and accountability for inter-governmental agencies (IGOs), such as the World Bank and the IMF.[6] The *New York Times* columnist Thomas Friedman can exalt market liberalization as inherently benign and contend, in his whimsical golden arch theory, that "no two countries that both have a McDonald's have ever fought a war against each other since they each got their McDonald's."[7] Princeton political scientist Richard Falk, on the other hand, speaks forthrightly of a kind of predatory globalization.[8] Still others seek to contain the harmful initial effects of globalization and bring in reforms around a six-fold strategy: (1) containing negative globalization; (2) mitigating anarchic responses to globalization; (3) promoting new forms of global governance and functional regulating regimes; (4) expanding civil society input and access to inter-governmental organizations, such as the IMF; (5) linking globalization to democratization; and (6) working for codes of ethics for multinational corporations.[9] This volume does not include any neo-liberals, but some voices are more reformist and others more resistant to globalization.

A precise definition of globalization – an inherently contested process involving power and wealth rearrangements and proposed alternatives that harbour starkly competing definitions of justice – is not practical at this time. Yet this phenomenon must, at least, be delineated and situated to enable viable debates concerning globalization. It might be helpful to pay less attention at the beginning to what we hope to gain or lose from globalization. Do we want to increase it, tame it, resist it, reform it, or find global alternatives to it? Do we expect to gain greater integration of the world and expanded economic opportunities? Or do we expect to lose livelihoods, and experience creeping desertification of the land, homogenization of world culture, and a dumbing down to a consumerist, pop culture? Instead, it might be better to pose an alternative question: what seems to be happening to all of us, whatever our stance or normative judgment on the causes, costs, price, and benefits of globalization?

Let me venture a few helpful descriptions of the phenomenon we confront together:

> Globalization denotes a process in the course of which the volume and intensity of trans-boundary transportation, communication and trade relations are rapidly increasing. It is undermining the divisive connotations

> of national boundaries and intensifying the impacts of border crossing economic, social and political activities for national societies. Many pressing problems cut across territorial boundaries. More and more events are simultaneously perceived throughout the world, making themselves felt with increasingly brief delays in more and more places.[10]

The empirical data seem to indicate that this process is occurring. Trade and travel between nations increased four-fold between 1980 and 2000. The number of students who take part in studies-abroad programs continues to grow. Four hundred billion dollars in cross-border currency now change hands every six hours; more money passes in these exchanges in just six hours than was ever dispersed by the World Bank in its 50-year history. The number of migrants working in countries other than their own has grown; it is now roughly 30 million (legally admitted) and the estimates are that more than twice that number are non-documented cross-border workers. Refugees greatly inflate, again, these numbers. Remittances from migrant workers to relatives back home have also increased dramatically: three billion dollars a year pour back to India in this form and an equal three billion dollars yearly flow to Mexico, just from Mexican migrants in California. For some countries, such migrant remittances are their largest source of foreign investment. Indeed, in some countries (such as the Philippines), we can now speak of a globalized family system with family members working in places such as Saudi Arabia, Ireland, and the United States.

A boom in international NGOs has occurred. Some 50,000 NGOs are active at the global level (a 90 per cent increase since 1970: see Scott Appleby's chapter in this volume). Increasingly, scientific research projects involve international teams. Transboundary issues often elude any single national solution. These include the drug and private arms trade, arms control, terrorism, money laundering, pollution, refugees, common heritage issues concerning the ocean and its mineral and fish resources, and the atmosphere. Simultaneous and related problems across national borders concern population pressures and health and infectious diseases.

Globalization has been driven both by a self-conscious projection of the economic integration of a world market and by technology, especially information technology. The Internet serves multinational corporations, scientists and scholars, crime syndicates (such as the increasingly international forms of Russian, Italian, Colombian, and East Asian cartels that deal in drugs, smuggling, and the sex trade), reformers, and human rights and environmental moral entrepreneurs. Globalization, like God's sun, seems to shine on the good and the bad alike. The Internet played a decisive role in the international anti-personnel land-mine treaty, the World Commission on Dams, and the effective torpedoing by NGOs of the proposed Multi-lateral Agreement on Investment. The Internet also helped in the boycott of Nestlé's unhealthy marketing of baby formula in the Third World and – it can now be strongly asserted – in the fall of Communism.[11] New global financial rules combined with the Internet are a money launderer's or a porn and drug addict's dream.

Globalization has been as much a communications revolution as an economic one. Roland Robertson speaks of globalization as entailing a "rapidly increasing global connectivity on the one hand and fast expanding and intensifying reflexive global consciousness, on the other."[12] We have increasingly become a community of common fate and responsibility – if not a global village then a spaceship earth. Even if the neo-liberal project of economic integration were to fall into stasis or were abandoned, globalization would not cease to be a real issue because of travel, television, global warming, the Internet, pop culture, terrorism, and infectious diseases.

Globalization (mainly through electronic technical revolutions) acutely compresses time and space. Computer experts in California's Silicon Valley pick up the same work done through the night by their counterparts in India. The sun also never sets in this new globalized empire. We may not have seen the proclaimed end of history but, just perhaps, globalization is displaying the new end of geography. Geography as distance is eclipsed, although it remains important when we think of it as a home, as our land, and as the source of climate and resources.

Globalization has both positive and negative effects. The positive effects of globalization include increased consciousness of being one world. Information is also more democratically available, and human rights language now permeates a wider global consciousness.

Among the alleged negative effects of globalization is its insensitivity to human suffering – a strong theme in Fernando Franco's essay in this volume with his haunting remark that, in India, globalization will always be remembered by its victims. Globalization will not be remembered for the new proliferating cybertech and biotech companies in India or as a blissful transition to a higher stage in humanity's life, but as a time of traumatic political and economic changes. A second negative effect involves the inattention (by multinational corporations in extractive industries) to ecological sustainability, although there is now strong evidence that ecologists are among the most effective NGOs as they combat environmental deterioration.[13]

A third negative effect entails polarization (both political and economic as well as in terms of life chances) between and within cultures. The gap between the poorest and richest nations has been growing, not declining. The inequalities even within sectors of the developed world have been growing.[14] There is an immense Internet gap between the rich and the poor. The facts, once again, are glaring: less than one per cent of Africans have ever used the Internet and Tokyo has more telephones than all of Africa. Forty per cent of Latin Americans still cannot read or write. As Canadian social scientist Pierre Hamel writes: "Uneven development trails globalization like a shadow.... The buzzword is globalization but we inhabit a divided world."[15] We may dream about some global unified cosmos but we do not now live in this cosmos. A strong fear is that the poorest countries of the world (and, in the case of Africa, entire world regions) will become marginalized in the process, so that there will be both greater world integration and lost societies that are almost completely left out in a kind of globalized apartheid.

Finally, people fear an erosion in the abilities of states to provide for societal needs, as traditionally expected of the state. These are physical security (especially in the growing number of failed states – an issue raised in Bryan Hehir's chapter in this volume), economic welfare and opportunities for human betterment, a social safety net, and distributive justice. As we will see, states remain indispensable actors if globalization is to be civilized and humanized. But, as Wolfgang Reinicke, Director of the UN Vision unit on Global Public Policy and Senior Partner and Economist in the Corporate Strategy Group of the World Bank, writes: "Forces of globalization confound and complicate traditional governance structures, challenging the operational capacity and democratic responsiveness of governments."[16]

Change in our social and economic realities has outpaced change in the political institutions and processes that once firmly embedded them. One other working definition of globalization might help here:

> Globalization, simply put, denotes the expanding scale, growing magnitude, speeding up and deepening impact of trans-continental flows and patterns of social interaction. It refers to a shift or transformation in the scale of human organization that links distant communities and expands the reach of power relations across the world's regions and continents. But it should not be read as pre-figuring the emergence of a harmonious world society or as a universal process of global integration in which there is a growing convergence of cultures and civilizations. For not only does the awareness of growing inter-connectedness create new animosities and conflicts, it can fuel reactionary politics and deep-seated xenophobia. Since a substantial proportion of the world's population is largely excluded from the benefits of globalization, it is a deeply divisive and, consequently, vigorously contested process. The unevenness of globalization ensures it is far from a universal process experienced uniformly across the entire planet.[17]

We may not be able to agree on a precise definition of globalization but few can doubt that globalization is, empirically, a real phenomenon. "There is no commonly held definition [of globalization], let alone a comprehensive conceptual framework, that would enable decision makers to consider the possible implications of globalization for public policy."[18] Yet there is abundant empirical evidence that, in some real sense, individuals, corporations, NGOs, and nation-states seem to be able to reach around the world farther, faster, deeper, and cheaper than ever before. Few can also doubt that new global units or actors – IGOs such as the World Trade Organization (WTO), and NGOs such as Doctors Without Borders, Amnesty International, Transparency International, and Greenpeace – have grown quickly and changed many of the perceived rules of the game for economics, geopolitics, ecology, and individuals.

The key issue becomes this: how do we humanize globalization and make it serve our habitat and humanity? We need to bring about an ethical and just world order with an economy that serves people. We might judge the process of globalization, as we see it unfolding, to be simply incapable of reform or redemption. How do we effectively resist its inhuman or cruel consequences and what do we propose in its place? To the pressing question, "Is the earth still governable?" the empirical facts of globalization – whatever one's varying definition or project for it – force the answer: clearly not by the old rules or with the old cast of characters. Multilateralism is the new game since no one nation – not even the dominant US – can address and solve by itself the transborder issues of poverty, illness, global security, crime, terrorism, financial stability, secure health, and ecological degradation.[19]

II. Catholic Social Thought and Globalization

Catholic Social Thought is both older and broader than the papal social encyclicals, which began with Leo XIII's encyclical on the labour movement, *Rerum Novarum*, in 1891. It includes, as well, a panoply of regional and national episcopal documents and pronouncements on social issues that have been issued by episcopal conferences in Europe, Canada, the US, Zambia, Brazil, Chile, and the Philippines. These social issues include full employment, inflation, Third-World development and debt, the death penalty, just war, the environment, and the family.[20] Catholic reflection on what it means to be authentically human in history and culture began in the second and third century with the fathers of the Church. This continued with Augustine, Aquinas, and the Spanish Scholastics (Suarez and Vittoria who helped forge the first rudiments of an international law). This concern includes an immersion in a web of relationships that are continuously connected with work, family, the economy, civil society, and the state. It should not be surprising that all of our authors in this volume feel that this tradition can offer much wisdom as they address the new issues of globalization.

Official documents are not the only, or even the richest, source of Catholic social teaching. Catholic institutions, think-tanks, and what are in effect religious NGOs (both national and international) around the world engage in lobbying on special issues; mount protests against injustices; provide social and humanitarian relief; and imagine an alternative world of peace and justice. Pax Christi, Catholic Charities USA, or Catholic Relief Services are, in this sense, as much a part of CST as are the official documents. This is especially the case if we take with some seriousness the remarks of Pope John Paul II that social Catholicism is found not just in social doctrine but "in her concrete commitment and material assistance in the struggle against marginalization and suffering."[21]

While authors differ on the precise number and exact terminology they use for the core social principles of Catholicism, these key social principles tend to boil down to the following eight. At the risk of a pedestrian review of what many may already know, I delineate them briefly here to show the apparatus that CST brings to globalization debates.

(1) *Human Dignity*: Every human person (believer or not) has been fashioned in the image and likeness of God and is called to be an artisan and co-creator of society and culture. Related to this seminal notion of human dignity is the rich sense of human rights (enumerated in a number of social encyclicals but principally in *Pacem in Terris*). Catholic human rights theory differs from a purely liberal theory in insisting on an important set of social and economic rights. This includes what are called positive rights to satisfy basic needs and encourage prosperity and not just the negative rights to liberty from coercion and state restraints. Social Catholicism also closely links rights to responsibilities because of the social embeddedness of human dignity. We are radically and not just incidentally interdependent beings.[22]

(2) *The Social Nature of the Human*: CST embraces a species of communitarian liberalism. Human rights entail fundamental liberties to facilitate effective human agency. But social Catholicism nurtures a strongly social sense of the human as a creature that is deeply embedded in families, associations, culture, and civil and economic organizations. As Catholic philosopher Alasdair MacIntyre expresses it, the human is a dependent and interdependent, rational, and symbol-using animal.[23] As created in the image of the Trinitarian God, the human is called to become what God is: a relational node and person within a society of persons. Humans are to be a communion that reflects and honours legitimate diversities. Catholic support for the rights to one's own culture and language flow from this Trinitarian grounded social sense of diversity as a good, in itself, that should be nurtured within the unity of society.

(3) *The Common Good*: CST espouses the notion that the common good is central to the good society, a well-functioning state, and international order. Lisa Cahill's essay in this volume shows how this concept of the common good can be indispensable in debates about globalization. The common good can be defined as a state of the system – the sum total of appropriate institutional arrangements that guarantee, enable, and facilitate human flourishing. This Catholic notion of the common good embraces a subordinate idea that at least some goods are public goods. It endorses, therefore, the priority of a common possession of the goods of the earth over a legitimate, but derivative, right to private property. As Pope John Paul II frequently re-iterated, "There is a social mortgage on private property." To be sure, the state has an important role to play in defining and promoting the common good, although it has no monopoly on either the definition or embodiment. The notion of the common good pushes Catholicism away from overly restrictive concepts of a minimal caretaker state. The state has positive responsibilities to care for justice, security, equal opportunity, minimal welfare for all, and social peace. The societal community, in this view, becomes an overarching and encompassing value into which the economy, the police, and autonomous organizations of civil society need to be situated. Catholics also espouse a robust ideal of an international common good.[24]

(4) *Subsidiarity*: The Catholic concept of subsidiarity includes a theory of societal pluralism, envisioning a civil society that does not totally depend on or

derive from the state its authoritative actions and power. Subsidiarity states that higher forms of governance must not co-opt or dissipate the proper roles of more local units. Catholicism assumes, for example, that the ultimate source or authority for the Church and the family comes directly from God, not just from the good graces of the state. Moreover, subsidiarity presumes that the local and grassroots are, ultimately, an important source of creativity and rooted wisdom. Other non-state organizations (such as labour unions, commercial associations, and voluntary groups for civic betterment) also receive their founding charter directly from the radically social nature of the human. Subsidiarity warns against overly distant bureaucracies (the national state and IGOs such as the WTO) swallowing up or too deeply curtailing local and associated activity in free public spaces. A corollary of subsidiarity is the affirmation of the limited state (or *pari passu*, which is a limited sovereignty for the emerging arena of IGOs). Clearly, subsidiarity would enter as an element in any discussion about the increase or design of new, more global, governance.[25]

(5) *Solidarity*: An account of the Catholic moral virtue of solidarity can be found in John Paul II's important encyclical *Sollicitudo Rei Socialis* #40 ff. This virtue stems from the radically interdependent social nature of the human ("no man [or woman] is an island, sufficient unto him[her]self") and also from a strong notion of the common good. Solidarity assumes that humans have real, pressing imperfect obligations (in Kant's sense of that term) to come to the aid and support of others, even when these others do not, strictly, have formal and explicit rights to such succour and aid.[26] John Paul II, for example, repeatedly remarked that "it is necessary to globalize solidarity, too." Solidarity is closely aligned with the next principle, the preferential option for the poor.

(6) *The Preferential Option for the Poor*: Catholicism privileges those who lack voice and resources and, for example, puts the priority on care for the basic needs of the poor and marginalized instead of advancing the opportunities for the wealthy and privileged. This preferential option for the poor gives CST a bias for the victims of history.[27] Catholicism assumes that taking the side of the poor is not against equal justice but represents a kind of participative justice. This enables the voiceless to have some real chances to weigh more equally in voice and effect. In the realities of power and class, they are most often marginalized as truly equal citizens and decisions about them are made without their input. Ultimately, this principle of preference for the poor has deep theological roots in God and Christ's own preferential identification with the poor. This is seen in the last judgment scene in Matthew 25 and in Jeremiah 22:16 where the prophet says of King Josiah, "He judged the cause of the poor and the needy; then it was well. Is not this to know me? says the Lord."

(7) *Catholic Theories of Justice*: Catholics follow the classic and ancient tri-partite sense of justice: (a) commutative justice is justice based on fulfilling promises and contracts; (b) distributive justice is defined as justice based on a fair allocation of burdens and benefits in society and a guarantee that parties to bargains have some relatively equal weight as moral agents; and (c) social justice,

which is the care for constructing the institutional arrangements that guarantee and enable fair contracts, distributive justice, and the common good. Moreover, recent CST has included a strong statement about justice as participation; this means that human agency and dignity simply demand that people have some genuine voice and input in determining the arrangements of society that shape and determine their lives and opportunity structures. No one can be allowed to become a non-participant or, effectively, a non-person or non-citizen who does not count. In this Catholic scheme of justice, distributive justice can never be limited to a mere contract but includes a legitimate moral claim from human need.

(8) *An Integral Humanism*: Catholicism tends to seek integrations, foster holistic views, and speak of an integral humanism. This view does not reduce the human or allow the economy to be cut off and abstracted from culture, ecology, the society and state, family, and work. In his encyclical about inculturation, *Evangelii Nuntiandi*, Pope Paul VI evoked an "integral liberation" and in his *Populorum Progressio* "an integral development of the person." John Paul II named a related notion of "authentic human development" in *Sollicitudo Rei Socialis* # 4. This typical and congenially Catholic adjective – integral – militates against any one-sided reductionist views of human persons as purely economic (or essentially interest-maximizing) animals and as autonomous choosers simply uprooted from their social relationships, detached from their social, cultural, and linguistic roots. Additionally, human persons are participative subjects or artisans of human social structures, and not objects. Using integral adjectives militates against any causal social science explanatory schemes that are equally reductionist.[28] In his encyclical *Centesimus Annus*, Pope John Paul II claimed that an integral globalization will pay due attention and not divorce its analysis from the six factors he used as a lens to look at the emerging, post–Cold War, and new world order in that encyclical. These six factors are politics, society, economics, culture, the state, and the environment.

Clearly, social Catholicism does not fit nicely with neo-liberal theories of a mainly autonomous economy unrelated to legitimate state regulation for the common good or with libertarian rights for autonomous individuals who are cut off from being embedded in their society and culture. It also does not mesh with overly vigorous statist and communitarian doctrines that deny, stringently restrict, and restrain justice as participation and subsidiarity.

While the authors in this volume differ somewhat on how much they think this framework of social Catholicism needs to be expanded or reconceptualized in the face of globalization, all appeal, in some fashion, to these eight central principles. I, for one, think the major building blocks or components for a vision of integral globalization can be found in a number of CST resources. *Gaudium et Spes:* Introduction and chapters 1-3 is the most fully rounded and theologically grounded presentation of the theological anthropology Catholics bring to issues of the person and society, government and economics, and culture. *Sollicitudo Rei Socialis*, parts 4-5, are important sections on Authentic Human Development and A Theological Reading of Modern Problems. *Centesimus Annus* #25-29 and parts

4-5 deal with economics (including the business firm and the market), culture, and interdependence among nations. Long before the term "globalization" became fashionable, CST had been dealing with a number of key issues on a continuing basis. These included development within the poorer nations, immigration and migration, population growth, the arms race and weapons of mass destruction, war, addressing basic human needs, the right to participation, and the need for new structures to guarantee a global common good. All have now become uppermost in globalization debates.

All of the core ethical elements needed to address issues of an integral globalization from a Catholic theological-moral foundation can be found, in germ at least, in these three documents. Yet, if CST is not only about fixed horizons of ethical orienting principles but also demands a careful reading of the signs of the times – a point Bill Ryan underscores in his concluding chapter, employing a discernment model as suggested by Paul VI in his social letter *Octogesima Adveniens* – then all is not in place for Catholic social teaching to address the new realities of globalization. Ethical principles need to be refined, take on new contours, and be reformulated when they are applied to real-life cases. Discernment expands and nuances principles and does not just deductively apply them. Careful correlation between CST and the new realities of globalization is a task still to be undertaken. Too often, the connection between CST core principles and the more mundane realities of new financial instruments of future derivatives, economic strategies of leveraged buy-outs and mergers, or the proliferation of IGOs and NGOs does not get made. This volume attempts to begin that process of making the connections between globalization and CST.

There is not yet, however – despite various attempts to address it – any truly rounded document on the major salient issues of globalization nor one that addresses the phenomenon as a social process of integration, a breaking down of borders, and a reconceptualization of the state. So, a number of conspicuous lacunae exist in the three documents I mentioned to move this debate about globalization forward. One is the broad issue of global governance. As early as the 1960s, Pope John XXIII in *Pacem in Terris* signalled glaringly unfinished business in this arena. "Under the present circumstances of human society, both the structure and form of governments as well as the power which public authority wields in all the nations of the world must be considered inadequate to promote the universal common good." (*Pacem in Terris* #135). Although this shortcoming is noted, no systematic thought has yet been given to the contours of institutions that might yield a global governance that is not some world government (which would violate, presumably, subsidiarity and constitute a threat to the Catholic sense of a limited government). A second unchartered issue in CST is how it can more adequately address (out of its theories of subsidiarity, justice as participation, and a civil society based on an associational principle rooted in the very social nature of the human and not just the benevolence of the state) the new entities in global society: NGOs and the related IGOs. What are their remit and competence in forging a global common good? Scott Appleby's essay probes this central challenge to CST. A third issue, found in a number of chapters in this book, is CST's need for a more radical approach to ecology. To be sure, as Mary Evelyn Tucker's fine appendix indicates and Joe Holland discusses in his essay in this volume, papal encyclicals (especially *Centesimus Annus*) and thoughtful pastoral letters on ecology by the Canadian and US bishops have brought this important topic more to the centre. But it continues to be seen mainly as a derivative of justice thinking and not addressed squarely as an issue relating to the integrity of God's creation. Even if one clearly distinguishes the human from other creatures, no anthropocentric view does justice to the fullness of God's glory in and through the creation of the whole cosmos that was not created simply for human use. Stewardship does not exhaust the depth of the ecological as a mirror of God's glory. These themes are strong in both Tucker's and Holland's essays. As Bill Ryan notes in his chapter, we need to resituate economic thought within the more encompassing category of ecology – our common habitat. If the environment sinks into degradation, the world economy will collapse.

Another suggestion in this volume to bring the tradition of CST forward to address globalization focused on the need to engage more vigorously in inter-religious consultations and action (a point in Tyndale's and Baum's essays). Johan Verstraeten's chapter in this volume is a plea to anchor CST more firmly in its deep, root, and fundamentally theological metaphors. Other suggestions are to find better ways to translate Catholic discourse on globalization more fully into effective action networks and to motivate and supply a justice-ecology spirituality for lay Catholics. The authors of this volume have some disagreement on a central disputed issue of CST: is CST a theologically grounded ecclesial set of principles or is it a set of principles derived from natural law and available to all men and women of good will?

Finally, a more solid look at the phenomenon of the multinational corporation seems needed. John Paul II, to be sure, addressed business firms in a generic way in *Centesimus Annus*. But the multinational corporation is not just a more extensive venue for trading; it involves a new organizational form of the business firm that has never been systematically addressed by Catholicism. For the purposes of this introduction, it seems to me useful to step back a bit from the current Catholic discourse on globalization to ask: How does globalization affect Catholicism itself? What are its resources (and drawbacks) as it acts globally for a more just and humane economy and world society? I turn now to that important, and insufficiently developed, theme.

III. The Roman Catholic Church as a Global Actor

The Roman Catholic Church is, quintessentially, a transnational actor. As the Welsh political scientist David Ryall puts it: "The church has been involved, as a primary agent and subject of globalization, for at least as long as any other body." Moreover, "In Catholic political culture qualified and pooled sovereignty, transnational structures, subsidiarity and devolution have long been familiar concepts."[29]

Yet, paradoxically, Catholic voices – except on the issue of debt relief for poorer nations as found in the Jubilee 2000 initiative – seem fairly muted on the major globalization campaigns concerning human rights, the environment, transparency, and the women's movement.[30]

I want to broach, in this section, four main topics: (1) the Roman Catholic Church as a transnational actor; (2) how globalization affects the Church; (3) Roman Catholic discourse on globalization; and (4) some limits to the Church's role in the globalization debates.

Patterns of Catholic population increases reflect its global reach. While global population grew 117 per cent in the last half of the twentieth century, Catholics increased by 139 per cent. The fastest growing areas of Catholicism have been in Africa, the Americas, and Asia. In Asia, Catholic population grew 278 per cent, compared to general growth in Asia of 104 per cent. These demographic shifts are increasingly mirrored by more representative proportions of non-Europeans in the College of Cardinals, the Roman Curia, and the college of world bishops. The present number of bishops is 4,541, compared to 2,500 in 1963. The numbers show 14 per cent from Africa, 40 per cent from the Americas, 13 per cent from Asia, 30 per cent from Europe, and 3 per cent from Oceania. In 1950, half of all Catholics lived in Europe. Today, while Europe is 41 per cent Catholic, it represents only 27 per cent of world Catholicism. The Americas are 63 per cent Catholic and now contain half of all Catholics in the world. Hillaire Belloc's famous boast that Europe is the faith and the faith is Europe no longer holds.[31]

The Church is partially anchored in a miniscule, yet sovereign, nation-state: Vatican City. This has allowed it to have permanent observer status at the UN and to exchange ambassadors with some 170 nations. Catholicism, it has been claimed, is the world's largest NGO. This is, in part, misleading since the Vatican is also a sovereign state. Within Roman Catholicism, specialized transnational religious cadres (such as the Jesuits, Opus Dei, Focolare, and Pax Christi) also serve to feed into and implement policies of the Vatican or to pursue parallel or independent initiatives for regions or global developments. At diocesan levels, a rich network of institutions – schools, health organizations, social welfare bureaus, and human rights and social justice commissions – tends to situate the Church close to the ground on local issues. In many places in the Third World, Catholic institutions for health and education outflank similar state institutions. At national and regional levels, bishops' conferences issue study papers or lobby about issues of debt relief for poor countries, arms control, land reform, and AIDS. Documents on globalization have been issued by the bishops of Asia, Canada, Spain, the Philippines, and Brazil; they have also come from interregional conferences of bishops in Africa, the Americas, and Europe.[32]

Roman Catholicism has been an interested participant in debates about development, immigration, the relation between religions, refugees, arms control, population growth, and global governance. Especially since the 1980s, Catholicism has made human rights a decided centre of its diplomatic and teaching strategies. Some secular international relations specialists could even claim, with

Samuel Huntington, that the Church has been at the vanguard of the global human rights revolution. Church representatives (from both official and non-official groups) come regularly to UN sessions on issues of the environment, population, and development aid, or they go to the World Social Forum, which was itself cofounded by a Brazilian who was a member of a Brazilian Church Commission on Justice and Peace. Catholicism, clearly, both mirrors and reflects on the forces of globalization: interdependency, rapid communication, and the growing awareness of being part of a single global community.

Both within the Roman Curia and outside of it, Catholicism maintains specialized agencies concerned with globalization debates. Catholic Relief Services and Caritas International assist refugees and provide humanitarian aid. Worldwide consultations on globalization have been held by the Vatican Pontifical Commission on Justice and Peace, and the Papal Academy of the Social Sciences has already held two consultations on globalization. Frequently, church commissions include lay Catholic experts, such as Michael Camdessus who is the former Director of the IMF. In recent decades, there has been a remarkable growth in transnational Catholic networks and exchanges of all kinds that cross national and regional borders, often bypassing Rome as they cross these borders.

Church people have become acutely aware of the varying impacts of globalization. These have included members from countries that suffer a debt burden, Kerala Catholic fishermen whose livelihoods have been threatened by corporate trawlers invading their waters (as Tyndale's chapter notes), Brazilian rubber tappers in the Amazon, or streams of new immigrants. The Church, moreover, encompasses semi-autonomous, transnational religious movements, centres of learning, and intellectual networks in Rome, Toronto, Louvain, Berkeley, Santiago, Nairobi, Manila, and Puerto Allegre.

Notoriously, globalization involves what has been called a simultaneous glocalization, which is defined as movements for identity formation or resistance at more local levels. On every papal visit, John Paul II endorsed the right to maintain the indigenous culture and language. Catholics have played key roles in a number of indigenous resistance movements such as the Zapitistas in Chiapas.[33] Especially in Africa, Asia, and Latin America, calls for more local autonomy and subsidiarity within the Church are increasingly voiced even if the cautious and wary responses from the Church's centre belie its stance, elsewhere, of supporting secular movements of indigenized localization.

Social network activists tend to emphasize the following salient themes for building a more humane globalization: (1) working toward a global ethic; (2) devising more just world systems; (3) collaborating with the UN in attempts to improve global governance; (4) developing interreligious dialogue in initiatives to avoid or overcome what Samuel Huntington ominously prophesies as a coming " clash of civilizations"; (5) a new concern for the environment to protect biodiversity, the ozone layer, and global temperature; and (6) movements for the emancipation and education of women.[34] Catholic voices have been active – but with the exception of human rights and inter-religious dialogue, never dominant or truly notable – in all six areas.

The Commission of the European Catholic Bishops' 2001 document, *Global Goverance: Our Responsibility to Make Globalisation an Opportunity for All,* endorses a need for a global ethic.[35] It follows Hans Kung's reasoning: no world order without a global ethic, no world peace without peace between the religions, and no peace between the religions without dialogue between the world religions.[36] This document is basically a reformist document similar, in many ways, to the famous charter *Our Global Neighborhood,* issued in 1995 by the Committee on Global Governance. The European bishops' document draws on strands of Catholic social teaching to underscore common values for a global world: human dignity, solidarity, responsibility, human rights, a care for the common environment, accountability, participation, and transparency.[37] It calls for the creation of a UN special agency – similar to the WTO and the International Labor Organization – that is devoted to global environmental issues. To this point, *Global Governance* is the most sophisticated and explicit CST source dealing with that topic. The Vatican – and many national Catholic groups both in the developed and the developing world – joined other religious groups in arguing strongly for debt relief for the poorest countries in the Jubilee 2000 movement. Pope John Paul II issued a joint pronouncement with the Orthodox Patriarch of Constantinople on the need for a code of environmental ethics.

The papacy maintains very close relations with the UN. The organization has been repeatedly endorsed and both Paul VI and John Paul II made special state visits to it. Clearly, the UN has played a very special role in shaping NGO responses to major globalization issues – such as women's development, population, and a sustainable environment. In very large part, the kind of civil society response that Scott Appleby's chapter discusses has flowed from UN forums and initiatives. The papacy has also strongly endorsed the new International Criminal Court and continues to support efforts to strengthen international law. Since Vatican Council II, inter-religious dialogue and joint work with non-Christian groups have grown rapidly, both at higher levels and at very local regional levels (as detailed in Baum's and Tyndale's chapters in this volume). The French and Canadian bishops have condemned discrimination against Moslems, and everywhere the Vatican pushes for a universal right to religious freedom.

Incipient Catholic discourse on globalization tends to see it as a complex, rapidly evolving, ambiguous phenomenon – in itself neither good nor bad. Significantly there is not, as yet, any truly rounded treatment of the issue in Catholic social teaching. "It will be," in John Paul II's frequently reiterated throwaway line, "what people make of it."[38] The papacy insists that globalization has great possibilities and potential risks. "For all its risks it offers exceptional and promising opportunities, precisely with a view to enabling humanity to become a single family, built on the values of justice, equity and solidarity," declared John Paul II.[39] As sociologist Jose Casanova notes: "The Catholic Church has embraced globalization, welcoming its own liberation from the strait-jacket of the territorial sovereign nation-state which had restricted Catholic universal claims. But the embrace is not uncritical."[40]

The Church's public voice insists that globalization must serve solidarity and the common good, be truly global, fully respect the human rights of all persons, and provide for participation according to appropriate responsibilities. Catholicism distances itself from neo-liberal projects of globalization, although it fully accepts the role of markets and entrepreneurship. It notes the deficits in current globalization: threats to welfare and a decent minimum to meet human needs, the inability of globalization – to this point – to reduce world poverty, the dangers of a homogenization of culture, the need for socially responsible investment, and a democratic deficit. In much repeated slogans, Catholics claim they want a globalization without marginalization, a globalization with a human face, and a globalization that does not homogenize culture. Catholic voices endorse a notion of civil society and embrace the concept of subsidiarity in any global governance. In general, Catholicism seeks a religious voice in global civil society without assuming that civil society will be, itself, explicitly religious.[41]

Msgr. Frank Dewane, the Under-Secretary of the Pontifical Council for Justice and Peace, asserts that

> There are different starting points [in debates about globalization] for Churches as opposed to businesses and these need to be clearly articulated. The Churches' concern must be for the poor, those not able to benefit from the goods of creation and human inventions which God originally designed for all people. Churches must be concerned very much with how wealth is distributed. Comments of Churches on the complex questions like economic progress and growth and for that matter on all aspects of globalization should be critical: critical of received wisdom, critical of the current consensus and critical of new theories.... Global governance without sufficient subsidiarity is like the seed that falls on the rocks. It is without staying power. Governance by its very nature and meaning implies ownership and ownership begins locally.[42]

Yet there may be also some severe limits to any role Catholicism might play in globalization debates. The truly jejune treatments of religious groups or Catholicism in the burgeoning literature on globalization (with the exception of the Jubilee 2000 campaign to reduce poor nations' debts) is extremely striking. Religious voices seem absent or terribly muted in the globalization literature. Indeed – considering Catholicism's size, global reach, and armory of rich theoretical and institutional resources – what is striking is how marginalized, in many ways, Catholicism remains in globalization campaigns and debates. Why is this so?

Some of it may reflect a blindness on the part of secular Enlightenment thinkers as to what religion can bring to policy debates.[43] In part, also, the Church still longs, in places, for a religious hegemony that is foreign to a cosmopolitan globalization. Like many religious groups, it is jealous of its own autonomy and is not, as a large institution, a very good networking partner. Social scientist John Clark says of religious groups that, unlike other NGOs and despite some clear issues uniting faiths, they tend to be competitive with regards to other religions. "They tend to find it easier to collaborate with secular NGOs than with other faiths."[44] Catholicism remains, as a world organization, much too cumbersome and slow to be the kind of resource for alternative information flows and quick networking that have been such effective tools of NGOs in global civil society.[45] In general, successful NGO global networking (about issues such as landmines, sweatshops, and child labour) is non-hierarchical, involves wide partnerships, and remains truly flexible. The Church remains distrusted by international women's groups and groups working on population questions, and the Church is seen to suffer, itself, from a democratic deficit. Hence, semi-autonomous and more local Catholic subgroups are more likely to be the major Catholic actors in activist global networks that work on the environment, human rights, and similar issues. Beyond pronouncements or some key interventions concerning peace or human rights, the international Church is not likely to engage strongly. To the extent that the hierarchical Church attempts to rein in or control such local Catholic NGOs, their own flexibility for networking and initiative will be stifled. Thus, again with a few exceptions such as the Jubilee 2000 campaign, Catholic groups tend generally to play subordinate, supportive roles in someone else's network concerning globalization.

Globalization is also a mixed blessing for Catholicism. Jose Casanova notes its threats to religion: "Globalization also represents a great threat insofar as it implies the de-territorialization of all cultural systems. Globalization threatens to dissolve the intrinsic link between sacred time, sacred space and sacred people common to all world religions and with it the seemingly essential bonds between histories, peoples and territories which have defined all civilizations."[46] Moreover, more secular NGOs encroach on religious groups as moral spokespersons for a new global order.

As Emory sociologist Frank Lechner sees it, global civil society does not really seem to provide ample opportunities for religious groups to shape agendas and mobilize movements. Religious actors tend to be active in various branches of other, largely secular, advocacy networks. No single global problem is defined mainly by religious actors from a religious standpoint. Yet, Lechner notes, religious globalization critiques do stand out by the way they are embedded in larger visions of another world order. They appeal to a distinctively transcendent and holistic horizon. Global religious voices have also begun to address some moral issues not well addressed in equally systematic fashion by secular globalization critics (particularly the issue of distributive justice). The religious voices call for universal solidarity, demand global religious freedom, inspire care for God's creation, and express the interests of humanity as such (and not just specialized interests). Secular thinkers, too, have not hesitated to insist, in the globalization debates, that "another world is possible" (the slogan of the World Social Forum). But religious thinkers and actors tend to think, argues Lechner, of this other world more concretely and precisely and are guided by more definite, if still somewhat general, overarching worldviews or guiding root metaphors. Thus, religious actors in globalization debates do provide a crucial legitimation for a free, independent global civil society critically engaged in reform from within the existing world order. They infuse global civil society with important and expressive symbolic support as they participate, prophetically, in specific movements, converge with secular critics of globalization, and articulate new forms of global community.[47]

As Richard Falk contends, the prevailing bankruptcy of the predominant global schemes provides room for a religious voice. "The best of secular thinking falls short of providing either a plausible path to travel in pursuit of humane global governance or a sufficiently inspiring vision of its elements to mobilize a popular grass roots movement for drastic global reform."[48] For Falk, religions contribute the following key components for a humane globalization: (1) They take suffering seriously and respond to real people who suffer; (2) They tap into a civilizational resonance, striking deep roots in popular culture; (3) They anchor an ethos of solidarity; (4) They provide normative horizons based on a transcendent ethic; (5) They rely, in overcoming pessimism, on the transformative power of faith; (6) They foster a sense of limits (and human fallibility); (7) They provide people with rooted identities in a runaway world; and (8) They believe in both justice and the need for reconciliation. Thus, avers Falk: "It is in the end the possibility of a religiously grounded trans-national movement for a just world order that alone gives hope."[49]

IV. The Organization of the Book

The rest of the book uses the following organization. Chapters 2 and 3 by Verstraeten and Cahill give the CST. Then the next chapters move to central themes of globalization: (a) the economy – James Hug; (b) military security – Brian Hehir; (c) ecology – Mary Evelyn Tucker; (d) culture – Joe Holland; (e) global civil society – Scott Appleby, and (f) religion – Gregory Baum. These central chapters look at globalization through a sectoral lens of the economy, military, ecology, culture, politics, and religion. Linked to Baum's chapter on religion are the first two case study chapters, both on religion: Tyndale's case studies of an attempted collaboration between the World Bank and religion in promoting development, and Rajaee's treatment of religion and building a democratic society in Iran. These two authors lend an ecumenical and interreligious character to the volume. Four case studies look at diverse geographical regions to see how globalization has affected them. Franco treats globalization in India, Sosa deals with Latin America, Campbell-Johnson with the Caribbean and Central America, and Henriot looks to Africa. Towards the end I present a short chapter on global governance, states, and multinational corporations. Bill Ryan's chapter is a final look at the themes and motifs that tie the volume together, and he draws on his own rich experiences working in development economics and global think-tanks in the US and Canada.

In the end, this volume will have succeeded if it provokes sharp conversation about globalization and what is happening in our world. It will be worth publication if people do make the connections, more keenly, between CST and globalization. Most of all, it will hit its mark if people move from mere conversation to a true engagement that makes ours a more humane habitat and globalization a project for the empowerment of people.

2

Catholic Social Thinking as Living Tradition that Gives Meaning to Globalization as a Process of Humanization

Johan Verstraeten

Each epoch has its own keywords that function as hermeneutical keys for public debates. In the 1960s, the keywords were the Cold War and development; in the 1970s, liberation was the keyword, and in the 1980s and 1990s, the keywords were management and structural adjustment. Today, globalization is the keyword, and its apparently opposite concept – the clash of civilizations – is also important.[1] For the Catholic Church, which defines itself as *kat'holon* or universal, the process of globalization is particularly challenging.

The essential question, which is not merely ethical but also theological, is: how can the Church as hermeneutic community contribute to clarifying the soteriological meaning of the process of globalization? This article will demonstrate that the problem of meaning and the quest for an ethic of globalization are intertwined.[2]

Globalization and "Scrutinizing the Signs of the Times"

Catholic Social Thought (CST) is a continuing learning process based on a method described in *Gaudium et spes* as "scrutinizing the signs of the times and interpreting them in light of the gospel" (GS 4).

Scrutinizing the signs of the times does not refer to a neutral analysis or an evaluation in the perspective of an impartial or judicious spectator. It is based on the commitment of the Church to be "truly linked with mankind and its history by the deepest of bonds" (GS 1). This commitment to be a real participant in the concrete history of humanization is characterized today by globalization as a process of socialization and increasing interdependence in the economic, political, cultural, and religious realms (cf. *Mater et Magistra* 59, *Sollicitudo Rei Socialis* 38). This process of humanization cannot be interpreted as a linear progress. Holocaust theology and post-modern philosophy have sufficiently demonstrated that the modern idea of progress is highly problematic. Human history is characterized by ambivalence and even by the possibility of radical evil. In this context, it is crucial to discern between positive and negative developments, and between life-enabling trends and forces leading to a culture of death. As Pope John Paul II put it: "Globalisation is neither good nor bad. Everything depends on what people make of it." Positive developments can be soteriologically confirmed and articulated as signs of the times that anticipate the kingdom of God, which is on earth "already present in mystery" (GS 48). Destructive tendencies, such as injustices and a radicalization of identities, must be criticized.

This discernment is not merely ethical, but also theological and soteriological.

On the one hand, there can "be no meaningful theological evaluation without an adequate understanding and ethical evaluation [of] this world, its expectations, its longings, and its often dramatic characteristics."[3] In other words, a theological judgment necessarily presupposes and includes analysis and ethical argumentation. Theological judgments on globalization cannot be made on the basis of faith alone.[4] Without social analysis a faith perspective loses touch with reality or leads to the construction of a world of pious ideas that might be more an expression of social alienation than a solution for it. "A vision must track the contours of reality; it has to have accuracy, and not simply imagination or appeal."[5] But, the opposite is also true: without the perspective of faith (and, as we will see later, its critical potential), social analysis lacks depth and runs the risk of being disturbed by ideological biases (cf. *Octogesima Adveniens* 38-40). In this regard, it is most significant that *Gaudium et spes* not only refers to scrutinizing the signs of the times, but also to "interpreting them *in light of the gospel*" (emphasis added).

In Light of the Gospel: Towards a New Vision and New Root Metaphors[6]

The biblical stories and particularly the gospels are more than a reservoir of citations that can be used as illustrations of moral insights. They are more than historical texts that are a sort of fossilized testimony of Christian thinking in the first stage of its development, as MacIntyre suggests.[7] To understand what is meant by interpretation in the light of the gospel, we must start from the actual and living hermeneutic relationship of faith communities with biblical texts by means of a continuing remembrance of the biblical narratives in liturgy or memorializing celebration. As Karen Lebacqz puts it, "If the story is not told, justice will die."[8] It is not sufficient to say that telling the story is important. One must also clarify the living and actual relation between community and text, and that means understanding how the texts open a new world of meaning.

Pope John Paul II seemed to have understood this well in his encyclical *Sollicitudo rei socialis*. He wrote that CST not only has the task to condemn actual injustices in the light of an adequately understood concept of human dignity, but must also proclaim a meaningful new future (SRS 42).

Something new is announced, a vision that opens our closed hermeneutic horizon, stimulates our imagination, and allows us to discover new and unexpected possibilities for change; this is not simply from our own perspective, but from the perspective of God. To put it in the words of one of the martyrs of our time, Archbishop Oscar Romero, "We are prophets of a future that is not our own."[9] This visionary aspect does not mean, as Elsbernd and Bieringer contend, that the Church would propose something completely strange to human experience. On the contrary, vision is "already present in human longings, desires, and hopes."[10] The most important aspect of the Christian vision is its capacity to produce semantic innovation.

The dialectic of the already known and not yet known is particularly present in biblical metaphors (also their predicative form of stories). These metaphors not only express what people experience, but also suggest new meanings and new perspectives on reality.[11] In general, good metaphors are a combination of two dimensions: epiphor and diaphor. "An epiphor is a metaphor that achieves its meaning by expressing experience that is analogous to that of the hearer (...) His response is: 'Yes, that is precisely the way I feel' or, 'Yes, that is a way of looking at things that I have never considered before, but I am sure that it is right.'"[12]

A diaphor, on the other hand, is a metaphor that suggests possible meanings rather than expressing meanings that are confirmed by the hearers. "It remains suggestive rather than expressive of experience and when interpreted literally always produces absurdity."[13]

All metaphors are composed of these two dimensions. There are no pure epiphors, otherwise they become pure analogies that do not suggest anything more than what they say. There are also no pure diaphors, otherwise, it would be difficult to understand the meaning. The biblical narratives and the gospel offer generative metaphors that contribute to a vision about what has not yet occurred.

Their poetic dimension makes a new and more meaningful understanding of reality possible. This semantic turn is neither purely theoretic nor a matter of a new objective knowledge that is not available otherwise (in moral matters this would contradict the reflective capacity of human beings and underestimate the role of reason). It leads, on the contrary, to a growing discernment about how God is at work throughout the history of humankind and how God wants his people to contribute as leaven to a transformation and humanization of a given historical context that otherwise would remain deterministically locked in its own immanency.

With regards to globalization, the text of the Bible suggests several inspiring root metaphors that are particularly interesting because they challenge the dominant root metaphors. A root metaphor is the most basic assumption about the nature of the world, society, or experience that we make when we are trying to understand it. "The function of the root metaphor is to suggest a primary way of looking at things or experience and this way of looking at things assists us in building categories or in creating art forms that will express this insight. Our very notion of what is true and what is meaningful rests upon our underlying assumptions about the nature of reality. Without such assumptions knowledge would be impossible, for we would have no way of organising our perceptions into a coherent whole."[14] A shift of metaphors implies a change in our perception of life and the world.

The Invisible Handshake Versus the Invisible Hand

One of the most powerful root metaphors in economic thinking is the invisible hand. It belongs to a mechanistic and deistic universe dominated by the imagery of an engine. It interprets society as an aggregate of individuals who try to calculate their self-interest and whose individual decisions are guided, by means of an invisible hand, to the realization of the greatest good for the greatest number. When we substitute the invisible hand for the biblical metaphor of the invisible foot or boot (referring to the oppression of the poor as criticized by the prophets), or, in a more positive perspective, for the invisible handshake (Charles Handy), our interpretation of society changes. It breaks through collective individualism and points to covenant and solidarity as primordial features of society. The image of God is also totally different; the deistic God of the mechanistic worldview is substituted for a God who is community and creates community.

This new imagination, based on solidarity, leads to a fundamental reinterpretation of social frameworks, such as the human rights tradition, which, as Hollenbach has explained, can be transformed from a tradition based on the claims of individuals into a tradition that defends human rights as basic conditions for life-in-community-with-others.[15] In this regard, the appeal by Pope John Paul II for a globalization of solidarity has great merit.

The House of Love Versus the House of Fear

In the context in which the concept of the clash of civilizations has potential to become a new paradigm, the suggestion of Henri Nouwen to replace the dominant metaphor of the house of fear by the metaphor of the house of love is most significant. In his book *Life Signs*, Nouwen observes how fear drives us, controls us, and blocks our capacity to imagine a new future.

> We are often seduced by the fearful questions the world presents to us. Without fully realizing it, we become anxious, nervous, worrying people caught in the questions of survival.... Once these fearful survival questions become the guiding questions of our lives, we tend to dismiss words spoken from the house of love as unrealistic, romantic, sentimental, pious, or just useless. When love is offered as an alternative to fear we say: 'Yes, yes that sounds beautiful, but...'. The 'but' reveals how much we live in the grip of the world, the world which calls Christians naive and raises 'realistic' questions. When we raise these 'realistic' questions we echo a cynical spirit which says 'Words about peace, forgiveness, reconciliation and new life are wonderful but the real issues cannot be ignored. They require that we do not allow others to play games with us, that we retaliate when we are offended, that we are always ready for war.... Once we ac-

> cept these questions as our own, once we are convinced that we must find answers to them, we become more and more settled in the house of fear .... Fearful questions never lead to love-filled answers... Fear engenders fear. Fear never gives birth to love.[16]

For Nouwen, the house of love engenders a different history – a history not based on our survival instinct but on a victory over our anxiety in anticipation of the kingdom of peace. In this praxis, prayer is a central act. Prayer is, according to Nouwen, a real act of death and rebirth that leads us in the midst of the world to a different attitude and the proclamation that "we are not afraid, because we have already died and the world [of fear] has no longer power over us."[17]

Moving from the house of fear to the house of love has practical consequences – it leads to a different way of thinking about security. With his metaphor of the house of love Nouwen implicitly responds to the suggestion of Theodore R. Weber that we do not only need new theories of international relations, but also new theological symbols of the international order.[18] According to Weber, we must think beyond the pessimism of the Lutheran concept of the international order as an emergency order of the fallen creation (preservative mode). In this order, the anarchy of states, or a balance of power between states, is necessary to prevent all power (and consequently also the corruption of power) from being concentrated in one centre. The state of the world is even interpreted as "antichrist." On the other hand, Weber also criticizes the radical optimism of some proponents of the Catholic tradition; he especially criticizes those who project a spontaneous evolution towards a higher level of institutional completeness (the creative mode). As an alternative, Weber proposes a third symbolization based on the redemptive mode of God relating to the world. This mode, rather than the creative and preservative modes, "sees the nature of the [international] order in the persistent struggle to bring the human oneness established in Christ to transforming historical concreteness in the relationships that actually exist among human beings and their groups."[19]

Such a redemptive way of thinking is clearly present in the writing of Pope John Paul II. In *Sollicitudo rei socialis* (1987), after his description of the reality of the mechanisms of evil, he writes that "the Church must strongly affirm the possibility of overcoming the obstacles which ... stand in the way of development." And she must affirm her confidence in a true liberation "based on the Church's awareness of the divine promise, guaranteeing that our present history does not remain closed in upon itself but is open to the Kingdom of God" (SRS 47). This theological interpretation is the heart of his social discernment.

The Earth: More than Matter and More than a Sacred Space

A mystic anthropo-cosmological understanding of the Earth avoids two extreme interpretations. On one hand, the earth can become an object totally void of any religious meaning, a measurable and useful *res extensa* at the mercy of economic and technocratic powers.[20] On the other hand, the earth can become so sacralized that it returns to what Levinas has called the *ivresse du sacré* (religious drunkenness) and the superstition of the place (which can include a denial of the universality of human rights). Or it may become a purely pagan perception of the world that explicitly, but unjustly, rejects the Jewish or Christian interpretation of the universe as the main cause of radical anthropocentrism.[21] In extreme cases, such a vision can even lead to sacrificing human dignity for the well-being of the ecosystem.

A biblical-theological perspective, which includes the redemptive mode described earlier, contributes also to elucidating the more subtle problem of the reduction of globalization to an infrastructural material process in which the cultural, ethical, and religious aspects would be nothing more than secondary, superstructural representations.[22]

Such a materialist interpretation of globalization is as unilateral as the Weberian thesis. For Weber, religious, ethical, and cultural values or practices have an essential influence on economic behaviour (compare *The Protestant Ethic and the Spirit of Capitalism).*

A mystic understanding of the earth does not admit an either/or option. It suggests that the so-called infrastructural and superstructual aspects are intertwined and interacting. As much as economy or technology have an influence on globalization, the very possibility of thinking globalization and interpreting it as meaningful is shaped by fundamental ideas and interpretative frameworks.

An excellent example of such an interpretatative framework is the metaphorization of the earth by Pierre Teilhard de Chardin, inspired by the cosmic-mystic intuition of Ignatius of Loyola. In his *Spiritual Exercises*, particularly the culmination point of the meditation about receiving love, Ignatius writes: "Consider *how God is present in all creatures,* in all elements through giving them the possibility to exist, in plants through giving them vitality, in animals through giving them the capacity of observation, in human beings through giving them reason and so on, and so also in me through giving me existence, life and perceptive faculties and through giving me the possibility to think." Ignatius continues, consider "*how God is carefully at work in all creatures on the surface of the earth* (...). Everything comes from God *"like the rays come from the sun and the waters from the well of love"* [emphasis added]. This pantheistic, cosmic-mystic intuition of Ignatius, more than a belief in a sort of linear progress ideology, has influenced Pierre Teilhard de Chardin, particularly in his text *La messe sur le monde* written in August 1923. Travelling in the Gobi desert, he wanted to say mass. Having no real bread and wine at his disposal, he offers human work as bread and human pain as wine and prays for the unification of the globe. The metaphorization of the earth is most interesting here: "My chalice and my paten are the depths of a soul, which is in a very broad sense open for the forces which, in a moment, will elevate themselves from all extremities of the Globe and which will converge towards the spirit."[23] In his offertory, he connects them with "innumerable masses of the living, all those who surround and support him [Teihard] with their knowledge, those who come and go, particularly those, in truth or in error, who believe in the plenification of things and passionately strive for it in their office, in their laboratory, in their manufacture."[24] Also in his offertory he includes "all what in this world increases, all what will diminish, all what will die."[25] And he prays to God that the not-yet-unified bread of the world would be transformed into unity and that the wine of human striving and suffering would be elevated by God's force to a living unity. "Receive, Lord, this total Host which creation, moved by your attraction, tenders to you by this new day-break. This bread, our effort, which is, I know, in itself nothing else than an immense disaggregate. This wine, our pain, which is, alas, still a dissolved brewage. But in the depth of this formless mass you have put … an irresistible and sanctifying longing which makes us all crying … Lord make us one."[26]

In the Eucharistic prayer, he asks that all life that springs up everywhere in the world, everything that grows and flourishes, would become the body of Christ and that all dead and suffering would become his blood. In this way a new humanity would be created in and through the divine process of transformation. In this cosmic-mystic text, globalization is interpreted as a spiritual process of transformation that takes place, not outside the material world or the material aspects of life or outside the world of work and science but incarnated in it. "In the new humanity generated today, the [divine] Word has prolonged its never ending act of birth and through its immersion in the heart of the world the great waters of matter are filled with life, without trembling. Nothing has (apparently) trembled under the influence of the ineffaceable transformation. And yet, in a mysterious and real way, the universe, having become an immense bread, has become flesh through the substantiating word. All matter is, from that moment on, incarnated, my God, by your incarnation."[27]

The metaphors of bread and wine and the prayers for a Eucharistic transubstantiation of the globe by God's Spirit enable us to see and interpret the process of globalization as being not merely a material happening, but an anthropo-cosmic drama. In this drama, the incarnation of God's spirit transforms the globe into a divine milieu on its way to become fulfilled in Christ, who is the Alpha and Omega of history. As has been the case since the earliest stages of the geosphere, the process of humanization in and through the process of globalization is not merely the result of anonymous processes, but a creative process in which God, connected with the earth, plenifies and transforms everything to what it ultimately is destined to become in Christ: love community (amorization). In this perspective, globalization is not a process outside us but part of our own self-becoming as human beings who are connected to all that is and who are moved and brought to unity by God's life-giving spirit. "For those who can see," Teilhard writes in *Le milieu divin*, "nothing here on earth is merely profane"![28]

It would be most interesting to connect this mystic intuition about the globe with contemporary deep-ecological and eco-feminist theories in which the metaphors of the earth and of the house (*oikos*) play a central role. But this connection requires a critical conversation since the biblical image of God is ethically qualified and not a matter of pure immanentism.

Pentecost versus Babel

In its document *Maîtriser la Mondialisation*, the French commission for Justice and Peace writes that globalization makes its way throughout history as a choice between two universalisms. On the one hand there is the dangerous and totalitarian perspective of Babel, on the other hand the liberating way of Pentecost.[29] What direction will globalization take? According to Justice and Peace France, the future remains open. "The logic of profit and the tendency to return to identities inclines to the way of Babel. The birth of a planetary nation, and the development of authentic human autonomy, goes in the direction of Pentecost."[30] Those who choose this way must do all they can to stop Babel from becoming the way. "We can not accept a new universalism which would be merely based on money and profit at whatever price, we must refuse Babel and its forms of violence. But, Globalisation can become the carrier of a new humanism, based on all peoples, all cultures, all diversities ... and finally all religions; but that implies a no to a destructive wild liberalism. We have the task to civilise it, loyal to the spirit of Pentecost and in the hope which is opened by the promise of the book Apocalypse: 'See how I will make everything new'"[31]

The four suggested metaphors (invisible handshake, house of love, earth, and Pentecost) enable us to give meaning to globalization. Since they also challenge the dominant root metaphors, they also urge us to more semantic vigilance.

The Interplay Between Semantic Innovation and Semantic Vigilance

As long as we interpret globalization and its apparently opposite processes – such as the return of extremist and/or fundamentalist religious ideas in politics[32] – in the perspective of the dominant hermeneutical horizon of our own time, we run the risk of getting stuck in a way of thinking. Instead of giving hermeneutic keys for the future, this way of thinking reinforces already existing conflicts and misperceptions influenced by anxiety.[33] In particular, the speed of the globalization processes and the fundamental changes of lifestyles and habits, as well as extremist and fundamentalist reactions to it, make people uncertain.

A number of factors create a sphere of uncertainty and anomie that often leads to anxiety. These include extreme flexibility in the work sphere, delocalization leading to unemployment of workers in the West, and (bio-)technologies that cause a new but uncertain agricultural revolution and also challenge our very understanding of what it is to be human. Other important factors are more elitist patterns of decision-making by experts challenging democracy and migrations leading to fundamental cultural changes. But, as Nouwen suggests, fear is a bad master. Social psychologists have demonstrated that, particularly in times of revolutionary changes and instability, anxiety leads to defensive or even wrong perceptions of reality and to biased information. Other products of anxiety are stereotyping (compare how we think about Islam), scapegoating strangers, and, not the least, a denial of meaningful alternatives or schemes of interpretation.[34] An example of such a way of thinking is the metaphor of the domino effect used during the Cold War. Rooted in a paralyzing fear of communism, it has influenced the escalation of violence in Southeast Asia (the Vietnam War) and Latin America (theory of national security and violent military dictatorships).

Today a bifurcation of the world in terms of Huntington's clash of civilizations risks generating the same sorts of effects and leads to the misunderstanding of Islam. Anxiety and a disturbed perception of reality are also present in the cynical use of euphemistic expressions – such as nuclear umbrellas, peace-shields, smart nukes, and clean wars. These give a false impression of safety and accuracy, while producing a virtual reality that makes people blind to the real cruelty of violence.

For example, defensive perceptions of reality are used in conversations about the use of genetically modified organisms (GMOs). For a long time, multinational corporations have provided the world with scientific arguments confirming the safety of their products. At the same time their pretended objectivity was the ideological expression of pure self-interest. They excluded scientific or rational, as well as ethical, arguments leading to opposite conclusions. Religious values or ethical convictions were totally disregarded, despite the fact that they constitute important social facts such as massive rejection (the rejection of GMOs by public opinion in Europe). On the other hand, opponents of GMOs have walked into the same sort of ideological trap, rejecting well-founded scientific arguments. Only a different attitude and a new imagination have opened a way out of the impasse and generated new dialogue among all the partners involved.

A last example concerns the apparently universal and objective standards used today in the globalized economy to evaluate people, including in the academic world. This includes criteria based on measuring performance and compliance with ethical standards, accountability of scholars, impact factors, and numbers of citations. These concepts function, in fact, as metaphors of a biased worldview: the gradgrind worldview as described by Martha Nussbaum, expressing a reductionist economic, utilitarian, and quantity-oriented approach of reality that, to some extent, changes the world into a sort of Benthamian panopticon.

Ideological interpretations of reality born out of anxiety cannot simply be unmasked by scientific evidence or modern rationality, since science and its rationality are partially enclosed in the narrow hermeneutic horizon of our time. To understand what is really at stake, we need access to a different hermeneutic horizon that is powerful enough to break open the narrow frameworks of interpretation through which we give meaning to our world. Without a radically different imagination (inspired by deep remembrance mediated by metaphoric texts and narratives), even the Church – like any other establishment – runs the risk of becoming caught in the illusions of a certain time or even in a mind-blocking status quo. This would make the Church the guardian of the thought and legitimation of the established disorder.

But the community of Christians has the real possibility to see with new eyes and to avoid ideological pitfalls. With a hermeneutical relation to a horizon of interpretation, which is different from the dominant hermeneutical horizon of our time, it is possible to develop a critical attitude.

I would like to distinguish my view from that of Dennis McCann. McCann defended the role of theology in applied ethics from the perspective of its capacity to unmask the ideological pitfalls of modern rationality on the basis of its access to a hermeneutical horizon that is older than that of modernity.[35] The point is not that this horizon is older. The Christian social tradition refers to narrative texts and stories that are actually present and transcend the original meaning given to them by the original authors (such as Ricoeur's distinction between *parole* and *texte*). The actual process of reading occurs when poetic or metaphoric texts open another world of meaning. Having access to a differing horizon of interpretation makes a confrontation between two different horizons of meaning possible; this can be more conflictual than suggested by Gadamer's concept of fusion of horizons. The friction between different horizons is what breaks through the established meanings and generates the already described capacity – creatively to reimagine the world. This leads to an apparently paradoxical situation.

Christian communities can function as an inspiring and healing force in the concrete history of women and men. This depends on the extent to which the communities are fully connected with the world and on the way that they make a difference by interrupting time-bound hermeneutic schemes (particularly by way of proclaiming new life). To express this in the words of Elsbernd and Bieringer: vision is not an extension of present possibilities into the future, but rather "the future reaching out to meet the present as an annunciation of something more or as a disjuncture from what is."[36] Creative friction, between vision as the source of renewal and reality, will always exist. One could even say more: precisely because the Christian vision is different from merely secular interpretations of reality (although not alien to human experience), it is capable of semantically enriching secular thinking. In this regard, Charles Curran's thesis about a dual audience in CST is not adequate. He makes a distinction between the language one can use in Christian communities and the language used when the secular world is the audience. In the first case, the community of Christians can express its own distinctiveness and refer to the gospels. In the second case, a more general and rational language can and must be used.[37] Far from denying the necessity of a universal language or of a form of natural law thinking (including a human rights discourse), this dualism makes it impossible to assess the particular challenge that Christian thinking presents to a secular society as a source of semantic and practical innovation. Insights that are universal, and thus valid for everyone, are also historical and not merely a matter of abstract or thin principles. The universal gets continuing meaning from particular traditions that provide meaning for the thin categories. What today is not yet considered as universal, can become universally acknowledged as reasonable under the influence of an enriched understanding of our own humanity.

An example is the perspective of the cross. The perspective of the Cross is not something particularistic or irrational. In this regard, Klaus Demmer rightly contends that the acceptance of the scandal of the cross can lead to a better understanding of human persons and their universal nature "under the conditions of a kenotic existence."[38] The cross, moreover, opens our eyes to the perspective of the victims of history: more precisely, today it is to the victims of globalization. The concern for the poor and victims, and respect for their interpretation of facts and their longing for liberation, is not merely a Christian attitude; it is of concern for us all.

Looking at the cross also opens our eyes to the tragedies of history. It is a warning against all manner of aesthetic minimization of suffering, ideological misuses, or a too optimistic and too linear interpretation of history. It urges us to pay attention to the depths of human suffering to which our societies can descend, and to the possibility that utopian ideas and political moments for a better future can lead to catastrophic and irreversible decisions (see Hans Jonas' *Principle of Responsibility*). The dangerous memory of the cross, which opens a dangerous future, urges us to fight against perversions of memory and ideological deformations of reality. It shapes a prophetic company of critics who remain vigilant with respect to meanings that risk being perverted by the logic of the market or technology.

Think Globally, Act Locally: The Problem of the Conflict of Interpretations in CST

The Catholic Church, defining itself as *kat'holon,* wants to be a major defender of a universalistic ethic in a world that has divided interpretations. Articulation of such an ethic was, from the beginning of his pontificate, one of the central concerns of Pope John Paul II. According to him this ethic must be based on the truth about real and historical human persons, understood in light of their redemption in Christ. One could call this a soteriological type of natural law: in Christ we are all destined to the same dignity. An articulation of some sort of universalistic ethics, grounded on something more fundamental than the arbitrariness of decisions or prudential judgment (compare with Apel's *Tranzendentalpragmatik*), will always be a challenge as a necessary condition of the humanization of globalization.

But any sort of universal ethics becomes too abstract if it does not sufficiently take into account the concrete, historical person about whom the universal truth is proclaimed.[39] A meaningful universalistic teaching about human dignity cannot be detached from the real life-context and faith-experience of the people who are victims of the great transformations of the world.

No doubt most of the new developments are steered top down by economic powers and experts. But that does not remove the fact that their decisions often fail to take into account the experience of people at the grassroots level – people who often become the intended or unintended victims of instrumental rationality. Yet these people are, as are the experts, stakeholders of the world.

While the universal magisterium of the Church intends to think and act globally, it should simultaneously think and act locally by taking seriously the experience of millions of people at the grassroots level. Their active participation in the global discernment process is indispensable. The neglect of their voice is a real problem, as James Wolfensohn, president of the World Bank, acknowledges: "You hear talk about a new financial order, about an international bankruptcy law, about transparency and more... but you don't hear a word about people.... Two billions of people live on less than two dollars a day.... We live in a world that gradually is getting worse and worse. It is not hopeless, but we must do something about it now."[40]

The people mentioned here are also victims of abstract ideolological discourses on topics such as more freedom, private property, workfare instead of welfare, and so on. What does the reality behind these words really mean in terms of the quality of life of the poor? What would happen if more freedom becomes an argument against social security? Suppose that private property becomes an argument to exclude the poor from the goods and services they need to fulfill their basic needs (compare the confrontation between pharmaceutical firms claiming patent rights against poor countries that are defending the rights of their citizens). What does workfare mean when there are no jobs or wages are extremely low? Does it mean an inhuman life for single parents (in most cases, women) who have to work themselves to death for the basic survival of their children but do not have enough income to give their children access to good schools? The meaning of words changes according to the interest they hide and the context in which they are used. This is also valid for the most beautiful ethical principles propagated by the Church.

Precisely in this regard, the honest acknowledgment of Pope Paul VI in *Octogesima adveniens* (4), has lost nothing of its meaning. He admitted that a pope cannot utter a unified message in which he would put forward a solution that – as the text literally says – would be in congruity with all local situations (qua solutio, omnibus locus congruens, proponatur). According to Paul VI it is "up to the *Christian communities* to *scrutinize* (perscrutentur) with objectivity the situation which is proper to their own country, *to shed on it the light of the gospel's unalterable words* and to draw principles of reflection (principia cogitandi), norms of judgment (iudicandi normas) and directives for action (regulas operandi) from the social teaching of the Church.... It is up to these Christian communities [and not only bishops' conferences], with the help of the Holy Spirit, in communion with the bishops, who hold responsibility, and in dialogue with other Christian brethren and all men of good will, to *discern* (discernere) the options and commitments which are called for *in order to bring about the social, political and economic changes* seen in many case to be urgently needed (OA, 4)." [emphasis added]

With these words Paul VI has given a full-fledged legitimacy to a perichoretic "top-down–bottom-up" approach in which the sapiential life experience of people is valued. But such an approach unavoidably engenders a conflict of interpretations, since interests and experiences differ according to the world or the social group to which one belongs. This conflict of interpretation should not be bypassed. It even urges us to acknowledge a tragic aspect in the teaching of the magisterium.

When it speaks in all too general terms, its message remains too abstract or open to ideological misuse. When it becomes too concrete it unavoidably takes sides and the question is then: in favour of whom? Nothing is more misleading than pretending to escape or transcend conflicts of interest in the name of a universal message.

A striking example of this problem is the universal criticism of the social assistance state in the fifth chapter of the encyclical *Centesimus Annus*. [To avoid misunderstanding I must explain that I don't deny the role of the civil society and I do appreciate the pope's rejection of the duality between individual and state. I also fully accept the validity of the principle of subsidiarity, although it is applied quite differently from John XXIII who, in *Mater et magistra,* defended a sort of social assistance state.]

The criticism of the social assistance state is partially valid for countries such as Belgium, France, or Germany. There an excessive bureaucratization has produced negative side effects. It is not valid in so far as it becomes an extraordinary strong universal rejection of the social assistance state.

The universal criticism of the social assistance state becomes ideological for three reasons. First, it does not take into account the historical merits of the social assistance state in organizing a system of solidarity in an industrialized world that could not resolve its problems on the basis of the older forms of solidarity in the agrarian society. Secondly, although it was not the intention of the writer, it becomes an argument for those who obstinately reject any sort of social security or health care and who think, like some nineteenth-century paternalist industrialists, that charity is sufficient and no legal or structural reforms are necessary. Thirdly, it joins the analysis (and interests) of Catholic writers such as Michael Novak who is oriented towards the corporate world. One of the striking aspects of the work is that it is literally more inspired by the text of the lay letter against the American bishops – defending the interests of corporate America – than by the original and gospel-based vision of the American bishops in *Economic Justice for All* (1986). A failure to indicate the limited contextual meaning of the rejection of the social assistance state unavoidably leads, in a globalized world, to ideological misuse.

Conclusion

CST is a living tradition of practice and thought that has legitimacy on its own, but also has the potential to become an inspiring voice in the great debates of our time. The Church serves the world not by sticking to a univocal reiteration of principles, but by developing a social ethic. This ethic is based on discernment and reading the gospels as source of moral imagination capable of moving people beyond the status quo, as the status quo is determined by narrow frameworks of interpretation. Drawing on its narrative and metaphoric sources, the Church enables people to look at social, political, and economic realities with new eyes. Having access to a hermeneutical horizon that is different from the dominant interpretative frameworks of our time, and inspired by new root metaphors, it can contribute to transforming globalization into a process of humanization. Theological discernment as hermeneutic process is a necessary, but not a sufficient, condition. It has to be supplemented by a careful analysis mediated by social sciences, ethical reasoning, and a search for concrete solutions. This reflexive work has to be more than merely top-down thinking. It must be rooted in the sapiential experience of the victims of globalization and in the life of the Church as a concrete community of communities (synod of 1985) that takes into account the diversity of real life contexts.

3

Globalization and the Common Good

Lisa Sowle Cahill

The concept of the common good is the centrepiece of Catholic social thought (CST), having assumed special prominence during the pontificates of John XXIII and Paul VI. With its companion concept – human dignity or the dignity of the person – common good provides a moral vision for CST and action. That vision accentuates an objective morality, including criteria of justice and of a good society that can be known by all reasonable persons. Justice is seen as a real historical possibility, implemented incrementally along a spectrum of communal affiliations from the family to the nation and to the international order. Within the common good, the dignity and rights of the individual and the welfare and cohesiveness of the social body are balanced and seen as interdependent and mutually necessary. From the 1960s onward, the concept of the common good has been designated as the universal common good, and it has grounded a universalizing and ameliorative view of human relationships and social structures. Likewise, it has funded an optimistic view of the possibility of benign and accountable government – distributing goods, ensuring participation, and mediating conflicts among members of communities from the local to the global.

The positive, forward-looking vision of the recent Catholic common good tradition reflects general trends in Western (North Atlantic) cultures in the 1960s and 1970s. In the decades after World War II, economic expansion, technological innovation, civil rights movements, decolonization, and mass communication among cultures were part of a period of relative peace, prosperity, productivity, and equality in North America and Europe. Members of these societies enjoyed a sense that the world is open and on the road to democracy. The term "participatory democracy" was coined in a manifesto drafted by Tom Hayden for the Students for a Democratic Society in 1961. Historian Francesca Polletta observes that the concept became one of the era's most influential ideas, uniting groups across class lines to challenge the status quo and to change policies at both the local and national levels.[1] The social consciences of religious persons looked ahead to the rapid development, in a more democratic and participatory mode, of social reforms that had actually begun in the late-nineteenth century, with the Social Gospel movement and the initiation of the social encyclical tradition by *Rerum Novarum* (1891).

A book with the intriguing title, *Faith and Freedom: The Life and Times of Bill Ryan, S.J.*, has a subject who became a catalyst for Catholic social action in Canada, the Jesuit order, and the Catholic Church as a whole. Ryan took his inspiration from the 1971 Synod of Bishops' *Justice in the World*. That document proclaimed, "Action on behalf of justice and participation in the transformation of the world fully appear to us as a constitutive dimension of the preaching of the Gospel."[2] One should also add, in respect to the common good, that this very concept was the necessary condition for Catholic optimism about the success of the transformative process. This process, announced by the Synod, took its lead from the engagement of Vatican II with the modern world in a spirit of collaboration toward social change. Although social transformation was depicted as part of Gospel identity, it was also seen in mid-twentieth–century social teaching as possible to accomplish historically because similar moral values and aims could unite Christians with peoples around the world. Christians could join with others in a quest for the common good, achieving practical agreement on the shape of a better future.

Unfortunately, however, the authors of *Faith and Freedom* concede that the momentum that propelled many Catholics to commit themselves to theology, religious life, and social ministries around 1971 (the year after I entered graduate studies in theology) has now "simply stalled." According to their analysis, this is due to the "self-perpetuating and unaccountable leadership" of the Roman Catholic Church, "whose prevailing response to change has historically been to hunker down and adopt a siege mentality."[3] If concepts like the human person and the common good are to be relevant to politics today, they must be advanced in the public forum in more innovative ways. Catholic spokespersons and episcopal conferences seem selectively to emphasize sexual ethics and pro-life issues, such as civil recognition of gay unions and embryo research, in constructing their social agenda. More visibility in the area of health care reform and global access to health resources, and a much increased presence on issues of global economics, are necessary for CST to have a significant impact on globalization. Perhaps the Catholic voice in these spheres is inhibited because the meanings of personal dignity and common good seem more elusive and difficult to connect to practical policy recommendations about global political and social issues, than they do in areas where more simple and absolute teachings can be invoked.

About five years ago, I participated in a small international study group on genetics, biotechnology, ethics, and Catholic theology that had Catholic theologian and political scientist Bryan Hehir as an advisor. Hehir is an expert on CST (see his essay in this volume). At one of our meetings, he posed a provocative question. To paraphrase, "Can CST survive globalization?" Hehir's point, as I understood it, was that the Catholic concept of common good depends on a theory of society as a system of distinct, hierarchically arranged groups, whose relations are structured by ascending and more comprehensive levels of government, with ultimate authority residing at the top. The key political actor on the modern scene is assumed to be the nation-state, and globalization is met by projecting a global authority that parallels national governments by overseeing regions, provinces, and states within nations. Hence John XXIII and Paul VI called for a UN and a World Fund as part of a public authority that had global reach and was able to ensure that justice is served. Given the now-evident limits of these international agencies and the weakened authority of the nation-state itself, the Catholic framework for promoting "action on behalf of justice and participation in the transformation of the world" (*Justice in the World*) may have reached the end of its road.

At this point, my own view is that CST is alive, well, and influential, even though the formal framework of hierarchical and encompassing government provided in the papal encyclicals is, in large part, obsolete. The concept of common good is not limited to that particular elaborative framework. (For one thing it antedates the modern nation-state by centuries, coming from the distinctive social visions of Augustine and Aquinas.) The notion of the common good has always begun from the experienced needs and goods of human beings, and from insights into the sorts of social relationships that promote human welfare. It has always included subcategories like mutual accountability, subsidiarity, and participation. Thus it provides for social action and responsibility at the local level and anticipates collaboration toward broader structural patterns and lines of authority. And it has always envisioned the interpenetration of the human and societal common good with Christian virtues of charity and solidarity, providing for the engagement of religious communities and churches with the common good on the many levels at which the common good itself is actualized.

One of the main things that has changed in the era of globalization is the public and practical perception of who takes care of the common good, by what authority, and with what means. Aquinas defined law as "an ordinance of reason for the common good, made by him who has care of the community, and promulgated."[4] While, in the Middle Ages, an emperor, monarch, or local lord may have single-handedly taken care of the community, the age of revolution, independence, and democratization vested care of the community in representative bodies or figures. The age of globalization is characterized by new communications technologies that compress time and space and by the integration of the world economy under global capitalism.[5] It has at once expanded and consolidated the means of control over human relations (both social and material) and decentralized authority over the means of control. The age of globalization has also displaced the idealized view of authority as consisting precisely in an office of care for the common good and replaced it with a realistic reading of authority as power propelled by self-interest. This has caused the lack of trust in national officials, elected or not, to work for the common good and a lack of confidence in international institutions and to be able to accomplish the common good even if they intend to do so. An additional problem is the fear of multinational corporations and the World Trade

Organization, whose power and authority not only serve their own interests (only occasionally even invoking the pretext of the common good), but are exceptionally effective in achieving their aims.

The continuing vitality of CST and the concept of the common good cannot be discovered by employing a model of society or of social theory that works with the old top-down, orderly, and hierarchical categories of social structure and social authority that globalization renders more and more irrelevant. Synods of bishops, episcopal conferences, elite think-tanks, government policy, and even papal encyclicals are no longer the only, or even the primary, loci from which leadership in Catholic social ethics is exercised. Instead, the common good is being redefined and implemented along a spectrum of networks for social change under the guidance of (Catholic) moral values like dignity, equality, social participation, meeting of basic needs, openness to transcendent values, and solidarity. In these networks, Catholics are cooperating with other religious and cultural traditions to seek the common good locally and globally.

In an astute analysis called "Retrieving or Re-Inventing Social Catholicism," John Coleman provides many examples of Catholic presence on global social issues: Catholic schools and hospitals, Catholic Charities, Pax Christi, Network, the Catholic League for Civil Rights, and church-based, community-organizing groups.[6] One could add international ventures like Caritas International, the Jesuit Refugee Service, San Egidio, Trocaire, AIDS ministries and services, and men's and women's religious congregations engaged in work for the common good across national boundaries. In all these cases, theory and reflection are combined with action that accomplishes, both locally and more globally, what official episcopal and Vatican teaching seems less able to carry off. Although sometimes it can, and should, influence specific social policy (as Coleman hopes), the global civil society movement is showing that local and mid-level forces for social change do not necessarily wait for legitimation by national and international legal, judicial, or regulatory systems. Sometimes those systems respond to demands or actual changes "from below" that pressure compliance "from above."[7] The challenges for CST are, first, to accommodate this changing reality of social authority and change within its theoretical framework, and second, to acknowledge the fact that CST itself is developing and operating in a parallel, more pluralistic, decentralized, and practical manner.

I believe there are at least four interdependent questions that CST must answer to restore power to the concept of the common good as the foundation of a Catholic social ethics with a global face. These questions concern four related aspects of the common good: substance (human goods), procedures (government and participation), dispositions (solidarity and hope), and efficacy (effective action with other traditions and movements). The questions are: 1) What is the substance or content of the common good? Is there a global basis from which to define human needs, goods, and obligations, and to arrive at a substantive view of the common good or good society? 2) Is there a practical means to achieve the common good? Is there a global sociopolitical structure or government through which the common good can be implemented? 3) Is there genuine commitment to the common good, in contrast to self-interest? Is there the moral will, manifest in dispositions of solidarity and hope, to implement the common good globally for all? 4) What is the present and future effectiveness of CST in achieving the common good? If CST is not in decline, then how does it interface ecumenically with other traditions and movements to influence the renewal of the common good?

Usually the orientation of leading questions or theses can be better understood if the adversaries against whom they are formulated are identified. So, before discussing these questions at greater length, I will indicate their contexts. My concern with goods is a reaction against postmodern deconstructions of hegemonic moral theories, which have the lamentable, if unintended, consequence of underwriting relativistic agnosticism about what justice is and requires. CST can provide a realist approach to morality that is neither abstract nor unduly partisan. My concern about structures is a reaction against political realism with its claim that self-interest does, and should, govern international relations. It is also a response to the fact that the structures of international governance, focused for more than 350 years on the nation-state, are breaking down. New forms of global civil society are needed if anarchy and the exploitation of gaps in the international system are to be avoided. CST affirms the moral, and not merely coercive, basis of global relationships; with the concept of subsidiarity, it also suggests new ways to think about global social institutions.

My concern with dispositions is an attempt to offer an alternative to a theological ethics whose strong doctrine of sin leads, in either a neo-Augustinian or a sectarian vein, to the denial of any real possibility of social transformation or progress. Catholic tradition remains committed to the project of persuasively changing human behaviour for the better. My concern with efficacy arises from the need to make this commitment bear fruit at the practical level. The "how" of a more just world order goes beyond ethical principles and ideals, and far beyond naïve evolutionary views of history to question whether we can achieve more than futile gestures toward human reasonableness and cooperation. Though CST has sometimes been guilty of impotent moralism, recent Catholic thought pays more attention to practical activism and to interreligious cooperation, giving stronger evidence that the ideals it projects can shape global realities. Interreligious and intercultural work for justice tests the premise that humans do share certain needs and values that must be respected in any just society. That a realist, reasonable, and practical concept of the common good is true, and that it can be recognized and accomplished (at least partly) is the aim of CST.

Now, a discussion of the four orienting questions will be offered in defence of my conviction that the wager can be won.

1. Substance. Is there a common basis on which to define human needs, goods, and obligations?

In CST, the dignity of the person and the common good are correlative concepts that keep the individual and society in balance. The social encyclicals specify the requirements of the common good in terms of rights and duties, which are based ultimately on the law of nature.

> Any human society, if it is to be well-ordered and productive, must lay down as a foundation this principle: that every human being is a person; his nature is endowed with intelligence and free will. By virtue of this he has rights and duties of his own, flowing directly and simultaneously from his very nature, which are therefore universal, inviolable and inalienable. (*Pacem in terris*, 9)
>
> ...The common good touches the whole man, the needs both of his body and of his soul (57)....The common good of all embraces the sum total of those conditions of social living whereby men are enabled to achieve their own integral perfection more fully and more easily (58; see also *Gaudium et spes*, 26).

These concepts imply the protection of specific personal and social goods that are necessary to fulfill the person and provide well-being for a society (the common good). John Boswell calls personal and common good the gateway concepts of CST, while Francis McHugh refers to "the dignity of human nature" and "the common good" its "guiding visions."[8] Basic human goods are required by human nature and known by human reason; they also define justice as social relations in which material and social goods are distributed fairly, conflicts resolved, and violations compensated. Traditionally, justice was subcategorized as distributive (what society owes to individuals), commutative (relations among individuals), and legal (what individuals owe to society). Contemporary CST, since *Quadragesimo Anno*, works with the more comprehensive but looser term, social justice. It has introduced the concept of contributive justice (as a reinterpretation of legal justice) to capture the importance of active participation by all members in a definition of a good society (beyond merely obeying laws).[9] The way that CST has specified basic goods and justice has varied over time. Early social encyclicals adopted a more hierarchical view of society and, hence, of access to goods. Later encyclicals adopted a more egalitarian view, with an emphasis on participation by previously excluded classes and groups.

The modern phenomenon of globalization resulted, at least in part, from worldwide communications technologies. These same technologies, in the form of mass media, also display cultural pluralism and, along with widespread trends toward democratization and the expansion of civil rights, have prompted identity-based resistance movements as well as postmodern and post-colonial philosophies. All of these contest the idea that one conception of nature and goods can be developed to apply to the whole world. Moreover, they maintain that the normative view, or views, promulgated by the post-industrial societies that were the agents of globalization should be resisted as hegemonic and oppressive. Therefore the very premise of the common good – that there are goods common to all people, the specification and protection of which constitute social justice – has been undermined.

In *The Common Good and Christian Ethics*, David Hollenbach states that "the issue we face is whether it is reasonable to hope that adherents of different religious and cultural traditions can identify aspects of the good life that are common to the lives of all human beings."[10] Robert Schreiter articulates the dangers of a failure to do so. "Denial of difference can lead to the colonization of a culture and its imagination. Denial of similarities promotes an anomic situation where no dialogue appears possible and only power will prevail."[11] Clearly, any approach to defining the content of the common good that will be persuasive and useful today must be inductive and dialogical. It must seek a better comprehension of human goods, the priorities among them, the routes of fair access to them, and resolution of conflict situations by means of an interaction among different cultural perspectives. The interaction called for is not primarily theoretical or intellectual, but practical, arising out of a shared commitment to resolve problems that beset local communities, ethnic groups, nations, or humanity as a whole. Hollenbach defines such a process as "dialogic universalism."[12] Schreiter reminds us that meaning and truth are established through practical social judgment and grounded in the narratives of living communities that sometimes mesh, complement, challenge, or correct each other.[13] Some feminist activists and legal scholars have coined the term transversalism (rather than universalism) to denote what happens when identity politics are transcended without losing their own rootedness and values, and without homogenizing their dialogue partners or the group to which they belong.[14]

The wager of the Catholic common good tradition must be that this more pluriform and multilayered approach to human nature will yield a basis of agreement not too dissimilar to the tradition's conception of the common good. It will have more credibility if it is inductively elaborated and continually revised, than if it is dogmatically announced and preemptively enforced. The capabilities theories of Martha Nussbaum and Amartya Sen are examples of a dialogical approach to the content of the common good that incorporates a variety of cultural experiences without being morally relativistic. Nussbaum has offered several revisable versions of basic human capabilities that need social protection to protect and support human functioning and flourishing. She believes intercultural social consensus should be possible on these capabilities and their importance for everyone. They include life; bodily health; bodily integrity; senses, imagination, and thought; emotions; practical reason; affiliation, which is a relationship to others that includes the social bases of self-respect and dignity; relationship to other species; play; and political and material control over one's environment.[15]

While Nussbaum's enumeration and explication of basic capabilities reveals a liberal bias to prioritize human freedom, the Catholic common ground tradition has a strong commitment to the intrinsic sociality of persons and, hence, to the common good. Nussbaum is an important corrective in that she stresses the equality and rights of women, which are necessary to women's equal participation in society with men. The recognizable similarity of these approaches, however, along with their differences, demonstrates that some intercultural consensus on human goods and the good society is possible, and that such a consensus must always be critically revised – especially in view of the needs and voices of excluded persons and groups.

2. Structures: Is there a global sociopolitical structure or government to implement the common good?

The key point here is that implementation of the common good, considering the fact of globalization, cannot and does not reside under the authority of a global government, or even of an aggregate or coalition of national governments. Other alternatives are emerging, however, that are treated in the chapters by Scott Appleby and Bryan Hehir on civil society and the new world order. Obviously, not all forms of global civil society work for the common good. However, the questions are whether, on the whole, emerging social movements and alliances foster the engagement of those who otherwise tend to be marginalized by globalization and whether, on the whole, such engagement tends to disrupt unjust patterns of exploitation and serve basic human needs rather than the reverse.

Looking at the historical evidence, it is hard to answer this question decisively. Since the practical viability of the normative common good concept of CST depends on an affirmative answer, I am going to concentrate on providing it, while granting the ambiguity of the results. In the words of Immanuel Wallerstein, "We are in effect being called upon to construct our utopias, not merely to dream about them. Something will be constructed. If we do not participate in the construction, others will determine it for us."[16] The political scientist Richard Falk believes that such utopianism is rooted in reality and not merely fantastical.[17] The emergence of a new global order provides conditions under which realignments of power and association can yield another Grotian moment. An equally creative and normative consensus can emerge around "widely shared human values," values that can be implemented through new forms of agency and "globalization from below."[18] Emerging global civil society and forms of transnational and international action might address a number of specific concerns. These include a revenue base to support global public goods, including the environment; treaties to uphold human rights; and the enhancement of participation and representation in global policies by means of citizens' organizations and other transnational networks. Other concerns address regulatory cooperation to protect those "victimized by capital and monetary flows" and mechanisms of accountability for national governments, such the International Criminal Court.[19] Falk realizes that utopian visions fly in the face of conventional wisdom and realist politics, but he nonetheless urges us to enter "self-confidently into the dialogic space between entrenched political power and transnational social forces," granting autonomy to neither.[20]

Margaret Keck and Kathryn Sikkink supportively contend that international advocacy networks have already improved the situation for women's rights, indigenous rights, labour rights, and human rights in general, as well as for the environment. They argue that successful networks give centrality to values and principles, make creative use of information, and involve non-governmental actors that use sophisticated political strategies in their campaigns.[21] Feminist legal theorists Hilary Charlesworth and Christine Chinkin cite, with approval, Falk's invocation of a Grotian moment. They suggest that "feminist approaches to international law can contribute to the modern Grotian project" by "recasting the role of international law so that it can transform ideas about justice and order in the international community."[22] Keck and Sikkink confirm Falk's interest in new forms of transnational agency as constituting a powerful reformist trajectory. Charlesworth and Chinkin show that social projects emerging from below and from grassroots networks that gather momentum and gain organization across borders ultimately have a positive effect on international institutions and agreements. Responsive policy at higher levels, in turn, helps shape the horizons and the conditions of local experiences.

In CST, the element that best reflects this dynamic is the principle of subsidiarity. Hollenbach captures this principle as reflecting the limits of government and as implying that "civil society" is "the soil in which the seeds of human sociality grow." The subsidiarity of local communities and associations is necessary to "the common good of participatory government."[23] Yet government still has a responsibility to reign in or modify subsidiary action that is detrimental to the good of the whole or injurious to the welfare of some members.[24] In the globalization era, what has changed is the idea that a global public authority can ensure this balance.[25] Therefore, subsidiarity has to be reconceived so that its connotation of a vertical dynamic of influence is expanded to include horizontal and "transversal" exercises of authority and efficacy, characterized by "power-sharing."[26]

3. Dispositions: Is there the moral will to implement the common good globally?

Protestant theologians with a strong sense of human incorrigibility, such as Karl Barth and Reinhold Niebuhr, have long accused CST of naïveté and excessive optimism in its approach to social reform, not to mention Pelagianism. Niebuhr famously declared original sin to be the only Christian doctrine susceptible of empirical verification.[27] If the critique had not hit home, the brave defence of reformist civil society put forward by Falk and others would be unnecessary. To the extent that their descriptions of pro-social historical trends are accurate, the criticism has been met.

One specific contribution that CST can make to enhance the moral will to change is to advance a worldview rooted in Christian symbols and narratives – such as image of God, brotherhood of Christ, and hospitality to the stranger.

Another very important contribution is to connect these images to expressions that carry a wider resonance or valence in a religiously pluralistic global culture – some examples are solidarity, preferential option for the poor, and social mortgage on property.[28] In a development of the natural law tradition of earlier social encyclicals, Christian themes and virtues engage with and inform a wider social milieu without giving up their integrity and distinctive character, or denying or overriding the other religious contexts into which they are received.

Robert Schreiter speaks of four important interreligious global theological flows in which Christian narratives, symbols, and practices participate: theologies of liberation, feminism, ecology, and human rights. Religions are providing concerted anti-systemic action, and are especially effective when global systems do not live up to their promises of progress, equality, and inclusion. Religious discourses are not uniform because they are rooted in specific cultural and social contexts; yet religions share a drive toward coherence, contain prophetic elements that resist exploitation of the powerless, and set human projects against the horizon of transcendent meaning. They can also be intelligible to other cultural discourses that are resisting the same kind of effects of globalization and mounting the same kind of protest.[29] Critics from Reinhold Niebuhr to Scott Appleby have shown that religious symbols of ultimacy can be co-opted by political and social forces aiming to acquire or consolidate violent social power. However, I believe, with CST, that it is still true that religion is a potent conversionary force that can form virtues of solidarity and hope.[30]

According to John Boswell, the distinctiveness of CST lies in the pre-eminence of solidarity within the inseparable triad of justice, subsidiarity, and solidarity. Justice defines right social relations, while subsidiarity guarantees that corrupt authority, an ever-present danger to justice, submits to correctives. Solidarity enlivens the just society, sustaining subsidiarity, the most practical test of the realization of the common good. Solidarity imparts to other values – such as justice, human rights, freedom, and subsidiarity – a distinctive character of altruism and compassion without which "Catholic social thought is impossible."[31]

While both charity and solidarity have a long history in CST,[32] as religiously inspired social virtues essential to authentic realization of the common good, the virtue of solidarity has acquired special prominence in the writings of John Paul II. In *Sollicitudo rei socialis*, he defines the virtue of solidarity as "a firm and persevering determination to commit oneself to the common good," in recognition of the interdependence of all and the mutual responsibility of all. This virtue overcomes the thirst for power and profit, but, according to John Paul II, is only possible with "the help of divine grace" (38). He elaborates the meaning of this virtue with references to the gospels, and characterizes it as "undoubtedly a Christian virtue" (40). In *Centesimus Annus*, John Paul II connects solidarity with charity, the love of the Lord Jesus Christ, and the "preferential option for the poor" (11). Yet he still sees it as valid "both in the internal order of each nation and in the international order" (10). There may be a tension here, as the dominant natural law and reason language that promoted the concept of the common good in earlier encyclicals up through Paul VI, gives way (without disappearing) to John Paul II's favoured biblical and faith themes. The special emphasis on solidarity as a Christian virtue, one contingent on religious conversion, may isolate the Catholic social message from the broader audience John Paul II envisions and play into the negativity toward broad, concerted social change that usually accompanies religious sectarianism. Yet, on the other side, John Paul II's message comes through clearly. He says that the availability of mechanisms of change will not actually bear fruit in the practical common good of the world's peoples if recognition of interdependence as a positive and normative element in human well-being cannot be evoked more widely.

The virtue of hope, important to feminist and other liberationist ethics, is the disposition to act habitually as if the attitude of solidarity and the practice of cooperation were viable possibilities. Margaret Farley says that underneath any claim on our compassion is a claim on our hope. "Human persons are the sort of beings who cannot live without hope – without, that is, a sense of future."[33] Not fanciful or delusional, but rooted in emerging solidaristic and collaborative practices, the virtue of hope makes it possible to live by the positive evidence while not ignoring the negative. Hope as a theological virtue is rooted in the experience of a transcendent power that sustains and completes frail human virtues, making possible what seems out of reach. Hope as a human virtue is rooted in the experience of historical openness and possibility, in the glimpse of fellowship and joy through cracks in walls of separation and confinement that used to seem impenetrable.

As a final point, despite evidence of newly developing structures of civil society and despite the cultivation of the virtues of solidarity and hope, social conversion and reform will never be complete. Thus, an element to be accentuated in social teaching of the future – more than in that since the 1960s – is the occasional, but still very definite, need for coercion to secure justice in social relations. Still needed is a principle of forceful intervention that is similar to the principle that undergirded the traditional just war theory. Once again, though, the structures of social agency have changed in the age of globalization; coercive authority is not limited to the nation-state, a comprehensive public authority, or international institutions. Activist networks and non-governmental organizations, along with dissenting national governments, can challenge and even coerce some aspects of global systems, at least some of the time.[34]

4. Efficacy: How can CST interface ecumenically with other traditions and movements to advance the global common good?

This question has already been addressed by the argument that Catholic theology is participating in a global theological flow, an interreligious movement that challenges some effects of globalization and is partly enabled by the same technologies that drive globalization. The question of CST's future influence should be connected with the analysis, already given, of emerging forms of global civil society. Just as civil government now takes place in a more multidimensional and multi-levelled way, so does the exercise of Catholic authority. Borrowing from John Coleman, I have already mentioned several examples of the way Catholic presence around the globe is advancing Catholic social ideals at the practical level, interfacing with and learning from other movements in a variety of cultures. Robert Schreiter reminds us that the theological identity of tomorrow is almost sure to be hybrid, as interaction destabilizes received perceptions and convictions.[35]

John Boswell resists the relegation of the "non-official, non-ecclesiastical stream" of CST to the margins of the tradition and the assumption that the latter consists primarily of pronouncements of the magisterium.[36] Defenders and critics alike concede, wrongfully, that authority emanates from the centre and that remedies for shortcomings likewise await the action of the magisterium. Boswell notes that prior to Vatican II, a number of non-official expressions, such as "trade unions, professional bodies, action groups and political parties" were highly visible purveyors of CST. Further, new variants such as "organisations in the areas of anti-poverty, justice, peace and overseas aid," may yet rise up as replacements.[37]

Schreiter envisions a positive, reconstructive task for theology, after the fact of globalization, and in pursuit of a more adequate and participatory instantiation of the common good. Similarly to Falk's Grotian moment, Schreiter believes globalization may present an axial moment when change is possible under a new normative construction of global relationships.[38] Corresponding to the increasingly pluralistic face of social agency, both in global religious life and in global civil society, Schreiter proposes several tasks for theology in this process. These tasks do not have to be fulfilled simultaneously or in a given sequence by the same agents or within the same social locations or institutions. They are the tasks of resistance, denunciation, critique (social analysis), advocacy, and reconstruction.[39]

Reconstruction involves developing "the means for new forms of cooperation…in the name of justice and in the hope for a renewed situation for humanity."[40] Within this task, Schreiter introduces the concept of "middle axioms," developed by J.H. Oldham for the World Council of Churches in the 1930s,[41] and retrieved periodically by other theologians (usually Protestant), including John C. Bennett[42] and, recently, Charles Villa-Vicencio.[43] Although sometimes middle axioms have been interpreted as deductive principles by which basic premises of Christian theology are applied to concrete situations (Bennett), Oldham, Villa-Vicencio, and Schreiter do not employ the term on a deductive model. Rather, middle axioms – which may be, perhaps, a poor choice of phrase – are interactive points of interdisciplinary collaboration when social needs and Christian values reach a working arrangement or equilibrium, and it is possible to propose a sort of intermediary vision of what a renewed society would be like. Thus, the specific content of a middle axiom must vary with the circumstances. Middle axioms are operative in and through mediating institutions that work to reconstruct societies in contemporary situations of injustice, conflict, or disarray.[44]

In the category of dispositions, the importance of interreligious cooperation has already been introduced. Many traditions, perhaps all traditions, include symbols, narratives, and practices that can enhance compassionate, inclusive, and just action. In fact, the interreligious piece will be an important facet in the development of the notion of common good in Catholic perspective in this millennium. It is a piece that affects goods, structures, and efficacy – not only dispositions. As is illustrated by Wendy Tyndale's chapter in this volume, communities come together in participatory social action when they decide to confront together threats to goods valued by all. Effective action is often accomplished through structures formed in solidarity and reflecting collective agency at the local level; this, then, develops or connects with institutional counterparts at higher or more comprehensive levels. For instance, Tyndale recounts the mobilization of fishworkers in the Indian state of Kerala, at first under Roman Catholic leadership, then evolving into an interfaith organization that was in fact able to resist efforts by subsequent local Catholic leaders to curtail the organization's political effectiveness.[45]

> Inherent to the theology of the Christians who acted as a catalyst for the fisher people's movements in Kerala is the importance of giving power to those who are powerless – that is – enabling people, as far as possible, to make their own choices about matters which affect their lives....
>
> Many of the values...are, of course, shared by people of other religions or of none. The Hindu and Muslim fisher people would certainly identify wit the view that development is about enabling people to sustain a livelihood in harmony with other people and with the natural resources around them. Moreover, in both these religions there is a strong tradition of sharing with the poor.[46]

In summary, CST today becomes concrete and functional within local and collaborative ventures. Local and mid-level experiences of participation in the common good refine and communicate CST in their own right, but they also eventually inform the official formulations that, in reality, have always been interdependent with them. The importance of the multifocal character of social Catholicism is especially important in a global Church. Only through the conduit of the local, in communication with other sites of social and ecclesial agency (including pope and bishops), can the fullness of Catholic Christian experience, belief, practice, and theology come to bear on the common good. The global common good, to be served by CST, is participation of all peoples in a diverse and differentiated, yet solidaristic and collaborative, world society. The global common good is both a normative ideal and an incipient form of life, embodying the cooperative and just interdependence of all human beings and cultures, and also of all that is human with the entire created universe.

4

Economic Justice and Globalization

James E. Hug S.J.

Social Location

I approach this topic not as a student of globalization literature but as an activist for global economic justice. Although I began my professional ministry in academia, teaching theological social ethics, most of my professional experience of globalization has come from personal involvement in the negotiations and civil society activities at eight global conferences. I have also followed the policy negotiations at the UN, the World Bank (WB), the International Monetary Fund (IMF), and the World Trade Organization (WTO) over the last fifteen years with my colleagues at the Center of Concern and our partners in at least seven active international networks.

My theological training brings me to the topic of globalization with an assumption and a commitment. First, I assume that there is a disconnect between the concept of economic justice our Catholic Christian tradition embraces and that of the US and some other Western cultures. In the US, for example, economic justice requires that each person have an equal opportunity to participate and compete. Its focus is upon the fairness of the process. From the Christian biblical and social traditions, economic justice requires more; it requires that each person also have adequate resources, insofar as they are available to the community, to survive, to develop and thrive, and to give back in service to the community. This Christian understanding of economic justice looks for fairness and adequacy in the outcomes of economic activity as well as in its competitive process. It defines a minimum acceptable quality of life for each person. This inevitably leads to differences in judgment with those whose sense of justice demands only equal opportunity and fairness of process.

Secondly, I must acknowledge with many other people of faith a preferential commitment to collaboration in solidarity with those in poverty worldwide in the struggle for economic justice. This demands special attention in structural analyses of the causes and dynamics of injustice to the roles of gender, race, and class. These observations will help to clarify the perspective, the selection of issues, and the conclusions in the pages to follow.

New Historical Context

While there have been other waves of globalization in history, such as the ages of exploration and empires, important characteristics of the contemporary period raise new challenges and offer new promise and serious danger. The technologies of this age have extended the global interconnections farther than ever before, made global communications nearly instantaneous, and generated pressures for institutions and laws of global governance that represent a new phase in human political history.

The international processes and arenas are where the struggles over the shape and control of this new stage of political life are being engaged and where I deal with the economic justice questions that contemporary globalization raises. This highly conflictual situation is substantially different from the conflict in which Catholic Social Thought (CST) developed in the last century.

Through much of its development during the twentieth century, CST claimed a centrist position between harsh forms of liberal capitalism and collectivist forms of socialism or communism. In pre-1989 Catholic social teaching, great care was taken to criticize the errors of both systems and promote the values of both, calling for an integration of the best features of each in some form of social market system.

That historical context no longer exists. Through the 1980s and into the 1990s, China began experimenting cautiously with forms of freer local and national economic markets. In 1989 the Soviet Union, the other major historical carrier of collectivist socialism, collapsed.

As these two dramatic historical transformations were unfolding, the dominant form of capitalism claiming victory and assuming unchallenged hegemony over the developing globalization of economic structures and networks was that promoted for a decade in the West. This capitalism developed under the political direction of Margaret Thatcher in the UK and Ronald Reagan in the US. This ideological vision proclaimed the social welfare state of the previous decades a failed experiment. It set about restructuring the national economies of the US and the UK according to a neo-liberal vision of export-oriented development characterized by market liberalization, the cutback and privatization of social services, and the reduction of the role of government to protection and service of the market.

The floods of petro-dollars into poor developing nations in the 1970s and the debt crises of the early 1980s, with their roots in the oil crises, gave the Reagan and Thatcher governments a unique opportunity also to restructure the economies of poorer nations. With dominant voting power on the boards of the WB and IMF, they were able to require a package of neo-liberal structural reforms as the condition for desperately needed debt relief.

These Structural Adjustment Programs (SAPs) oriented the debt-ridden economies toward participation in global markets to earn enough hard currency to repay their debts – or at least service them. Often, small farmers were displaced as the best lands were set aside for export crops. Export earnings flowed from the poor nations of the South to the large banks, governments, and multilateral institutions of the North. The wealth of the impoverished nations was being drained off, rather than invested in the development of the people.

The debts of the poorest nations, often illegitimate for many reasons, became levers of power in the hands of the wealthy nations of the West. They used this power to reshape national economies and build a neo-liberal form of global economy at the cost of increased hardship and suffering for people in some of the worst poverty around the world. Fifteen years of growing social protests have forced some modification of SAPs and the introduction of various debt relief programs. Fundamentally, however, the situation of poor indebted nations remains desperate. And their debt remains an instrument of control in the hands of creditor nations and institutions.

To put it in an unvarnished way, then, the functioning economic system, which took the reins of globalization processes in 1989 and retains them to this day, was the most extreme form in a century of the type of laissez-faire capitalism CST finds objectionable. Socialist collectivism is no longer a serious opponent, either ideologically or politically. The Catholic community can no longer locate itself in a centrist position, carefully balancing its critiques of competing systems in broad general terms. It must now directly criticize injustices at all levels of the political economy within which it lives and operates. It must offer moral guidance for all socio-economic actors in determining future economic structures and policies, and it must model the justice it calls for in its own structures and activities.

The Catholic community is not alone in its critical approach to this context, however. Over the last two decades, a growing number of non-governmental organizations (NGOs), civil society organizations (CSOs), and broad-based social movements – such as the women's movement, labour movements, and the environmental movement – have emerged to challenge destructive economic, social, and ecological impacts of the neo-liberal political economy. These organizations and movements have raised severe critiques of the SAPs and the neo-liberal trade agenda. They grew in strength and coherence through the recent fifteen-year series of UN world conferences and now focus, as well, upon the regular meetings of the multilateral institutions. The World Social Forum has become their highest-profile annual gathering.

These organizations and social movements are in broad general agreement on the need for alternative approaches to development. They judge poverty around the world to be less the result of personal or local failure to climb a ladder of development and more the result of active impoverishment caused by neo-liberal policies. The activities of the powerful and the wealthy result – sometimes knowingly and sometimes unknowingly, sometimes deliberately and sometimes accidentally – in the impoverishment of vast numbers of people.

The critics of neo-liberal globalization are widely dubbed anti-globalizers or the anti-globalization movement. This is a transparent – and, unfortunately, fairly successful – effort to discredit the movement and divert attention from the important insights in its critique. Using the technological tools of globalization, the movement is more properly a movement for a more just form of globalization – a movement for global justice.

Under the pressure of the movement critique, the Washington Consensus – a current name for the neo-liberal, export-oriented, and free trade approach to development – is more and more broadly recognized as a failure. The WB and IMF, the major implementers of the Washington Consensus, have increasingly acknowledged these failures. People in 54 nations under the sway of the Washington Consensus are poorer now than they were a decade ago, according to the UN Development Program's *Human Development Report 2003*.[1]

The Washington Consensus remains the dominant policy approach to development, not because it is economically superior, but because the WB and the IMF that impose it both have plutocratic governance structures: the majority of decision-making power resides with the wealthy nations. The Washington Consensus survives today because of the international institutional power of the wealthy nations who benefit from it most.

At the same time, the most democratic of the multilateral institutions, the UN, has been deliberately discredited by the wealthy nations in recent decades. The WTO, which is also constitutionally democratic in structure, has been controlled by the wealthy nations through a distressingly large array of deceptive and bullying tactics, as detailed in a 2003 joint NGO study produced in Geneva.

The primary economic justice issues at this stage of the globalization process, then, are political or power issues. To understand them better, evaluate them, and recommend useful directions for future action, it will be helpful to clarify the dynamics that have created this situation and are driving it.

Major Dynamics

Technological developments are at the foundation of globalizing forces over the last four decades. The advances in technology revolutionized production, communications, and transportation. Machines replaced workers, increasing reliability and efficiency in production while reducing the power and leverage of organized labour. As communications improved, it became possible to coordinate activities in various parts of the world quickly and reliably. As transportation became faster and cheaper, it became possible to transport goods produced at most places in the world to most other spots at affordable costs.

Labour, then, became the major variable in the cost of production. Machines could be moved from country to country – wherever there was adequate power, infrastructure, and skilled labour for them to work. And so corporations moved their production facilities to cheaper, cooperative labour. Debate raged in the 1970s over the emergence of the global factory and the resulting de-industrialization of America. What could or should be done about the workers and what could be done for the communities left in ruins by the departure of their local industries? But the process could not be stopped. Workers in different parts of the world were turned against each other in competition for basic livelihoods.

As corporations opened operations in various parts of the world, it became less possible for national governments to regulate them. The transnational corporations (TNCs) were able to transfer profits through intra-company trading and various accounting processes to those nations where taxes were lowest. They were able to locate production to avoid labour regulations and environmental constraints. They learned to take advantage of their mobility and increasing wealth to negotiate even more favorable conditions from poor nations desperate for jobs and vulnerable to bribery and corruption. In effect, TNCs had slipped beyond the control of national governments. They took advantage of the situation to increase their wealth and power. As more companies went transnational, the competitive pressures of the market forced many others to follow.

Throughout this period, a cultural shift was in process that was providing greater and greater legitimation for corporate freedom and the dominance of market values and systems. Through the labour struggles of the early part of the twentieth century, the stock market crash of 1929, and the Great Depression and its New Deal antidote, the US cultural understanding of the role of government became clarified and firmly entrenched in the national psyche: the role of government was to make up for the deficiencies of the market in service of the common good.

By the 1980s and 1990s, that cultural assumption had been turned on its head. Government had long been under attack as bloated and inefficient. A patient campaign has been waged over more than five decades to wrest control of the commanding heights of the economy from the hands of government back into the hands of corporate leadership. The success of that effort is witnessed in the current conventional wisdom in the US and much of the West where the private sector can do almost anything better than government: the market should be trusted to make up for the deficiencies of government and serve the common good.

This careful tilling of the cultural ground made it fertile for the emergence of neo-liberalism just as communist socialism collapsed. The balanced social system or political economy of the West, in which corporations were authorized to pursue profit maximization within a framework of government regulations that guided their energies into service of the common good, had broken down. With new cultural legitimation, increased transnational freedom, growing wealth, and political power, TNCs joined the ranks of the most powerful global actors, able to influence national governments to serve their profit goals. National governments could no longer adequately protect social and environmental values from private sector excesses.

Needs of TNCs in a Global Market

While deregulation and market freedoms are perennial refrains of corporate leaders, the fact remains that corporations require certain regulatory frameworks to function and succeed. A wide-open frontier context is a threatening environment for enterprise. Corporations need to know that terms and concepts used in business contracts and other international negotiations have common meanings and that agreements they enter into can be enforced. They need to know that their investments and profits cannot, or will not, be expropriated. They need protection from ruthless behaviours of other entrepreneurs. They need, in other words, an international regulatory system.

In recent decades, TNCs have pressed national governments to establish a system of global governance to serve their trade needs. That infrastructure requires a systematization of critical economic concepts – such as ownership, property rights, and so forth – and local or national systems of regulatory legislation.

The Uruguay Round of the Global Agreement on Tariffs and Trade (the GATT) established the WTO as the multilateral institution to bring about an integrated global trade infrastructure. Independent of the UN system, its mandate is global trade liberalization. It organizes negotiations and judges international trade disputes. Either corporations or nation states can bring cases before it. Its unique power to levy sanctions makes it the most powerful multilateral institution in the global arena. It can judge local or national laws – such as those protecting workers or the environment, or supporting local or national enterprises – to be illegitimate restraints on free global trade, and it can impose heavy penalties.

Systemic Imbalances

This sets up dangerous systemic imbalances at the international level. First, it constitutes a global governance system that effectively subordinates human rights, social values, ecological concerns, and all other dimensions of the common well-being of the planetary community to the economic needs and interests promoted by powerful corporate interests through their national governments. In effectively subordinating all other governance responsibilities to the demands of economic liberalization, it has created a materialistic, economistic global governance system.

Second, the most powerful corporations and the most influential national governments through this globalization process are Western. This has meant the promotion of processes of systematization dominated by Western cultural notions of ownership, wealth, property rights, legal protections, and so forth. The negotiation processes have revealed no efforts to study the variety of cultural understandings of ownership and exchange processes and to build a global system drawing on, and integrating, the best in all of them. Western concepts and processes upon which the wealthiest and most powerful corporations are built are being laid down as the form of the global trading system into which all nations are being ushered.

This new form of global governance is a clear case of cultural imperialism with immense economic repercussions.

Third, the wealth, power, and cultural advantages of the TNCs in these processes allow them to promote global trade policies that serve their interests above those of less powerful actors such as smaller economies, indebted nations, or small and vulnerable national enterprises. The rules are being developed to ensure the continued dominance of the wealthy and powerful, as much as that can be envisioned.

Finally, in pressing to address the legitimate trading needs and concerns of TNCs and larger industrial and service economies, the wealthy nations at the WTO are forcing issues that poorer nations are not equipped to understand adequately or negotiate in ways that would protect the interests of their people. As a result, global institutions and policies are currently being promoted around competition policy, investment policy, government procurement, and trade in services that could structure poorer nations into permanent economic dependency, undermining any possibility of their designing or implementing home-grown development strategies that are better oriented to their local needs.

The Challenge of Creating a More Just Globalization

Pursuing economic justice in this stage of globalization, then, has several serious challenges. We must address the domination of economic values and institutions embodied in the unaccountable power of TNCs, the WTO, WB, and IMF. We need to offer an alternative vision of development values and institutions capable of shaping a more just future. We must lay out the proper relationship of the institutions of the private and public sectors to achieve this alternate vision and point toward how they should be organized and established. We need to extend this vision and our approaches toward establishing it to current areas of conflict and negotiation in global political arenas. We must promote solidarity, rather than competition and conflict, between workers and peoples of different nations. And we must find ways to help a religious ethic of globalization evolve through cross-cultural interfaith dialogue.

Catholic Social Thought: Initial Reflections

These challenges give rise to a number of initial observations. First, the imbalance in power among nations calls into question the justice of their agreements. In *Rerum Novarum* (#45), Pope Leo XIII had warned that agreements between unequal partners are not necessarily fair just because they have been entered into by mutual consent. Pope Paul VI applied that principle "with equal force to contracts made between nations." (*Populorum Progressio*, #59) The development of a global trading system must be based on more than treaty agreements. It must enshrine the commitment to justice in its global rules – justice that guarantees that all, especially those in poverty, have what they need to survive and develop. Current agreements, insofar as they are not just, are illegitimate and must be replaced.

Second, CST has a strong critique of neo-liberal economic polity, placing the Catholic community among the social movements that are critical of contemporary forms of globalization.

Third, CST brings a more developed ethical framework than many of those social movements and can help them situate, refine, correct, and develop their intuitive critiques. At the same time, CST can find in the insights and demands of the social movements a rough form of social and moral discernment of the signs of the times, learn from them, and incorporate them into its development.

Fourth, many of the worst abuses and problems experienced in contemporary globalization would dissolve if people, corporations, and nation states were to abide by well-established CST principles. Many of the evils involved are not the result of inadequate thought or lack of knowledge; they are easily traceable to temptations of greed and power.

Finally, the important issues raised by the social movements and central to the formal negotiations among nations are the critical ethical issues of globalization today that CST must address. In the following sections, I will address several of the most important.

CST and Social Movements: Seeking a More Holistic Model of Development

The slogans of various social movements for global justice are many and include the following: "Trade for People, not People for Trade"; "People not Profits"; "Our World Is Not for Sale"; and "Another World Is Possible." They point to the conviction that the neo-liberal approach to development through market primacy and trade liberalization violates essential human values. Strategies focused only on economic growth not only cannot achieve development, they harm and prevent it.

Development is a dynamic social reality. It involves personal and community growth and maturation within the planetary context. These do not result automatically from increased trade or economic growth. In an effort to reach development more attuned to the rich complexity of human persons and communities, some civil society groups and NGOs promote the evaluation of development by a triple bottom line, which adds social and environmental issues and concerns to economic ones.

The social bottom line includes respect for human dignity and protection of the human rights and fundamental freedoms that flow from it. These are widely acknowledged to include rights to the essentials required for survival and development: food, clothing, shelter, health care, education, work or employment with a just wage, leisure, freedom of speech, religion, association, migration, and participation in society. Universal human dignity also demands that each person support the fundamental rights and freedoms of every other person.

The international women's movement has further elaborated the social dimension of development under the rubric of social reproduction. Social reproduction includes all those activities that are essential for human development and community well-being but are not part of the formal economy: domestic chores, basic family education and health care, care of the elderly, and the passing on of culture, faith, and traditions. In 1995 the UNDP *Human Development Report*[2] estimated that the unpaid, or care, economy – the world of social reproduction – provided an essential support to the money economy: a $16 trillion subsidy to the $26 trillion money economy. Feminist scholars have shown the destructive effects of neo-liberal economic policies on social reproduction.

These insights express the richly differentiated character of human development. Human rights and responsibilities are grounded in human dignity and share its sacred character. They are not given by governments and not earned or won in the marketplace. Governments and markets must respect and support them.

Evolving CST has presented authentic human development as embracing the social, cultural, political, and spiritual dimensions of human life. It involves each person developing skills and gifts for community service. Pope John Paul II insisted that the development of the person in the process of working is more important than the object or service produced.

Environmental organizations and ecological movements have worked against the negative impact of neo-liberal policies on the essential ecological foundations of planetary life now and in future generations. Indigenous peoples and many NGOs and social movements are fighting corporate efforts to commodify life forms by patenting them. The ecological bottom line assesses what happens to these values under different approaches to development.

In recent years, CST has become more outspoken on ecological issues, arguing that authentic human development includes living in a healthy, non-exploitive relationship with the global ecology. CST's vision of authentic development is being enriched and made more adequate by integrating ecological issues and concerns. Its vision will be further enriched in essential ways by incorporating the insights of the global women's movement on social reproduction. They flesh out and specify in fuller ways the dimensions of sacred human dignity and social development and focus attention on important, but too often hidden, moral issues.

With that enrichment, CST will be all the more clearly a natural ethical home for those demanding "People, not Profits"; "Our World Is Not for Sale"; "Trade for People, Not People for Trade"; and "Another World Is Possible." For more than a decade, Pope John Paul II insisted that there are certain things that must not ultimately be subject to market dynamics. He characterized the dominance of market values and principles in social organization as a form of idolatry. He proclaimed it a "strict duty of justice and truth" to guarantee that anything essential to survival and to authentic development must not be simply under market control. (*Centesimus Annus*, 34). The well-being, or common good, of people must always command higher priority than market profits.

CST and Social Movements: The Role of Government

For CST, the protection and support of the authentic human development of all people and of the social, cultural, economic, political, and ecological conditions essential to it is the role of government. Government is to serve and preserve the common good. It cannot achieve authentic development for anyone; people must be active subjects in order to develop. But it can protect the rights of all and support the conditions for development as far as possible.

CST envisions a complex, multi-layered society founded on individual initiative and shared responsibility that expresses itself through participation in a vast variety of organizations and social movements. The interrelationships of those organizations must be coordinated in such a way that they actually serve the common good of all and protect the global commons of the human community. That coordination constitutes the role of government.

Guiding these complex social relationships is the principle of subsidiarity, articulated by Pope Pius XI in 1931. (*Quadragesimo Anno*, 80) In part, this principle insists that it is wrong for higher levels of social organization to do for individuals and groups what they can accomplish by their own initiative and hard work. Social activity is meant to enable the participants to develop themselves and care for their families and communities. The principle of subsidiarity supports grassroots social development. Each community must develop the form of social institution most appropriate to its own people. The responsibility of government is not to supplant this process, but to support and facilitate it.

This responsibility takes priority over repaying debts to wealthy institutions and governments. CST insists the repayment of debts must not require draining national resources essential to meeting the basic needs of impoverished people for food, shelter, health care, and education. CST demands that national governments first respond to those needs under their fundamental human rights commitments.

Here CST stands firmly among the NGOs, social movements, and developing countries resisting the imposition of a single model of neo-liberal development by global institutions. It opposes the WB, IMF, and WTO, driven by wealthy nations and their corporate interests, imposing a one-size-fits-all approach to development on the smaller and poorer nations of the world. This system is affecting the smaller and poorer nations by destroying their cultures and ecologies, disrupting their social systems, undermining their national economic development, and violating their national sovereignty.

NGOs that have been following the international negotiations have been struggling to democratize those decision-making processes to open political space for other approaches to development. They are demanding access to information and documentation, transparency in negotiations, participation for governments and peoples' organizations in the decisions that affect them, and means for holding decision-makers accountable. Participation, transparency, and accountability have become the global strategy for breaking the neo-liberal dominance.

CST stands in full support of these demands and grounds them systematically. The opportunity for democratic participation in decision-making is the best way to respect the dignity of people. Participation in government is one of the major instruments by which people cooperate in order to achieve the common good. Fostering the international common good requires frameworks and opportunities for participation in international organizations as well.

In the current context, smaller and poorer nations do not have the ability to protect their needs and concerns in the financial and trade decisions that affect their welfare. CSOs essential to holding national and international institutions accountable are given little opportunity to participate in the financial and trade-policy decision-making processes. Their participation is all the more essential in light of the corrupting power of big money over governments. Participation, transparency, and accountability in support of local and national self-governance are essential demands in the CST vision of a possible, more just, world.

CST and Social Movements: World Government

Beyond insisting on widespread participation and a bottom-up approach to social development, the principle of subsidiarity requires that what individuals and local organizations cannot do for themselves to secure the common good must be done by higher forms of social organization or government. CST demands higher levels of organization and authority when lower ones cannot support the development of each person and serve the common good.

In other words, CST does not consider national sovereignty absolute. If nation-states cannot adequately regulate TNCs, global governance institutions become essential both to facilitate TNC activities and to regulate them in service to the global common good. Church leaders since Pope John XXIII in the early 1960s have pointed out the historic need for global government to provide for the universal common good of the whole human family – arguing for it on the basis of the principle of subsidiarity. (*Pacem in Terris*, 140; *Centesimus Annus*, 15, 48).

This is a corrective to some NGOs and elements of the broad social movements that call for an end to global institutions in the name of national sovereignty. Global governance institutions are essential at this stage of human development precisely to protect the common good where sovereign nations no longer can. Those NGOs and social movements are correct in this, however: the WTO, WB, and IMF are currently usurping decisions and policy-making that belong at the national and local levels. These institutions need to be reorganized so that they safeguard all legitimate forms of national sovereignty under the principle of subsidiarity.

The various institutions of global governance need to be reintegrated as well to better reflect all values of authentic human development and work together to protect them. They must give structural governance priority to human rights and fundamental freedoms, including the right to development, while regulating transnational economic actors in ways that facilitate their activities yet channel them into serving the universal common good. Increased authority for the institutions committed to protecting human rights and ecological integrity must supplant the current dominance of the WTO with its trade liberalization mandate.

Many NGOs and social movements in the global North – wealthy, industrial nations – seek to use a different approach to correct the power imbalance by demanding labour and environmental standards as integral parts of trade agreements. It is a pragmatic strategy: the WTO has the power of enforcement and is the most powerful international institution. Therefore, the easiest way forward is to use its power to enforce labour and environmental standards.

But NGOs and social movements in the global South – poor, developing nations – and some of their colleagues in the North reject that strategy. First, they note that the standards can be used as a means of protectionism to exclude Southern exports. They point out, second, that the inclusion of labour and environmental standards developed in the North is a form of cultural imposition by the powerful nations upon the weak. Third, including labour and environmental standards in trade agreements simply increases the power and reach of the WTO. They do not change the fact that labour and environmental concerns will be subordinated to the WTO's primary mandate – trade liberalization – rather than orienting trade liberalization to the service of human rights, environmental health, and the global common good. The real way to correct the imbalance among global governance institutions is to give greater power to the multilateral labour and ecological institutions, integrating them under the UN.

The Universal Common Good

Concern for the global, or universal, common good immediately raises an important issue for human development: the massive disparity in wealth and power within countries and between countries. Pope John Paul II often called attention to it as a grave injustice. The universal destiny of the goods of creation – the insistence that all the resources of creation were given to the human community as a whole to meet the needs of all people – is a foundational principle of CST. People have a right to those things that are essential for their survival and development. Essentials must not be subject simply to the laws of the market.

Policies to govern trade in several of these essentials are currently under negotiation in the Doha Round of WTO trade talks and in various regional and bilateral trade negotiations. They are generally grouped under three broad headings: agricultural trade, trade-related intellectual property rights (TRIPS), and trade in services.

Agricultural Trade

The negotiations over trade in agricultural products have been stalemated for many years. A few wealthy nations or groups of nations – especially the US and the European Union (EU) – have massive agricultural support programs. The US and the EU have different systems of support, however, which has enabled them each to attack the other's system while protecting its own.

The nations of the global South have been forced, through structural adjustment programs and rigged trade rules, to reduce their farm supports and tariffs on food products while those of the US and the EU have been protected. Current policies under negotiation at the WTO and in various regional trade negotiations would open markets in the South even more without significantly affecting those of the North.

This effectively puts small farmers in the South, who constitute the vast majority of the economy in most poor nations, into competition with highly subsidized and protected agribusinesses in the North. The North American Free Trade Agreement (NAFTA) has shown that they cannot compete: tens of thousands of small farms, related businesses, and rural communities were lost in Mexico in the years following the implementation of NAFTA due to the influx of subsidized US agribusiness. Most small economies or poor nations cannot offer alternative employment for those displaced, leading to urban and international migration and contributing to the growth of poverty, as seen in many countries following the neo-liberal model.

The universal common good demands that the food security of every person be assured. How can food security be guaranteed? How must agricultural trade be structured to guarantee that everyone has the food they need? It is not enough to simply have adequate food supplies in markets everywhere if people in poverty cannot afford it. Farms have been lost. Government food programs have been cut in most poor nations as part of the reduction of the government sector in the economy. Hunger is increasing.

Some are advocating food sovereignty, which would guarantee to national governments the right to put into place a set of policies guaranteeing food production and food security for all their people. Some governments, in accord with this approach, are demanding the right to exempt certain special products from trade liberalization agreements and the right to protect certain production processes so that they can provide jobs.

This latter approach is consistent with CST's approach to development from the bottom up. It stresses the right of the individual to the essentials for survival, but also the importance of each person having the opportunity to work and develop his or her gifts and talents. And it stresses local and national sovereignty, wherever possible, since it can be more sensitive to local resources and needs, more participatory, and more accountable.

TRIPS

The TRIPS debate concerns medical essentials for survival, but its implications stretch much further. TNCs have now begun patenting some basic life forms and are attempting to obtain property rights to various forms of traditional and indigenous knowledge.

At the Doha Ministerial meeting of the WTO in 2001, nations reached an agreement on essential medicines. It states that any WTO member can override pharmaceutical patents when necessary to provide essential medicines at affordable prices in public health crises such as HIV/AIDS, tuberculosis, and malaria. It urged the Council on TRIPS to find ways for poor nations, unable to produce the medicines themselves, to meet these needs.

Since then, the US alone has been raising every possible legal barrier to implementing this declaration, working to protect the interests and profits of pharmaceutical companies. The ethical conflict here is over the extent and limits of property rights in the face of human need.

As already noted, CST has long insisted that the right to private property is limited by the universal destination of goods and the special application of that principle in the case of items essential for survival and development. CST, then, clearly condemns the actions of the US and the pharmaceutical companies, supporting the right of people to essential medicines.

This extension of these principles to intellectual property is a new and important development. It asserts a social claim on knowledge as well as on material goods. This is especially important in knowledge-based economies where information and expertise are the key source of wealth. The basic principle remains: people have a right to what is essential for survival and this takes priority over the right to private property. But the extent of its applicability – for example, what knowledge really is essential? – will surely be contentious for years to come.

The issue of TRIPS in relation to traditional or indigenous knowledge raises other questions. First, there is the issue of cultural imposition. The patent system enforced by the WTO is a Western creation foreign to many cultures. To recognize how foreign a concept it is, it is enough to note that 97 per cent of all patents are held by individuals and corporations in the West.

As TNCs use the patent system to lay claim to indigenous medicines and traditional healing procedures, a groundswell of resistance is arising. NGOs, social movements, and governments in developing countries are struggling to stop exploitation of their resources and of the knowledge passed down through generations that they consider their rightful heritage.

Their resistance is not simply to the most obvious abuses. In these situations, TNCs come into an area, study local medicines and healing practices, exploit what they find, patent it, profit from it, and then control access to it. This is a modern form of piracy. The resistance also is an effort to secure space to honour another, more communal, form of ownership.

CST's concepts of property and ownership clearly reveal the Western cultural identity of its ethical thought. It is culturally incarnate in Western forms, which raises the issue of cultural relativity in any ethical evaluation of globalization, an issue to which we must return.

Trade in Services

The current negotiations over trade in services centre around the effort to open national markets to TNCs to provide services such as water, health care, education, energy, and finance. Many of these services are essential to human development and the work of social reproduction in society. Privatizing them excludes those in poverty from access to them. In addition, opening markets for TNCs to provide these services too often eliminates the possibility of developing strong national service industries more closely tied to local communities. In both cases, these violate the fundamental principles of authentic development put forward by CST.

In addition, the current proposals offered for negotiation favour the movement of highly skilled professional people while maintaining restrictions on the movement of semi-skilled personnel. This enables wealthy nations to siphon off the most skilled talent from poorer nations while excluding those most in need of basic employment and income. The commitment of CST to the sacred right of each person to the essentials for survival and development imply an ethical demand for the right to migrate freely in pursuit of those rights.

A Globalization of Solidarity

In calling for a globalization of solidarity, Pope John Paul II articulated a foundational belief of CST: all people constitute one family under God. Creating greater economic justice in this age, then, presents a major challenge to workers and policy makers. The difficulty is how, in an economic system based upon competition in which the price of labour is a principal variable in the cost of production, to prevent workers in one nation from fighting those in others for their very survival.

Unfortunately, the strategies of organized labour are too often driven by their members' demands to protect job security and income no matter what the cost to workers elsewhere. In *Economic Justice for All: Catholic Social Teaching and the U.S. Economy*,[3] the US bishops had no simple solution to the tensions involved. However, they did point out, in accordance with the preferential concern for and with those in poverty, that a wealthy nation such as the US has more resources with which to provide for displaced workers than impoverished nations do.

Unfortunately, the political will to provide that help is lacking. For some, divisions among workers strengthen the hand of management and capital. For others, the individuals are responsible for themselves, and larger society has no responsibility for them. Pope John Paul II was clear, however, that the indirect employer, or society at large, is responsible for the well-being and development of all workers, and he called for international collaboration to reduce the imbalances in the standard of living for workers around the globe (*Laborem exercens*, 18).

In this context, the Catholic community needs to encourage organized labour to build international alliances with labour in other parts of the world. The International Labor Organization (ILO) has launched a global campaign for decent work for all; it brings labour, management, and governments together to work out solutions. The campaign offers hope for building global labour solidarity for a more just economy.

People in the wealthy industrial countries, especially members of faith communities, must also re-evaluate lifestyle preferences. Ecologists estimate that for all people on earth to lead a middle-class Western lifestyle would require between three and nine more planets the size and wealth of earth. Pope John Paul II called for an end to superdevelopment of the few so that the majority of the world's people may have enough to survive and develop (*Sollicitudo Rei Socialis*, #28).

This is a major challenge to Christian spirituality in the West. Progress toward achieving it will probably require the exposure of people in the North to the lives of people in the poor nations of the South and the building of relationships of solidarity with them. The Catholic community also needs to develop a spirituality of solidarity for impoverished people that reaffirms their sacred dignity and calls them to the struggle for justice to claim their rights.

Intercultural Interfaith Dialogue

CST offers an important vision of an alternative approach to development with principles designed to evaluate progress in justice and guide implementation. It is, however, a Western cultural product. Its foundational concepts and the principles articulated from them arose in the European context and are most at home in the industrial nations of the West.

This does not necessarily diminish their universal claims or religious insight and importance. However, it does raise the legitimate questions about cultural relativities, biases, and blind spots. We cannot presume that CST is not affected by our Western cultural limitations or that it provides adequate ethical insight and guidance across cultural differences. And it is obvious that it does not carry the rational and symbolic persuasiveness for people of other faiths and cultures that it can for the Western Catholic community.

The globalization process is bringing the world's religious faiths into closer daily interaction. They share many foundational values and concerns. An adequate ethic for the age of globalization must be forged through interfaith and intercultural dialogue. The goal cannot be the victory of one religious ethic over the others. It must be the mutual enrichment of each in dialogue with the others in a common search for a more just globalization that serves the development of each member of God's family.

Conclusion

This is a truly momentous period in the development of the global economy. Policies and institutions are being shaped that will govern economic, social, cultural, and political activities for years to come. The decisions made now on technical, and at times arcane, topics through difficult international negotiations will determine how billions of people will live and in many cases when and why they will die.

The forces engaged in these negotiations have very different degrees and types of wealth and power. They are pursuing different values and visions that are too often incompatible. It is, as in all times of major social change, a time of grave danger and immense opportunity.

The best contribution of the Catholic faith community at this time will be the promotion of CST's universal vision of solidarity in dialogue with the other faith communities of the world. CST offers a challenging and promising message at the same time as it is being invited into a globalizing process that will enrich and enlarge its vision, its ethic, and its religious adequacy. This honest dialogic process carries the only hope for true economic justice globally and lasting peace among all peoples.

5

Conflict and Security in the New World Order

J. Bryan Hehir

The issues of war and peace – what would be called in contemporary parlance security issues – are among the oldest topics in Catholic moral and social teaching. Reflections of the topic can be found in the New Testament, and a systematic discussion began with St. Augustine (+430), and continues to the present time.[1] The period since World War II had been a particularly intensive development in Catholic teaching, cutting across the Cold War and post–Cold War eras. This development has been driven by internal and external forces as the Church, under the direction of the papacy, has sought to renew Catholic teaching, and the world has presented a challenge of dramatic political and strategic changes.[2]

This chapter will seek to chart the internal developments in Catholic teaching and to describe the principal changes posed by the international system. In light of both, the chapter will close with a look what Catholic teaching can bring to contemporary security challenges.

War, Peace, and Security: Catholic Themes and Ideas

Few religious traditions have invested the amount of time, effort, and authority on issues of power and security as has the Catholic tradition. In the context of the Christian scriptures, it was not possible for the Church to avoid these issues. Considering the international role that the Church has played in the modern era, there has been an explicit demand for a coherent body of religious and moral reflection on issues of peace and security.

The demand was met by drawing on the past and supplementing it by using the resources of religion and morality to prevent war and build peace. The past teaching, inherited as a legacy from the work of magisterial texts and theological reflection, is rooted in the New Testament. It has been decisively shaped by Augustine and Thomas Aquinas (+1274); extended into the modern era by Vittoria (+1546) and Suarez (+1617); and taken up again in the twentieth century by popes, councils, and scholars, beginning with the work of Pius XII (1939–1958).

To convey a sense of the contemporary teaching on peace and security, I will look at the contributions of Pius XII, John XXIII (1958–1963), Vatican II (1962–1965), and John Paul II (1979–2005).

Pius XII

The rapid election of Pius XII in the conclave of 1939 was due in part to the widespread perception in the College of Cardinals that war was imminent and the Church needed a skilled diplomat as its leader. Pius XII brought to the papacy a lifetime of diplomatic service in the Church and the mind of an international lawyer. These two resources shaped his contribution to Catholic teaching on issues of international morality and security. Like the diplomats who gathered at the end of the war to found the UN, Pius XII had a basic sense that the era of Europe as the centre and controlling force in world politics was drawing to a close. While this vision of the future was embryonic, it did contain the basic truth that a truly global system of international relations was emerging. Faced with this truly new prospect, Pius XII shaped Catholic teaching in the style of an international lawyer informed by the Catholic moral vision. The keynote of his teaching – found in his *Christmas Addresses* and in scores of specialized discourses to groups visiting the Holy See[3] – was the need for a new jurisprudence. He felt that this structural vision of morality and law should be able to direct the development of our expanding international system of states and peoples.

The jurisprudential character of his contribution was manifested in both the structure and the scope of his writings and addresses. Structurally, he moved Catholic moral teaching in the direction of human rights, embracing the concept of rights and extending his embrace to a much more positive evaluation of democracy than any of his predecessors. During the war, he focused the Christmas addresses on the need for shaping the international and internal life of states, using the twin resources of human rights and democratic institutions. The proposal was not elaborated in detail, but the crucial contribution was opening the door to these ideas after two centuries of resistance to modern conceptions of rights and democratic polity. Precisely because Pius XII was carrying off a significant shift in Catholic teaching, his discourse was filled with distinctions designed to make clear that the endorsement of both rights and democracy should be understood within carefully circumscribed limits. Most notable among the limits was the absence of any acceptance of the right of religious freedom.

The limits of the teaching were less important, however, than the full scope of its reach. Here Pius XII was on familiar Catholic ground, asserting that the basic moral category for directing law and policy should be the human community as a whole. The new jurisprudence had to posses the scope and the strength to meet the needs of a global order of states.[4] Nothing less than attending to the needs, aspirations, and legitimate expectations of the whole human community would suffice for a legal and political order in the second half of the twentieth century. In retrospect, there were limits to the Church's sense of the pace of change needed to meet the moral expectations it set forth. The Holy See was not all that far ahead of others in preparing for the speed with which decolonization occurred. While the process was espoused and legitimated in Catholic teaching from Pius XII forward, the next two pontificates were needed to match Catholic action with its teaching in particular instances. Within the context of this structure and scope, Pius XII made two significant contributions that would provide a baseline for his successors.

First, he defined the basic jurisprudential problem that lies behind what international relations theory describes as the problem of anarchy. The term refers to the fact that the international order is comprised of independent political units that acknowledge no superior authority and, therefore, constitute a law unto themselves. The perennial political-strategic problem, then, is how to maintain peace and order in a context of anarchy. The moral-legal problem that Pius XII identified at the root of the anarchy problem was the lack of any centre of political authority adequate to address the expanding needs of a changing international order. The absence of such a political authority eroded the force of international law and left the security of states to a system of self-help. By default, independent states had to rely upon their own resources and, therefore, claimed the right to use force in their defence.

Recognizing that this basic long-term problem was in place, Pius XII's second contribution was to revive the traditional Catholic teaching on the use of force and adapt it to the changed landscape of military technology. In a classic article, John Courtney Murray S.J. set out a detailed commentary on Pius XII's ethic of war.[5] In Murray's view, the Pope's contribution lay in reasserting the basic principle of Just War teaching: the belief that the only legitimate use of force had to be a limited use – limited in its purpose and its methods. Having recalled that principle, Pius XII then advanced the moral doctrine by setting new limits on the ends or purposes of war. The traditional norm had legitimized a war of defense, a war of punishment, and a war of recuperation of unjustly taken goods. Pius XII reaffirmed only the first objective. Finally, he sought to use the principle of proportionality to draw the line between just and unjust means of warfare. In retrospect, the Pope's contributions lay in the first two points – calling the Catholic community to attend to the ancient teaching and recognizing new limits on the legitimization of war. His analysis of the means of warfare failed to delve deeply enough into the authentically new issues posed by weapons of mass destruction.

John XXIII

Commentators on the papacy often stress the difference between the pontificates of Pius XII and John XXIII. Multiple examples support this contrast but teaching on international ethics is not one of them. The legacy of John XXIII on these questions is found in his two crucial encyclicals: *Mater et Magistra* (1961) and *Pacem in Terris* (1963).[6] I will focus on the latter. The primary point to be made is the dependence of John XXIII on the teaching of his predecessor. *Pacem in Terris*, the Pope's last document, has had a long-term systematic impact on Catholic social thought (CST). Without doubt it moved quite beyond Pius XII's vision, but it also used his vision as a baseline. The connection, involving both continuity and change, was three-dimensional. First, John XXIII took the teaching on human rights to a new level of systematic analysis, understood as both the specification of which rights belonged to the person and an articulation of the relationship among different kinds of rights. Second, John XXIII analyzed the jurisprudential problem cited by Pius XII in greater detail and with more extensive implications. He cast the problem in terms of the universal common good, a phrase first used in *Pacem in Terris*. The phrase built upon the traditional concept, but highlighted the fact that the increasing interdependency of global politics and economics had created the conditions for asserting a common good that went quite beyond that of individual societies to encompass the human community as a whole.[7] It can rightfully be held that such an affirmation was always implicit in the very idea of the common good, but its explication made the new dimensions of international ethics more clear and urgent. In John XXIII's terms the gap between the emerging needs of the universal common good and the absence of any global political authority constituted a structural defect in world politics that could not be ignored. Creating an adequate political authority required attention to the classic principle of subsidiarity. Such an authority neither could be imposed on others, nor would it totally usurp the legitimate independence of existing sovereign states. While *Pacem in Terris* did not move forward to specify how such an international political authority should be established, it did identify the UN as an institution that exemplified the kind of structure that would be needed.

Third, *Pacem in Terris* addressed more extensively than Pius XII did the unique challenge posed by weapons of mass destruction, particularly nuclear weapons. Part of this difference lay in the generalized learning curve that engaged analysts on all sides of the nuclear age. One of the motivating causes of *Pacem in Terris* was John XXIII's response to the Cuban Missile Crisis, the most dangerous encounter of the superpowers during the Cold War. Part of the distinctiveness of John XXIII's teaching was the tone of urgency, even radicalism, that he gave to the encyclical. While never rejecting the traditional framework of the Just War ethic, which Pius XII relied upon exclusively, *Pacem in Terris* – by its tone and themes – opened a new chapter in the Catholic analysis of issues of war and peace. Over the next 40 years, two distinct lines of analysis flowed from this letter. One line moved in the direction of a Catholic style of non-violence and pacifism. A second line stayed within the structure of an ethic of limited war, but significantly constricted the limits imposed on modern warfare.[8]

Vatican II

The Second Vatican Council's treatment of issues of international security reflected both changes in the Church and in the world. The relevant text of the Council, *Gaudium et Spes* (1965), devoted a chapter to "The Fostering of Peace and the Promotion of a Community of Nations." The title joined the question of security, war, and peace, to the broader problem of building the fabric of peace in the whole range of issues that tied nations and peoples together in the new global order intuitively seen by Pius XII, but fully confronted by Vatican II. The challenge was not only to prevent recourse to war, but to address those political, economic, and social problems that prepare the way for war. The Council addressed the double challenge in a traditional formulation:

> Peace is not merely the absence of war.... Instead it is rightly and appropriately called "an enterprise of justice"(Is. 32:7). Peace results from that harmony built into human society by its divine Founder and actualized by men as they thirst after greater justice.[9]

This positive conception of peace, in which peace is the fruit of justice and justice is the product of rightly ordered relationships at every level of society, runs through the Catholic tradition from Augustine to *Pacem in Terris*. It particularly reflects the need to address the socio-economic dimensions of international relations that Pope Paul VI emphasized throughout his pontificate under the rubric "Development is the new name for Peace."[10] The conciliar text was, in effect, bringing together in one document two distinct dimensions of twentieth-century CST: the ethics of war and the ethics of social justice.

Because of the changing patterns of international politics, this synthesis was particularly needed by the 1960s. The two great wars and their consequences dominated the first two-thirds of the twentieth century. The founding documents of the UN reflected the pervasive concern for establishing structures dedicated to preserving security among states. The Cold War gave this problem particular urgency and complexity. But the double development of decolonization in the southern hemisphere and the growing interdependence of the post-industrial economies of the northern hemisphere raised the standing of international political economy (in its empirical and ethical aspects) to the status of high politics, complementing the security issues of the 1960s and 1970s.

In retrospect, one can see that the interdependence of the 1960s was only the first stage of the political and economic change that is now termed globalization. The teaching of Vatican II, therefore, opened a new chapter in CST. Without precisely stating the case, the Council's concern with peace and the building of a community of nations highlighted the need for a more tightly integrated linkage of the ethics of war and the sources of conflict in the socio-economic order. Having identified the emerging question, the Council offered guidance that was uneven in quality. Its treatment of the ethics of war and peace became recognized as a defining moment in the long history of these questions. On the one hand, the Council reaffirmed the Catholic argument that had held sway from Augustine through Pius XII and was reflected in a more complex form in *Pacem in Terris*. Essentially, it acknowledged the duty of the state to provide security for its people and territory and, therefore, the right of the state to use force because, in the language of *Pacem in Terris,* no international political authority existed. This quite traditional Catholic argument was then complemented by a recognition of the legitimate moral position of conscientious objection to the use of force, provided the needs of the common good could be met. This legitimation provided for a nonviolent option on behalf of the claims of personal conscience, but was not a fully developed, religiously based position of Christian pacifism. In the development of Catholic thought and opinion after Vatican II, however, a significant segment of the Church moved in this direction. It is not possible to claim either that authoritative Catholic teaching is pacifist or that anything near a majority of Catholics hold this position. However, the concilar text, joined with themes from *Pacem in Terris* and specific positions taken by Pope John Paul II, has provided the basic elements for some Catholic scholars and citizens to articulate an approximation of Christian pacifism.

The unevenness in the contribution of *Gaudium et Spes* lies in its failure to develop adequately the theme of building a community of nations, as promised in the chapter heading of *Gaudium et Spes.* While the theme is addressed both in this chapter and in the chapter on socio-economic life, most of what is said recapitulates the prior papal social teaching of the twentieth century. This constitutes a respectable statement, but it does not advance the intellectual argument in the face of the growing interdependence of the world noted in *Mater et Magistra* (1961) and developing with some rapidity in the study of the world economy throughout the 1960s and beyond.[11] In brief, *Gaudium et Spes* promised a bit more than it produced in its proposal for both a security ethic and an ethic of promoting peace.

John Paul II

As he had in multiple areas of Catholic teaching, Pope John Paul II made his own contribution to both dimensions of the question identified by *Gaudium et Spes.* He has stressed repeatedly in his teaching that the social tradition of the Church must manifest both continuity of themes and a developing edge of new ideas and new applications of the moral tradition. Some commentators have found his stress on continuity overplayed, but no one doubts that the body of Catholic social and moral teaching was enhanced in this papacy.

The Pope did exhibit a direct line of continuity in his ethics of war and peace. His own position reflects the basic premises of both *Pacem in Terris* and *Gaudium et Spes*. In both his thematic analysis and his casuistic commentary on specific situations, John Paul II emphasized the imperative of seeking non-violent methods of resolving conflicts, particularly within nations but also in relations between countries. For countries as diverse as Ireland, Latin America, Southern Africa, the Balkans, Central Europe, and the Middle East, John Paul was a voice for non-violence. His position was controversial, engaging his teaching with multiple communities. Scholars of Just War theories have found some of his positions unsettling. Activists facing apartheid in the 1980s were at odds with his opposition to the use of military means. US presidents found his opposition to both the Gulf War and the Iraq war a serious political challenge, and architects of the Latin American Theology of Liberation had to address his critique about appeals to class conflict.

In all of these instances, particularly in his praise of the non-violent role in the collapse of communism, John Paul II developed ideas first advanced by John XXIII and Vatican II.[12] But continuity was also visible at strategically important moments when the Pope would reaffirm the logic and necessity of Just War principles in a still anarchic world polity. In his 1982 World Day of Peace Message, in his response to the war in Bosnia, and in his commentary on the terrorist attacks of September 11, John Paul II reaffirmed the validity of proportionate use of force to defend life and fundamental social values.[13] By the end of his pontificate, John Paul II had extended the framework of *Gaudium et Spes* as the basic context for Catholic analysis of security issues. He left in place a Just War ethic of states and international institutions, a legitimized position to press non-violent alternatives at the policy level, and specific space for a non-violent personal position for individual Catholics.

His contribution to the work of fostering peace and building a community of nations was his more decisive contribution to Catholic teaching. He moved the argument of the ethics of international community and international political economy ahead on two fronts: his teaching on human rights and on solidarity. John XXIII had systemized the Catholic conception of human rights. He had taken the elements of an argument in Pius XII and moved the issue of human rights into the heart of CST as well as advancing that position in terms of religious freedom and the role of socio-economic rights.

By word and deed, John Paul II appropriated this foundation and vastly expanded its significance in the life and work of the Church. John Paul II made human rights the principal category through which he sought to defend human dignity in the politics of nations and interstate relations. This was shown in his address to the UN in 1979 and his encyclicals of the 1980s and 1990s. Also important was his direct public engagement on behalf of human rights, especially in Poland but also in Latin America, Africa, and the multiple forums of the UN and the Bretton Woods institutions. The right of religious freedom was affirmed as the cornerstone of human rights. Civil and political rights were asserted with new emphasis, and socio-economic rights were given a secure foundation in Catholic teaching and advocacy.

The Pope joined his analysis and advocacy for human rights with his signature theme of solidarity. This category had been invoked previously in Catholic teaching by Pius XII and Paul VI, and the use of it in John Paul II's encyclicals *Sollicitudo Rei Socialis* (1987) and *Centesimus Annus* (1991) has been much expanded.

The contribution of rights and solidarity was a principal theme in the Pope's teaching on economic justice. The idea of solidarity as a moral-religious category has many meanings. Here I emphasize its structural character as it applies to both the socio-economic life of nations and among nations. John Paul II described it as "one of the fundamental principles of the Christian view of social and political obligation." It is fundamental because it builds upon the religious conviction that all human life derives from God and each life has sacred dignity. The principle moves from that conviction to an assertion of universal moral responsibility: each person has duties toward others that transcend nation, culture, and geography. Those duties have a hierarchical ordering; we have different duties to different individuals and groups. But solidarity affirms a universal common good within which "we are all really responsible for all."[14]

The articulation of how that responsibility is to be defined for individuals, states, and international institutions is the work of a theory of human rights and the theory of justice. Specifying that analysis goes beyond the scope of this chapter, but the Pope's basic vision is summarized in his idea that interdependence and globalization must be morally shaped and structured by the concept of moral solidarity.

The Challenges of Politics and Security: Globalization and Beyond

The organizing theme of this anthology is the challenge that globalization in world politics poses to the tradition of CST. The topic of this chapter, security issues, is related to globalization, but globalization is seldom taken as the framework for analyzing the political-military issues of security. There is no question, however, that a new and different order has replaced the structure of world politics that dominated the second half of the twentieth century. The task of defining this version of a new order includes the reality and role of globalization. Some are inclined to equate the new order and the fact of globalization. I believe such a move invests globalization with greater influence, and more interpretive power, than it actually has in the contemporary international system. A better explanation would place globalization as one of two defining changes in world politics. The first change, the collapse of the bipolar order of world politics, has inaugurated a process of competition that may not yet have reached a stable term. The debate about the structure of power in the new order has been a central theme in the diplomatic and academic worlds for the last decade.[15] The overwhelming power of the US has led many to conclude that the world is unipolar. But this conclusion must be qualified to be sustained. It is accurate in military terms, but in the broader dimensions of world politics it can be misleading. US power is unique, but not simply unipolar.

The second change, achieved over four decades, has been the movement from interdependence to globalization. The arena in which this has occurred has been principally in the relationship of politics and economics. The term interdependence entered the lexicon of both political science and church teaching in the 1960s. It referred to the growing influence of both transnational problems – economic, environmental, and demographic – and transnational actors – corporate, humanitarian, and so forth – in the life and policies of nation-states and international organizations.[16] This basic meaning of interdependence – the way in which the lives of people are connected in spite of geographical, cultural, and political differences – took on qualitatively new dimensions in the 1990s.

Globalization constitutes a new stage of integration in world politics. The integration in its fundamental sense occurred in the material order; a mix of economics, technology, communication, and transportation combined to erode the significance of distance, time, and national sovereignty as an organizing principle of international life. This material meaning of globalization is captured in the definition that the International Monetary Fund uses for it: "Globalization is the growing economic interdependence of countries worldwide caused by the increasing volume and variety of cross-border transactions in goods and services and international capital."[17]

While the definition fits and frames one central aspect of globalization, it fails to acknowledge the fact that both the idea and the reality of globalization are contested territory. This contest involves both empirical and normative dimensions – both the understanding of globalization and the evaluation of it. The material description of globalization fails to address its political, social, and cultural dimensions. Pope John Paul II stressed that these aspects of the term "globalization" need as much attention as the economic meaning of the term.

Beyond the empirical definition of the term lies the even more complex territory of the moral analysis of globalization. The spectrum of evaluation runs from those who find the phenomenon self-evidently positive to those who see it as inevitably destructive of human values. These positions do not capture the centre of the ethical debate. The centre is closer, I believe, to a view that globalization, like other major components of world politics, is a complex phenomenon that must be evaluated in terms of the ends it seeks, the means it engages, and the motives that drive it forward. CST has encountered other phenomena analogous to globalization: the sovereign state, the use of force, and the multiple forms of governance in states. In these cases, the structural moral vision of Catholicism has demonstrated a capacity to engage, evaluate, and direct these secular forces. Globalization constitutes a new chapter in this narrative. As in other instances, the tradition needs to grow and expand to address a new reality.

Those who possess the tradition and those who are designated to teach it must work to develop its scope and power. Many of the essays in this volume focus on this challenge posed by globalization. By arguing that it is only one of two basic changes in world politics, however, I have implicitly taken a position in the globalization debate. To be explicit, let me say that I am not persuaded by the argument that the concept of globalization is adequate to capture the structure and dynamic of world politics in this new century. The issues of security and conflict are those that do not find explanation within the ambit of globalization.

That is not to say that there is no linkage between the elements of globalization and security issues. Such linkage clearly does exist. The topic of the causes of war is a perennial topic in international relations. There is no doubt that among the causes of war are the socio-economic questions of poverty and oppression, distribution of resources, and deprivation of hope that afflict more than three billion people on the globe today. The exact relationship between the elements of globalization and the causes of war remains to be played out, and it lies beyond my capacities to explain. But the recognition that security and globalization are mutually related should shape and influence both empirical and moral analysis of international relations, even if precise linkages remain to be defined.

One way to frame the issue is to draw upon Professor John Lewis Gaddis's proposal to examine international relations in terms of the forces of integration and fragmentation at work within states and among states.[18] This broad thematic suggestion does not deny the role of states, international institutions, or non-governmental organizations, but it provides a different lens that cuts across multiple issues in world politics. Fragmentation, in my view, should be understood at two levels. At the first level is the fragmentation within states that followed upon the end of the Cold War and is most visibly evident in the Balkans and in Africa in the 1990s. The second level is the fragmentation between the major powers in world politics and the rest of the globe. At least in the 1990s, the major states were defining their vital interests in a way that placed significant distance between them and the very fragmentation going on in broad sectors of the world. To some degree, the post–September 11 response to terrorism caused a renewal of interest and called attention to the material linkage between fragmented or failing states and the upper reaches of the hierarchy of world politics.

The process of globalization has been symbolized by increasing integration in world politics. While the rhetorical comparison of fragmentation vs. integration seems to give a distinctive ethical edge to globalization, it is now widely recognized that simply allowing globalization and integration to run their course will not necessarily enhance the welfare of individuals or the well-being of their nations and states.[19]

The challenge facing both Catholic teaching and the wider international community of states, advocacy groups, international institutions, and analysts is to define policies that provide structure, direction, restraint, and response to both fragmentation and integration in world politics. Obviously, these two challenges pose quite different tasks, but neither can be addressed without defining the moral responsibilities incumbent upon different sectors of the international community.

A comprehensive conceptual framework, encompassing both normative and empirical elements, that addresses each side of the international equation – fragmentation and integration – and then seeks to define the relationship of the two is not possible here, even in outline fashion. While acknowledging the need for such a framework, I must focus on the security issues that lie primarily in the fragmentation agenda. The goal of a just and effective security policy is, of course, to overcome fragmentation – both within societies and among states. My purpose is to define the major security challenges that exist in the first decade of a new century and to provide the lines of response that emerge from the development of Catholic teaching on war and peace to each major challenge.

In other writing I have defined the security challenges as the product of three legacies.[20] First, the legacy of the Cold War: weapons of mass destruction (WMD) produced promiscuously during the Cold War, with a life span that continues in today's new context long after that chapter of world politics has been closed. Second, the legacy of the 1990s: the yet unfinished debate about humanitarian military intervention (HMI), itself a product of the double fragmentation described above.

Third, the legacy of the 21st century: terror, and the double problem of how to prevent or resist terror and how to do so within morally acceptable limits.

The Legacy of Weapons of Mass Destruction

Weapons of mass destruction, as their name implies, constitute a unique strategic and moral problem in any setting. The term encompasses nuclear, biological, and chemical weapons, each of which was the product of the twentieth century. I will concentrate here on nuclear weapons as representative, and the most extreme, of the three. From their appearance on the stage of history in 1945, nuclear weapons constituted a unique challenge for strategists and moralists alike.[21] One can trace a halting learning curve in both groups as they come to grips with weapons whose destructive capacity literally changed the meaning of war. The product of the learning among strategists was the conviction that the weapons were unusable, but by the very fact of their existence they could defend their owners by deterrence. This conclusion then posed a challenge for the traditional ethic of war; it is possible to trace a learning curve in Catholic teaching from Pius XII to *Gaudium et Spes*. Now individuals had to evaluate not only the ethic of war (use of weapons) but also the ethic of keeping the peace (deterrence policy).

The recitation of this history is well under way on the strategic and moral sides of the narrative, but the problem today has a different context. The political context that deterrence was designed to address was the clearly bipolar world of US–Soviet (and by implication NATO–Warsaw Pact) competition. That context has been swept away by the welcome end of the Cold War. Now WMD exist in a less structured political context that potentially includes all major areas of the globe. The former superpowers no longer control access to WMD as they once, practically, did. The new political context is systemic. The knowledge of how to produce these weapons is now readily accessible, and fissionable material is only selectively policed. The nuclear club has expanded to include India, Pakistan, and Israel. The commonality of self-interest once shared by the US and the Soviet Union is not self-evidently shared by existing or prospective non-state actors in search of WMD. How does contemporary Catholic teaching address this legacy of WMD in a new context?

First, from *Gaudium et Spes* onward, Catholic teaching, and most theological reflection, was not at peace with deterrence. The conciliar text and key statements of John Paul II acknowledged a limited role for deterrence, but the emphasis of the teaching had the character of accommodating a transitional ethic – what could be tolerated but not accepted in principle. Second, the end of the Cold War has been seen as an opportunity to move aggressively against WMD even to the point of seeking to eliminate them from state arsenals. This objective was received with skepticism among professional strategists. Third, the Holy See has traditionally supported the diplomatic method of addressing proliferation – agreements and treaties executed under international legitimization. This traditional diplomatic approach is now in some tension with US strategies of the 1990s that involve ideas of coercive nonproliferation; this is defined as considering the use of force to prevent some potential proliferating states and organizations. Fourth, the clear linkage between security and socio-economic issues, which the Holy See and Catholic theology has expressed, is the condemnation of the expenditures of the arms race in a world of massive unmet human needs.

The Legacy of Humanitarian Military Intervention

The end of the Cold War brought multiple surprises, multiple expectations, and some unexpected events and consequences. One of them was a large-scale conventional war – the Gulf War. A second, occurring throughout the 1990s, was the process of fragmentation that led to the debate, decision-making, and debacles surrounding HMI. Fragmentation within states – for example, Yugoslavia and Somalia – created a demand for external international action to prevent widespread killing, looting, and destruction of human life and basic values. The secular political debate – which arose early in the decade around Bosnia, continued through the genocide in Rwanda, and returned again to the Balkans in Kosovo – was shaped by the clash between moral claims and positive international law. This legal tradition, arising from the sixteenth to the eighteenth centuries, was built on a norm of nonintervention in the internal affairs of states.[22] The historical memory that sustained this norm was the widespread violence that had engulfed Europe during the wars of religion. This was the fact of a world of sovereign states constantly in danger of resorting to force because, as the traditional Catholic ethic understood, no central authority existed to guarantee security. The strength of the non-intervention norm lay partly in the common ground it created among contesting views of world politics – liberals, realists, international organizations, and emerging states all found utility in the norm. During the 1990s, calls for military intervention were met with an initial rebuke from defenders of nonintervention. By the end of the decade, after multiple arguments and several failures to meet the challenge of fragmentation, there was an emerging consensus, but not a triumphant one, to override nonintervention in specific cases.[23]

How does Catholic ethics fit into the HMI debate? In the first place, two characteristics are evident in a Catholic analysis of HMI. The first characteristic is a reflection of the post–Vatican II tension between continuity of Just War ethics and a conviction that non-violent responses to conflicts should be given significant weight in deciding policies. The second characteristic was a refusal to grant either sovereignty or nonintervention the kind of absolute character that some voices in the secular debate accord them.

The second response by Catholic ethics is the conviction, shared by several contributors to the theological analysis of HMI, that the structure of the Just War ethic could be analogously used to shape a Just Intervention ethic. In the process, the nonintervention norm would be accorded significant weight, but a series of justifiable exceptions would be developed.[24]

In the third response, other voices in the Catholic discussion were skeptical of the promised benefits of military intervention and stressed, instead, the need for an ethic of peacebuilding and reconciliation. They were willing to endorse only non-violent responses to the dilemmas of fragmentation within states.

Fourth, John Paul II and other Vatican statements could be invoked to support both the second and third positions summarized. The Pope, himself, was generally reluctant to endorse the use of force, but, as noted earlier, he believed certain extreme situations illustrated the need for a legitimate military option.

And in a fifth ethical response, Catholic statements at various levels of authority, analysis, and advocacy in the Church linked security and socio-economic themes when they addressed HMI. The statements highlighted ways unaddressed socio-economic conditions were a contributing cause of fragmentation within states or, as in Africa, of whole continents.

The Legacy of Terror

The challenges of HMI were substantially different from the issues of WMD, but neither foreshadowed the crises faced after September 11, 2001. The fact of terrorism has been evident in the politics of states since the nineteenth century, but the scale and scope of transnational terrorist capability demonstrated by the attack on the US constituted a new problem. The first response to 9/11 by states, alliances, and international institutions was a united response. The later response was an increasingly contested debate culminating in the invasion of Iraq in 2003.[25] The urgency and scope of the arguments about ways to respond to terrorism pushed HMI debates into the background, while adding a new dimension – linking terrorist groups to WMD – to the nonproliferation strategy. Even summarizing the secular story is beyond the limits of this survey; instead we need to ask again where the Catholic response fits.

As with the HMI discussion, the Catholic response emerged from multiple sources. The Holy See, episcopal conferences, theologians, and advocacy groups were all part of the Catholic conversation. First, John Paul II consistently condemned terrorist strategies and actions and called for means to resist them. In his World Day of Peace Message for 2002, he systematically developed a position that had three aspects. It 1) acknowledged the right of self-defence and proportionate means to guarantee it; 2) stressed that defence must be matched with capacity for forgiveness; and 3) emphasized pursuit of justice, which is understood as bringing terrorists to justice and creating conditions of social justice in world politics.

In a second response to the legacy of terror, theologians were often more specific in articulating the right of self-defence, particularly in the support given to the immediate response against Al-Qaeda and the Taliban government. In a third response, support for action against Afghanistan did not necessarily extend to proposed responses to terror beyond Afghanistan. In the debate leading up to and into the Iraq invasion by the US and its allies, the opposition of the Holy See (including John Paul II) was persistent and vocal. The theological debate fractured the initial support given to the Afghan invasion. US policy had its theological defenders, but it also met significant opposition. Fourth, as in the HMI debate, much of the Catholic response was noticeably more explicit in tying security issues to arguments that the roots of terrorism – for example, socio-economic injustices – must be addressed in any successful response to terrorism. This argument was not necessarily shared in some of the secular debate.

In summary, all of the major security issues evident in this new century find some response from Catholic teaching. The Catholic discussion reflects the themes struck by Vatican II, stressing the need to locate any ethic of force within the broader vision of international community, human rights, and international social justice.

Resources of Catholic Moral Teaching

The theme of this chapter has been to trace a very ancient dialogue that has entered a substantially new stage of development. Security is an essential need of every political community; maintaining security almost certainly means the possibility that force must be used. Defining why, where, and how that decision should be made has engaged Catholic thinkers and teachers for centuries. In the face of the changed security environment outlined above, what are the resources and expectations for Catholic teaching in the immediate future?

(A) The sovereign state remains the basic unit of reference on security issues, but the sovereign state today exists within the normative framework of the UN Charter. The norms of the Charter (limiting and authorizing force) are crucially important, but the institutional capacity of the UN to enforce the Charter is marginal. Some norms may be in need of revision – for example, on humanitarian intervention. The institutional capacity of the UN certainly stands in need of enhancement, but this will be done through states not in spite of them.

(B) The potential for the use of force in international relations will remain all too evident for the foreseeable future. My conviction on this point is based on, first, the theological anthropology of the Just War ethic – compare Augustine's concept of war as the result of sin and the remedy for a sinful world. The second important factor to me is the abiding insight of realist political thought that the international system is anarchical, that is, without a legitimated organizing centre.

(C) Both the conviction about the abiding nature of the state and the pervasive possibility of force, however, are open to some modification. The state today is surrounded by institutions organized above it (international institutions) and around it (NGOs) as well as by forces within it (constitutional restraints). This complex fabric is the subject of much empirical analysis that needs to be incorporated into any moral analysis.

(D) The concepts of preventive diplomacy or peacemaking – while in the early stages of development – have capacities to provide at least a direction in which the international system should be shaped.

(E) The basic strength of Catholic teaching on international relations may be its scope; it addresses force, economic equity, human rights, and international order. In addition, the Catholic style is to join desirable normative objectives to needed institutional structures. Finally, strength lies in the potential contributions of diverse local churches to an overarching international vision.

(F) One limit of the teaching is at its frontiers – what is not yet addressed or does not have the ready conceptual tools to address. A second is in the generalizations that make up the teaching and are not often brought to the level of specificity that would give the general norms directive power in the density of debate that characterizes the theory and practice of global politics.

6

Globalization and the Environment

Mary Evelyn Tucker

It is difficult to imagine a period more challenging than our own in terms of understanding the multiple effects of globalization, especially in its economic forms. We are inheriting both a gradual historical process of globalization along with a current rapid process of globalization that is now changing the face of the planet in a very short period of time. To understand our current environment, we need to first take a step back and look briefly at the historical trajectory of globalization over the last 2,000 years of human history. We begin with the integration of the Eurasian continent along the Silk Road, and then move to the emergence of European colonization in the age of exploration 500 years ago. These two earlier phases of gradual globalization have now become an accelerated phase of rapid globalization in the last 50 years since the end of World War II. This acceleration is especially due to the increased travel, communication, and financial exchange made possible by technological advances.

Within the framework of this larger historical perspective, we can then see that current patterns of globalization share aspects of earlier globalization – namely, social, cultural, religious, and political interchange along with economic exchange. Like earlier periods of globalization, our present one involves numerous mixed motivations and consequences that are both intended and unintended. As in earlier periods, moral judgment is clearly needed to evaluate the mixed aims and outcomes of the recent forms of rapid globalization. Such moral reflection and insight on the limits and benefits of our current situation may be an indispensable component in a genuinely sustainable future.

Historical Perspectives: From the Silk Road Exchange to the Columbian Exchange

With the emergence of trade along the Silk Road during the Han period in China (202 BCE–220 CE) and the Roman Empire in the West (100 BCE–550 CE), the Eurasian continent was linked with other world cultures for the first time. This great thoroughfare for the exchange of goods, ideas, and culture gave birth to a more globalized network with its intricate patterns of multiple influences.

Alternating between periods of peace and warfare and between decentralized tribal groups and imperial control (from the Chinese and later the Mongols), this region bears the imprint of global interchange over countless centuries. In this region, Buddhism made its lengthy passage from India to China and became transformed in the process. The invention of paper and printing, which contributed to the flourishing of the Renaissance and Reformation, occurred in this region. In this region, Islam met Confucianism and used the latter's ideas to spread its faith. And through this region, Chinese decorative arts seeped into Persian carpets and later into the chinoiserie tastes of European china and gardens. Indeed, a culminating period of this global exchange is evident in the influence of Confucian ideas on the eighteenth-century *philosophes* in France, and the subsequent birth of modernity in the form of an enlightened secular humanism in the West. Globalization as the intricate interaction of cultures, ideas, and goods has a considerable history that world historians – such as William McNeill, Ross Dunn, L.S. Stavrianos, Linda Schaefer, Jerry Bentley, Phillip Curtin, Alfred Crosby, and others – have been clarifying for us over the last several decades.

From the Silk Road exchange to the Columbian exchange, beginning 500 years ago, globalization escalated from a Eurasian phenomenon to an intercontinental reality. With the age of exploration initiated by the Europeans, the planet became gradually linked and the interchange of species, as well as goods and culture, became more evident. The complex connections between the Old World and the New World, and between Africa and the North and South Americas, burgeoned forth with all the mixed legacy this has entailed. This legacy has ranged from aspirations to embrace Enlightenment ideals of democracy and religious freedom to the abhorrent reality and enduring consequences of the introduction of diseases, the oppression of Native peoples, and the subsequent enslavement of Blacks.

Similarly, with the expanded globalization resulting from colonialization and industrialization of the last several hundred years, the ecological consequences have been long lasting and the economic inequities enduring. Environmental destruction, marginalization of large numbers of people, endemic poverty, and control of wealth by the few are the contemporary legacies of these centuries of colonial control and industrial exploitation. At the same time, it might be said that in the last several decades the spread of democratic ideals, the hopes to alleviate poverty, the desire to reduce war and insecurity, the linkages of modern communication, and the dispersal of culture across boundaries have brought numerous benefits to millions.

In short, our current patterns of rapid globalization are distinctive in many ways and global communication networks and international travel have transformed us in ways that happened in no earlier period. At the same time, we are also part of a larger history of the Columbian exchange and its colonial legacy. We are also reminded that decolonialization is relatively recent. Most Western powers only relinquished control of their territories after World War II with the assistance of the UN Trusteeship Council. The deleterious patterns of colonial control and economic exploitation have a long historical reach, as do the enduring aspects of intellectual, cultural, and religious exchange, which have left behind both benefits and problems. Our challenge is to evaluate present modes of globalization in a context mindful of multiple historical tributaries and attuned to complex contemporary currents.

Contemporary Modes of Globalization

While it is clear that current discussions of globalization are dominated by a concern for its economic forms, we are also aware that the global interconnections of our planet at present may be described as a vast web with many strands. As in earlier periods, these include the globalization of societies, cultures, religions, politics, and the military, along with economies. Each of us, no doubt, has had experiences reflecting the remarkable strands of globalization in which we now dwell. The positive and negative dimensions of these strands of globalization are ever present. For example, an experience of the social and cultural mixture of a society like Malaysia – with Chinese, Indian, Southeast Asians, Europeans, Japanese, and Middle Easterners – is to witness one of the richest exchanges of humans to ever occur. At the same time, many cultures, especially indigenous ones, are being marginalized and diminished at a rapid rate. Moreover, the fact that some 40 million people a year are migrating across the globe in their search for a more stable life is sobering. This migration is causing enormous tensions – cultural, social, political, and economic – in many parts of the world, particularly Europe, where immigration issues are volatile.

Similarly, observing Russians in Beijing buying silk products to sell back in Moscow and seeing fish from South America available in the markets of Urumqi in central Asia helps us to realize how widespread our system of global economic exchange has become. At the same time, the more invisible processes of financial markets and institutional policies of the World Bank and the International Monetary Fund are reminders of the growing consequences evident in the destruction of the environment and the impoverishment of peoples. The report by the International Forum on Globalization, titled *Alternatives to Economic Globalization* (2002), forcefully expresses this.

What is emerging with the multiple strands of expanded economic globalization is a picture of ever-greater inequities between the developed and the developing nations. This is evident throughout the world in vast pockets of poverty (both urban and rural), the agricultural breakdown of small scale and organic farming, the widespread creation of imagined needs through advertising, the rampant waste and emptiness of mindless consumerism, and the relentless deterioration of the global environment. For all these reasons, the growing tension between the developed countries of the North and the developing countries of the South remains the critical issue of contention in the UN.

In the UN conferences at Rio (1992) and Johannesburg (2002), the path to resolving these growing disparities has been termed sustainable development, which is itself a much-contested term. The Brundtland Commission report on *Our Common Future,* issued in 1987 in preparation for the Earth Summit in Rio, defined the term sustainable development as "paths of progress which meet the needs and aspirations of the present generation without compromising the ability of future generations to meet their needs."[1] However, many people feel this concept has been co-opted by multinational corporations and international financial institutions to push forward development that does not take into account social or environmental costs.

A central challenge is how to see economic development and environmental protection as integrated issues promoting social equity, not as diametrically opposed movements encouraging wealth for the few. Ecological economics is working toward that end, as are numerous groups such as the Coalition for Environmentally Responsible Economics (CERES), the Global Reporting Initiative (GRI), and Socially Responsible Investing.

Key questions remain for defining sustainable development, namely, development for and by whom and at what cost to both humans and the environment. In other words, what are the goals and processes of development and what are the consequences, intended or unintended? While poverty alleviation may be a development goal of governments, non-governmental organizations (NGOs), and international financial institutions, the means to such alleviation are radically different. As the anti-globalization movement has emphasized, some of these means may have disastrous results for the environment, for democratic processes, for human rights, and for social equity. With the amount of human suffering spreading due to increasing poverty and growing environmental degradation, the need for a thoughtful moral response is urgent.

Moreover, while most analysts describe current globalization as the interconnection of market forces driven by corporations and financial institutions, it also has many other dimensions – social and cultural, political and military, and religious. These need to be brought more fully into the analysis and critiques of our current circumstances. In addition, the ironic reality of our global historical movement should be kept in mind. Just as we are awakening to a new global consciousness that recognizes our profound interconnection as a species with other species and our radical dependence on healthy ecosystems for our survival, rapid economic globalization is pushing us to the brink of destruction of our natural environment on a monumental scale. This dual realization brought on by globalization – both threat and opportunity – is defining our period as a watershed for future directions of our planet and our species.

Indeed, the emerging global consciousness has given birth to an awareness that our common future rests on creating the basis for a sustainable and multiform planetary civilization. Neither the nation state nor transnational corporations can do this, but religious communities, which have always shaped and dynamized civilizations, can make important contributions to this great work. They can do this by encouraging civil societies in their efforts to create institutions and programs promoting sustainability. They can also do this by supporting the movement toward an inclusive global ethics, which is represented in the Earth Charter (www.earthcharter.com). Our emerging planetary civilization will require a global ethics that respects both pluralism and common goals. The very fact that such a comprehensive, internationally negotiated document as the Charter was developed signals the concerted efforts of humans to define our planetary moment as one requiring an inclusive global vision, an integrated ethical framework, and realistic suggestions for implementation. Representatives of all the world's religions had input in the three-year drafting process from 1997 to 2000.

The Earth Charter opens by making us aware of the importance of our historical moment: "We stand at a critical moment in earth's history, a time when humanity must choose its future. As the world becomes increasingly interdependent and fragile, the future at once holds great peril and great promise. To move forward, we must recognize that in the midst of a magnificent diversity of cultures and life forms we are one human family and one Earth community with a common destiny." The Charter's Preamble highlights the cosmological context of the evolution of the universe and the Earth: "We are part of a vast, evolving universe. Earth, our home, is alive with a unique community of life." The three central parts of the Charter suggest an interconnected way forward by protecting ecological integrity; promoting economic and social justice; and fostering democracy, non-violence, and peace. Catholic social and environmental teachings can make a contribution to reshaping current globalization trends within this framework of an emerging global ethics and an attempt to create a sustainable planetary civilization.

Significance of the Environment

In thinking about globalization in its many forms, it is becoming increasingly clear that the environment emerges as a key issue that will determine all others. For without a healthy biosphere that can sustain ecosystems and nurture life in its myriad forms, all other issues remain secondary. If the life-support systems are destroyed irreparably, water shortages increase, food supplies decrease, fisheries are depleted, forests are clear-cut, and topsoil lost there will be no lasting security, and military violence or terrorism will erupt. This issue becomes ever more urgent as the environment continues to deteriorate radically and rapidly in many parts of the world.

Thus, in rethinking the various interrelated strands of globalization now engulfing the planet, it is critical that we recognize that our common future rests, in very particular ways, on our common ground – the planet itself. The quality and availability of air, water, and soil will be determining factors in the survival and flourishing of life. We cannot realistically create a second biosphere for the entire planet, and we have seen the gross inadequacy of this experiment to do so on even a small scale in the Arizona desert. Nor is it likely that we can recreate Earth's life systems on other planets. Life is far more intricate, delicate, and mysterious than our technologies can even approximate.

What is at stake here cannot be minimized. Our radical dependence on interrelated ecosystems is being made abundantly clear as we are unraveling the web of those ecosystems in ways that reflect multiple motivations – including blindness and ignorance as well as greed and arrogance. Moreover, we have had cornucopian expectations of nature's limitless capacity for use and renewal and an abundant faith in the saving power of science and technology as agents of progress. These have led us to the brink of destruction – not only of human life, but also of all other forms of life.

The Scope of the Problem

The scope of our challenges and the scale of our current environmental degradation cannot be stated often enough. Perhaps the litany of air pollution, toxification and loss of soil, eutrophication of water, desertification of land, clear-cutting of forests, and over-fishing of seas will arouse us from our slumbering personal concerns toward a genuine hope for our common future. As the Earth Charter suggests, and the last ten years of UN conferences make clear, more than any other time in human history the fate of the planet and future generations lies in our hands. This is the great challenge for religious communities – to activate a level of response that is commensurate with the scope of the challenges.

We can enter the discussion of globalization and our current environmental crisis from many angles. Here we will examine two macrophase issues that for many years have remained invisible but are now dawning on human consciousness. These are the planetary problems of global climate change and of species extinction. Increasing industrialization, destruction of ecosystems, rapid use of resources, and population explosion are causing both of these crises. The deleterious effects of these two issues have resulted in such radical alterations to the biosphere and atmosphere of the planet that scientists are now suggesting we are at the end of a geological era.

To observe that we are at the termination of the Cenozoic Era as we enter the 21st century is to help us understand the scale of the destruction we are causing. As Peter Ravens, the Director of the Missouri Botanical Garden, wrote, "We are Killing Our World." The Harvard scientist E.O. Wilson asked, "Is Humanity Suicidal?" Bill McKibben's book *The End of Nature* raises similar questions.

Climate Change: The End of Nature

Leading international scientists are now warning us that climate change is certainly occurring and they report that we are contributing to it in significant ways. The International Panel on Climate Change (IPCC), composed of high-level scientists from around the world and sponsored by the UN, has said this definitively in their report in the summer of 2002. Whether we continue to debate the rate of climate change or the amount of humanly induced (anthropogenic) change, it is clear, as the Kyoto Protocol would suggest, that at a minimum the precautionary principle should be operative. In other words, we should work to reduce greenhouse gases, conserve energy, and utilize alternative energy sources. The aim is to prevent the warming of the planet; the flooding of coastal areas; the sinking of island nations; more frequent and violent storms; further deterioration of ecosystems; disruption of life cycles of flora; and changes in the migrating patterns of birds, fish, and mammals.

While the churches are just beginning to respond to these enormous problems, there are as yet few Catholic social and environmental teachings available to guide the discussion. An exception is the statement of the US Conference of Catholic Bishops from June 15, 2001, "Global Climate Change: A Plea for Dialogue, Prudence, and the Common Good." The campaign launched in 2000 by the National Council of Churches to promote awareness of the growing impact of climate change and the moral implications of the issue is another important start (www.webofcreation.org/ncc/index.html). The *Daedalus* issue of Fall 2001 – "Religion and Ecology: Can the Climate Change?" – looks at this issue from the perspective of the world's religions as well as from those of science, public policy, and global ethics. (http://www.daedalus.amacad.org/issues/fall2001/fall2001.htm)

Further work clearly needs to be done regarding:

1) slowing the rate of energy consumption and encouraging alternative energy use in the developed world (the US with 4 per cent of the world's population uses 25 per cent of the world's energy resources);

2) mitigating the impact on the poor in the developing world who will be most adversely affected by climate change, as is already evident in coastal flooding, especially in Bangladesh;

3) encouraging mindfulness of future generations who will inherit a legacy of a vastly altered biosphere.

Species Loss: A Sixth Extinction Period

The other large-scale issue that is beginning to penetrate the consciousness of more and more people is the rapid loss of species on a global scale. Scientists are now observing that we are living in the midst of a sixth extinction period where we are losing some 30,000 species a year (www.massextinction.net). The cause of all other extinction periods, which are known from the geological and fossil records, were meteors or climate change such as the ice ages. The last geological period, the Mesozoic, ended with the destruction of the dinosaurs 65 million years ago. This was most likely caused by a meteor that hit a region of the Yucatan peninsula in Mexico and it launched the next geological period, the Cenozoic, which is now being brought to a close by the massive extinction spasm currently taking place on the planet.

The scientific community is not in denial about this reality nor is it debating the particulars, as they have been about climate change. In fact, the Hall of Biodiversity at the American Museum of Natural History in New York has a plaque noting this vast loss. The plaque observes that, while humans are causing this extinction, we have the potential of "stemming the tide of destruction." The exhibit illustrates that the choice is ours by giving arresting examples of both current devastation and restoration of the environment. A wake-up call to the museum staff to become more outspoken on these environmental issues came in 1998. At that time, in the search for an ornithologist as a curator, it was discovered that four of the six finalists for the position had witnessed their birds go extinct while they were studying them.

It is now clear, as many scientists have warned, that natural selection has been halted by the impact of humans around the globe. We have become a macrophase presence that will determine which species survive as well as which ecosystems flourish and which waters remain pure. The awesome responsibility for the continuity of life – in all its forms – is now in our hands. Whether the great apes – our nearest primate cousins – become extinct in our lifetime, as is now predicted, is a question we have not begun to address. The massive loss of species already taking place is a reality we have yet to absorb fully, much less to mourn. Nonetheless, the radical diminishment of life is leaving us orphaned of our ancestral lineage and deprived of the great voices of biodiversity with whom we share the planet. How will we respond to future generations who may only know these life forms in zoos or aquariums?

Response of Religious Communities

Religious communities are only beginning to awaken to what it means to participate in a sixth extinction period stemming from the effects of economic globalization. The reframing of human-Earth relations, which is required as a response to this diminishment of life, can be helped by the moral insights and persuasive force of the world's religions. Specifically, the extension of moral concern to all life forms can be evoked as grounds for stemming the tide of destruction and participating in programs of conservation. In addition, spiritual resources and ritual practices will need to be developed for mourning the loss of life on such a profound planetary scale. The conference held at Harvard on World Religions and Animals in May 1999 was a small step in these directions as is the volume that will be published from the conference papers entitled *A Communion of Subjects.*

There has also been significant progress in the field of animal ethics and animal rights to promote conservation and protection of other species. Clearly the work of Jane Goodall, Marc Bekoff, Richard Wrangham, Barbara Smuts, and numerous other scientists represent the drive of the human community to recognize and honour our deep connection to what David Abram calls the "more than human world." The publications and website of the Biodiversity Project (www.biodiversityproject.org) in Wisconsin also signal important progress in seeing the responsibility to other life forms as a moral issue of enormous significance. Once again, Catholic social and environmental teaching can make important contributions in this regard.

By touching on two of the most troubling macro-scale environmental problems caused by rampant economic globalization, we are highlighting the need for Catholic teachings to be equally comprehensive in response. Many of the topics discussed in this volume, including conflict and security, and economic justice, may best be seen within the framework of the primacy of the security and protection of the environment and of the equitable use and distribution of natural resources for present and future generations. This is the only possible basis for a sustainable future. As many are noting, conflicts in this century will increasingly be over resources; beyond oil, water is emerging as the resource of paramount importance for life. Similarly, food security will depend on our fundamental attitudes toward soil, water, and pesticide use as well as issues of genetic manipulation and fair distribution.

Beyond land issues, the oceans and seas are in peril.[2] This is evident in the massive collapse of fisheries throughout the world, where 90 percent of commercial fish stocks have been depleted within the last 50 years. It is also seen in the destruction of major seas (the Black Sea is virtually dead from eutrophication and the Aral Sea has been radically depleted by irrigation), and dead zones and a red tide of algae bloom threaten marine and human life in many coastal areas. Additionally, the diminishment of coral reefs by bleaching due to global warming and by dynamiting as a fishing method, as well as the overfishing by deep-sea drag nets and bottom trawling resulting in strip mining of the oceans, are warning signs that cannot be ignored.

The only religious leader to speak out consistently on the rapid destruction of the oceans, seas, and rivers is the Greek Orthodox Patriarch Bartholomew; he has spoken especially in the five symposia he has convened since 1995 on the Aegean, the Danube, the Adriatic, the Baltic, and the Black Seas. His speeches have been collected by John Chryssavgis in the volume *Cosmic Grace, Humble Prayer: The Ecological Vision of the Green Patriarch, Bartholomew I* (2003). The representatives of the Vatican that have participated in these symposia include Cardinals Cassidy, Casper, and Etchegaray, and Sister Marjorie Keenan. Again, Catholic teachings on the environment have an important contribution to make, as is evident in the Venice Declaration signed at the end of the Adriatic Symposium in June 2002 by both the Patriarch and the Pope.

Where to Begin: Humility and Hope

It might be said that religious communities need to begin with humility, recognizing that we are late in coming to the problems of the environment and that our responses have not been adequate to the enormous challenges we face. This is in part because we are not always fully informed about the size and scale of the problems, nor have we absorbed the particulars of the scientific or ecological discussions of environmental issues. It is time, then, for both re-education and rethinking. We cannot simply apply CST to massive and complex environmental problems. We need to start with a thorough examination of the problems themselves and then suggest a creative reappraisal of human-Earth relations in light of what we are facing. Moreover, we need to expand CST to include the environment as a primary context for sustaining life on the planet.

The questions are multiple, but we might ask ourselves: What can stem this tidal wave of an octopus-like presence on the planet devouring the possibility of the continuity of life itself? Humans are shutting down the processes of natural selection and diminishing life forms; destroying the biosphere and unraveling ecosystems; and polluting the air, water, and soil so that areas of land and water have become uninhabitable. What principles and practices can help us to reshape the direction of human-Earth relations and provide a moral urgency concerning our present circumstances? What are the contributions of religions to these discussions? These are some of the questions that have guided the Harvard project on World Religions and Ecology that has held a series of conferences. The papers from these conferences have been published in a ten-volume series, and a major website under the Harvard Center for the Environment is now available in eight languages (http://environment.harvard.edu/religion).

In addition to humility and moral urgency, religious communities can offer hope to those participating in movements toward building a sustainable future. These include international efforts (such as UN conferences and agencies and also environmental and developmental agencies), national organizations and NGOs providing assistance and relief, and grassroots groups struggling to maintain and restore their local environment. To build a sustainable future in these multiple ways is to recognize that our historical moment is defined by numerous efforts to create a multiform planetary civilization; that is shaped by international, national, and local organizations that will contribute to the flourishing of the Earth community. This is a process that is imperfect at best, emerging in groping and uncertain forms, but which promises to be our greatest hope for the generations that will follow. They, no doubt, will inherit this process and move it forward in ways that we cannot yet envision; but it is up to our generation to sculpt the contours of a sustainable future. No generation has been called to such a monumental task and there are no blueprints to guide us in this venture. It will require careful reflection and imaginative vision to give birth to new modes of human-Earth relations. It is within this context and in response to this call that Catholic teachings – social and environmental – will make a distinctive and enduring contribution.

How to Approach the Problem

In inviting Catholic social and environmental teachings to participate in the larger shaping of a multiform planetary civilization, we can begin by recognizing the present contributions and limitations of these teachings. We can observe that at the beginning of the twentieth century, Catholic teachings were aimed at a relatively contained audience of Catholics in Europe and North and South America. At the opening of the 21st century, this audience has shifted well beyond those confines to embrace Catholics in Africa and Asia – and those in Latin America who have now been influenced by liberation theology. The challenge, then, is for these teachings to build on the significant Catholic social and labour teachings of the early twentieth century and the rich social justice and civil rights statements of the mid-twentieth century. Additionally, liberation theology, ecofeminism, and the emerging ecotheology of the late twentieth century have broadened that discourse. A major task at hand is to draw on these teachings but to reframe and expand them in light of economic globalization and our massive environmental crisis.

The reframing that will be required is to move beyond strictly human-centred language and concerns to an awareness of the larger planetary community. Understanding our cosmological context will be central to this process – namely that we participate in ecosystems held in the vast web of evolutionary life. To recognize that we are derivative from, and dependent on, these life systems will require major changes in attitudes and awareness. Our anthropocentric concerns need to be integrated into ecocentric concerns and our economic aspirations to be seen in relation to ecological limits. We need to expand our political hopes to include not just national security but planetary well-being. Our human drives and desires will need to be reframed within an acknowledgment of a larger common good that rests in the flourishing of the whole Earth community. Our highly developed sense of Western individualism will need to give way to an acknowledgment that individuals cannot survive physically or thrive economically except in relationship to others in the human, and the more than human, world. This shift of consciousness and concerns will require the astute guidance of the religious communities. It is here that Catholic teachings – environmental and social – can play an indispensable role.

In the move beyond anthropocentric thinking and acting, Catholic teachings and theology are poised to assist in the changes needed to shape this new planetary civilization. We can identify several key areas, which are already present in Catholic thought, that are vital for reframing human-Earth relations.

Overarching Principles

1. The affirmation of the sacredness of creation

2. The acknowledgment of the intrinsic value and interdependence of life in all its forms

3. The importance of thinking on behalf of future generations

Ethical Choice and Creative Action

4. The recognition that the environmental crisis is a moral crisis and, thus, the need for ecological conversion

5. The highlighting of responsible care for creation in the concepts of stewardship and *imago Dei*

6. The need for meaningful work for humans as co-creators with Creation

Critique of Market Economics and Unrestrained Use of the Environment

7. The identification of the various links between poverty and the environment

8. The advocacy of equity and distributive justice in the use of resources

9. The urgency of limiting consumption and exercising restraint

10. The problematic role of the free market in increasing inequity and wasteful consumption

Ways Toward Integral Development

11. The importance of integral development as a foundation for peace

12. The problem of war as a cause of environmental destruction.

While these resources are present in many of the recent statements by the Vatican (see pp. 101-112) and the bishops, much more remains to be done to build on these teachings and the context of discussion needs to be expanded. This is currently taking place through the work of various theologians and ethicists as represented in the Harvard volume on *Christianity and Ecology* (2000) and the volume published by the US Catholic Bishops' Conference, *And God Saw That It Was Good* (1996), edited by Drew Christiansen and Walter Grazer.[3] What has not been adequately addressed, however, is the question of population growth in relation to the environment or the role of the education and empowerment of women in this regard. The work of Daniel Maguire at Marquette University is an important exception.

There is also a need to respond to the critical challenges of the environment in language that is not only steeped in Catholic theology and piety but speaks beyond the boundaries of the Catholic world. If religious leadership is to be truly effective with regard to the sustainable future of the planet, it needs to speak in language that moves the minds and hearts of those who yearn for guidance and direction on these issues. There is enormous potential for effective leadership regarding globalization and the environment within the Catholic community by theologians, laity, and the hierarchy. This leadership should be drawn upon so that the fuller expression of these teachings may be realized as they are translated out of the framework of Catholic piety and into the living world of emerging global ethics. Catholic teachings cannot afford to be narrow, circumscribed, or ghettoized. While rooted in the richness of the tradition, they need to reach out and participate in the currents of planetary dialogue now shaping a sustainable future. The influential role of the Church, well beyond its own members, needs to be recognized as we seek a language to awaken and inspire the human community to respond to the enormous environmental challenges we are facing at present.

Apart from the World Council of Churches, there is no other religious institution besides the Catholic Church so well placed with such vast global resources and extraordinary educational potential poised to assist in reshaping the course of human-Earth relations. This is the case, despite all the failings, limitations, and scandals within the Church – both historically and at present. It is important to remember, as well, that the Jesuit community itself has an opportunity of unique proportions to contribute to the flourishing of the Earth community. With their highly educated and deeply committed members and their excellent colleges, universities, and secondary schools around the world, the Jesuits can educate future generations in a period of ecological awakening that will redirect and enhance human-Earth relations. This is no small mission, but one well worth striving toward. If Ignatius called forth the energies needed for the Counter-Reformation, so now we need the energies for an ecological reformation. Who can give better intellectual leadership and moral guidance to this effort than the Jesuits?

Ecological Reformation

The challenge is how to respond creatively with fresh vision and invigorating moral force to an ecological reformation. This will require a retrieval and re-examination of the resources of Catholic teaching. At the same time it will demand a reframing and expansion of those resources. The retrieval process will involve a re-examination of the resources of

1. The Bible, such as covenantal theology and stewardship and care for creation. What indeed does "dominion" or "be fruitful and multiply" mean for our times?

2. Sacramental theology, such as Eucharist as thanksgiving for food that sustains life and Baptism as purification by water. Can these be sacraments with genetically modified food or polluted water?

3. Christology, such as the notion of the Cosmic Christ of St. Paul and the incarnational theology of the Logos in all creation of John's Gospel. If all reality is infused with the Logos, can we destroy it? In what ways is matter sacred?

4. Ethics, such as the notion of environmental ethics as a necessary expansion of human-centred ethics. If we have developed ethics for suicide and homicide, why not for biocide or ecocide?

5. Natural theology, namely, exploring the revelatory quality of the natural world and encouraging ongoing dialogue with science. How does natural theology contribute to our understanding of our embeddedness in an evolving universe?

The reframing and expansion of the resources of the Catholic tradition may include:

1. An openness to the cosmological context of the universe itself as revelatory of sacred mystery (the perspective of Pierre Teilhard de Chardin).

2. An embrace of the evolutionary scale of universe history and Earth history (*The Universe Story* by Brian Swimme and Thomas Berry).

3. An awareness of the need for ecological conversion in seeing the environmental crisis as a moral crisis (the call of John Paul II).

4. An acknowledgment of the need for a comprehensive global ethics to guide the emerging multiform planetary civilization (such as the Earth Charter).

5. Recognition of the critical role of humans as responsible for the continuity of life in all its forms, thus an intergenerational ethics (an ethics for future generations as advocated in papal statements).

Conclusion

Our historical moment is defined by a growing realization that we dwell simultaneously in the midst of the awesome beauty of evolutionary time and the devastating destruction of environmental space. We are presently awakening to our unique connection to the 13-billion-year unfolding of the evolutionary story and our embeddedness in 4.6 billion years of Earth's history. At the same time we are struggling to absorb the scale of destruction we have wrought in a very short period due to unlimited economic globalization and mindless environmental degradation. As we grope to find the appropriate response of religious voices to these issues, it may be the case that the most important contribution we can make is to engender hope in the possibility of a sustainable future that so many no longer envision for themselves or their children. For it is this hope that will engage human energies for the great work of shaping a vibrant multiform planetary civilization for the flourishing of the Earth community.

Appendix

Summary of Contributions and Limitations of Catholic Social Teachings on the Environment Through the Lens of *From Stockholm to Johannesburg: An Historic Overview of the Concern of the Holy See for the Environment 1972–2002.* (Note: Italics are as they appear in book, bolding is the emphasis of Mary Evelyn Tucker.)

At the end of the Jubilee Year 2000, John Paul II issued an Apostolic letter, *Novo Millennio Ineunte*, which contained the plea: "…how can we remain indifferent to the prospect of an ecological crisis which is making vast areas of our planet uninhabitable and hostile to humanity? Countless are the emergencies to which every Christian heart must be sensitive (51)."

A. Contributions

John Paul II issued a strong critique of globalization in January 1999: "However, if globalization is ruled merely by the laws of the market applied to suit the powerful, the consequences cannot but be negative. These are, for example, the absolutizing of the economy, unemployment, the reduction and deterioration of public services, the destruction of the environment and natural resources, the growing distance between rich and poor, unfair competition which puts the poor nations in a situation of ever increasing inferiority. While acknowledging the positive values which come with globalization, the church considers with concern the negative aspects which follow in its wake." (page 131, *From Stockholm to Johannesburg*)

In the move beyond anthropocentric thinking and acting Catholic teachings are poised to assist the changes needed in shaping an emerging multiform planetary civilization. There are several key areas we can identify as already present in Catholic teaching which are vital for reframing human-Earth relations in response to current patterns of economic globalization and environmental deterioration.

I. Overarching Principles

1. The affirmation of the sacredness of creation

"Nature speaks to us of God. 'The ear of the heart must be free of noise in order to hear this divine voice echoing in the universe…Nature too, in a certain sense, is the *book of God.*' One cannot but see the order that governs the cosmos and the dynamism that marks relations between the macrocosm and the microcosm. This visionary and contemplative approach must however lead us to rediscover our kinship with the earth. 'If nature is not violated and degraded, it once again becomes [our] sister.'" (pages 74-75)

Message of Pope Paul VI to the Stockholm Conference, 6/1/72:

"How can we fail to recall here the imperishable example of St. Francis of Assisi and to mention the great Christian contemplative Orders, which offer the testimony of an inner harmony achieved in the framework of **trusting communion with the rhythms and laws of nature?"** (page 91)

Dilecti Amici: Apostolic Letter of Pope John Paul II, 3/31/85:

14 "...contact with the visible world, with nature, is of immense importance. In one's youth, this relationship to the visible world is enriching in a way that differs from knowledge of the world 'obtained by books.' It enriches us in a direct way. One could say that by being in contact with nature we absorb into our own human existence the very mystery of creation which reveals itself to us through the untold wealth and variety of visible beings, and which at the same time is always beckoning us towards what is hidden and invisible. Wisdom – both from the inspired books as also from the testimony of many brilliant minds – seems in different ways to reveal the **'the transparency of the world'**. It is good for people to read this wonderful book – **'the book of nature'**, which lies open for each one of us. (pages 106-107)

"Man today, especially in the context of highly developed technical and industrial civilization, has become the explorer of nature on a grand scale, often treating it in a **utilitarian** way, thus destroying many of its treasures and attractions and polluting the natural environment of earthly existence. **But nature is also given to us to be admired and contemplated**, like a great **mirror of the world**. It reflects the Creator's **covenant** with his creature, the centre of which has been, from the beginning, in man, directly created 'in the image' of the Creator." (page 107)

Message for the 1990 World Day of Peace: Pope John Paul II 12/8/89

14 "***Finally, the aesthetic value of creation cannot be overlooked.*** Our very contact with nature has a deep restorative power; contemplation of its magnificence imparts peace and serenity. The Bible speaks again and again of the goodness and beauty of creation which is called to glorify God (cf. Gn 1: 4ff.; Ps 8: 2; 104: 1ff.; Wis 13: 305; Sir 39: 16, 33; 43: 1,9)." (page 121)

2. The acknowledgement of the intrinsic value, unity, and interdependence of life in all its forms

Justice in the World: Second Synod of Bishops 11/30/71

Chapter I Para 2 "Moreover, men are beginning to grasp a new and more radical dimension of **unity**; they perceive that their resources, as well as the precious treasures of air and water – without which there cannot be life – and the small delicate biosphere of the whole complex of all life on earth, are not infinite, but on the contrary must be saved and preserved as a unique **patrimony belonging to all mankind**." (page 84)

Message for the 1990 World Day of Peace: Pope John Paul II 12/8/89

IV. No. 14 "Even men and women without any particular religious conviction, but with an acute sense of their responsibilities for the common good, recognize their obligation to contribute to the restoration of a healthy environment. All the more should men and women who believe in God the Creator, and who are thus convinced that there is a well-defined unity and order in the world, feel called to address the problem." (page 122)

Ecclesia in Asia: Post-Synodal Apostolic Exhortation of Pope John Paul II 11/6/99

No. 41 *The Environment.* "When concern for economic and technological progress is not accompanied by concern for the balance of the ecosystem, our earth is inevitably exposed to serious environmental damage, with consequent harm to human beings. Blatant disrespect for the environment will continue as long as the earth and its potential are seen merely as **objects of immediate use and consumption, to be manipulated by an unbridled desire for profit.** It is the duty of Christians and of all who look to God as the Creator to protect the environment by restoring a sense of **reverence** for the whole of God's creation." (page 132-133)

3. The importance of thinking on behalf of future generations

Message of Pope Paul VI to the Stockholm Conference: 6/1/72

"Our generation must energetically accept the challenge of going beyond partial and immediate aims to prepare **a hospitable earth for future generations. Interdependency must now be met by joint responsibility**: **common destiny by solidarity**." (page 90)

"Thus, instead of seeing in the struggle for a better environment the reaction of fear of the rich, they would see in it, to the benefit of everyone, an affirmation of faith and hope in the **destiny of the human family gathered round a common project.**" (page 92)

Evangelium Vitae: Encyclical Letter of John Paul II 3/25/95

No. 42 "As one called to till and look after the garden of the world (cf. Gn 2: 15), man has a specific responsibility towards *the environment in which he lives*, towards the creation which God has put at the service of his personal dignity, of his life, not only for the present but also **for future generations**. It is the *ecological question* – ranging from the preservation of the natural habitats of the different species of animals and of other forms of life to 'human ecology' properly speaking – which finds in the Bible clear and strong ethical direction, leading to a solution which respects the great good of life, of every life." (page 128)

II. Ethical Choice and Creative Action

4. The recognition that the environmental crisis is a moral crisis and thus the need for ecological conversion and ecumenical and interreligious cooperation

Message of Pope Paul VI to the Stockholm Conference: 6/1/72

"But all technical measures would remain ineffectual if they were not accompanied by awareness of the necessity of **radical change of mentality.** All are called to clear-sightedness and change. Will our civilization, tempted to increase its marvelous achievements by despotic domination of the human environment, discover in time the way to control its material growth, to use the earth's food with wise moderation, and to cultivate real poverty of spirit in order to carry out urgent and indispensable reconversions? We would like to think so, for the **very excesses of progress lead men**, and significantly, the young particularly, to **recognize that their power over nature must be exercised in accordance with ethical demands.**" (pages 90-91)

Message for the 1990 World Day of Peace: Pope John Paul II 12/8/89

I. No. 5 "People are asking anxiously if **it is still possible to remedy the damage which has been done.** Clearly an adequate solution cannot be found merely **in a better management or a more rational use of the earth's resources**, as important as these may be. Rather, we must go to the source of the problem and face in its entirety that profound **moral crisis** ***of which the destruction of the environment is only one troubling aspect.*** (page 117)

IV. No. 13 "**An education in ecological responsibility is urgent:** responsibility for oneself, for others, and for the earth. This education cannot be rooted in mere sentiment or empty wishes. Its purpose cannot be ideological or political. It must not be based on a rejection of the modern world or a vague desire to return to some 'paradise lost.' Instead a true education in responsibility entails a **genuine conversion** in ways of thought and behaviour. Churches and religious bodies, non-governmental and governmental organizations, indeed all members of society, have a precise role to play in such education. The first educator, however is the family, where the child learns to respect his neighbour and to love nature." (page 121)

IV. No. 14 "Today the ecological crisis has assumed such proportions as to be ***the responsibility of everyone***. As I have pointed out, its various aspects demonstrate the need for concerted efforts aimed at establishing the duties and obligations that belong to individuals, peoples, States and the international community. This not only goes hand in hand with efforts to build true peace, but also confirms and reinforces those efforts in a concrete way. When the ecological crisis is set within the broader context of *the search for peace* within society, we can understand better the importance of giving attention to what the earth and its atmosphere are telling us: namely, **that there is an order in the universe which must be respected**, and that the human person, endowed with the capability of choosing freely, has **a grave responsibility to preserve this order for the well-being of future generations**. I wish to repeat that ***the ecological crisis is a moral issue.***

> ... Christians, in particular, realize that their responsibility within creation and their duty towards nature and the Creator are an essential part of their faith. As a result, they are conscious of a vast **field of ecumenical and interreligious cooperation opening up before them**." (page 122)

Ecclesia in Asia: Post-Synodal apostolic Exhortation of Pope John Paul II 11/6/99

No. 41 *The Environment.* "**The protection of the environment is not only a technical question; it is also and above all an ethical issue**. All have a moral duty to care for the environment, not only for their own good but also for the good of future generations. ..." (page133)

5. The highlighting of responsible care for creation in the concept of stewardship and imago Dei.

Sollicitudo Rei Socialis: Encyclical Letter of Pope John Paul II 12/30/87

No. 29 "Thus man comes to have a certain affinity with other creatures: he is called to use them, and to be involved with them. As the Genesis account says (cf. Gn 2:15), he is placed in the garden with the duty of cultivating and watching over it, being superior to the other creatures placed by God under his dominion (cf. Gn 1: 25-26). But at the same time man must remain subject to the will of God, who imposes limits upon his use and dominion over things (cf. Gn 2: 16-17), just as he promises his mortality (cf. Gn 2: 9; Wis 2-23). Thus man, being the image of God, has a true affinity with him too. On the basis of this teaching, development cannot consist only in the use, dominion over and indiscriminate possession of created things and the products of human industry, but rather in subordinating the possession, dominion and use to man's given likeness and to his vocation to immortality." (INSERT PAGE #)

Evangelium Vitae: Encyclical Letter of John Paul II 3/25/95

No. 42 "In fact, 'the dominion granted to man by the Creator is not an absolute power, nor can one speak of a freedom to 'use and misuse', or to dispose of things as one pleases. The limitation imposed from the beginning by the Creator himself and expressed symbolically by the prohibition not to 'eat of the fruit of the tree' (cf. Gn2: 16-17) shows clearly enough that, when it comes to the natural world, we are subject not only to biological laws but also to moral ones, which cannot be violated with impunity.'" (page 128)

6. The need for meaningful work for humans as co-creators with Creation

Populorum Progressio: Encyclical Letter of Pope Paul VI 3/26/67

No. 27 "The concept of work can turn into an exaggerated mystique. Yet for all that, it is something willed and approved by God. Fashioned in the image of his Creator, '**man must cooperate with him in completing the work of creation and engraving on the earth the spiritual imprint which he himself has received.**'" (page 86)

Message of Pope Paul VI to the Stockholm Conference: 6/1/72

"To rule creation means for the human race not to destroy it but to perfect it; **to transform the world** not into a chaos no longer fit for habitation, but **into a beautiful abode where everything is respected.**" (page 91)

Laborem Exercens: Encyclical Letter of Pope John Paul II 9/14/81

"The word of God's revelation is profoundly marked by the fundamental truth that man, created in the image of God, ***shares by his work in the activity of the Creator*** and that, within the limits of his own human capabilities, man in a sense continues to develop that activity, and perfects it as he advances further and further in the discovery of the resources and values contained in the whole of creation." (page 104)

Centesimus Annus: Encyclical Letter of Pope John Paul II 12/30/87

No. 37 "Instead of carrying out his role **as a co-operator with God** in the work of creation, man sets himself up in place of God and thus ends up provoking a rebellion on the part of nature, which is more tyrannized than governed by him." (page 124)

III. Critique of Market Economics and the Unrestrained Use of the Environment

7. The identification of the various links between poverty and the environment

Message for the 1990 World Day of Peace: Pope John Paul II 12/8/89

IV. No. 11 "It must also be said that the proper ecological balance will not be found without ***directly addressing the structural forms of poverty*** that exist throughout the world. Rural poverty and unjust land distribution in many countries, for example, have led to subsistence farming and to the exhaustion of the soil. Once their land yields no more, many farmers move on to the clear new land, thus accelerating uncontrolled deforestation, or they settle in urban centres which lack the infrastructure to receive them. **Likewise, some heavily indebted countries are destroying their natural heritage, at the price of irreparable ecological imbalances, in order to develop new products for export.** In the face of such situations, it would be wrong to assign responsibility to the poor alone for the negative environmental consequences of their actions. Rather, the poor, to whom the earth is entrusted no less than to others, must be enabled to find a way out of their poverty. This will require a courageous reform of structures, as well as new ways of relating among peoples and States." (page 120)

Centesimus Annus: Encyclical Letter of Pope John Paul II 12/30/87

52 "For this reason, **another name for peace is *development***. Just as there is a collective responsibility for avoiding war, so too there is a collective responsibility for promoting development. Just as within individual societies it is possible and right to organize a solid economy which will direct the functioning of the market to the common good, so too there is a similar need for adequate interventions on the international level. For this to happen, ***a great effort must be made to enhance mutual understanding and knowledge, and to increase the sensitivity of consciences***. This is the culture which is hoped for, one which fosters trust in the human potential of the poor, and consequently in their ability to improve their condition through work or to make a positive contribution to economic prosperity. But to accomplish this, the poor – be they individuals or nations – need to be provided with realistic opportunities. Creating such conditions calls for ***a concerted worldwide effort to promote development***, an effort which also involves **sacrificing the positions of income and of power enjoyed by the more developed economies.**" (page 126)

Incarnationis Mysterium: Bull of Indiction of the Jubilee of the Year 2000 11/29/98

No. 12 "There is also a need to create a new culture of international solidarity and cooperation, where all – **particularly the wealthy nations and the private sector**– accept responsibility for an economic model which serves everyone. There should be no more postponement of the time when the poor Lazarus can sit beside the rich man to share the same banquet and be forced no more to feed on the scraps that fall from the table (cf. *Lk* 16: 19-31). **Extreme poverty is a source of violence, bitterness and scandal; and to eradicate it is to do the work of justice and therefore the work of peace.**" (page137)

8. The advocacy of equity and distributive justice in the use of resources and the insufficiency of mere economic progress

Justice in the World: Second Synod of Bishops 11/30/71

Chapter I, Para.5 "The strong drive towards global unity, **the unequal distribution which places decisions concerning three quarters of income investment and trade in the hands of one third of the human race**, namely the more highly developed part, **the insufficiency of a merely economic progress and the new recognition of the material limits of the biosphere** – all this makes us aware of the fact that in today's world new modes of understanding human dignity are arising." (page 85)

Message of Pope Paul VI to the Stockholm Conference: 6/1/72

"For this reason the care of offering everyone the possibility of access to **a fair share in the resources**, existing or potential of our planet must weigh particularly on the conscience of men of goodwill. Development, that is the complete growth of man, presents itself as *the* subject, the keystone of your deliberations, in which you will pursue not only ecological equilibrium but also **a just equilibrium of prosperity between the centres of the industrialized world and their immense periphery**. **Want, it has rightly been said, is the worst of pollutions.**" (page 91)

9. The urgency of limiting consumption and exercising restraint

Redemptor Hominis: Encyclical Letter of Pope John Paul II 3/4/79

No. 16 "Man cannot relinquish himself or the place in the visible world that belongs to him; **he cannot become the slave of things, the slave of economic systems, the slave of production, the slave of his own products**. **A civilization purely materialistic in outline condemns man to such slavery**, even if at times, no doubt, this occurs contrary to the intentions and the very premises of its pioneers. The present solicitude for man certainly has at its root this problem. It is not a matter here merely of giving an abstract answer to the question: Who is man? It is a matter of the whole of the dynamism of life and civilization. It is a matter of the meaningfulness of the various initiatives of everyday life and also of the premises for many civilization programmes, political programmes, economic ones, social ones, state ones and many others." (page 96)

Evangelium Vitae: Encyclical Letter of John Paul II 3/25/95

No. 42 "…'the dominion granted to man' by the Creator is not an absolute power, nor can one speak of a freedom to 'use and misuse', or to dispose of things as one pleases. The **limitation** imposed from the beginning by the Creator himself and expressed symbolically by the prohibition not to 'eat of the fruit of the tree' (cf. Gn 2: 16-17) shows clearly enough that, when it comes to the natural world, we are subject not only to biological laws but also to moral ones, which cannot be violated with impunity." (page 128)

10. The role of the market in increasing inequity and wasteful consumption

Octogesima Adveniens: Apostolic Letter of Pope Paul VI 5/14/71

No. 9 "**Unlimited competition** utilizing the modern means of publicity incessantly launches new products and tries to attract the consumer, while earlier industrial installations which are still capable of functioning become useless. While very large areas of the population are unable to satisfy their primary needs, **superfluous needs are ingeniously created**. It can thus rightly be asked if, in spite of all his conquests, man is not turning back against himself the results of his activity. **Having rationally endeavored to control nature, is he now not becoming the slave of the objects which he makes?**" (page 88)

Redemptor Hominis: Encyclical Letter of Pope John Paul II 3/4/79

No. 16 "It is a matter – as a contemporary philosopher has said and as the council has stated – not so much of 'having more' as of 'being more'. Indeed there is already a real perceptible danger that, while man's dominion over the world of things is making enormous advances, he should lose the essential threads of his dominion and in various ways **let his humanity be subjected to the world and become himself something subject to manipulation in many ways** – even if the manipulation is often not perceptible directly –through the whole of the organization of community life, through the production system and through pressure from the means of social communication." (page 95)

Message for the 1990 World Day of Peace: Pope John Paul II 12/8/89

IV. No. 13 "**Simplicity, moderation and discipline**, as well as a spirit of sacrifice, must become a part of everyday life, lest all suffer the negative consequences of the careless habits of a few." (page 121)

Vita Consecrata: Post-Synodal Apostolic Exhortation of Pope John Paul II 3/25/96

No. 90 "… evangelical poverty forcefully challenges the idolatry of money, making a prophetic appeal as it were to society, which in so many parts of the developed world risks losing the sense of proportion and the very meaning of things. Thus, today, more than in other ages, **the call of evangelical poverty is being felt also among those who are aware of the scarcity of the planet's resources** and who invoke respect for and the **conservation of creation by reducing consumption**, by living more simply and by placing a necessary brake on their own desires." (page 130)

IV. Ways Toward Integral Development

11. The importance of integral development as a foundation for peace

Sollicitudo Rei Socialis: Encyclical Letter of Pope John Paul II 12/30/86

No. 34 "A true concept of development cannot ignore the use of the elements of nature, the renewability of resources and the consequences of haphazard industrialization – three considerations which alert our consciences to the moral dimension of development." **(page 100)**

Address: Pope John Paul II, the United Nations Centre (Nairobi, Kenya) 8/18/85

No. 2 "The use of natural resources must aim at servicing the integral development of present and future generations. Progress in the field of ecology, and growing awareness of the need to protect and conserve certain non-renewable natural resources, are in keeping with the demands of true stewardship. God is glorified when creation serves the integral development of the whole human family." (page 109)

No. 7 "Two kinds of assistance are needed: **assistance which meets the *immediate needs*** of food and shelter, and assistance which will make it possible for the people now suffering to resume responsibility for their own lives, to reclaim their land and to make it once more capable of providing a stable, healthy way of life. Such ***long-range programmes*** make it possible for people to regain hope for the future and a feeling of dignity and self-worth." (page 113)

No. 8 "'Development is the new name for peace.' Yes indeed, ***integral development is a condition for peace***, and environment programmes for **food and housing** are concrete ways of promoting peace." (page 113)

12. The problem of war as cause of environmental destruction

Message for the 1990 World Day of Peace: Pope John Paul II 12/8/89

IV. No. 12 "But there is another dangerous menace which threatens us, namely *war.* Unfortunately, modern science already has the capacity to change the environment for hostile purposes. Alterations of this kind over the long term could have unforeseeable and still more serious consequences. Despite the international agreements which prohibit chemical, bacteriological and biological warfare, the fact is that laboratory research continues to develop new offensive weapons capable of altering the balance of nature.

"Today, **any form of war on a global scale would lead to incalculable ecological damage.** But even local or regional wars, however limited, not only destroy human life and social structures, but also damage the land, ruining crops and vegetation as well as poisoning the soil and water. The survivors of war are forced to begin a new life in very difficult environmental conditions, which in turn create situations of extreme social unrest, with further negative consequences for the environment." (pages 120-121)

B. Limitations

1. Otherworldly goals

Gaudium et Spes: Pastoral Constitution of the Church in the Modern World 12/7/65

No. 57 "Christians, **on pilgrimage toward the heavenly city, should seek and think of these things which are above**. This duty in no way decreases, rather it increases, the importance of their obligation to work with all men in the building of a more human world. Indeed, the mystery of the Christian faith furnishes them with an excellent stimulant and aid to fulfill this duty more courageously and especially to uncover the full meaning of this activity, one which gives to human culture its eminent place in the integral vocation of man." (page 82)

2. Subduing the Earth

Gaudium et Spes: Pastoral Constitution of the Church in the Modern World 12/7/65

No. 57 "When man develops the earth by the work of his hands or with the aid of technology, in order that it might bear fruit and become a dwelling worthy of the whole human family and when he consciously takes part in the life of social groups, he carries out the design of God manifested at the beginning of time that he should **subdue** the earth, **perfect creation** and **develop** himself. At the same time he obeys the commandment of Christ that he place himself at the service of his brethren." (page 83)

Populorum Progressio: Encyclical Letter of Pope Paul VI 3/26/67

No. 22 "In the very first pages of Scripture we read these words: **"fill the earth and subdue it."** This teaches us that **the whole of creation is for man**, that he has been charged to give it meaning by his intelligent activity to complete and perfect it by his own efforts and to his own advantage." (page 85)

Redemptor Hominis: Encyclical Letter of Pope John Paul II 3/4/79

No. 15 "Why is it that the power given to man from the beginning by which he was to subdue the earth turns against himself, producing an understandable state of **disquiet**, of conscious or unconscious **fear** and of **menace**, which in various ways is being communicated to the whole of the present-day human family and is manifesting itself under various aspects?" (page 94)

3. Use of nature for humans

Gaudium et Spes: Pastoral Constitution of the Church in the Modern World 12/7/65

No. 69 "**God intended the earth with everything contained in it for the use of all human beings and peoples**. Thus, under the leadership of justice and in the company of charity, created goods should be in abundance for all in like manner. Whatever the forms of property may be as adapted to the legitimate institutions of peoples, according to diverse and changeable circumstances, attention must always be paid to this universal destination of earthly goods. In using them, therefore, man should regard the external things that he legitimately possesses not only as his own but also as common in the sense that they should be able to benefit not only him but also others. On the other hand, the right of having a share of earthly goods sufficient for oneself and one's family belongs to everyone. The Fathers and Doctors of the church held this opinion, teaching that men are obliged to come to the relief of the poor and to do so not merely out of their superfluous goods. If one is in his extreme necessity, he has the right to procure for himself what he needs out of the riches of others." (page 83)

Populorum Progressio: Encyclical Letter of Pope Paul VI 3/26/67

"Now if the earth truly was created to provide man with the necessities of life and the tools for his own progress, it follows **that every man has the right to glean what he needs from the earth.** The recent Council reiterated this truth: "God intended the earth and everything in it for the use of all human beings and peoples." Thus under the leadership of justice and in the company of charity, created goods should flow fairly to all." (page 86)

Address: Pope John Paul II, the United Nations Centre (Nairobi, Kenya) 8/18/85

No. 4 "The Catholic Church approaches the care and protection of the environment from the point of view of *the human person*. It is our conviction, therefore, that all ecological programmes must respect the *full dignity and freedom* of whoever might be affected by such programmes. Environment problems should be seen in relation to the needs of actual men and women, their families, their values, their unique social and cultural heritage. For the ultimate purpose of environment programs is to enhance the quality of human life, ***to place creation in the fullest way possible at the service of the human family.*** " (page 110)

4. *Necessity of industrialization and progress*

Populorum Progressio: Encyclical Letter of Pope Paul VI 3/26/67

No. 25 "The introduction **of industrialization**, **which is necessary for economic growth and human progress**, is both a sign of development and a spur to it. By dint of intelligent thought and hard work, man gradually uncovers the hidden laws of nature and learns to make better use of natural resources. As he takes control over his way of life, he is stimulated **to undertake new investigations and fresh discoveries**, to take prudent risks and launch new ventures, to act responsibly and give of himself unselfishly." (page 86)

5. *Dualism*

Redemptor Hominis: Encyclical Letter of Pope John Paul II 3/4/79

No. 16 "The essential meaning of this 'kingship' and 'dominion' of man over the visible world, which the Creator himself gave man for his task, consists in the priority of ethics over technology, in the primacy of the person over things, and in **the superiority of spirit over matter.**"

7

Toward a Global Culture of Life: Cultural Challenges to Catholic Social Thought in the Postmodern Electronic-Ecological Era

Joe Holland

Introduction

In this chapter I share the fruit of my ongoing study of Catholic Social Thought (CST) in relation to modern, and now postmodern, culture. My approach has been predominately philosophical by focusing on the historical evolution of cosmologies with their underlying root metaphors as the deepest dimension of all human cultures. As such, this approach to culture explores the evolution of humanity's cosmological cultural eras, within which the rich and diverse plethora of smaller regional, sectoral, and ethnic cultures find their own evolving context. Because the subject of this essay is so vast, it will be feasible here only to summarize the proposed analyses. Therefore, this chapter will refer to essays or books where I have presented more extended statements.

My reflection is indebted to the grace-filled opportunity to learn from the experience and wisdom of prophetic Catholic lay leaders across the planet – thanks in part to the Center of Concern, where I worked for a decade and a half, and thanks also to the global Catholic lay movement known as Pax Romana, of which I have been privileged to have been a member for some 45 years. In particular, I thank young Catholic lay leaders among the Aymara and Quechua peoples of the high plains of the Andes in Bolivia and Peru, who have been my most recent and profoundly wise teachers.

This chapter is mostly devoted to reflecting on the deep cosmological shift from the modern cultural era of nationalism to the postmodern cultural era of globalization, a shift precipitated by the still unfolding Electronic Revolution. This reflection identifies three past cosmological eras of human culture and evaluates contending postmodern strategies that are presently attempting to define in different ways the new, and fourth, postmodern era now emerging across humanity's bioregionally, ethnically, and religiously diverse cultural heritage.

Then, in response to the above cultural exploration, the chapter reflects briefly on the historical unfolding of CST as seen in the papal encyclical tradition from its genesis in 1740 to the present. This reflection is based on a series of two sequential books that I have written on the historical development of CST in the papal encyclical tradition from 1740-2000; one book is already in print and the other should be published in the near future.[1]

Finally, in a conclusion drawing on the fresh postmodern response of CST, the paper proposes that the Holy Spirit is calling us to serve a planetary culture of life. Alternately described here as a culture of regeneration, this call is seen as inviting all disciples of Jesus, and indeed all of humanity, to be liberated from the pervasive and threatening culture of death generated by the simultaneous climax and crisis of Western culture's globally hegemonic modern bourgeois era.

Postmodern Globalization

The Electronic Revolution

Though it seems best not to define globalization – since it is still an unfinished, fluid, and multi-dimensional process – I believe that the contemporary emergence of globalization has been precipitated by the Electronic Revolution. The Electronic Revolution has made globalization possible by creating the new technological possibilities of intense and rapid global networking in transportation and communication.

Further, although I do not see the Electronic Revolution as determining the ultimate deep cultural shape of globalization, I do see it as establishing technological parameters for cultural possibilities and cultural limits. For example, the Electronic Revolution favours global networking in a way that is simultaneously local and global, or decentralizing and centralizing, but with a still contentious strategic debate over which direction will be favoured and in what manner.

Neo-liberal Global Capitalism

In my view, the neo-liberal global stage of capitalism, still guided by what I describe as the now crisis-ridden modern mechanistic cosmology, favours the global centralization of an often spiritually and ethically empty market culture. This happens particularly through centralized corporate media systems, with the planet's local bioregions cast into the role of locally fragmented and globally manipulated consumers of the global market culture. By contrast, I see the technological miniaturization of the Electronic Revolution as favouring, in the long term, a very different process – namely the development of relatively self-reliant, locally bioregional, and community-centred cultural processes dialogically joined in conversation with other cultures across the planet by a vigorous global electronic networking.

In this proposal, the recent global triumph of modern industrial capitalism, though taking advantage of the technological achievements of the postmodern Electronic Revolution's early stage, needs to be seen culturally as a late-modern phenomenon and as one that is already entering into terminal ecological, societal, and spiritual crises.[2] As management theorist Peter Drucker has argued, the future is already "post-capitalist."[3] To appreciate this possibility, however, it is necessary to step back and develop a rough generalized map of the overall cosmological evolution of human culture.

Cosmology and Culture

The deepest dimension of our human cultures is the telling of our communal human story in response to basic human questions. Who are we? Where do we come from? How do we relate to each other? How do we fit into our environment? Where are we going? What is the meaning of all this? And, particularly, where do we find the nourishing presence of the sacred? Such are the basic questions behind all cultural stories.

The cultural responses to these questions ultimately form a comprehensive narrative of time and space in relation to the sacred, with all shaped by the predominance of a particular root metaphor. Such comprehensive narratives in their broadest form shape philosophical cosmologies. Cosmologies constitute the deepest guiding cognitive dimension of human cultures.

In a Hegelian dialectical sense of broad cultural eras, I will sketch a generalized map of three great past cosmological eras of human cultures and then describe the postmodern period of globalization as the birth of a new, and fourth, cosmological era. Though actual human reality can never be so neatly or simply segmented, such a map of cosmological eras is, nonetheless, a useful tool to have on hand as we enter an entirely new period in the human journey.

Thomas Berry has identified four cosmological eras – tribal cultures, the great classical civilizations, modern techno-industrial culture, and now the post-Cenozoic ecological era. Marshall McLuhan identified four eras of communications – speech, handwriting, mechanical printing, and now electronic. Linking Berry's and McLuhan's two eras provides a cultural map that also weaves together evolving root metaphors, forms of social organization, and shifts in sexual symbolism with deep implications for technology and spirituality.

Since there is not space here to elaborate in detail on this broad map, I will simply summarize its basic elements. Note, however, that this proposal of four evolving cultural eras rejects the modern mechanistic-liberal interpretation of historical evolution as uprooted progress from a supposedly backward past – the liberal theory of progress in which an emancipated rational future supposedly frees a society from the chains of pre-rational roots.

Evolution of Cosmological Eras

Since early humanity's development beyond the social structure of the small hunter-gather familial band (itself a rich and foundational source of human wisdom, and one that still survives in fragile vestiges on planet Earth), the human family has experienced, as proposed above, the maturation of three major cultural eras. It is now entering a fourth era.[4] Let us begin by examining the three past, but still living, eras.

Although I refer to these past eras as still living, they might better be called concentric circles forming the organically interrelated rings of a living cultural tree. Just as a living tree does not loose its earlier inner rings when it grows new outer ones, so, in this perspective, new human cultural eras do not eliminate prior ones, but instead incorporate the rooted legacy of the still living past and the living energy of new rings into richer wholes. Past and future are thus seen here within an organic whole; each new cultural era forms a new and living ring organically connected to the still living rings of the tree of humanity's evolving cultural energy. The past, rather than being a restraint on the future, is seen here as its creatively nourishing tap root. The still-living past three cosmological eras of the human journey may be briefly described as follows.

Primal-Organic Era of Speech

This is the ancient era of the relatively egalitarian tribe, developing sedentary horticulture with speech as the basic communications technology. Cultivating a symbolically feminine and matrifocal culture of ecological immanence in both technology and spirituality, its underlying cosmology is shaped predominately by the cosmological root metaphor of organicism. (Note that technology and spirituality are seen here as two sides of the same coin of human culture; spirituality is its subjective energy system and technology is its objective embodiment.) Known especially through the primal Earth-Mother Goddess and closely linked with the cycles of biological life, this cultural era in its degraded form faces the temptations of fatalism and human sacrifice to deified natural powers.

Classical-Hierarchical Era of Handwriting

This is the classical era of the urban-centred and dualistic, aristocratic, agricultural, and imperialist civilizations; it is grounded in the communications technology of handwriting. Cultivating a symbolically masculine and patriarchal culture of transcendence in technology and spirituality, its underlying cosmology is shaped by the cosmological root metaphor of anthropological and sociological hierarchy, though the organic tradition continues strongly within the still vast matrifocal peasantry. Known especially through the classical Sky-Father God transcendent beyond the cycles of the natural world, this cultural era in degraded form faces the temptation of ethnic domination and enslavement by violent force, in turn deifying in an exploitive, and even murderous, way an imperialist aristocratic hierarchy.

Modern-Mechanistic Era of Printing

This is the modern nationalist era of more vastly urban-centred, but now bourgeois, industrial nation-states, with the most powerful ones developing industrial imperialism. This era eventually cultivates within its market cultures an increasingly totalizing (and possibly even totalitarian) hyper-masculine symbol system that manipulates, marginalizes, and undermines the organic heritage of symbolically feminine and primal, peasant, and cultural values. Grounded in the communications technology of mechanical printing, this era promotes a culturally schizophrenic dualism of instrumental and expressive styles for technology and spirituality. The instrumental style predominates in the cosmological root metaphor of a symbolically masculine technological mechanism, while the expressive side is guided by a secondary, but profoundly interrelated, root metaphor of symbolically feminine emotivism, particularly in spirituality.

The era is guided by a mechanistic root metaphor, emerging initially in its modern form with the philosophy of medieval European Nominalism and known as the *via moderna*. For this root metaphor, the machine, like the deist cosmos, can take any shape chosen by its engineer, whose will is not confined by any cognitive parameters. Thus, though the mechanistic metaphor appeals publicly to an instrumental or utilitarian rationalism, its determining choices (guided only by the pleasure-pain principle) are ultimately non-rational and expressive – that is, voluntarist and emotivist. Hence, cognitively blind emotivism is the non-rational secret underlying bourgeois, instrumental rationality.

Marxism, socialism, and communism are seen here as radically rationalist variants of the mechanistic metaphor of the modern bourgeois project. They are included in the category of bourgeois nationalist industrialism and even, in a broad sense, within the category of industrial capitalism as well as within the broad framework of modern liberal ideologies. Thus, when speaking of modern industrial capitalism, we might speak of two variants. One variant is a corporate-centred capitalism and the other a state-centred capitalist variant; intermediate positions are available, but all share, in various ways, in the same modern mechanistic cosmology.

Initially, in this bourgeois era, the so-called private institutions of family and religion are assigned responsibility for the emotive side, beginning with the medieval *devotio moderna*. In late modernity, however, emotive energy is increasingly guided by the capitalist global media in service of the ethically and spiritually empty market culture. As the modern bourgeois era climaxes and enters into profound ecological, social, and spiritual crises, and as the public power of mechanistic secularization advances, the degraded market culture faces the temptation of inflicting upon the planetary system a pervasive culture of death, perhaps eventually in neo-totalitarian form.

Feminine and Masculine Cultural Energy

Within these three eras, the long primal era may be described predominately as the communal women's revolution – seeing the natural and human world as woven together in a single web of life. It lays the abiding and indispensable organic foundations for human culture, using biodegradable materials and sacramental ecological spiritualities. Similarly, the shorter classical era and very short modern era – both based on progressive advances in metallurgy – represent two sequential waves in the hierarchical-mechanistic men's revolution. Using non-biodegradable stone, metal, and, later, petrochemical synthetics, the two eras of the men's revolution emphasize mining below the earth and phallic projects upon its surface.

The gifts of the men's revolution are to challenge both naturalistic fatalism with human sacrifice in the names of history and justice and to awaken humanity to our awesome and even divine-like power to intensify geological and biological evolution through technological evolution. But, because it shuts itself off from the primal organic roots in idolatries of hierarchy and mechanism, the men's revolution enters into its own degraded temptations of violence and oppression.

The late-modern bourgeois stage of the men's revolution, though willingly embracing women but only on male terms, divorces humanity's technological evolution from its geo-biological matrix. By so doing, it foments the late-modern culture of death, which simultaneously inflicts ecological, societal, and spiritual devastation. Those who most feel the pain of this devastation are the young, who are threatened by alternating between rage and despair.

Chart 1: Four Concentric Circles in the Evolution of Human Culture

ERA	COMMUNICATION	SOCIETY	GENDER	SPIRITUALITY
PRIMAL 40,000 BCE?	Speech (organicism)	Egalitarian tribe	Women's revolution	Biological immanence
CLASSICAL 5,000 BCE?	Handwriting (hierarchy)	Aristocratic empire	Men's revolution-1	Ontological transcendence
MODERN 1,500 CE	Printing (mechanism)	Bourgeois nation	Men's revolution-2	Mechanistic exteriority vs. emotive interiority
POSTMODERN 2,000 CE	Electronics (creativity)	??????? Planet	Partnership (women + men)	Holistic co-creativity

I propose that the authentic postmodern culture that is still emerging calls humanity to a new, never-before-existing feminine-masculine partnership, both symbolically and among real women and men; this includes the diverse cultural experiences of human gender. Before exploring that development further, however, let us first look at the contending postmodern strategies seeking to shape the cultural future of humanity in the new planetary era.

Postmodern Cultural Debate

Presently there are four contending strategies promoted by various societal elites attempting to define the newly emerging postmodern planetary cultural era within the logic of the previous modern cosmology. Each of these contending elite strategies emphasizes a particular area of human experience and tries to define the human reality though its cosmological interpretation of that area. These same areas, however, are also addressed by alternative cosmological visions supported by less elite alternative movements. I propose that these alternative movements, with their alternative cosmological approaches, are proving most resourceful for creation of a regenerative culture of life on a planetary scale.

Economic Neo-liberalism

First, there is the ideological strategy pursued by most business elites of the new global stage of capitalism who are seeking to create what has been called a neo-liberal global system guided only by market culture. This attempt seeks to reduce all human goods and all human meaning to the modern capitalist financial calculus of the mechanistic cosmology's utilitarian ethics. Karl Marx labelled this development the commodity fetish.

In my analysis, this neo-liberal strategy is not truly postmodern but rather late-modern, ultra-modern, or in the language of Charlene Spretnak, hyper-modern. It represents the nearly total global triumph of the modern mechanistic metaphor on its objective side. Thus, this strategy reveals the objective side of the late-modern culture of death by promoting the marginalization of the poor, the devastation of the ecosystem, and the alienating spiritual despair experienced by so many young people.

Alternative movements to this ideological strategy include the development of a truly postmodern science of ecological economics that rejects the central mechanistic tenets of the dominant modern liberal economics in its various right- and left-wing forms. Also included are decentralized ecological technologies and sustainable community-centred forms of business, including micro-enterprises and micro-finance, that are all made feasible by the Electronic Revolution.

For example, as we will see later, the new scientific cosmology requires a radical revision of the underlying scientific assumptions of modern economic theory. Human economic science needs to become a subset of general ecological science. In modern economic theory, whether it is liberal or Marxist, the world of nature is unscientifically seen in alienated form only as a collection of resources for utilitarian human economic use. In reality, the global natural ecosystem precedes, and is deeper than, the global human economic system. The failure to recognize this reality is truly unscientific and, I propose, economically catastrophic.[5]

Academic Deconstructionism

Second, there is the academic strategy of many university elites who rightfully seek to celebrate diversity and difference. Beginning, originally, as a rich literary movement in Peru during the 1930s and then migrating to a circle of poets in the United States, this strategy has presently expanded across the world into the human sciences and philosophy. Now presented by many as a comprehensive cosmology, it is best known by its French proponents as deconstructionism or post-structuralism.

Despite its freeing celebration of diversity and difference, this strategy philosophically rejects the possibility of any broad human meaning as defined by the term meta-narratives. As such, it reveals the subjective side of the crisis of late-modernity by collapsing, albeit unintentionally, into relativism and nihilism.[6]

The dominant global media in their expressive projects now promote and celebrate in their artistic expressions the deconstructionist cosmology in service of the commodity fetish of the market culture. With this development, the main source of meaning celebrated by the dominant global media increasingly becomes purely voluntarist, and empty, human self-construction. As a result, there remains, despite emancipatory slogans, no philosophical restraint on the will of the economically and politically powerful. Thus, the public media culture moves toward the judgment that might makes right. In this process, the late-modern culture of death, while claiming to be emancipatory (particularly from institutions rooted in the past), begins in opposite fashion to articulate the philosophical justification for a frightening global domination.

Gratefully, alternative postmodern philosophical movements are already exploring a renewed sense of moderately realist inter-subjectivity, of moderately realist subject-object communion, and of moderately realist embodiment.[7] Other alternative philosophical movements, in interrelated fashion, are exploring the new creative cosmology emerging from post-Newtonian physics and from postmodern developments across the natural sciences; more about this later.[8]

Such alternative philosophical movements, which I describe as authentically postmodern, break out of the long aristocratic wave of Platonism (and the even deeper wave of Pythagoreanism) that has so strongly influenced Western culture – particularly its spiritualities – since classical times. These alternative philosophical movements also break out of the bourgeois form of neo-Platonism that was foundational for the modern European Renaissance, the modern European Scientific Revolution, and the modern European Protestant Reformation, with its combination of heightened Nominalism and heightened Augustinianism. All of these fed so powerfully into creating the spiritually and ethically empty market culture of modern capitalism – in neo-Platonic form celebrating a mysticism of numbers abstracted from any real societal or ecological context.

Religious Restorationism

Third, there is the religious strategy of many clerical elites who, across multiple world religions, seek in the postmodern context to restore classical patriarchal spiritual values as a critique of modern secularization. At the extreme, this attempt has been called fundamentalism; in more moderate versions it has been called restorationism.

Though rightfully pointing to the primacy of spiritual values and their powerful implications for public life, for better or worse, this strategy largely appeals – sometimes in violent form – to the patriarchal imagination of classical masculine warrior civilizations.[9] This restoration of classical patriarchal values is incorporated into an attempted late-modern revision of the liberal ideology on its instrumental or political-economic side over against its expressive side. Often described as neo-conservative, this attempt seeks to provide a defensive apparatus of religious security for late modern global capitalism, despite its threatening and terminal crises.

Alternative healing and symbolically more feminine forms of spiritual energy are also arising, I propose, out of humanity's common African roots and out of symbolically feminine inspiration. Earth is becoming electronically networked in the postmodern era and recent biological, archeological, and anthropological studies are converging in their conclusions that all humans have a common African origin. As the human race becomes conscious of its familial unity as children of Mother Africa, large sectors of humans return to drink from ancient African cultural sources, which carry a strongly matrifocal cultural heritage. This symbolic attraction to African roots can be seen, for example, in the development of a planetary youth culture, rooted musically in Rock and its subsequent mutations up to Hip-Hop, all tracing their deep roots in some form to ancient African cultural inspiration.

For the religious sphere, we see a resurgence of the religious energies of the African Diaspora and, most importantly, the explosion of a new cultural form of Christianity – namely Pentecostalism. Pentecostalism, of course, draws profoundly on African cultural roots, strongly empowers women (according to multiple analyses), and is now the fastest growing religious movement in the world.

The Holy Spirit, who is central for Pentecostalism, may in turn be seen as the cultural re-emergence of the feminine face of God proclaimed in Genesis 1:28. The feminine face of God as the Holy Spirit was celebrated initially in the primal era as the Earth-Mother Goddess and then kept alive in lesser form within classical era by Catholic and Orthodox veneration of Mary as the Theotokos, or God-bearer. Later, this feminine aspect of the Holy Spirit was strongly suppressed by the dominant Protestant evangelical form of modern Western Christianity, but this aspect is now re-emerging with social power in global Pentecostalism.

Yet another symbolical feminine movement has been emerging for more than a century; this is the so-called New Age movement, which actually began in the late 1800s. Although it initially drew on Indian images of the Earth-Mother Goddess, which were made accessible to the West by nineteenth-century British colonialism, this movement has taken on a more bourgeois character. As such, it faces the threatened late-modern bourgeois temptation to seek anti-realist escape into an expressive-individualist consolation that fails to provide outer-directed energy for authentic healing of the global ecological, societal, and spiritual crises.

Scientific Bio-engineering

Fourth, there is the scientific strategy of many technocratic elites in the frontiers of the natural sciences, and especially biology, to place science completely at the service of the great capitalist corporations, and in that process only to be guided by the crass utilitarian values of the global market culture. Already much of science and technology seems to have been used by the market culture, and science has become no longer a neutral actor but one often corrupted by the profit motive. In some cases, large universities are abandoning any guidance by traditional humanistic ethics and are being drawn into crassly utilitarian corporate partnerships guided only by the neo-liberal ideology. In other cases, giant corporations are attempting to replace universities with their own corporate research institutions. Again, the only remaining guide is the clearly bankrupt utilitarian ethics of late capitalism. Thus, it should come as no surprise that sensitive utilitarian ethicists, such as Professor Peter Singer of Princeton University, now offer "compassionate" ethical arguments for the execution of handicapped children.

But that is not the whole story of contemporary science. Alternate voices speaking from within science and about science have begun to articulate a post-Newtonian and authentically postmodern scientific cosmology that is at once relationally holistic, artistically developmental, and mystically humble; it is grounded ethically in what would have traditionally been called natural law.

This postmodern cosmology is arising from philosophical reflection upon the new scientific observations by the more sophisticated scientific instruments of the Electronic Era. Primal cosmology was based on folk wisdom; classical cosmology was based simply on the systematic observations of an aristocratic priestly class; and modern cosmology was based on systematized observation magnified by optics, such as the microscope and telescope. Postmodern cosmology is based on systematized optical observation enhanced by electronics, such as the electron microscope. With each of these cosmologies, the cosmological interpretation of time, space, and the sacred profoundly shifts.

The book by theologian Thomas Berry and physicist Brian Swimme called *The Universe Story* contains a useful overview of the authentically postmodern scientific cosmology, especially for physics and biology. Other scientific exponents include the late physicist David Bohm, biologist Rubert Sheldrake, and physicist Fritjof Capra. In the humanistic disciplines important voices include eco-feminist philosopher Charlene Spretnak, eco-feminist theologian Sallie McFague, and eco-feminist historian Carolyn Merchant.[10]

In light of these developments, as Thomas Berry and Brian Swimme have so eloquently narrated, human cultures are now called to tell our evolving human story, that is, our meta-narrative. They are also called to set our human story within the larger and evolving geo-biological story of our garden, planet Earth, and, in turn, to set that story within the even larger and evolving cosmic story of our universe.

Chart 2: Non-authentically Elite Postmodern Strategies

STRATEGY	VISION	PERSPECTIVE	THREAT
Economic neo-liberalism	Mechanistic coloni-zation of planet	Ultramodern (objective-instrumental)	Ecological-social devastation
Academic decon-structionism	Deconstruction of all meta-narratives	Ultramodern (sub-jective-expressive)	Ethical relativism and nihilism
Religious restorationism	Reassertion of patriarchal values	Secure defence of ultramodern	Authoritarianism and militarism
Scientific Bio-engineering	Scientistic conquest of life	Total triumph of autonomous reason	Neo-totalitarianism

Chart 3: Authentically Postmodern Alternative Movements

STRATEGY	VISION	PERSPECTIVE	GIFT
Bioregional economics	Global network of diverse bioregional communities	Authentically postmodern	Sustainable economic creativity
Neo-realist philosophy	Recovery of practical wisdom rooted in ancient traditions	Authentically postmodern	Rerooting education in communal needs
Charismatic-prophetic religion	Celebration and defence of culture of life	Authentically postmodern	Celebratory-prophetic spirituality of life
Holistic-evolutionary cosmology	Co-creative participation in evolutionary holism	Authentically postmodern	Ecological-mystical consciousness

Postmodern Cosmology

In this postmodern cosmology, which is the fruit of the globalizing Electronic Revolution, we are beginning to glimpse for the first time the depth and breadth of the evolving human story, of the evolving Earth story, and of the still richer cosmic story. We are seeing the human story and its spiritual meaning as an integral part of the wider and richer evolutionary story of our garden planet Earth and of its wider matrix in the entire cosmos.

In this postmodern cosmology, the universe is now seen as relationally holistic, artistically creative, and immersed in mystery. In turn, humanity is perceived in the new cosmology as the reflective consciousness of Earth's own evolution, which is itself a part of the wider, evolving cosmic evolutionary process and, in turn, part of the wider evolving cosmic process.

The new scientific cosmology has much in common with the ancient spiritual-cultural traditions of the tribal or indigenous peoples of Earth. For example, leading Irish theologian Sean McDonagh, faithful to the ancient tribal Celtic Christianity of his roots, has reflected extensively on the new cosmology's effect on Catholic theology.[11] Tragically, however, the rural Celtic path for Christianity was suppressed in the early Middle Ages by the cultural-spiritual imperialism of the urban Latin path.

In sum, we are presently living within the deep shift from a modern, print-based culture centred in the North Atlantic nations and grounded in a mechanistic-emotive cosmology to a fresh postmodern electronic-based culture giving birth to a truly planetary civilization that is grounded in an ecological-artistic cosmology. The new planetary civilization is at once globally networked and ethnically and religiously diverse in its countless bio-regional localities. Within this diverse networking, the new planetary civilization is called to be ecologically sustainable, economically just, politically democratic, and culturally holistic in character. But what does this mean for CST?

Catholic Social Thought

Postmodern Stage

The papal encyclical tradition, with CST as central, begins in what Michael Schuck has called its pre-Leonine stage that coincides with the emergence of early laissez-faire capitalism in its local stage.[12] CST in this period represents a largely pre-modern aristocratic reaction to the modern European bourgeois Enlightenment, with its new philosophical cosmology of mechanism underlying its modern ideology of liberalism. The strategy of CST in this period is to defend a Europe aristocratic "Christian Civilization" as an indispensable foundation for the evangelization of human culture.

Next, after the European aristocracy is finally routed across Western Europe, a process complete by the time of Pope Leo XIII's election in 1878, CST enters what Schuck has called its Leonine stage, which coincides with the emergence of the national stage of modern industrial capitalism.[13] In this period, CST attempts to develop a reforming adaptation to the modern bourgeois culture of liberal democracy and liberal capitalism. In this process, under the initial leadership of Pope Leo XIII and with the help of a Jesuit intelligentsia, a comprehensive strategy was designed to reform modern liberal culture into a bourgeois adaptation of Eurocentric Christian Civilization.

The Leonine strategy pursues what would eventually become a six-pronged strategy that includes the following elements:

1. definition of socialism, and its radicalization in communism, as the primary enemy;

2. anti-socialist alliance with the moderate bourgeoisie;

3. Thomist philosophy as the philosophical ground for a bourgeois neo-Christendom;

4. Christian democracy, supported by Catholic Action, as the vehicle;

5. Social Catholicism, a contested element, to retain the loyalty of the working class;

6. repression of liberal penetration within inner-ecclesial consciousness.

Lastly, in what Schuck calls the post-Leonine period, but which I prefer to call the Johannine period because it began with the election of John XXIII in 1958, the concept of both a Eurocentric and a Christian Civilization is abandoned on behalf of a new postmodern humanistic global civilization. This civilization is later called by John XXIII a global "culture of life" and by Paul VI a global "civilization of love." This period, of course, correlates with the emergence of the global stage of capitalism and the Electronic Revolution. Vatican II is central for launching this new strategic stage, but thus far the Johannine strategy has been handicapped by bitter ecclesial polarization.

Spirituality of Life

The first great postmodern challenge to CST appears in the foundational area of spirituality. The old Catholic Action movements of the Leonine strategy, which include lay groups like Pax Romana, were based on both the classical spirituality of transcendence and the modern spirituality of interiority. They were, in turn, placed at the service of the attempt to create a modern but reformed bourgeois form of European Christian civilization. Following the old Platonic dualism, the temporal sphere of the apostolate, to which lay Catholic Action was to be directed, was not seen as a source of spiritual energy itself but only as an a secular object to which spiritual energy could be extrinsically applied.

A series of bourgeois European revolutions – the Protestant Reformation, the scientific revolution, the philosophical Enlightenment, and finally the combined assault of the modernizing democratic and industrial revolutions – spelled the doom of the classical Catholic aristocratic rule on which European Christian civilization had been based. The loss of the Papal States at the close of the nineteenth century, during the papacy of Pius IX, was the final step in the defeat of the European Catholic aristocratic power. In response, Catholic leadership from Leo XIII through to Pius XII pursued the ambitious but ultimately unsuccessful strategy of attempting to create a bourgeois form of Eurocentric Christian civilization. Jacques Maritain described this project as a Neo-Christendom. By the middle years of the twentieth century, however, it was becoming clear that this modernizing attempt was collapsing in traumatic failure.

Now, however, with the collapse of the dualistic paradigm, a Christian appropriation of the postmodern cosmology begins to see all of creation as holistic and sacred. In essence, it is considered sacramentally charged across space and time and as participating in God's creative presence, though also in need of healing from the wounds of human sin. Further, God's own creativity is seen not simply as shared with the human sphere, but also as present across all of cosmic creation. Thus, both the wider natural world and within it the human family are, at different levels, co-creators with God in the ongoing evolutionary process of cosmogenesis.

This means that the fundamental human tasks of work, family, and citizenship are not simply areas of ethical responsibility. They represent, more profoundly, sacred experiences of mystical communion with the Creator's own creativity, though they are also subject to demonic deformation. Further, Christians in their mystical communion with the Creator's own creativity need to follow a prophetic path in the arenas of work, family, and citizenship – seeking to heal the wounds of sin that scar and block humanity's ecological, social, and spiritual co-creativity with the Creator.

As this postmodern spirituality unfolds in a single, worldly, spiritual whole, the old concepts break down. These were dualistic and hierarchical concepts of a metaphysical separation between sacred and secular spheres, as well as between clerical and lay states or alternately between spiritual and temporal orders. There is no longer a valid cosmological distinction between spiritual and temporal, sacred and secular, or clerical and lay. There is only one creation, participating holistically in creative Divine energy, though wounded by sin and crying out for holistic healing.

In the context of this new scientific cosmology, the community of Jesus' disciples begins to recover its originally and exclusively lay character. This lay character was obscured when the Jesus movement was overlaid in the Roman imperial period with imported pagan and non-evangelical doctrines of clerical and religious states of life. In the emerging postmodern cosmology, however, the so-called religious life, though not lay intentional communities, and so-called clerical state, through the lay sacrament of ordination, enter into cultural-spiritual crises. As the dualistic cosmological constructs of the clerical state and religious life break down, the Christian healing of the evolutionary process by the proclamation and ministry of Jesus' Gospel returns to its original understanding as a lay movement. In this movement, the lay state is seen as the only one available in God's sacred creation.[14]

Women and Men

The second great challenge to CST is supporting and celebrating the co-creative mutuality of women and men. With the postmodern turn, women and men have, for the first time, the possibility of developing a true partnership of co-creative mutuality. This means that the three sacred areas of human co-creativity – namely, family, work, and citizenship – are called to become spheres of increasingly balanced and co-creative feminine-masculine partnership.

For Christians, the deepest theological grounding of this partnership, as the philosopher Hegel appreciated, is the understanding of the doctrine of the Trinity. In one metaphorical interpretation, with the Holy Spirit seen as feminine, the Trinity may be described in sexually symbolic terms as the eternal fertile embrace – the eternal co-creative sexual communion of the feminine and masculine faces of the Divine Mystery, eternally birthing new life. The creative dialectic of the Trinity is then echoed, as Hegel celebrated, across the creativity of all creation. This metaphorical interpretation of the Trinity recovers, I suggest, the deep meaning of Genesis 1:28: "In God's own image they were made; male and female they were made." In this metaphor the Holy Spirit represents, of course, the feminine image of God.[15]

Consistent Ethic of Life

As modern culture enters into profound ecological, societal, and spiritual crises – and rapidly infects the entire planet with these crises – Pope John Paul II proclaimed that we are threatened globally with a culture of death. The alternative, he proposed, is a culture of life, served by the Gospel of life.[16] In support of this vision, the late Cardinal Joseph Bernadin of Chicago spoke of a consistent ethic of life.

The culture of death is the very opposite of a culture of life. Applying the perspective to society at large, we may say that it represents the expansion of deadly addictive processes to institutions and professions in their late-modern form. Increasingly today, for example, many schools of higher education seek to train future professionals simply to succeed in what is increasingly becoming a culture of death. Similarly, as the ecological, societal, and spiritual crises intensify on a global scale, large sectors of the professions – in massive acts of ever-deepening denial – become enablers of the threatening processes of ecological, societal, and spiritual breakdown. This is the negative face of the end of the modern cultural era.

But there is also a positive face where fresh, postmodern hope and life appear. Within the professions themselves, and in the training programs that prepare candidates for them, new experiments are already underway that represent fertile seeds for a regenerative planetary civilization of life. For example, in the area of human work, think of solar energy and other ecological technologies in engineering, of restorative justice in law, of complementary medicine in health care, of micro-finance in banking, and of micro-enterprises in business.

The same struggle against the culture of death by the culture of life goes on in the related spheres of family life and citizenship. On one side, young couples, increasingly pressured by crushing demands from hyper-masculine institutions pursuing the neo-liberal ideology, find their parenting undermined and even their marriages threatened. So, too, there arise within political circles new movements of xenophobia, racism, and scapegoating.

But the opposite is also true. On the other side, young couples across the planet are developing new and more supportive patterns for parenting and marriage, sometimes at great financial sacrifice but also with priceless emotional and spiritual rewards in their relationship. So, too, young leaders across the planet are exploring creative alternatives to the late-modern drift into ecological, societal, and spiritual breakdown. They are forming new solidarities to resist sexism, racism, classism, and ecological devastation, and also new models of socially and ecologically sustainable community.

Conclusion

To sum up, I have proposed that a new postmodern era is now being born; it is at once electronic and ecological, grounded culturally in a postmodern scientific cosmology of evolutionary and mystical holism, and encourages a fresh planetary civilization. In service of this new global civilization, I further propose, the Holy Spirit has raised up CST as a creative, transnational prophetic guide, though also as a still-developing and unfinished tradition.

To follow the inspiration of the Holy Spirit, we first need to boldly recognize that we live within a deep cultural shift from the global hegemony of a modern-nationalistic culture, centred in the North Atlantic nations, to a fresh postmodern and multipolar planetary culture. The new global civilization flowing from this postmodern cosmology is called to be ecologically sustainable, economically just, politically democratic, and spiritually meaningful. Since cosmology has always grounded civilization, we also need to share in the fresh dialogue between science and spirituality in a way that remembers the cosmological wisdom of humanity's ancient tribal traditions. At the birth of this new planetary culture, I further propose that CST faces three strategic challenges:

1. to perceive family, work, and citizenship as sacred arenas of our co-creativity with other humans, with the rest of the natural world, and with the Divine Mystery;

2. to perceive women and men, with each representing one of the two faces of God (Genesis 1:28), as called to celebrate true partnership across family, work, and citizenship; and

3. to see the postmodern, planetary era as a call to promote a culture of life at every level from the womb to the planet by means of the consistent ethic of life that returns to the natural law of ecology in both its environmental and societal expressions.

As we form a new Catholic-Christian and more broadly human solidarity across the multiple divisions of gender, class, ethnicity, religion, age, and geography, let us listen humbly and prayerfully to the Holy Spirit. We need to follow her wisdom as she leads us out of the late-modern mechanistic culture of death into a co-creative and authentically postmodern culture of life for the new planetary civilization.

8

Global Civil Society and the Catholic Social Tradition

R. Scott Appleby

The question to be considered in this chapter is whether the notion of global civil society is a misleading contradiction in terms – an unfortunate, rather than an illuminating, paradox. That is, does the assertion of a global civil society obscure, rather than clarify, what it seeks to comprehend by trivializing civil society, evacuating it of its meaning, and exiling it from its natural habitat in local, face-to-face communities that are engaged in ongoing, interpersonal public discourse and interaction? Is the concept of a global civil society flawed in much the same way that the idea of the global village displayed insufficient reverence for the traditional character of the village as essentially a real (as opposed to a virtual or transparently constructed) human community?

To phrase the point slightly differently: Is it true that a suitably robust civil society must be embedded always and everywhere in the stubborn particularity of the local? Is civil society, understood through the lens of Catholic Social Thought (CST), inherently resistant to globalization?

Befitting the emerging reality they seek to name, definitions of both globalization and civil society have been fluid and unstable. Globalization admits of several overlapping definitions, each highlighting a different dimension – political, economic, cultural, and social – of the fundamental phenomenon. One definition is the erosion of the spatial and temporal barriers to human interaction, unprecedented in its scale and speed, that may be leading to the greater integration of markets, political systems, and cultures across national boundaries.

Civil society, a slightly more mature concept, is more precise. As recently as the mid-1990s – when the concept was being tested, explored, and applied beyond its original Western European boundaries in analyses of post-Soviet Eastern Europe, Communist China, Latin America, and the Islamic world – social scientists developed several definitions of civil society:

a) "an attempt to theorize about a specific historical experience: an ongoing, uninterrupted tradition of a core of socioeconomic and political institutions (interconnected with some key cultural dispositions) in some North Atlantic nations dating back at least two to three centuries" (Víctor Pérez-Díaz);

b) "a rich social fabric formed by a multiplicity of territorially and functionally based units" (Philip Oxhorn);

c) "that set of diverse non-governmental institutions, which is strong enough to counterbalance the state, and, whilst not preventing the state from fulfilling its role of keeper of the peace and arbitrator between major interests, can nevertheless prevent the state from dominating and atomizing the rest of society" (Ernest Gellner);

d) "a historically evolved sphere of individual rights, freedoms, and voluntary associations whose politically undisturbed competition with each other in the pursuit of their respective private concerns, interests, preferences, and intentions is guaranteed by a public institution, called the state" (Salvador Giner).[1]

Despite the range of emphases in these definitions of civil society, a focus comes into view and that focus raises the question of complementarity with the process of globalization. Does globalization provide a context within which civil society might develop in a direction congenial to a Christian vision of human flourishing, or does it inhibit that development?

Civil Society and Catholic Social Thought

Variations in the definitions of each term aside, are globalization and civil society complementary, mutually reinforcing social realities? On the face of it, globalization in its cultural and social dimensions would seem to be an ally and agent of civil society – a transnational, potentially global extension of zones of free, unfettered enterprise and interaction. Consider some of the candidates for new forms of civil society. These include the international women's movement, the environmental movement, and transnational religious movements from Al Qaeda to Socially Engaged Buddhists. Surely these movements, presumably unimpeded (or less impeded) by the regulatory canopy of the nation-state, provide a remarkably robust zone of freedom and association and space for self-determination and political empowerment.

From the perspective of the CST, however, one must proceed with a degree of caution in declaring globalization an ally of civil society. If one places appropriate emphasis on the territorially and functionally based character of civil society, in contrast to the pan-territorial nature of globalization, the two forms of interaction seem less reconcilable. They also seem less alike if the stress is on the organic relationship between civil society and the state, in contrast to the transnational dynamics of globalization, with its inexorable integration of nation-states and consequent erosion of national sovereignty.

In standard usage, civil society refers to the array of voluntary associations that stand between the state and the individual or family. During the latter half of the twentieth century, the Church shifted orientation from partnership with the state – concordats, diplomatic alliances, political parties, and so forth – to transforming presence within civil society – within, that is, schools, labour unions, civic organizations and the like. It was precisely the normative character of civil society that made it the Church's natural public habitat. Catholic intellectuals – such as José Casanova, David Hollenbach, and John Coleman – celebrated civil society precisely as a zone of freedom, a public space within which the pursuit of (citizens') respective private concerns, interests, preferences, and intentions could be discussed, debated, and formed. As mediator of the complex and otherwise unequal relationship between the individual or family and the state, civil society was the realm within which subsidiarity, the common good, and the limited but appropriate role of the state and other bedrock principles of CST were enacted. Or so Catholics presumed.

Happily, they were joined by non-Catholics in the presumption that vigorous communal life and social solidarity – albeit contested in their scope – are essential to a truly liberal, pluralist, democratic, and free society. To political philosophers such as Robert Putnam and Samuel Sandmel, the glue of civil society was inter-communal, interpersonal relationships whose meaning derived largely from being part of the same local or state community.

The concept was transnational in theory, though not in practice. Inclusive, non-sectarian public discourse could thrive in any cultural soil. Indeed, Ashutosh Varshney's groundbreaking study of communal violence in India demonstrates that the Hindu-Muslim violence, which ravaged several Indian states from the 1950s through the 1990s, was virtually absent in some cities, towns, and villages. These cities, towns, and villages had developed voluntary, inclusive, cross-religious, and cross-ethnic networks of associations that characterize civil society at its most vibrant. Varshney argues that such strong, associational forms of civic engagement – including trade unions, political parties, integrated business organizations, and professional syndicates – functioned collectively as an agent of solidarity and peace by restraining those, including powerful politicians, who sought political gain by polarizing Hindus and Muslims across communal lines.[2]

Globalization and Solidarity

How does globalization comport with this set of practices and values? Does it promote forms of civil society congenial to a Catholic Christian vision of authentic human flourishing? Pope John Paul II said that "globalization, a priori, is neither good nor bad. It will be what people make of it."[3] What, then, are people making of it?

In the US and Europe, the early theorists were pragmatists, utilitarians, and garden-variety liberals. Diverse groups in society hold together, notes Bernard Crick, because they practise politics – not because they agree about fundamentals or some such concept too vague, too personal, or too divine ever to do the job of politics for the group. The moral consensus of a free state is not something mysteriously prior to or above politics; it is the activity, the civilizing activity, of politics itself. Or, as Albert Hirschman has claimed, the community spirit that is normally needed in a democratic market society tends to be spontaneously generated through the experience of tending the conflicts that are typical of that society.

However, it could be argued that globalization reduces the incentives to tend to such conflicts. By reducing the civic engagement of internationally mobile groups, globalization loosens the civic glue that holds societies together and exacerbates social fragmentation. "Globalization," writes the political economist Dani Rodrik, "delivers a double blow to social cohesion – first by exacerbating conflict over fundamental beliefs regarding social organization, and second by weakening the forces that would normally militate for the resolution of these conflicts through national debate and deliberation." [4]

This dynamic is painfully on display in most developing countries. Jorge Castañeda, for example, speaks of "a new cleavage that is rapidly cutting across Mexican society." This split

> separates those Mexicans plugged into the US economy from those who are not.... It divides Mexicans who are highly sensitive to government macroeconomic policy from those who are indifferent to it. It separates those who correctly believe that politics and events in Mexico still determine their destiny from those who just as rightly understand that the decisions most critical to their lives are made in Washington and New York.[5]

Mexicans who remain on the margins of global flows of capital, goods, and services – even if they are not on the margins of society – are increasingly alienated from Mexicans who are steadily being integrated into those flows. "This growing group of Mexicans oriented toward the United States," Castañeda laments, "is isolated from much of the country's economic tribulation and relatively complacent about its political travails."[6]

If the Mexican experience suggests the corrosive effects of globalization, it is worth noting that the literature on civil society suggests that solidarity of any duration or depth is by no means a guaranteed outcome. Indeed, civil society is routinely envisioned as consisting in "the forging of links which are effective even though they are flexible, specific, and instrumental" rather than organic, principled and deeply embedded in the social fabric.[7] Such "links," accordingly, can be paper-thin, temporary, and ultimately self-interested arrangements rather than reliably structured commitments capable of creating and sustaining a community of common purpose.

Scholars have identified five prominent dimensions of mature civil society. In these dimensions, one notes both the points of tension with the fundamental principles of CST, and the similarity to the essential features of unregulated globalization. The first dimension is individualism, which understands individuals as sovereign components of the polity; the second dimension – privacy – is understood as the legally sanctioned distinction between public and private spheres. The third dimension, market, is defined as the spontaneous and anonymous process of countless contractual transactions in the economic, intellectual, political, and cultural spaces for the production of social life. Pluralism, the diffusion of power throughout society, creating relatively autonomous individuals and associations and a culture of wide-ranging and tolerated beliefs and practices, is the fourth dimension; and class, the unintended consequence of citizenship in a pluralist society, is the final dimension. Although various commentators see free markets as the salient structural feature and organizing principle of civil society, the notion of a global civil society – as distinct from civil societies transformed by globalization – is a contested notion.

Is There a Global Civil Society?

This is the question posed recently by, among other theorists, the political scientist John Keane. He answers the question in the affirmative by arguing that one can indeed discern a "thick web of associational ties shared by people rooted in a particular place and time" emerging on a global scale. This civil society hovers above and extends across national boundaries, even as it sinks roots and embeds itself in local communities. This form of global civil society, Keane argues, carries with it a powerful and enduring political vision. His analysis of the emerging global civil society and his description of its political trajectory are worth pondering, for they help us to identify the opportunities for extending CST and practice within this new global social order.

By "global civil society" Keane means "a dynamic non-governmental system of interconnected socio-economic institutions that straddle the whole earth, and that have complex effects that are felt in its four corners." Neither "a static object nor a fait accompli," it is an unfinished project that consists of "sometimes thick, sometimes thinly stretched networks, pyramids and hub-and-spoke clusters of socio-economic institutions and actors who organise themselves across borders, with the deliberate aim of drawing the world together in new ways." Thus far, Keane's definition resembles those we have already reviewed. But he adds a normative dimension: "*These non-governmental institutions and actors tend to pluralise power and to problematise violence; consequently, their peaceful or 'civil' effects are felt everywhere, here and there, far and wide, to and from local areas, through wider regions, to the planetary level itself.*"[8]

Five interrelated dimensions of this definition are noteworthy. While global civil society is composed, first, of non-governmental actors, Keane restricts the application of non-governmental to those entities that conform to a second dimension of the definition. In this dimension the actors constitute a society – "a dynamic ensemble of more or less tightly linked social processes." By definition, the members of a global civil society interact with one another in complex patterns that reflect the fact that they are "interrelated and functionally interdependent." As "a society of societies," global civil society is larger and "weightier" than any individual actor or organization or combined sum of its thousands of constituent parts – "most of whom, paradoxically, neither 'know' each other nor have any chance of ever meeting each other face-to-face." Global civil society, Keane insists, is "a highly complex ensemble of differently sized, overlapping forms of structured social actions…a vast scenario in which hundreds of thousands…of individual and group adventures unfold, sometimes harmoniously through cooperation and compromise, and sometimes conflictually." The key point, he adds, is that "General Motors plus Amnesty International plus the Ruckus Society plus DAWN (Development Alternatives with Women for a New Era) does not equal global civil society. Its social dynamics are more intricate, more dynamic and more interesting than that."[9]

These social dynamics oblige the various actors in global civil society "to refrain from certain actions, as well as to observe certain norms…." A third characteristic of global civil society, Keane avers, is one such overriding norm, namely, civility. Indeed, his analysis rises or falls on his claim that the following statement is descriptive rather than merely aspirational or normative. Global civil society, he asserts, "is marked by a strong tendency to both marginalise or avoid the use of violence or to take pleasure in violence." Notwithstanding the fact that globalization provides convenient hideouts – pockets of incivility – for gangsters, terrorists, war criminals, arms traders, and other purveyors of death and destruction, global civil society is "a complex and multi-dimensional space of nonviolence."[10] Keane points to the empowering of innumerable organizations and social initiatives that specialize in repairing the torn fabric of global civil society, including NGOs that battle child prostitution, pornography, the spread of HIV-AIDS, arms trafficking, and other social predators. He devotes an entire chapter to document the following claim:

> The actors of global civil society, in their own and varied ways, admire the peaceful. All of them more or less observe the rule that non-violent respect for others overrides any considerations of their national identity or skin colour or religion or sex, or that murder and other forms of violence against others is undesirable, and should be minimised, or strictly prohibited. Thanks to such shared norms, the participants within this society are prone to exercise physical restraint, to mix non-violently with others, "foreigners" and "strangers" included. Normatively speaking, the killing rituals of hunting and gathering orders, or tribal violence, or mafia thuggery tend to have no place within this society. Its extra-governmental institutions and forms of action are marked by a proclivity towards non-violence and respect for principles of compromise, mutual respect and even power-sharing among different ways of life…. Factually speaking, this society encourages compromise and mutual respect…. Insofar as these various actors have a more or less deep sensitivity towards violence and violence-prone institutions, they enable global civil society to be "civil" in a double sense: it consists of non-governmental (or "civilian") institutions that tend to have non-violent (or "civil") effects.[11]

Nonetheless, Keane acknowledges, global civil society, being inherently pluralist, contains within it the seeds of fragmentation, disorder, and conflict. This fourth characteristic of global civil society – its heterogeneity – complicates the picture of a potentially peaceable, civil, and even harmonious pattern of relationships interacting within the parameters of a "global community." No such single community exists. Rather, a multitude of sub-communities thrives under the aegis of institutions that create "social 'homes' or 'nests' within which individuals and groups fashion and re-fashion their identities, familiarise and make sense of each other, find meanings in life, get their bearings through activities that cross borders…." Keenly aware of the fluid and unstable nature of these sub-communities, the participants within global civil society recognize that it is neither spontaneously self-regulating nor self-reproducing. "They are more or less reflexively aware of its *contingency*," Keane notes. The structures, rules, and even the norms of the society "are subject to strenuous negotiation and modification, through complex processes." This sense of contingency also "feeds social conflict, thus ensuring that global civil society stands precariously between the boundaries of social equilibrium and disorder at the edge of chaos." [12]

The fifth defining characteristic of global civil society – its global scale and scope – poses an additional challenge to its potential for fostering genuine civility, solidarity, and peacebuilding. Drawing upon many different actually existing societies, global civil society is both integrated and decentred. Its development, furthermore, has been uneven. In certain geographical zones – Keane mentions Afghanistan, Chechnya, Sierra Leone, and Burma – global civil society is weak or virtually absent.

Yet where global civil society is present, its dynamics deepen the interdependence of peoples. The resulting linkages " 'socialise' actors in ways that 'thicken' or increase the density of social interactions across political borders."[13] For example, transnational social movements are a prototypical product of globalization and a stimulus to the development of global civil society. Such movements generate international non-governmental organizations of every size, shape, and cause that form a virtual, or embryonic, cross-cultural society. Often these movements are efforts by clusters of relatively marginalized actors to promote some form of social or political change. Movements promoting different goals not only vary in the actors they mobilize and in their degree of formal coordination, but also face different political opportunities in national, intergovernmental, and transgovernmental decision-making arenas, and these factors influence the strategic choices they make.

Significantly, the intervention of transnational social movements in national, intergovernmental, and transgovernmental political processes alters decision makers' perceptions of problems and of the costs and benefits associated with different policy choices.[14] Indeed, Louis Kriesberg has argued that such movements have radical implications for the global spread of democratization; they increase global integration, converge and diffuse values, and proliferate transnational institutions. The democratization trend is evident in social systems at the organizational, community, national, and global levels. And shared values, including respect for human rights and individual dignity, are disseminated into corners of the world where they were previously unspoken.[15]

The shared sets of values promoted by various transnational movements and organizations are, for the most part, overlapping and mutually reinforcing. Take, for example, polls indicating far stronger popular support for non-governmental organizations (NGOs) like Amnesty International than for governments, business, and media; or the participation of significant numbers of people in anti-globalization and anti-war demonstrations and protests. The "battle for Seattle" in 1999 and the global protests against the invasion of Iraq in 2003 were "symptomatic of the rebirth of civic actions that tend to grow into social movements, on a global scale."[16]

Rather than one world movement, the global process generates a wide variety of discrete movements engaging diverse policy areas – for example, clean water, human rights, trade laws, post-war reconstruction. They also draw on a spectrum of activists possessing a range of political and religious loyalties – from deep-green ecologists to Christian pacifists, and social democrats to Buddhist mediators. Employing the means of advanced communication, the movements of global civil society "comprise a clutter of intersecting forms: face-to-face encounters, spider-web-like networks, pyramid-shaped organisations, hub-and-spoke structures, bridges and organisational chains, charismatic personalities." Marked by a cross-border mentality, the participants in these movements refuse to see their concerns as confined within a strictly bounded community or locality. Rather, "they are convinced that toxic chemicals and human rights and debt relief...know no borders. For them the world is one world. So they nurture their identities and publicise their concerns in 'translocalities,' as if they were global citizens." [17]

In sum, while transnational social movements do not in themselves constitute a new form of global civil society, clearly they are constituent elements thereof. That is, they contribute to the creation of an autonomous social space within which organizations and groups can alter existing power relations and advance the good of a certain kind of universalizing community marked by practices such as civility, equality, criticism, and respect for human dignity.[18]

What, Then, Is Missing?

From the perspective of CST, as we have noted, a globalized civil society must foster the thick web of associational ties shared by people rooted in a particular place and time who are responsible for that place and time. Place and time, of course, are precisely the conditions that globalization seeks to overcome or to render irrelevant; but they are, I am arguing, the binding glue of civil society.

John Keane has been an important source for the purposes of our inquiry because he presents global civil society as a new and dynamic means of empowering local peoples and communities. The main means to this is by linking them to transnational networks that are concerned, not with abstract causes, but with specific policies and practices as these are embedded in and affect local communities. Thus we come to a central question posed by this volume: Can new forms of transnational Catholic social movements participate in global civil society thus conceived? Do they or can they offer an alternative to the ungluing and disembedding effects of globalization? In the age of globalization and under its conditions, how might Catholic individuals groups, organizations, and movements contribute to the evolution of forms of civil society that are conducive to the flourishing of solidarity and the common good as envisioned in CST?

Transnational Religious Peacebuilding

There are signs of hope. As Lisa Sowle Cahill notes in Chapter 3 of this volume, "The common good is being redefined along a spectrum of networks for social change under the guidance of (Catholic) moral values like dignity, equality, social participation, meeting of basic needs, openness to transcendent values, and solidarity." One such hope-bearing sign of the times is the emergence of inter-religious peace-building, including representatives from the Catholic world, as a type of transnational social movement. The emerging contours of religious peacebuilding include, *inter alia*:

• The proliferation of faith-based NGOs that work across a spectrum of activities. These include faith-based diplomacy (for example, the International Center for Religion and Diplomacy), political and civic inter-religious mobilization (such as the World Conference on Religion and Peace, the Inter-Religious Council of Sierra Leone), and local education for peace (Sri Lanka Institute for Peacebuilding).[19]

• The development within Caritas Internationalis / Catholic Relief Services (CRS) of a justice lens. This is a set of criteria, drawn from the CST, according to which Catholic relief and development workers around the world plan projects and serve communities with an eye to addressing structural violence and social injustices. In 1997, CRS developed and implemented a peacebuilding lens that provides a mandate for each country staff to develop programs of conflict resolution and mediation, education for peace and justice, and interreligious dialogues. These were all set within the framework of CST but drew upon and evolved from local cultures of faith and practice.

• The emergence of transnational social movements for justice and peace within the major religions. Examples include the Community of Sant'Egidio (Roman Catholic), the Society of Engaged Buddhists, and the Christian Global Network. Such movements interact with locally rooted organizations such as Corrymeela and Christian Renewal Centre (Northern Ireland) or the Buddhist Reconciliation Centre (Cambodia).

• Theological and religio-legal ferment within religious traditions. An example is the efforts of Muslim jurists and academics to develop religio-legal warrants for non-violence within Islam. Other examples are the re-thinking, by Marc Gopin, Yezekial Landau, and others, of Jewish traditions of hospitality and forgiveness vis-à-vis their implications for peacebuilding, and the ongoing Christian interrogation of Just War categories, including the strengthening within Catholicism of non-violence as an ethical response to war.

• The establishment of a Catholic Peacebuilding Network. This network gives a name and a formal network to the hundreds of local-global peace and justice ministries and mission conducted by the faith-based NGOs, Catholic peace organizations such as Pax Christi and Maryknoll, Catholic bishops' conferences, transnational social movements, educational institutes, and the like.

Participation in these movements is transforming Catholic agencies and attitudes or, to state this better, participation is reinforcing certain post-conciliar directions and emphases. A central dimension of global religious peacebuilding, for example, is or should be familiar to Catholic theologians and public philosophers for whom the Vatican Council II was intellectually formative. I refer to the fact that transnational, faith-based activism for the common good and human solidarity is unfolding within a larger context of human rights, feminist, ecological, and other global movements for social justice – making Richard Falk's talk of a Grotian Moment and rooted utopianism plausible.

Moreover, this little corner of global civil society is grounded in concrete collaboration between Catholics and their non-Catholic partners, sometimes working within the same Catholic NGO, and interlocutors who act from within other religious traditions and communities. Additionally, in joint action for social change a new bridging discourse is being forged, incrementally perhaps, but unmistakably. In this development, first-order symbols and discourse, which articulate the depth of the revealed or otherwise privileged truths of a particular religion, are being supplemented by a lexicon that opens out to the other without betraying the core beliefs and principles of the faith community. This emergence of a second-order discourse has been prompted less by official inter-religious dialogues than by the demands of humanitarian crises on the ground, faced by multiple communities that require practical collaborative responses. The gradual articulation of second-order discourses is entirely in keeping, of course, with the public theology of Catholicism – that is, with the claim that the Catholic worldview and social principles are fully accessible to and potentially persuasive within a pluralist society.[20]

The new Catholic presence in global civil society is instructive for transnational actors who come to see themselves as the agents of the development of civil society in local and regional settings. This is as opposed to being builders of some kind of transnational civil society whose temporary centres rotate among Beijing, Geneva, New York, and Rome. Some ponder the structural relationship between global access to cultures and their internal development as centres of local political participation, public discourse, and empowerment of the marginalized. For these individuals, Catholic wisdom about, and practice of, rootedness, sacramentality, inculturation, and local knowledge may show the way for the development of a global civil society understood as the proliferation of local, robust civil societies across the world.

Religion, like politics, is local. CRS knows that, as do Sant'Egidio, Pax Christi, Maryknoll, Jesuit Volunteer Corps, and the rest. In the age of globalization, however, the local is transformed by its inevitable proximity to the global. Catholic ministry to the suffering world has always been based on face-to-face encounters and actual presence with individuals trapped in unjust social structures and situations. This will not change – this must not change – as a result of globalization. Rather, Catholic agencies and social justice activists and practitioners must enhance their face-to-face service to the poor and marginalized by entering into the kind of transnational, internally plural, often provisional, temporary, and ad hoc networks and alliances that are coming to characterize global civil society. Participation in global civil society and local cultures simultaneously will require diversification, new skills, and growth of resources. The good news, however, is that Catholics are not, and will not be, alone in the effort. At last count, in 2001, some 5,000 world congresses were held annually and some 50,000 non-governmental, not-for-profit organizations were operating at the global level. [21]

9

Religion and Globalization

Gregory Baum

The troubling effects produced by the globalization of the free market economy, the spread of the US-based culture of consumption and entertainment, and the military prowess of the American empire are having a significant impact on the practice of religion all over the world. Some people in the West, disturbed by this troubling development, opt for the *fuga mundi* – the flight from the world – by following an otherworldly spirituality or by joining a sectarian community that shrugs off responsibility for society. For some men and women, even in the major churches, religion is becoming increasingly a purely private journey.

Because of the many incidents where religion is blessing the turn to violent action – in the Middle East, India, Sri Lanka, and Africa – some people in the West have come to believe that religion is a dangerous cultural product and that societies would be better off without it. By contrast, there are conservative Christians in the US who interpret the expansion of the American empire as America's "manifest destiny," sustained by God because America is good. The situation is different in the tricontinental world (Asia, Africa, and Latin America) where economic globalization widens the gap between rich and poor in dramatic fashion and spreads a culture of consumption that undermines the indigenous religious traditions. In these regions, the revitalization of religion that is taking place enables people to resist the invading materialism, protect their collective identity, and be proud of their own tradition even though it is regarded as backward by the arrogant West.

A disturbing development accompanying this revitalization of religion is the emergence of fundamentalist movements. Fundamentalists in all religions, including Christianity, adopt a rigid interpretation of their sacred texts, demand internal unanimity, repudiate the mainstream of their own tradition, and refuse to engage in dialogue with outsiders. To disagree with them is to become their enemy. Fundamentalism breeds the kind of religion that is capable of blessing violent action against people and powers perceived as an embodiment of evil.

Turning to Universal Solidarity

In this chapter, I want to discuss an entirely different religious reaction to the conditions created by economic globalization and the increasing spread of violent conflicts. What has happened is that significant movements in the world religions, including Christianity, are promoting peace, justice, and ecological care as an essential dimension of their religious commitment. Men and women involved in these movements recognize an intrinsic connection between their religious faith and the active concern for the well-being of society and the health of the earth.

This turn to universal solidarity is a fairly recent development in the Catholic tradition. In the past, the dominant neo-scholastic theology made a clear distinction between the supernatural and the natural orders. The former referred to the life of faith, hope, and love; the latter designated people's involvement in the world, including issues of social conflict and social justice. At that time, the books on the spiritual life used in seminaries, monasteries, and convents and recommended to Catholics in the pews dealt with prayer and the quest for personal holiness; yet they never mentioned unemployment, discrimination, exploitation, or oppression. Dealing with these problems was thought to belong to the natural order. They were to be rectified by the exercise of the natural virtue of justice, guided by papal social teaching, but they did not involve the spiritual life.

Movements among the laity and theological developments in the first half of the twentieth century led to the new teaching of Vatican Council II (1962–1965), acknowledging that Christian faith generates commitment to peace and justice. Christian discipleship includes responsibility for the world. In situations of grave injustice, the love of neighbour transforms itself into a yearning for justice and an impulse to act to lift the heavy burdens from the shoulders of the poor and oppressed. The spiritual life is now seen as sustaining practical involvement for the well-being of God's world. Since the Vatican Council, papal social teaching invokes not only the natural law (as it did in the past) but also the imperatives of the Christian gospel. The Church's official teaching now summons Catholics to universal solidarity. The commitment to peace, justice, and ecological care has become even stronger in the adverse conditions produced by the neo-liberal globalization and American unilateralism.

A similar spiritual development has taken place in the Protestant churches, especially at the Geneva-based World Council of Churches. A growing number of Protestant Christians understand their faith in Jesus Christ as an obedience to the divine call to do their utmost to promote justice and peace and to protect the integrity of the creation.

After September 11, 2001

A remarkable manifestation of this social faith has been the reaction of the American churches to the 11th of September and the military response of President Bush. A look at the websites of these churches revealed their sorrow over the thousands of innocent victims and their wish that the government not act hastily, not turn to military violence, and not overlook the maldistribution of wealth and power in the world. Ecclesiastical leaders were embarrassed by the apocalyptic images used by born-again President Bush interpreting his fight against terrorism as the struggle of good against evil. Instead of the bombing of Afghanistan, the churches would have preferred the initiation of an international cooperative police action to catch, judge, and punish the perpetrators of these crimes.[1] On November 14, 2001, the American Catholic bishops asked their flock to examine the military attack on Afghanistan in the light of the Catholic just war theory. This request led to a public statement published on December 17, 2001, signed by thousands of Catholics, objecting to the government's policy on moral grounds and asking for the creation of a commission to study the injustices and humiliations manipulated by the terrorists to justify their crime.[2]

Here are the Pope's words addressed to Catholics in America on November 6, 2001:

> The tragic events which have shaken the international community in the past two months have made us all aware once more of the fragility of peace and the need to build a culture of respectful dialogue and cooperation between all the members of the human family. I am confident that the Catholic community in the United States will continue to uphold the value of understanding and dialogue among the followers of the world's religions. As you know, the Church's commitment to this dialogue is ultimately inspired by her conviction that the Gospel message has the power to enlighten all cultures and to act as a saving leaven of unity and peace for all humanity. In a world of growing cultural and religious pluralism, such dialogue is essential for overcoming tragic conflicts inherited from the past, and for ensuring that "the name of the one God become increasingly what it is: a name of peace and a summons to peace" (*Novo millennio ineunte*, 55).[3]

Pope John Paul II opposed the bombing of Afghanistan. On October 15, 2001, Archbishop Raphael Martino, then the Vatican's Permanent Observer at the UN, made the following statement:

> We do a disservice to those who died in this tragedy if we fail to search out the causes.... Though poverty is not by itself the cause of terrorism, we cannot successfully combat terrorism if we do not address the worsening disparities between the rich and poor. We must recognize that global disparity is fundamentally incompatible with global security.... Poverty along with other situations of marginalization that engulf the lives of so many of the world's people, including the denial of human dignity, the lack of respect for human rights, social exclusion, intolerable refugee situations, internal and external displacement, and physical and psychological oppression are breeding grounds only waiting to be exploited by terrorists. In searching out the root causes of terrorism, we are in no way condoning terrorism. But any serious crime reduction effort cannot be

> confined only to intensified police work. Any serious campaign against terrorism needs to address the social, economic and political conditions that nurture the emergence of terrorism.[4]

To promote peace in these troubling times John Paul II invited representatives of the world religions, including the Native Peoples of North America, to join him in Assisi on January 24, 2002, to offer joint prayers for peace and justice in the world. The Pope then sent a letter to all heads of state and governments in which he called for international peace and the dialogue of civilizations. The letter included "The Ten Commandments of Peace," a remarkable statement of the Church's contribution to peacemaking for which there is no historical precedent.[5]

The Pope's emphasis on the dialogue of civilizations offered a reply to Samuel Huntington's theory of "the clash of civilizations," which is widely supported by right-wing circles in the US.[6] According to Huntington, all civilizations are shaped by the religion that founded them; because the values fostered by different religions are incompatible, the clash of civilizations – especially the clash between the Muslim world and the West – is almost inevitable. America is unprepared for the coming conflict, Huntington argues, because the secular spirit and multiculturalism have weakened its Christian foundation. He calls upon America to become, again, a Christian nation.

Contrary to this theory, John Paul II promoted the dialogue of civilizations. He believed that the quest for peace is inherent in all the world religions and that dialogue and cooperation among them will raise this quest to become a major common commitment.

President Bush's preemptive strike against Iraq in January 2003 was supported by the Southern Baptists and conservative Christians in the Republican Party, but opposed by mainline US churches. These were the Catholic Church, the Episcopal Church, the United Methodist Church, the United Church of Christ, the Evangelical Lutheran Church in America, the Presbyterian Church of the USA, the Disciples of Christ, the Orthodox Church in America, the Mennonites, and the Quakers.[7] Christian churches in other countries also opposed the preemptive war against Iraq. Pope John Paul II condemned a war in Iraq in strong language, saying that those who unleash the attack will have to answer for it before God. To prevent the war, the Pope made Ash Wednesday 2003 a day of fasting and prayer for peace. While there exists as yet no monograph on the reaction of the churches to the bombing of Afghanistan and the preemptive strike against Iraq, my impression is that their discourse critical of empire is without historical parallel. Admittedly, the leaders of the churches may not represent the majority of their members. The rise of American empire is likely to create deep divisions within Christianity.

The Church's response to September 11 includes the warning not to allow the campaign against the terrorists to create resentment against the nations, the ethnicity, or the religion to which these men belong. The anti-terrorist legislation in the US and Canada gives new powers to police. It allows them to arrest people on suspicion alone – suspicion created by their clothes, their beard, or their language; this suspends the century-old common law principle of Habeas Corpus.

The institutionalization of suspicion has disturbing cultural consequences, nourishing prejudice against people of Arab origin, of Muslim faith, or both. In this new situation, church leaders have expressed their solidarity with Arab and Muslim citizens and appealed to public opinion not to allow "the war against terrorism" to generate prejudice and discrimination against innocent people.[8]

Interreligious Cooperation

The turn to universal solidarity in the Christian churches is accompanied by a similar movement in the other world religions. Since I am writing this article as a Catholic theologian, I shall discuss the movement in the world religions rather briefly and then concentrate on new developments in the Catholic Church. Under the present conditions, how should Catholic social thought (CST) be expanded?

Fortunately, other authors in this collection have dealt with the compassionate movements in the other religions.

Peace

In his chapter, Scott Appleby makes many references to the peacemaking practices in various religions. In his ground-breaking study, *The Ambivalence of the Sacred*,[9] Appleby has examined religious movements that practise violence and, more importantly in the present context, the religious movements that wrestle for truth, justice, and peace in a non-violent manner. These movements are often led by charismatic personalities. Well known to everyone are Mahatma Gandhi and Martin Luther King. In his book, Appleby introduces the reader to Buddhist spiritual leaders such as Maha Ghosamande, Sulak Sivaraka, and Thich Nhat Hanh and describes the emergence of engaged Buddhism. He also studies religious personalities in other religions that have been active in non-violent conflict resolution.

The peacemaking potential in the Muslim tradition is explored in Mohammed Abu-Nimer's *Nonviolence and Peace-Building in Islam: Theory and Practice*[10] and Eknath Easwaran's *Non-violent Soldier of Islam,*[11] a biography of Abdul Ghaffar Khan. This remarkable man of prayer and simplicity, a friend of Mahatma Gandhi, organized a non-violent army to resist the British forces in India and later promoted peacemaking in Pakistan. He spent more than half of his long life in British and, later, Pakistani prisons. In two recent books, Marc Gopin has provided many examples of peacemaking practices in the world religions.[12] He argues that facilitators in conflict resolution trained at Western universities usually fail to find a hearing among people identified with a religious culture. Why? Because the Western agents operate on presuppositions that are purely rational and secular. Gopin demonstrates that every religion has peacemaking potential and that conflict resolution in religious cultures must draw upon the wisdom derived from people's own living tradition.

The fear of a nuclear exchange during the Cold War brought together representatives of the world religions in the World Conference of Religions for Peace, a thriving organization that has local chapters in many countries and has held global conferences at regular intervals. In their joint statements, the members confess that their religious tradition has often allied itself with political powers and legitimated injustice and violence, yet they profess that the deepest and most authentic values of their tradition promote justice and peace in the world. They now want to renew their religious tradition by giving priority to the commitment to peace. The website of the World Conference of Religions for Peace (www.wcrp.org) reveals their activities in various parts of the globe.

The World Conference is also aware that a problematic inheritance of all religions is the subordination of women, a cultural tradition that tolerates violent acts to "put women in their place." To counter this heritage, the website of the World Conference provides a global directory of women's organizations in the different world religions. The voices of women may help the religious traditions to recover their dedication to peacemaking.

Justice

The chapters in this book by Jim Hug and Wendy Tyndale mention interreligious cooperation in matters of social justice and human rights. In his discussion of social movements that oppose neo-liberal globalization and foster alternative models of economic development, Hug argues for the necessity of inter-cultural and interreligious cooperation. CST does not claim to be a universal wisdom – it is clearly a Western intellectual development – yet it wants to be in dialogue with non-Western traditions of economic justice and to support local and global cooperative practices. Tyndale has been the acting secretary of the World Faith Development Dialogue (WFDD), the official dialogue of the World Bank with representatives of the world religions. Her article reports the origin of this unusual interaction and her doubts about its usefulness. Will the World Bank change its policies or will it use the religions as stabilizing forces in the societies destabilized by its aggressive neo-liberal policies? The good thing this dialogue has produced is a significant literature revealing how the different religions view economic activity in the light of their ethical vision. The web of the WFDD (www.wfdd.org.uk) is a rich source of information.

The same themes are pursued in *Subverting Greed: Religious Perspectives on the Global Economy*, edited by Paul Knitter and Chandra Muzaffar.[13] Knitter, a Catholic theologian, had studied religious pluralism in philosophical terms. Yet in his more recent book, *One Earth, Many Religions*,[14] he is interested instead in common practices – for example, cooperative actions promoting justice, peace, and ecological care – and argues that common practices generate a new consciousness in religious participants that allow them to formulate their common convictions. The same action-oriented approach is adopted by Chandra Muzaffar, a Muslim scholar of Malaysia and founder of the International Movement for a Just World, which brings together religious people of different traditions who are committed to peace and justice.[15]

These experiences of interreligious dialogue in the context of common practices raise the question whether the efforts to formulate a global ethic in conceptual terms are premature. Most famous among these is the Declaration of a Global Ethic inspired by Hans Küng and produced by the Parliament of the World's Religions in 1993. This global ethic was further developed by Küng in a subsequent book.[16] Yet how widely is such an ethic received in the world religions? Should we not first multiply common practices and joint engagements to generate a new awareness that will allow us to formulate a set of common ethical norms? Still, Hans Küng's global ethic challenges the world religions and demands critical self-reflection on their part.

Ecological Care

The essay by Mary Evelyn Tucker puts great emphasis on the contribution of the world religions to the protection of the natural environment. While CST has long neglected issues of ecological responsibility, several statements on this topic from Pope John Paul II and bishops' conferences now exist. Tucker offers a list of these statements and provides information about the contribution of other religions to the environmental movement. As a bibliographical source, she mentions the fall issue 2001 of *Daedalus* and the website of the Forum of Religion and Ecology.[17]

Interreligious cooperation on behalf of peace, justice, and ecological care raises a theological question. Are Catholics allowed to rejoice in the plurality of religions as an expression of God's will or must they regard religious pluralism as a historical defect destined to be overcome by the conversion of non-Christians to the Catholic Church? We shall return to this question later.

Expanding Catholic Social Thought

How does CST respond to the impact of corporate globalization on the world religions? How should CST be expanded to make the Church's message more effective? I wish to make three proposals.

Peace: In a previous section I have shown that papal and episcopal teaching on peace has generated vigorous responses to the wars and threats of wars that mark the contemporary world. I again refer to John Paul II's remarkable "Ten Commandments of Peace" in the appendix of this article. Numerous Catholic groups and centres also engage in peacemaking, most famous among them Pax Christi Internationalis (www.paxchristi.net) and its American chapter, Pax Christi USA (www.paxchristiusa.org).

Another aspect of the Church's commitment to peacemaking, which is hardly ever thematized, is the effort to avoid a discourse of condemnation or exclusion that easily leads to violence. The most obvious example is the traditional Christian discourse regarding the Jewish people. In the New Testament, Jesus is reported to have said to the Jews, "Your father is the devil and your will is to do your father's desire"(John 8:44). The Apostle Paul writes: "The Jews who killed the Lord Jesus and the prophets… displease God and oppose all men, hindering us from speaking to the Gentiles...so as to fill up the measure of their sins, but God's wrath has come upon them at last" (1 Thess 2:15, 16). This discourse of rejection was continued throughout Christian history. Only after the Holocaust did Christians begin to ask themselves whether their hostile references to Jews had created a cultural prejudice in European civilization that Hitler was able to use in pursuing his murderous racist project. With profound remorse, Vatican II has rethought the Church's relationship to the Jews, recognized the ongoing validity of God's covenant with them, and asked Catholics to engage with them in dialogue, friendship, and cooperation.[18]

The Church committed to peacemaking calls for the review of its discourse in regard to outsiders and dissidents. This is well expressed in a letter written to Pope John XXIII by Cardinal Léger of Montreal in 1962, prior to the Vatican Council, in which he complained that the draft documents for the Council prepared by the Roman Curia were totally unacceptable.[19] He criticized, in particular, the many condemnations of the thought of outsiders and dissidents. To overcome a purely negative discourse, Cardinal Léger wanted Catholics to respect alternative world interpretations and search for the grain of truth contained in them. This call to dialogue inside and outside the Church was endorsed by Vatican II and formulated in systematic fashion in Paul VI's encyclical *Ecclesiam suam* (1966), which presented the Church itself as engaged in dialogue.

The universal vice of violence against women raises the question of whether the Church's discourse on women needs to be reviewed. In 1989 the Quebec bishops produced the public letter "Violence en héritage," admitting that Church had responded inappropriately to violence against women. When women complained to the priest that their husband had beaten them, he would counsel forgiveness, patience, and longsuffering. The letter assured women that priests are now being trained differently. When a woman reveals her husband's violent behaviour, the priest will encourage her to demand that her husband's behaviour must change or else to register a public complaint.[20]

According to a world-wide inquiry of the World Council of Churches, the patriarchal subordination of women, still practised in many places, assigns women a place among the less mature in need of guidance. It assigns men the responsibility to direct the behaviour of women and, if need be, discipline them like children for their own good.[21] The Catholic Church has made great progress in its teaching in regard to women. In his apostolic letter, *Mulieris dignitatem* (1988), John Paul II corrected patriarchal subordination and acknowledged the equality of men and women. Yet he still assigned them different vocations: men are called by their very nature to be fathers and exercise leadership while women are called by their nature to be mothers and followers.[22] A Church committed to non-violence may have to move one step further.

The relation of ecclesiastical discourse to violent action became a topic of public debate in Canada in the fall of 2003 when Parliament discussed a bill to outlaw language insulting to the homosexual minority by inserting a clause in the Canadian anti-hate legislation protecting ethnic and religious minorities. The arguments supporting the bill referred to the violence committed against homosexuals in contemporary society. The Canadian Catholic bishops and the Catholic Women's League of Canada appealed to the Minister of Justice and the members of Parliament to oppose this bill.[23] Why? Because they thought the Church's teaching on homosexual love might be interpreted as hate-producing and judged as criminal. Still, the bill was passed. The Church is beginning to ask itself whether its official teaching bears a certain responsibility for the suicides committed by people who discover their homosexual nature.

Because all religions, in one way or another, see themselves involved in a historical drama between the forces of good and evil, they often use a vocabulary for condemning evil that is easily used to legitimate violence. The peacemaking mission of the world religions calls for an alternative discourse. The message of Jesus that we must love even our enemies (Mt 5:44) and that saying to your brother *raca,* meaning "you fool," is a sin (Mt 5:22) may well be a summons to the Church to review its public discourse on outsiders and dissidents.

Justice

According to the chapters in this book, we are presently witnessing a multiplication of countervailing movements, often organized transnationally, that promote issues of social justice, the cause of peace, the emancipation of women, the observance of human rights, and the protection of the environment. These movements are in agreement that the present system defined by neo-liberal capitalism and American empire is leading us to humanitarian and ecological catastrophe, even if they are in disagreement regarding many issues of public policy. These movements work towards an alternative form of globalization – a globalization-from-below – that uses the new technology of Internet, e-mail, and jet transport to create world-wide cooperation in the pursuit of an alternative society. The concrete symbol of this cooperative effort is the World Social Forum that has held yearly meetings at Porto Allegre in Brazil, attracting each time more than 50,000 participants from all over the world.

Is involvement in these movements utopian? Do these movements simply satisfy the conscience of people who love justice, or will they have an impact on society as a whole? In his apostolic letter *Octogesima adveniens* (1971) Pope Paul VI argued that utopia can be an unrealistic dream that prevents people from effective action. But utopia, rightly understood, is a positive vision that criticizes the existing order, generates a forward-looking imagination, recognizes the as yet unrealized possibilities of the present, and supplies energy for the creation of a new future (# 37). Without utopia, there is endless repetition.

The alternative movements for peace, human rights, social justice, and ecological care create a new consciousness among the people engaged in them. Why? Because they are organized according to principles that are at odds with those operative in the dominant society. These movements are democratic and egalitarian: everyone is allowed to speak; they uphold the equality of men and women, which contests the patriarchal inheritance of society; and they practise cooperation across boundaries, a spirit at odds with the competitive spirit that drives contemporary society. They also make the participants conscious of their power to act as social agents, against the effort of capitalism to define people as customers and clients; and they generate solidarity across national boundaries and facilitate transversal activities, involving people internationally. These alternative movements may well be the training ground for the creation of an alternative global society – not immediately, but after the shock waves created by environmental disasters or the revolts of the excluded masses. These movements are utopian in the sense defined by Paul VI.

Until now, official CST has not recommended these movements. Official CST addresses Catholics and other people in the hope that they will promote these socio-ethical ideas in their society and urge their governments to put them into practice. In fact, a growing number of Catholics and many Catholic organizations participate in the countervailing movements. An exception to this general observation is a teaching document published by the Canadian bishops in 1983 that outlines the methodology of their critical approach:

> i) to be present with and listen to the experience of the poor, the marginalized, the oppressed in our society; ii) to develop a critical analysis of the economic, political and social structures that cause human suffering; iii) to make judgements in the light of Gospel principles and the social teachings of the Church concerning social values and priorities; iv) to stimulate creative thought and action regarding alternative visions and models fore social and economic development; and v) to act in solidarity with popular groups in their struggles to transform economic, political and social structures that cause social and economic injustices.[24]

It is significant that the 15th Latin American and Caribbean Conference of Caritas, held in Mexico City in March 2003, published a statement that calls for the involvement of Catholics in community development, the social economy, and ecological protection. It seems appropriate to ask that official CST be expanded to include support for these social movements.

In this context, I wish to mention the political economist Karl Polanyi (1886–1964), who offered a theoretical basis for community development and the social economy. In his major work, *The Great Transformation,*[25] Polanyi gives an original analysis of the harmful impact of liberal capitalism on the lives of people in traditional societies. He demonstrates that the extension of the unregulated market system disembeds people's daily work from their social matrix and, thus, undermines the culture that defines their values and their identity. People are lifted out of their villages and employed in factories and enterprises away from their communities. Polanyi shows that this happened at the beginning of the Industrial Revolution in Britain and, in subsequent decades, in many regions of the colonized world. Today's neo-liberal globalization intensifies the process of cultural disintegration, especially in parts of the world where the majority population relies on a subsistence economy for survival.

Polanyi's work offers a social theory in support of community-based models of economic development. According to him, the remedy for impoverishment-cum-cultural-disintegration is neither the social democratic transformation of capitalism nor the collective ownership of the means of production. The remedy is the re-embedding of people's daily work in their social relations. Such daily work creates friendship, trust, and solidarity and strengthens the bonds that unite a community. Here, the motivation for people's work is not so much its economic benefit but their desire to keep their recognized place in the community. According to Polanyi, the struggle for a more just society is first of all a social struggle, creating democratic organization of daily work that initiates people into a new consciousness. Only as this communitarian consciousness spreads, will the political struggle to change the dominant structures become a realistic possibility.

Today the search for democratic models of economic production is called the social economy or community economic development. It is of increasing importance in the regions of the South. Yet even in the capitalist countries of the North, community development and community economic development are playing an ever greater role.[26] Capitalist society is increasingly divided into three sectors: i) the families of the economic and political élites, ii) people with a good income – merchants, professionals, technicians, and organized workers, and iii) the so-called third sector made up of minimum wage workers, part-time workers, occasional workers, the unemployed, and the unemployable. In all capitalist societies, the third sector is growing. It is in this sector that a new vitality is emerging – the creation of a social economy that rescues people not only from impoverishment, but also from loneliness and despair.

This movement is greatly helped by volunteers. If a parish were acquainted with the community development in its own locality, parishioners with useful skills could offer their help and, through their modest involvement, enter into a new vision of society.

Religious Pluralism

The historical changes discussed in this article demand new theological reflection on religious pluralism. Interreligious cooperation is spontaneous in the movements supporting peace, justice, and ecological care. The growing poverty in the South has stirred up movements of emigrations that have brought a new religious pluralism to the metropolitan areas of Western Europe and North America. It is noteworthy that the mainline churches have not tried to convert the new Hindu, Buddhist, and Muslim citizens; instead the churches have defended their human rights and preached against prejudice and discrimination. Here practice seems to precede theory.

The questions Christians are asking today is whether religious pluralism is a defective historical condition that will eventually be overcome by the triumph of the Church or whether religious pluralism is a historical reality in which we may rejoice and see a reflection of God's infinite riches.

On the basis of the ancient Logos-Christology, revived by Henri de Lubac and Karl Rahner, Vatican II was able to honour insights and practices in the world religions as echoes of God's Word and capable of mediating salvation. This theology allowed Vatican II to recommend interreligious dialogue and cooperation and at the same time to profess the fullness of truth and grace in Jesus Christ, God's incarnate Word. Yet this theology, generous as it is, has led to unresolved problems in the Church's official teaching.

On the one hand, we have texts of John Paul II that respect religious otherness and promote peaceful co-existence among the world religions. Speaking to religious representatives invited to participate in a prayer worship at Assisi in 2002, the Pope seemed to praise religious pluralism.

> With daily renewed wonder at God's creation, we note the variety of manifestations of human life, from the complementarity of male and female, to a multiplicity of distinctive gifts belonging to the different cultures and traditions that form a multifaceted and versatile linguistic, cultural and artistic cosmos. This multiplicity is called to form a cohesive whole in contact and dialogue that will enrich and bring joy to all.[27]

John Paul II praised the respectful co-existence of Catholicism and Islam. Here are two quotations, one from a speech before Muslim leaders in the Great Omayad Mosque of Damascus on May 6, 2001, and the other from a speech given in Rome to an interreligious delegation from Indonesia, a largely Muslim country, on February 20, 2003.

> Christians and Muslims agree that the encounter with God in prayer is the necessary nourishment of our souls, without which our hearts wither and our will no longer strives for good but succumbs to evil. Both Muslim and Christians prize their places of prayer, as oases where they meet the All Merciful God on the journey to eternal life, and where they meet their brothers and sisters in the bond of religion.... It is my ardent hope that Muslim and Christian religious leaders will present our two great religious communities as communities in respectful dialogue, never more as communities in conflict.[28]

> At this time of great tension for the world, you have come to Rome, and I am grateful to have this occasion to speak to you. With the real possibility of war looming on the horizon, we must not permit politics to become a source of further division among the world's religions. In fact, neither the threat of war nor war itself should be allowed to alienate Christians, Muslims, Buddhists, Hindus and members of other religions. As religious leaders committed to peace, we should work together with our own people, with those of other religious beliefs and with all men and women of good will to ensure understanding, cooperation and solidarity.[29]

On the other hand, the Vatican has been critical of theological theories in Asia for being too open to the Asian religions and suggesting that the Church has something to learn from their spiritual practice. In the Apostolic Exhortation *Ecclesia in Asia*, published on August 6, 2000, John Paul II reminded the Asian bishops that the Church's mission was to convert the Asian continent to faith in Jesus Christ. On the same day, the Congregation *de doctrina fidei*, chaired by then-Cardinal Ratzinger, published the declaration *Dominus Iesus.* It recognized echoes of God's Word in other religions, yet emphasized in triumphalist language the universal significance of Jesus Christ and the universal mission of his one and only Church. To contain theological reflection in Asia, the Congregation *de doctrine fidei* subjected the person and work of the distinguished theologian, Jacques Dupuis SJ, to a long and humiliating investigation without ever finding anything objectionable in his writings.[30]

In *Dominus Iesus*, Cardinal Ratzinger lamented the spread of what he calls "an ideology of dialogue." He argued instead that interreligious dialogue is compatible with the intention to convert one's partner. This is how I responded to this proposal: "It would be utterly deceitful to lure partners into dialogue, attempt to create a community of trust in which they become willing to expose the weaknesses of their own tradition, and then abuse this confidence in an effort to persuade then to change their religion."[31] Interreligious dialogue is based on mutual respect. I am grateful to Pope John Paul II for including, in his liturgy of repentance on March 12, 2000, sorrow over the sins of the Church "against the rights of people and respect for their culture and religion."[32]

The lack of clarity in Rome demonstrates that the Logos-Christology does not allow us to escape the dilemma between proselytism and dialogue. We need a new theology that allows us to say that the Church preaches the Gospel to seekers, the confused, and people caught in destructive ideologies, but that its mission to the world religions includes witness, dialogue, and cooperation without any intention of converting their members to the Christian faith.

In many parts, this is already the Church's practice. In Indonesia, a largely Muslim country, the Catholic and Protestant churches respect the legal system of Pancasila, which gives official recognition to five religious traditions – including Catholicism and Protestantism – and proscribes attempts at proselytism in any direction.[33] I have already mentioned that the mainline churches in Europe and North America refuse to proselytize the Hindu, Buddhist, and Muslim immigrants living in their country. There exist today a variety of interreligious institutions where the participants trust one another, serve the same cause, and together rejoice in religious pluralism.

Allow me, at the end of this chapter, to propose a theology of pluralism faithful to the traditional doctrines of Incarnation and Trinity. This proposal is built on the ancient idea of *kenosis*. According to Philippians 2:7, Jesus emptied himself (*ekenosen*) by not clinging to his divine status and instead assuming equality with other human beings. Reading Jürgen Moltmann I encountered the idea, taken from kabalistic Judaism, that in creating the world God emptied himself – making room for the non-divine, even for human sin.[34] Through the divine kenosis, God's infinite being ceased to be total reality. John Paul II may well have been alluding to this divine self-contraction when he spoke of God's impotence before human freedom.[35] Yet if the eternal God embraces kenosis in the work of creation and if Jesus has embraced kenosis in his work of redemption, then the Church – Christ's earthly body – has a kenotic vocation: instead of clinging to its divine status, the Church willingly assumes equality with other religious communities. The Church must proclaim Christ's universal redemption, not in a triumphalist manner but in a kenotic discourse leaving room for other religions. While this kenotic ecclesiology is in keeping with the ancient creeds, it allows us to honour other religions for their difference and rejoice in religious pluralism.

Yet this theology of religious pluralism is incomplete if it does not recognize the need of all religions, including Catholic Christianity, to be delivered from their shortcomings and failures and renewed in accordance with their most authentic aspirations. When we speak positively of religious pluralism, we often forget that the world religions, including Catholicism, are highly ambiguous historical realities. In fact, we are grateful to the Enlightenment critiques of religion for the grain of truth they contain. There are, indeed, religious currents that legitimate injustice, flatter the seats of power, encourage racism, stand against human rights, humiliate women, justify slavery and colonialism, discourage collective self-criticism, and make people flee from their social responsibility. What the religions want to be, and in essence are according to their authentic inspiration, is indeed wonderful, but their empirical reality in the historical conditions of the different countries in which they exist is unevenly burdened. What is Hinduism in present-day India, Buddhism in Sri Lanka, Islam in Iran, Judaism in Israel, Protestantism in Northern Ireland, and Catholicism in Croatia? Even in more normal situations, and at the best of times, the empirical reality of the religions never escapes a certain ambiguity. In theological terms, religions in this fallen world are wounded by sin and in need of redemption.

What I propose is that interreligious dialogue and cooperation – in the service of peace, justice, and ecological care – rescue the religions from ideological distortions and make them more faithful to their deepest values. Dialogue of this kind is the locus of the Holy Spirit summoning the religions to engage in renewal and reform. The Church's kenotic vocation allows it to admit, without betrayal of its divine gifts, that it will be made more authentic and become more true to itself through peace-and-justice-oriented dialogue and cooperation with other religions.

Appendix

John Paul II: The Ten Commandments for Peace

February 24, 2000

1. We commit ourselves to proclaiming our firm conviction that violence and terrorism are incompatible with the authentic spirit of religion, and, as we condemn every recourse to violence and war in the name of God or of religion, we commit ourselves to doing everything possible to eliminate the root causes of terrorism.

2. We commit ourselves to educating people to mutual respect and esteem, in order to help bring about a peaceful and fraternal coexistence between people of different ethnic groups, cultures and religions.

3. We commit ourselves to fostering the culture of dialogue, so that there will be an increase of understanding and mutual trust between individuals and among peoples, for these are the premise of authentic peace.

4. We commit ourselves to defending the right of everyone to live a decent life in accordance with their own cultural identity, and to form freely a family of his own.

5. We commit ourselves to frank and patient dialogue, refusing to consider our differences as an insurmountable barrier, but recognizing instead that to encounter the diversity of others can become an opportunity for greater reciprocal understanding.

6. We commit ourselves to forgiving one another for past and present errors and prejudices, and to supporting one another in a common effort both to overcome selfishness and arrogance, hatred and violence, and to learn from the past that peace without justice is no true peace.

7. We commit ourselves to taking the side of the poor and the helpless, to speaking out for those who have no voice and to working effectively to change these situations, out of the conviction that no one can be happy alone.

8. We commit ourselves to taking up the cry of those who refuse to be resigned to violence and evil, and we desire to make every effort possible to offer the men and women of our time real hope for justice and peace.

9. We commit ourselves to encouraging all efforts to promote friendship between peoples, for we are convinced that, in the absence of solidarity and understanding between peoples, technological progress exposes the world to a growing risk of destruction and death.

10. We commit ourselves to urging leaders of nations to make every effort to create and consolidate, on the national and international levels, a world of solidarity and peace based on justice.

10

Some Reflections on a Dialogue Between the World's Religions and the World Bank with Reference to Catholic Social Thought

Wendy Tyndale

Jorge Simaj, a spiritual guide of the indigenous Mayan tradition, lives in a tiny market town in the northwestern highlands of Guatemala. As he opens a box of incense made at an Anglican monastery near Newbury in the South of England, he gently draws breath. "It has energy, a lot of energy!" he exclaims. Shortly afterwards, he asks for books in Spanish about Buddhism because it seems to him that "Buddhists come close to sharing many elements of our Mayan world view."

The process of globalization, through its agents of communications technology as well as air travel, has brought the world's religious and spiritual traditions closer together. At the same time, the economic and political project being furthered by this process – the globalization of capitalism – has meant that these same traditions are being made increasingly aware of global institutions, such as the World Bank.

This chapter looks at some of the critiques of mainstream development policies and practices offered by people of different faith traditions who are working with, and rooted in, materially impoverished communities. Their vision is a prophetic one of a different social, political, and economic world order, based on a different set of values from those that prevail today. Their viewpoints on development, arising from their position at the margins of their societies, do not always reflect those of their own religious institutions or hierarchies that may be more open to reforming the system from within the current framework. This does not mean that the grassroots groups we are dealing with are not prepared to take immediate practical action to improve conditions for the poor nor that they are unwilling to take advantage of the benefits offered by the modern world, but their vision goes beyond these measures.

In articulating the voice of these faith-based communities, I am not denying that many thoughtful people, both from the different religious institutions as well as from the mainstream development agencies, have worthwhile arguments of a different nature to put forward. Nor am I overlooking the real dilemma of the chasm that exists between the huge and powerful forces shaping the world and these communities that are often numerically quite tiny. I do, however, believe that their starting points, ways of working, and ultimate aims for development can guide us in the direction of a fundamental paradigm shift. This shift is necessary if we are to achieve global peace and harmony and even the survival of life on our planet.

Dialogue

In February 1998, Lambeth Palace was the setting for a memorable gathering of leaders representing nine different religious traditions from all over the world. Lambeth Palace is the ancient seat of the Archbishop of Canterbury and home of the leader of the Church of England and *primus inter pares* – senior representative – of the Anglican communion worldwide. The meeting was chaired jointly by George Carey, Archbishop at that time, and James D. Wolfensohn, President of the World Bank. The topic for discussion was Poverty and Development.

Characterized by caution veering towards mistrust and even hostility, the discussion highlighted the lack of collaboration in the field of development – both among the faith communities themselves and between them and the World Bank. Nevertheless, out of this discussion arose an agreement by all present that there should be further dialogue between the religious and the development world and that it should be loosely coordinated by a very small secretariat. The name later given to it was World Faiths Development Dialogue (WFDD).

WFDD has been carrying out a dialogue on two fronts: on the one hand among people from different religions who are engaged in development work, and on the other between them and the World Bank. Dialogue requires the will to move forward, genuinely searching for the truth together with neither side trying to win or to exert power over the other. However difficult the process, those involved have been convinced that in our contemporary context, in which isolation is no longer desirable or even possible, dialogue is an important tool for overcoming the global crisis that affects us all.

Interreligious dialogue

Interreligious dialogue has tended so far to be visible mainly through international conferences to which leaders from different religious backgrounds are invited. Such gatherings have been an important start but they can all too easily degenerate into symbolic events of an elitist nature that achieve little change, particularly as the same few leaders tend to appear at all of them. However, dialogues are going on at other levels that give grounds for more hope.

At an intermediary level, WFDD has been able to bring together people who are less well-known but who are actively engaged with poor communities in their countries. Some of these meetings have focused on contributing ideas to aspects of the World Bank's policies by contributing to the World Bank's "World Development Reports" or to the Poverty Reduction Strategy process. Other meetings have been held to discuss how different religious traditions can throw light on what development is actually about and how we should deal with specific development issues.

However, the most significant inter-faith encounters may be happening at the grassroots level. One example of these is in the highlands of Guatemala where Presbyterian women have invited Catholics and women of the indigenous Mayan spiritual tradition to join their project to cultivate flowers and strawberries for the local market. For these women, spirituality and work are not two separate spheres of their life. They all believe that the Creator – whether experienced as the Trinitarian God or as the Heart of the Earth and the Heart of the Sky – has given them life: "God gives us the wisdom to carry out our daily tasks," they say.

Another example is in Cameroon where a group of Christians has been giving a helping hand to the Muslim organization Sarkan Zoumountsi (Chain of Solidarity), which is working with people in an inner city area of Yaoundé. These Christians and Muslims share a strong sense of social justice and are committed to improving the lot of the poor. Then there are the Catholic fishworkers in the south of Kerala who took a theological as well as a political decision to open up their movement to fishworkers of all religions or none at all to form the National Forum of Fishworkers. "Different people bring a commitment from their own faith. Development cannot be one-sided. If Christians alone develop, then that is only one side of the face of God," explains Sister Philomine Marie, one of the nuns who works with them.[1]

All these are examples of people from different faith traditions who have joined together to take action to improve life for poor communities, to which, in many cases, they themselves belong. This kind of dialogue, carried on through action for a common purpose, is likely to form the strongest bonds between people of different religions. Here there is mutual respect because the people taking part in the dialogue and action have gained credibility and provided a basis for trust by showing that their commitment of service to others is stronger than any sectarian prejudices that might arise. The Catholic Church (*Redemptor Hominis* 11) does recognize that the various religions are "as it were, so many reflections of the one truth, 'seeds of the Word.'" Often Christians at the grassroots seem to experience the deepest experience of the enrichment of their own faith by a truly mutual sharing with people of other traditions with no intention of evangelization.

One of the most important challenges facing the incipient inter-faith movement world-wide is the danger that dialogue among progressive, or liberal, people from each tradition might alienate people and movements that are less open to interreligious relations and, thus, contribute to hardening their position still further. Experience seems to show that when the dialogue is focused on solving common problems and creating common benefits for everyone in a given geographical area, it will be more likely to broaden its membership.

Dialogue with the World Bank

The dialogue between people from different religions and the World Bank has been seen by many, both within the World Bank and within the religious world, as problematic. It must be noted that among the staff of the World Bank there are, of course, many deeply spiritual people. However, at the institutional level, religions are often seen – not without reason – as divisive, in opposition to modernity or progress, the cause of violence, an obstacle to development, and generally too politically risky for the World Bank to engage with.

Nevertheless, some World Bank staff have been keen to further the dialogue because they understand the important role of the faith communities – especially because of their grassroots networks and unequalled influence among the poor of the world. Indeed, it is probably true to say that in general the interest on the side of the World Bank in this dialogue has been more in finding ways to encourage faith communities to cooperate with its programs than in dialoguing with them about policy issues.

On the religious side there are many who show no interest in a dialogue with the World Bank as an institution on the grounds that it is unable to substantially change its policies and practice because it is so closely identified with the promotion of global capitalism. Many others, however, have been encouraged by the openness of James Wolfensohn to try to find ways to bridge the gap in understanding between the two worlds.

These people are convinced that every effort should be made to find common ground and to build on the idealism and good will that are to be found within the World Bank. They are aware that religious organizations that are working with the poor have a lot to learn from the expertise of such a large development institution in areas of analysis and planning. They can benefit from the huge fund of information that the World Bank has gathered from all over the world. They are also aware that such a dialogue provides an opportunity for the faith communities to voice their opinions about the policies and practices of official development agencies as well as to suggest alternatives.

Pope John Paul II was well aware of the importance of engaging religious institutions in the development debate at the institutional as well as grassroots level. In his encyclical *Sollicitudo Rei Socialis* (43) he said: "I wish to mention specifically: the reform of the international trade system, which is mortgaged to protectionism and increasing bilateralism; the reform of the world monetary and financial system, today recognized as inadequate; the question of technological exchanges and their proper use; the need for a review of the structure of the existing international organizations, in the framework of an international juridical order." In 42, he referred to "medical care and, above all, those without hope of a better future. It is impossible not to take account of the existence of these realities.

To ignore them would mean becoming like the 'rich man' who pretended not to know the beggar Lazarus lying at his gate (cf. Lk 16:19-31)."

The difficulties of the debate have been many, but one of the main obstacles has been trying to find ways of bringing together into a meaningful conversation people who often find each other's language and logic almost incomprehensible. Indeed, one of the biggest challenges facing the faith communities of the world today is the context in which they find themselves: the scientific and technological revolution that is having such a profound effect on how we live and has made the process of globalization possible. Science and technology may be intrinsically neither good nor bad but they do function according to their own particular logic. This logic tends to reduce our view of what is real to what is quantifiable – to what can be empirically proved, weighed, measured, and counted.

Along with the advance of scientific and technological knowledge, there seems to have been a withering of the knowledge that combines rational understanding with intuition, spiritual experience, and ethical awareness – the kind of knowledge traditionally known as wisdom. The faith and spiritual communities probably have their greatest contribution to make here: in bringing to the debate a different kind of consciousness and in raising people's awareness that the world's crisis is a spiritual crisis. Those who see things differently have the job of pointing out that the logic of technology, combined with the values of the market, has led us towards a false starting point for development. This starting point places a disproportionate emphasis on the economic dimension of life, and it has not resulted in an adequate solution to the hunger, lack of education and health, injustices, and environmental damage that we see all around us.

What Is Development?

The debate with the World Bank started with an interreligious contribution to the Bank's "World Development Report 2000/1: Attacking Poverty." One of the key issues, which is probably still the most important in the dialogue, was the question of the meaning of development. What are its goals? What kind of a process is it?

People from different religions have never before attempted to arrive at a consensual definition of development. The main message that those engaged with WFDD have wanted to give is that, if development is to have any meaning, it must embrace the social, political, environmental, cultural, and spiritual dimensions of life as well as the economic. Since all dimensions of human existence are brought together in the reality of the divine or the cycle of life, separating them makes no sense. As the strawberry growers in Guatemala say so beautifully: "We breathe, we move, we reap the harvest of our work, the earth, the heat, the water make the seed germinate and grow and produce its fruits: everything is in the hand of God and we put everything into God's hands."[2]

Another way in which development is described by people from the faith communities is as an awakening brought about by an internal process of self-transformation. According to Dr. A.T. Ariyaratne, founder of the Sarvodaya Shramadana Movement in Sri Lanka: "This awakening has to begin with oneself, with every individual, then extend to the family, the country, the nation, the world. The awakening must be an integrated whole where spiritual, moral, cultural, social, political and economic aspects of life are included."[3]

This awakening is to a vision of the potential of the individual and others. It is a realization of what is essentially important and of what reality is, and it certainly does not mean that overcoming material poverty is not regarded as a high priority. Sarvodaya (which means Welfare of All), like any human institution, faces all sorts of problems but it has brought material improvements such as roads, schools, housing, and water to thousands of Sri Lankan villages through programs based on Buddhist values, such as giving and service (*shramadana*).

The realization that without a spiritual dimension, material development will be meaningless, was expressed by Pope John Paul II. His vision went beyond the Enlightenment's duality of the spiritual and material worlds, which has been so dominant in many Christian churches since the eighteenth century. At the beginning of *Sollicitudo Rei Sociales,* he referred to "an authentic development of man and society which would respect and promote all the dimensions of the human person" and later in the same encyclical he wrote: "Following the example of my predecessors, I must repeat that whatever affects the dignity of individuals and peoples, such as authentic development, cannot be reduced to a 'technical' problem. If reduced in this way, development would be emptied of its true content, and this would be an act of betrayal of the individuals and peoples whom development is meant to serve." (41).

In practice there are very many faith-based groups that stand firm against the temptation to reduce development to a technical problem. Sarkan Zoumountsi in Yaoundé, Cameroon, is one of them. Two or three years ago its members were offered a substantial grant from the European Commission for a program to provide credit to small enterprises. When they realized that a condition for the grant was that they should charge interest on any money lent, Sarkan Zoumountsi rejected it because charging interest is against the rules of Islam. "The aim of our association is certainly to seek development, the well-being of individuals in society" they explain, "but not at any price, for in Sarkan Zoumountsi we take action following the great guide, Islam in general."[4]

Overriding what seems to be satisfactory development practice, from a technical viewpoint, is seen as irritatingly irrelevant by many people in development agencies who are impatient to improve the conditions of life for impoverished communities as quickly as possible. There is, however, a growing awareness that sustainable development without the full cooperation of those to be developed is impossible; this means that local cultural and religious customs and beliefs have to be taken into account.

The World Bank is not prone to giving direct answers to questions about the meaning of development, for fear of simplifying complex concepts, but its statement of purpose is: "Our dream is a world free of poverty." Few would quarrel with this as a laudable aim. Moreover, the oft-repeated recognition by the World Bank that poverty is a multi-dimensional phenomenon that includes social and political elements, as well as economic ones, has been widely welcomed. The quantitative targets of the Millennium Development Goals, approved by almost all the countries of the UN, are, in themselves, also considered a worthy aim for everyone. An example of a goal is that by the year 2015, the number of the world's poorest people must be reduced by half and all children of primary school age must be at school.

The faith community is not unhappy with the World Bank's aims and targets as such, but with the notion that still underpins the policies and programs of multilateral, governmental (and many non-governmental) development institutions. The assumption is that development is essentially the process by which the non-industrialized countries catch up with the standard of living of the more advanced nations. Many people from faith-based communities see this as a reductionist understanding that fails to take into account the context of the religions, values, and cultural heritage of both the developers and those supposedly being developed. Moreover, there is also a great deal of disagreement about the emphasis on economic growth that is to be achieved through integrating poor countries into the world's markets, which is the instrument by which this catching-up process is to be managed.

Is Global Economic Growth an Adequate Instrument to Bring About Development?

It must be said, however, that opinions within the faith community are divided, very often between those who find themselves in a position in which the benefits of globalization are more apparent and those who work most closely with those who are being marginalized. The Catholic nuns and priests working in Kerala, for example, have participated in the fisher people's experience of globalization through the arrival of multinational corporations whose vast trawlers deplete the fish stock along the Indian coasts and whose prawn farms ruin mangrove swamps and paddy fields. "We march to Delhi," said the banner of the National Forum of Fishworkers in 1998, "we, the labouring people from whom they are stealing our sand, sea and fish; from whom they are taking away our homes and occupations.... Give us the dignity of our skills, our work and our lives. Do not rob us of the sea – our only wealth."[5]

Pope John Paul II understood this suffering. "The first negative observation to make is the persistence and often the widening of the gap between the areas of the so-called developed North and the developing South," he writes. "This geographical terminology is only indicative, since one cannot ignore the fact that the frontiers of wealth and poverty intersect within the societies themselves, whether developed or developing. In fact, just as social inequalities down to the level of poverty exist in rich countries, so, in parallel fashion, in the less developed countries one often sees manifestations of selfishness and a flaunting of wealth which is as disconcerting, as it is scandalous." (SRS 14)

Crucial to the debate is the question of trust in the theory that global market integration will eventually bring benefits to all. Such speculation for the future also needs to be weighed against the imperative to meet people's immediate needs. The essential underlying argument, however, is about sacrificing human dignity and integral human development to material progress – a recurrent theme of papal encyclicals, at least since *Pacem in Terris* (1963).

Consumerism

The globalization of capitalism is based on an understanding that human beings are only out to promote their own self-interest. Capitalism encourages competition rather than cooperation and it relentlessly excludes those who are superfluous to the needs of the economy. However, the rampant consumerism being spread by this system throughout the world is precisely what many people view with abhorrence as a new form of idolatry that can never lead to peaceful contentment.

"The modernisation process creates new problems in rural communities," write Jane Rasbach and Pracha Hutanuwatr who work with the Buddhist Spirit in Education Movement in Thailand. "With roads passing through, consumer goods such as TVs, motorcycles and refrigerators reach villages, as well as middlemen who come in to sell other expensive products and buy cheap agricultural products. Soon after, villagers become indebted and the vicious cycle starts to destroy the fabric of rural village life, as alcoholism, drugs, ill health, prostitution, HIV and loss of hope move in."[6]

How closely John Paul II identified with this picture is shown by this comment:

> All of us experience firsthand the sad effects of this blind submission to pure consumerism: in the first place a crass materialism, and at the same time a radical dissatisfaction, because one quickly learns – unless one is shielded from the flood of publicity and the ceaseless and tempting offers of products – that the more one possesses the more one wants, while deeper aspirations remain unsatisfied and perhaps even stifled. (SRS 28)

Principles and Values

Jonathan Sacks, Chief Rabbi of the United Hebrew Congregations of the Commonwealth, agrees with Pope John Paul II and with many other religious leaders. Sacks says that the causes of the flaws in the present world order lie in the lack of ethical guidance given to us by contemporary politics and economics. "Beyond the freedom to do what we like and can afford, contemporary politics and economics have little to say about the human condition. They give us inadequate guidance in knowing what to do in the face of the random brutalities of fate." Sacks recognizes that religions are not our "sole source of morality" but he speaks of their important role in remaining "a significant space outside of and in counterpoint to a late-modern Western culture that tends systematically to dissolve the values and virtues that give meaning to a life."[7]

If the different faith communities are to be a living source of morality in our world of rapid change, however, they have to be clear about the differences between beliefs and practices that are essential to their faith and those which can now be seen as culturally or historically conditioned. They will also need to see what they can absorb from the modern world that might enhance the physical, as well as spiritual, well-being of their people.

One of the most difficult issues among many people who work with the poor, both inside and outside the faith community, is the prohibition by some religions of the use of artificial birth control. This prohibition comes in an era in which the world's population is growing at the unsustainable rate of 90 million people every year. Linked to this is the very difficult challenge of holding the deepest concern for the value of life in our age when so many millions of people are dying of AIDS every year, many leaving behind them poverty-stricken orphaned children. Many people within all religions react against the cultural standardization and the consumer society brought by the globalization of capital by withdrawing from the world's problems. Others are sacrificing many of the traditional values of their religions by succumbing to the consumer society with its craving for material goods and the status they are seen to bring with them. WFDD has been trying to find examples of communities that are engaged with the burning issues of the world but whose work rests on principles and values that are different from those of the dominant culture.

The Common Good

Catholic social thought (CST) rests on the central principle that the organization of society, including processes of development, should aim to attain the common good – the welfare of the whole group. The same idea is to be found in Judaism and Islam, with their strong bias towards the community and social justice. It is supported, too, though from a different starting point, by Buddhist philosophy and the Hindu Vedas, both of which point to the interconnectedness of all living beings that leads each person to a sense of their responsibility towards the rest. In practical situations, the common good is not always easy to define, but as a principle it is a starting point from which certain themes have risen to the fore in the debate about development.

Cooperation

The principle of the common good implies a world order that sets out to provide the basic needs for everyone, but this is being undermined today by competition as the essential incentive driving forward the global capitalist system. If care for one's neighbour is to be taken seriously, then competition must be accompanied by cooperation to ensure that the weakest are not crushed by the strongest. Moreover the rules of competition must be fair.

Pope John Paul II addressed this question by looking at ways in which poor countries may defend themselves from the competition of the rich. He recommended regional economic cooperation as a way forward: "It is desirable, for example, that nations of the same geographical area should establish forms of co-operation which will make them less dependent on more powerful producers…" (SRS 45)

Religious groups, in alliance with many others, have, however, found ways to show that it is possible not only to strengthen the weakest within a competitive framework but also to inject an element of solidarity into the market system. One of these ways is through the Fair Trade Movement that has created a solidarity market in industrialized countries. This is protecting millions of producers of products – such as coffee, bananas, honey, and cocoa, as well as handcrafts – from the most harmful effects of international competition based on the rules of supply and demand.

Similar principles of cooperation and solidarity are being applied to marketing programs set up by Comal, a group with Quaker origins in Honduras through which small farmers sell their produce directly, bypassing middlemen, to community shops. The farmers get a better price than they would from middlemen and the shops are able to sell products more cheaply than in the market. The same idea is behind a large Catholic-inspired program that markets indigenous produce in Ecuador.

People-centred Development: Service

The principle of the common good implies that the basic needs of all people should be met, but this does not mean that all people will define their needs in the same way. Father Christian Aurenche, the medical doctor and Catholic priest who leads the Project for Human Promotion among mountain tribal people in Tokombéré in northern Cameroon, focuses on the importance of an attitude of respect and trust on the part of the developers towards those who are to be developed. "No development project can give signs of hope if it has not regarded people as the agents of their own development," he says.[8]

This means that the persons who should define poverty are the poor themselves. As Deepa Narayan found out in her research for the World Bank, those who are poor very seldom point to economic poverty alone. "Poverty definitions focus on difficulties in securing food and livelihood," she writes. "What is striking, however, is the extent to which dependency, lack of power and lack of voice emerge as core elements of poor people's definitions of poverty."[9]

If the poor themselves should be given space to define poverty, then it is a mistake to suppose that experts from the developed countries, or even the elite of the developing ones, can define development better than the poor can. This does not, of course, mean that professionals should not put their expertise at the service of the poor. On the contrary, service to others is highly valued in all religions and, for many, as a way of expressing devotion to God whose spirit dwells within each person.

In 1979, the medical doctor Hanumappa Sudarshan went to live with the Soliga people in the Biligiri Hills in the Indian state of Karnataka. Sudarshan kept in mind the three requirements of a worker set out by his Hindu mentor, Swami Vivekananda: to feel the pain of his brothers and sisters as his own, to find a remedy for their ills and act upon it, and to constantly question his true motives.

After three years, the Soligas were confident that he understood their needs. The result of Sudarshan's patience has been the creation of the Vivekananda Girijana Kalyana Kendra (Tribal Welfare Centre) and its expansion from a small health program to a large integrated development scheme. Sudarshan is fully aware of how much he has learned from the Soligas. "Here," he says, "I have learnt to appreciate beauty and understand the regenerative power of love."[10]

Access to Services

The World Bank's promotion of the private sector as the driving force for the successful implementation of development strategies has received much criticism because it is seen to flout the principle of the common good.

People from various religious traditions have commented on the first draft of the Bank's World Development Report 2004, "Making Social Services work for the Poor." Drawing on these comments, WFDD concludes that while faith communities do not oppose privatization in principle, they urge that some degree of state control should be kept to ensure that the poor have access to all essential services.

The comment highlights a particular apposition to the privatization of water on the grounds that it must be made available to everyone. "Since it is essential for life itself, water has a special spiritual significance as a resource for the good of all and is not considered to be a tradable commodity," it says.[11]

For a long time, CST has emphasised that the ownership of property brings certain responsibilities. "It is necessary to state once more the characteristic principle of Christian social doctrine: the goods of this world are originally meant for all," wrote Pope John Paul II in *Sollicitudo Rei Sociales* (42). "The right to private property is valid and necessary, but it does not nullify the value of this principle. Private property, in fact, is under a 'social mortgage.'"

The Environment

The Abrahamic traditions have often been accused of undervaluing the importance of taking care of our natural environment because of their emphasis on human beings as stewards of nature rather than as an integral part of it. This is in stark contrast to the insights of indigenous spiritual traditions concerning Mother Earth as the sacred giver of all life and an insight shared by Buddhists and Hindus concerning the interdependence of all living beings.

Over the last 30 years, environmental crises – such as floods, droughts, soil erosion, and landslides – have brought a new realization about development. Unless development work is not merely environmentally friendly but is grounded in an awareness of humanity's place in the cosmos, not only animals and plants but the human species itself will perish. The idea that scientific and technical solutions will be found to replace what we need in nature is viewed as a dangerous illusion by all who believe that human beings depend on a life-giving force beyond themselves.

In *Sollicitudo Rei Socialis* Pope John Paul II acknowledged that care of the environment is an important part of any development strategy. He said, "A true concept of development cannot ignore the use of the elements of nature, the renewability of resources and the consequences of haphazard industrialization – three considerations which alert our consciences to the moral dimension of development." (34) Moreover Christians, Jews, and Muslims – as well as other faith groups all over the world – are now supporting programs such as organic composting, organic agriculture, and reforestation.

The World Bank has agreed to do an environmental audit on all its projects, but economic growth and the protection of the environment are not necessarily compatible. For example, even if trees are eventually planted alongside the pipeline that is being built from Chad to Cameroon, the pipeline is causing untold environmental destruction. The same is true of the many dams that have been built with World Bank money. The Buddhist Spirit in Education Movement has for years been supporting local protests against one such dam in Thailand.

The time has come to move beyond environmental audits and beyond environmental projects, even beyond the dualistic paradigm of stewardship itself, to a different vision – a vision that draws on the age-old wisdom of indigenous peoples from Australia to the Amazon and of eastern mystics. Their understanding that humanity can only exist as an integral part of the life of the planet is a safeguard against regarding nature in a purely utilitarian light. It also makes us aware that our survival depends on a relationship of true respect for our environment, an ingredient of which is an attitude of wonder and awe.

A Global Ethic?

Much common ground can be found among religions regarding the common good, the need for cooperation to temper competition, the value of service, the social use of property, and the need to protect the environment. This could lead to the conclusion that Hans Küng is right and that it is not only an imperative for world peace to find a global ethic but that it is possible.[12] The danger of the search for a global ethic from a Western perspective is that those seeking it will fall into the same trap as Western would-be developers – they will ultimately assume that their own values are universal.

When it comes to specific cases in which values have to be prioritized, there will not only be differences among the different religions, but also many profound differences within them. The latter are demonstrated in visible ways by disagreements within Islam, for example, about the right balance between compassion and justice within Sharia law or about the treatment of women. While Sarkan Zoumountsi in Yaoundé is working hard for women to be educated, some of the imams in the same city are preaching against such initiatives.

Within the Hindu tradition many people like Swami Agnivesh, the social activist who has worked hard for the freedom of bonded labourers from the stone quarry workers around Delhi, are doing everything possible to abolish the caste system in practice as well as in law. But many Hindus still support it. And within Christianity there is no agreement about the meaning for our era of the injunction to be in this world but not of it, let alone agreement about sexuality and family planning. Moreover, all institutionalized religions have deep internal disagreements about what inclusion means in terms of democratic decision-making with regard to the laity and, particularly, to women.

These differences make any dialogue between the world's religions and the World Bank a highly complex process. WFDD has tried to simplify things through its focus on people from faith-based groups who are actively working for improvements for the poor.

Criticism of Small Local Projects

With these faith-based groups the World Bank should be able to engage meaningfully about practical development work, since these are people who know what poverty is like from the inside and are working to improve life for those who suffer. Staff from the World Bank have, however, voiced their frustration on many occasions about the small scale of much faith-based development work. Many countries, particularly in Africa, have nation-wide networks of schools and hospitals run by religious communities, and Sarvodaya in Sri Lanka, for example, covers more than 11,000 villages. Nevertheless, more common are local village-based programs that are isolated from any national agenda and have little or no visible impact nationally, or even regionally, on reducing poverty. Many calls have been made, including one from the President of the World Bank himself, for the faith communities to scale up their work.

Should the faith communities act upon this call and be ready to take advantage of the offer of expertise made by the World Bank to help them do so? Since there is nothing particularly religious about being ineffective, an immediate reaction might be that they should. But many questions arise about how efficiency is understood in practice.

Many faith communities may, for instance, give higher priority to inclusiveness, compassion, and justice in their ways of working than to speed and technically cost-effective procedures. Since faith-based programs are concerned with the development of the whole human being, along with material benefits, they bring results such as hope, self-confidence, and a sense of dignity, that cannot be easily counted or measured.

An example is the story of a former pupil from the school run by the Project for Human Promotion in Tokombéré in Cameroon who was not able to continue his studies with many of his friends. He now has a small plot of land on which he keeps farm animals. "I am not disappointed, on the contrary!" he says. "I think each person is important in the place where he is. I have my place in the village and I can give some help towards development. I actively participate in the activities suggested by the Tokombéré Project and I can see that life is changing around me." Such a sense of belonging and purpose in life may, in the end, have a greater and more lasting impact on reducing poverty from one generation to another than projects that focus more narrowly on quantitative results, whether in health, education, or income generation.

Cooperation between faith communities and development institutions will only be beneficial to the poor if they preserve the central focus on people. The danger of scaling up local faith-based programs is that their vision of development and their particular qualities of personal contact, a sense of community, and the workers' sense of service might get lost.

Future Dialogue?

It is vitally important for people from different religious traditions who are working to improve the quality of life for the most impoverished people in our world to have a place at the table where policy decisions about development are made. They should also participate in the implementation of these policies. The dialogue will bring some searching questions to the Catholic Church, as well as to others. They will need to balance the tension between their vision of development, based on different values than those of advanced consumer societies, with an openness to the improvements that modern technology can bring to the material well-being of those who suffer most.

Another question will be how to engage with the powerful institutions of this world while holding fast to the wisdom in every religious tradition about worldly power being an illusion sought after only by the foolish. People from faith communities will be required to show their integrity by living according to the values that they insist should be the basis for all development programs. One of the greatest challenges to all traditions will be to ensure that women, who along with their children make up the majority of the world's poor, are recognized as leading players in the development process and fully participate at all levels in the development debate.

In the end, this is about people from faith communities engaging with the world through a commitment of solidarity with those whom the world has marginalized. But such an engagement will only be of real significance as long as it has a solid base in that space of which Jonathan Sacks speaks. The base is its sense of the sacred and its source of energy and inspiration – perhaps the only space that can never be taken over by the powers of the global market.

This is the space from which genuinely different visions can arise, and in which new perspectives are nurtured that challenge the religious as well as the secular institutions. The danger of dealing with development issues from within the framework of the world as it is, is that the room for these new perspectives will be reduced rather than enlarged. Also, the voice of those at the grassroots level who have prophetic insights into the possibility of a different way of ordering our lives will not be heard. This is a tension to be found in all religious traditions, the Catholic Church among them.

11

Muslims' Dialogue with Globalization: The Case of Iran

Farhang Rajaee

My aim in this chapter is to canvass what I consider to be the response of a group of Muslims to the challenge of modernity, which has now culminated in the process signified by the overworked notion of globalization. For myself or anyone else to assume that one can grasp what Muslims as a whole say or have done in response to or about this process is presumptuous. Since the internal cohesion of the Muslim world has been destroyed, the battle of world views among Muslims is so intense that recognizing and acknowledging the enormous diversity among Muslims is essential. More than 50 world states claim, in one way or another, to be living within the bound of the tenets of Islam. At the same time, many self-proclaimed Muslim groups challenge the claim and legitimacy of these states. Who can speak for Islam or Muslims? I think the answer is a paradox: no one and everyone. Because Islam does not recognize clericalism, in practice whatever Muslims display or express in words and deeds and within any given historical context is seen as representing Islam and Muslims. Here I will concentrate on the response of Islam-minded Iranians to this challenge.

I have a number of reasons for concentrating on Iran. Iran has had a successful revolution with the aim of institutionalizing an Islamic way of life. That revolution seems to best utilize the forces of globalization; after all, the cassette tapes carrying the message of Ayatollah Khomeini were the means of spreading the message of the revolution throughout the country. I agree with Canadian scholar Peter Beyer, that "the Iranian revolution represents an effort to give a marginal, 'Third World' region greater access to the perceived material and cultural (such as prestige, recognition) benefits of globalized systems, but in such a way as to enhance the cultural particularity that hitherto has been associated with marginalization."[1] Despite an eight-year war (1980–1988) fought by Iraq against Iran's new regime, the Islamic Republic of Iran has survived and is continuing with its goal of Islamization. The serious debate in Iran today is worth some attention. It not only addresses social justice, human rights, gender justice, and democratic deficit among

Muslims, but also the more sophisticated questions of epistemology, knowledge, and civilizational deficit. Additionally, both the clerical and more secular strata of Iranian intelligentsia have taken part in the debate. To capture the dynamism of this debate I will address the following questions. What is the context of the debate? What internal, national, or international contexts gave rise to the debate? Who are the voices in the debate? What is their main agenda? What is their diagnosis of the crisis in "the abode of Islam"? Do they propose any solution? These are some of the questions that guide the discussion in this chapter.

The Context

The year 1979, which marks the victory of the Islamic Revolution, should have changed the reactive approach to what is now known as the Islamic Movement. On February 1, 1979, an Air France Boeing 747 landed at Tehran's airport bringing with it the leader of the revolution. Amid an ocean of supporters, he went directly from the airport to the cemetery where the martyrs of the revolution were buried and declared, "I will appoint a government, I will crush the present government." Within ten days his provisional government was in power. Soon, in April, the Iranian people marched to the voting polls to participate in a referendum to decide the future form of government in the country. The leader of the revolution, the late Imam Khomeini, had asked the people to vote for "the Islamic Republic, not one word less and not one word more." Ayatollah Khomeini's "Eight Points Edict," was issued on December 1982 after the institutionalization of the main organs of the Islamic Republic, including the election of the Assembly of Experts on December 9, 1982. The latter was significant because, among other duties, it was entrusted with the authority to elect the new leader of the state. In his famous message, Khomeini called for the restoration of people's civil and economic rights, but more importantly he explicitly declared the end of the revolution and its revolutionary zeal. This day should have marked two significant events: the inauguration of a new regime and the beginning of the end of the Islamic revolution. It succeeded in the first but not the second. It began a new Islamic regime, and it should have begun the process of normal state building – an Islamic one, of course.

State building was postponed by a series of internal and external events. The new phase that was to implement the grand theories of the revolutionaries for Islamic banking, education, international relations, and the like had to wait because more urgent issues needed attention. Internally, at least three important trends did not allow for the return to the Iranian modernization process. One was the legacy of the Pahlavis's pseudo-modernization that was not at all authentic, and more importantly was not an inclusive approach. In terms of politics, as the Iranian scholar Asghar Schirazi writes, "The political legacy of the Shah's regime is evident in systems of values such as the primacy of politics, particularism, absolute authoritarianism and gigantism."[2] The pan-politics, exclusivity, arbitrary power of the rulers, and, worst of all, the practice of setting goals beyond one's means contributed a great deal to the revolutionary zeal that dominated politics in the first decade of the Islamic Republic.

A second trend was the change in the battle of ideas against the unholy alliance of internal pseudo-modernization and external America-centrism that had resulted in the emergence of the relatively monolithic voice of the opposition against the previous regime. It soon dispersed into competing groups who did not share the same intellectual framework (*mavazin*) and rules of the game (*qava'ed*). Thus, the unity of approaches and strategies of the initial phase of the battle of ideas turned into a bloody zero-sum game in a battle of world views. The struggle for power, terror, and assassination replaced the civility by which the revolution itself had been won. By the autumn of 1982, the juridical Islamists (*Eslam-e Fiqahati*) had won and had eliminated all other secular and non-juridical Islamists.

In the third trend, a byproduct of the previous two trends, the politics of Islamism emerged and proved as particularistic and absolute as that of the Pahlavis. The Islamists established what the late professor of philosophy and staunch follower of Heidegger, Seyyed Ahmad Fardid, termed "vertical democracy."[3] The authoritarian, absolutist, ideological, and, in some sense, militarist system of the Islamists only permitted one sort of politics (or pseudo-politics) – a politics of supplication to higher authorities. Little chance existed for what political philosophers term "horizontal voices"[4] to find expression or to flourish. These voices would have called forth the "we" feeling that had so powerfully manifested itself during and in the first couple of years of the revolution. They would have manifested a political identity that included synchronically all elements of Iranian society and diachronically the four components of contemporary Iranian identity: Islam, Iran, tradition, and modernity.[5]

Internationally, there were two initial effects of this revolution. First, the androlepsia[6] against the American diplomats in Tehran, lasting 444 days, unnecessarily intensified antagonism between Iran and the US and also Iran and the West. Further, it resulted in an American embargo on Iran that completely overshadowed Iranian foreign policy. Second, the real or perceived fear of the revolution and its exportation instigated a regional and international alliance to contain the revolution. The Iraqi invasion of Iran on September 20, 1980, drained Iran of its human and financial resources for almost a decade. Beginning with the formation of the Gulf Cooperation Council in 1980 to contain the Iranian Revolution, the mounting international pressures did not allow a natural unfolding of the new politics in Iran. The eight-year war was the most important impediment, because it gained priority over everything else. Every other impulse was subordinated to the war and all other considerations – such as the problems of agriculture, industry, labour, justice, education, welfare, and recreation – were deferred.[7]

Iran and Islam watchers who were keen to observe a new historical experience in the making had to wait for another ten years before Islam-minded Iranians could think of normal state-building processes and polity formation. Interestingly, like the political career of the Prophet of Islam, as long as Khomeini was alive and at the peak of power his personal charisma set the parameters within which the political game was played.

By the late 1980s, two major events led to the normalization of the life of the polity. First, the war came to a close. Second, the debate over the extent of the power of the Islamic government became a real issue. This led to an interesting debate and the normalization of the life of the polity. The unfolding debate was finalized in 1989, a year that was definitely a turning point: Khomeini died on June 5, the revised constitution was ratified, the new president was elected, the new leader designated, and the end of the revolution appeared in sight.

Although Khomeini died of abdominal cancer and heart problems, his death was an ordinary one. For one thing, he was the only Iranian leader who had died of natural causes in full power for a long time. King Nassau al-Din Shah (1831–1896) had died by an assassin's bullet, and Muhammad Ail Shah, Ahmad Shah, Reza Shah, and Muhammad Reza Shah have all died powerless and homeless somewhere outside of Iranian soil. The archetypical Iranian nationalist leader, Dr. Muhammad Mussadeq, died a natural death (1967) but at the time he was under house arrest and no one was allowed to publicly mourn his death. The case of Khomeini was different. On June 5, people mourned fiercely, freely, and, in fact, to the point of madness. The ocean of human flesh did not allow for a normal burial. This was the suppressed feeling of the century, which was now pouring out.

The government gave in to an unforeseen and unprecedented event: despite the Islamic injunction that any given corpse should be buried immediately, that of Imam Khomeini was displayed, inside a glass freezer, for a few days to allow the public to pay their homage. Even when the body was finally to be returned to the earth, it was impossible to break the sea of the dense spectators and mourners. The corpse had to be brought by a helicopter at the cost of ten deaths and 10,000 injured. Only the heavy container placed on the grave by a crane could save the body from the lamenting devotees. Afterward, I observed his shrine being erected practically in a flash. From hour to hour, one could see significant changes in the construction. It was incredible to see bulldozers, trucks, and heavy machinery at work in the middle of people who were crowding around it for pilgrimage. I visited regularly once a week and never stopped being astonished at the unfolding of the passion and feeling.

Khomeini's death was a test of the survival of the polity he had left behind. It was amazing to observe the government's hasty announcement that all activities must halt just after the news of his death was broadcast and, when the enormous support for this action was observed, that things began to relax. As the day wore on and masses of people began to pour toward the Imam's residence, the government gained confidence with the popular show of support. And since, erroneously I believe, he was seen as a man responsible for the continuation of the war and revolutionary zeal, his death opened the scene for a new form of radicalism that lasted until the late 1990s.

Another factor that came to play a rather significant role was the changing demands and expectation of the very same people who, in the words of their Imam, "had not revolted for the reduction of the price of watermelon." The mid-twentieth-century global concern for the future and the pressures of daily life had affected the revolutionary corps and the dedicated members of the Islamic movement. The end of the oil boom and a decade of economic recovery and development in the last days of the Shah also played a role in this conversion. Pursuit of university degrees, higher education, technical skills, and a welfare state were beginning to affect the psyche of the revolutionaries who were now beginning to reach their thirties and even experience mid-life crises, which know no race, religion, time, place, or culture. These concerns and demands became all the more acute since a post-revolutionary population explosion made the new Iran much younger than before, with more than half of the population under 20 years of age.

More important was a powerful resistance against the vertical democracy of Islamism by a coalition of four powerful elements in Iranian society: revolutionaries turned democrats, women, the youth, and the proponents of an Iranian modernity project who were empowered by the coming of the process of globalization. It may be an irony that the year 1989 was also a decisive year for the world. Many important developments pointed to the coming of what Muslim philosopher of history Ibn-Khaldun calls "the new creation."[8] This new creation resulted from the combination of communication technologies with the revolution in processing of data by computer, resulting in the emergence of a world of one-civilization/many-cultures.

Humanity as a whole now belongs to the process of technological civilization, but unlike that of industry, the new civilization allows for diversity of voices and a variety of players. As far as this discussion is concerned, the most important consequence of this new creation is that the existing system based on Eurocentrism has been shaken and its foundations have lost their legitimacy. Many conscience-minded thinkers had been questioning and analyzing the uni-dimensional nature of the dominant system, but as a result of globalization it became self-evident. The post-colonial, post-industrial, postmodern, post-structural, and post–Cold War world not only had to accept but also to welcome the horizontal voices – something that could not have been imagined even a decade before. A politics of us versus them has been replaced with a global politics of Earth-ship and the inclusive approach of humanity as a whole: human rights, social justice, gender justice, and ecology.

The changing internal and external contexts have given rise to a new generation of Islam-minded Iranians. This generation seems to have gone beyond the inactive and passive mind-set of the voices of the Islamic movement that dominated not only the Iranian public sphere but also that of the Muslim world in general. Some call this new generation progressive Muslims,[9] and I have called them, in another context, Islamic Yuppies.[10] Whatever one calls them, what is important is that they are trying to be proactive and have an appreciation for their own tradition as well as respect for traditions of modernity and the West. In the minds of the members of this generation, it is hard and even wrong to make generalizations about cultures or traditions. They believe in the dynamic life of any culture as well as an active dialogue within any given cultural milieu and among diverse and different civilizations. In this sense, what they have said or continue to say should not be seen as their response to globalization, but rather their dialogue with the forces and voices of globalization. In the rest of this chapter I will provide a glimpse at the views of some prominent voices of this generation in Iran.

The Voices: The Post-Islamist Generation

Who represents the post-Islamist generation? In the present phase of the revolution in Iran that coincides with the first decade of the new millennium, intellectuals have emerged who are at home with both the Irano-Islamic cultural milieu and that of the technological and postmodern globalized civilization. Many names come to mind, but here I concentrate on three individuals who, in many ways, resemble the first generation of Muslims who faced the challenge of modernity in the early nineteenth century. The latter concentrated on a restoration of Islam to its historical glory. The new generation also thinks in terms of restoration, but goes beyond it by hoping for regeneration and even renovation.

The three individuals are Muhammad Mujtahid Shabestari, Abdolkarim Soroush, and Saeed Hajjarian. All of them are significant voices at this juncture in the Islamic movement of Iran. The first has been a longtime member of the religious class who has decided to face the contemporary challenges. The second is a noncleric, Islam-minded intellectual who has been at the heart of controversy in post-revolutionary Iran dealing with the authority of the religious establishment in the public sphere. The last is a political activist and a practical actor in the revolution and in policymaking circles.

All three feel that they have to formulate a response to the challenge of modernity and, now, globalization. In the process, they seem to respond to three adversaries. The first are those who see tradition as something sacred in its totality that has to be obeyed uncritically with no need of rethinking. Other adversaries are those Muslims who have turned Islam into an ideology of revolution and terror. The third category of adversaries are those who feel that Muslims should submit absolutely to the demands of the globalized world and embrace the demands of capitalism and those of the free-market economy. These three adversaries could be termed traditionalists, Islamists, and modernists, respectively. Instead, the three Islam-minded Iranians treated here propose a renovated narrative of Islam that critically accommodates both Islam and the demands of modernity.

Muhammad Mujtahid Shabestari

The first individual, Shabestari, is a cleric and theologian who teaches in the Department of Theology of Tehran University. He has had a long career among Islam-minded Iranians who tried to revive Islamic teaching. He has become a prominent voice in the past decade because he has challenged the official version of Islam that became so dominant in post-revolutionary Iran and has a grip on power there today. Shabestari claims that there is no one version or one reading of any religion. He states in the preface of his book: "Indeed, any religion expression amounts to a reading of the religious text, and the fact is that the latter could be understood and interpreted in various ways."[11]

The first part of his book includes three essays dealing with the issues of religion and development, the rational reading of religion, and the official reading of religion. The first essay opens with this controversial sentence: "The official reading of religion in our society is in crisis" and lists two causes. The first is "the irrational and erroneous position that Islam as a religion is a comprehensive political, economic, and legal system based on jurisprudence, that is applicable to all times and has required Muslims to live by it in all aspects of their lives and in all times. The second is an emphasis on this erroneous claim that the duty of government among Muslims is to implement the ordinances of Islam."[12] Instead, Shabestari invites Muslims to see the reality of their lives in the face of modernity. For him, the main features of the modernity process have the following components. Human will and volition constitute the foundation, the new empirical and social sciences are dominant, and industry shapes the mode of production. Modernity also has long-term planning, the main discourses are a plurality of ideas and universal participation, and objective rules and regulations are at work. In addition, the state acts as a manager of scientific rules; justice has a new meaning; religion and development are compatible; and finally, contrary to traditional ways, the end result is never predictable.[13]

For Shabestari, freedom lies at the heart of this sophisticated process; this means that the notion of freedom is at the heart of his theology. Shabestari feels that freedom allows for any dialectic between tradition and modernity. Indeed, to grasp the internal logic of Shabestari's thought one needs to concentrate on his understanding of freedom. How is it defined and understood? For Shabestari, freedom means manifestation of the autonomous self, for which one has to note three issues: freedom from, freedom to, and freedom for. The first pertains to the removal of all forces either inside or outside the agent-actor that may create impediments to one's way of exercising volition. The second defines the realm where the agent-actor could display volition – that is "the realm of action." And the final form of freedom helps "securing of one's objective, which is nothing more than preservation of freedom of action." Although this appears repetitious and a tautology, it is another way of saying that freedom is both end and means, and it constitutes the very reason for humanity's life on earth. As Shabestari writes: "the reality of being human is 'to be free always.' To live as human means to live freely. Human being constitutes the essence of freedom and its very manifestation."[14] By this definition alone, Shabestari has embraced the most significant element of modernity and globalization, namely the free autonomous self.

To show the centrality of the notion of freedom, Shabestari then treats the relations of freedom to faith, the reading of any sacred text, and political thinking based on religious tradition. The relation of freedom and faith is significant because, for Shabestari, the essence of religion is faith and religiosity makes sense in "a religious experience" that is different from a collective movement or even a revival. He calls the latter "political movements" with religious colour.[15] Religions usually manifest themselves in the world either in forms of faith or in forms of beliefs or rituals. According to Shabestari, only through faith can one achieve presence to the divine, while beliefs and rituals are servants and facilitators of proximity to the divine and to its presence. "Religion means presence; beliefs, rituals, ethics, and ordinances of religion are but servants to this presence. Their value depends on the role they play in facilitating that presence."[16] The ultimate manifestation of such a presence comes with faith when one loses oneself in God. This frees one from the four earthly jails of history, society, language, and one's body, which is described best, according to Shabestari, in the Bible in Matthew (10:39) where it is stated that if one loses oneself one gains God.[17] In a way, faith is a conscious choice, and it remains so as long as it is in constant dialogue with other human experiences in a logical way. For a religious mind, no conscious effort happens without "serious criticism of the religion, religiosity, and the tradition dominating" the given society and where there is no limitation or "red light" on the path of criticism, and rethinking.[18]

But Shabestari believes that, just as unity with God happens through human experience, approaching any divine text and religious tradition happens through a similar process. Here is the logic of his argument. Any religious thinking is shaped by three elements that are, in turn, related to how human beings experience themselves, how they experience the world, and how they understand or experience revelation. "A Muslim could approach and experience the revelation," Shabestari writes, "only with the help of a particular understanding and experience of himself and the world. It is through the combination of these three that religious thought is formed."[19] No one can claim to have ever understood the true intention of the text because one is always reading the text with a particular pretext. The tacit dimension is always at work. In other words, any religious expression is a human phenomenon, and cannot be presented as something divine or sacred. This idea is very challenging to the traditionalist approach that claims to know the truth about religious teachings. It also paves the way for religious pluralism and for all other forms of plurality and toleration – the cultural, the social, the legal, and the political.

Shabestari then returns to freedom of religion. For him, freedom is engrained and is built within religion, which explains why various religious interpretations exist as part and parcel of religious history. The implication is that there is, and should be, interpretation of religion, but not guardianship or only one version of religion. As he writes, "Freedom of religion is related to the religion itself and not for the person to be free to chose a particular religion. Religion has to be free; personal freedom to choose religion is a social right that in turn is part of the principles of 'human right'."[20]

Abdolkarim Soroush

While Shabestari concentrates on freedom, Abdolkarim Soroush deals with all aspects of the contemporary secular world. This is his question: How could a religiously based polity deal with secularism? He positions himself within the greater project of religious revival among Muslims and thinks this question has been at its heart.[21] Soroush takes a multidisciplinary approach toward Islam and its place in the public square. While the other prominent leaders of the Islamic movement were each concentrating on one area, Soroush draws upon all human disciplines. For example, among prominent Muslim revivalists, Mehdi Bazargan (1908–1995) was a man of science, Ali Shari'ati (1933–1977) was a social scientist, and Murtaza Mutahari (d. 1979) was a man of philosophy. Soroush believes that a multidisciplinary approach makes it possible for Islamists and Muslims to live within the parameters of pluralism, because "the story of secularism amounts to the venture of non-religious reason; although not religious in character, it is not anti-religion."[22] In his mind, in a world where secularism is dominant, all emphasis is on rights, scientific management, rationalism, human progress, and worldly gain. Such a world begins with the introduction of ideas about the nature of things, and the discussion has shifted from concentration on God to nature and, obviously, to natural rights.[23] It is possible for a religious mind to live with, and even in, such a world, because none of these features contradict revelation.

Soroush is quick, however, to point out that combining secularism with liberalism would create a problem. "Any religious society that is bound by a creed, logically, cannot compromise with principles or derivatives of liberalism. The answer to any question in a liberal context is derived from examination and experiment, whereas for a religious society the answer to many questions is known ahead of time."[24] He has set out to explain how Muslims could accommodate secularism.

Soroush suggests combining three broad solutions. One is his controversial theory of "contraction and expansion of religious knowledge." He proposes the study of modern sciences, both the natural and the social sciences, for ascertaining the principles of religion, instead of the traditional studies such as the science of geneology (*'Elm al-Rejal*). Here is how he summarized his main purpose to the author in 1991 during the time his theory of "the Theoretical Contraction and Expansion of the Creed (Shari'at)" was just affecting, and subsequently shaping, the debate among Islam-minded intellectuals in Iran:

> In one way or another, the revivalists before me wanted to reconcile tradition with change.... I argue that in order to solve the problem of the relation between tradition and change, we should separate religion from the understanding of religion. The first is unchanging, but the second changes. In fact, we should try to establish constant exchange and interaction between the second and other branches of human knowledge and understanding such as sociology, anthropology, philosophy, history, and so on.[25]

On the surface, the idea is simple, but it has far-reaching implications. Two are worth mentioning. First and foremost, it allows for plurality. If one's knowledge of religion is temporal, one's understanding is as valid as any other. Thus, a plurality of interpretations would be inevitable, which in turn would open the door for democratization and political plurality. Second, no particular group could or should claim special authority, thus threatening the clerical rule that is dominant in Iran today.

The idea of the distinction between the changing and unchanging dimensions of religion is not new among Muslims, however. The Egyptian reformer and thinker Muhammad Abduh (d. 1905) had introduced this idea before. What distinguishes Soroush's ideas is that he has abandoned the defensive or apologetic attitudes that were dominant before, and has instead adopted a proactive posture in rethinking both Islam and modernity. He is critical of, and imaginative toward, both. He invites a complete revision of his fellow Muslims' understanding of secularity and Islam. Neither Islam nor secularity is holistic and a kind of totality that should not or could not be rethought or renovated. Any representation of either Islam or the modern world is simply a narration on the part of the person who expresses it. This is very postmodern indeed.

The second idea is Soroush's understanding of the nature of religion. In the past few decades, a powerful trend has been debated among Muslims that Islam is an ideology, and a totalitarian one at that. He is challenging this narrative by claiming that religion is far greater than any ideological system. He compares religion to an ocean, and ideology to a particular pool. Religions are mysterious symbols of truth, are not applicable to a particular historical epoch, contain inner meanings, and serve as criteria. In short, "religions are not manifestos, practical guides, plans for social engineering, and particular diet regimes, but rather are like waters that flow through rivers and waterways, but are not limited to them."[26] Religions can be turned to ideologies but at their own perils. An ideological religion may help you win a battle, but surely will make you lose the war. Humanity will prosper with the sense of awe that religion can give, but not with the sense of struggle that ideology provides.[27]

The third idea Soroush advances is the notion of selection as a strategy for construction of a renovated religious thought and society for Muslims today. Muslims should be daring to choose from their own tradition as well as from those of others. In what he calls a selective approach he suggests that one should select the truth wherever it is found, in the West, among Muslims, or in any other traditions. For Soroush "to select the truth requires insight and daring and it represents the noblest form of love toward the noblest lover."[28] This requires a critical mind that avoids any kind of generality, be it positive or negative, about any particular tradition.

In fact, he entered into a heated debate with a powerful conservative trend in Iran about the meaning of the West. Its proponents asserted that the evil essence of the West has threatened the sacred world of Muslims, whereas Soroush talked about complexities in the West as well as complexities among Muslims. Even if one could make any generalization about the West or Muslims, they are incidentals in history. Both regions are composed of a collection of discord and collaboration; interactions between political actors, religious groupings, scholars and professionals; and so on.[29]

Soroush's depiction of the complex world of Muslims and the distinction he makes between the essentials of religion and its accidental aspects run contrary to the views of those who consider a Muslim society as an undifferentiated mass of blind followers of the Islamic creed. On the other hand, his treatment of the West is similar for the modern, and now globalized, world. His careful reading of the evolution of modern sciences in the West is a serious attempt at depicting the complex world that people usually express with the overworked notion of the West. For him, the latter represents dynamism, secularity, and progress, but this does not mean one should prostrate before it, but rather one should exercise the "arts of analyzing it and learning from it."[30] The combination of the three ideas – contraction and expansion of religious creed, religion as mystery and not ideology, and finally the notion of selection – would enable Muslims to live within a secular framework. But while Soroush deals with generalities, our third thinker, Saeed Hajjarian, has been more specific in examining the relation between Islam and republicanism.

Saeed Hajjarian

Hajjarian is an influential Muslim revolutionary in Iran who worked for the ministry of intelligence and was deputy head of the Strategic Research Center of the President's Office. Hajjarian is also an adviser to President Muhammad Khatami. He began his studies by training in engineering but changed direction, both professionally and intellectually, finishing a Ph.D. in political science from Tehran University. He became a political activist and later a member of the intelligentsia in revolutionary Iran. He established a newspaper, *Sobheh Emrouz* (Today's Sun), in 1998. He survived an assassination attempt in 2002, when he was a member of the city council of Tehran, but was left half paralyzed. He continues to write and publish.

His main concern became the process by which a religiously inspired polity could deal with republicanism. Like the other two, he thinks that interaction between tradition and modernity, now globalization, constitutes the gravest challenge for Muslims the world over. And the polity that can best deal with such a challenge is an "Islamic Republic," provided the relation between the tenets of Islam and the principles of republicanism is worked out and a new jurisprudence that is a "jurisprudence of the commonwealth" (*fiqh al-masleha*) is formulated and implemented.[31] The way he describes his mission is as follows: "In our country a revolution occurred in the name of religion and even formed a polity. What it amounted to was the fact that the sacred came to the public domain in an age of secularism in the form of a revolution and a state. Naturally, the success and failure of a religious state and more so the fate of the sacred has become the main concern of a Muslim [like me]."[32] How should one deal with this dilemma?

According to Hajjarian, history tells us that there have been two ways of responding to this challenge. One is the path of constitutionalism and the other is that of republicanism. The first was born with the Magna Carta in England where the aristocracy resisted the absolute power of the king and demanded "participation in decision making" in accordance with "the taxes they were paying." Based on the new charter, many aspects of the "monarch's authority was delegated to the parliament."[33] The second path was born in the *Declaration of the Rights of Man and Citizens* inaugurated by the French Revolution of 1789. That revolution ushered in the age of "representation" and "citizenship" where human beings "have rights, the most significant one being that of sovereignty."[34] Originally, when Iran faced the challenge of modernity, people at the beginning of the twentieth century responded with constitutionalism. "The dominant discourse in the mind of Iranian intellectuals even until the Islamic Revolution [1979] was that of constitutionalism," but that discourse proved unsuccessful. "The very revolution itself," Hajjarian contends, "indicates that the crisis of legitimacy could not be resolved with conditioning the absolute power of the ruler with a constitution."[35] In his view, republicanism presents the most efficient solution. Not only does it solve the practical problems Iran is facing today, but also it guarantees the Islamic dimension of the polity in Iran. The following passage is very telling. "If one accepts that Islam is a religion of justice, and if one further accepts that justice means paying everyone their due, then if a mature and rightful nation is not allowed to determine its fate in a legal way, such a polity is not Islamic. In other words, if the Iranian regime after the revolution is not a Republic (that is, people do not determine their own fate), then it cannot be Islamic either."[36]

The logic behind Hajjarian's argument could be summarized as follows. He identifies three trends in the contemporary intellectual history of Iran. The first powerful trend holds that "tradition resembles a crumbling wall that should be destroyed completely, before it falls on the society. Criticizing or rethinking a tradition does not suffice. One has to eliminate it with 'a grenade of submission to the civilization of the Franks.' [For the intelligentsia of the time] there was no other way but to establish the new civilization on the ruins of tradition."[37] This trend was born in the aftermath of the wars between Iran and Russia from 1813 to 1828, and it became the dominant view until the first half of the twentieth century.

The second trend was born in the post-WWII period. In this era, the West lost its legitimacy for many intellectuals and instead the imperial and colonial dimension of modernism became a significant issue. The new trend emphasized "resurgence of tradition," which included replacing the notion of "the deconstruction of tradition" with "re-enchantment" of it and the notion of "return to the self." The ideas of dependency theory and authenticity gave more substance to some of the arguments.

Then came the third trend, which emerged after the Iran-Iraq War (1980–1988). Its proponents advocate "reconstruction of tradition." In Hajjarian's words, "the main concern of this discourse emphasizes presentation of a new narration of the old tradition in such a way that it would be useful for our present condition without hiding its utilitarian reading of [the local] tradition."[38] Hajjarian sees himself as a member of the groups of Muslims who advance this idea. The method he proposes is "reconstruction of tradition" that he defines as a method for reaching a synthesis between "deconstruction and resurgence" of tradition. "It is possible," he writes, "to utilize the dynamic aspects of tradition in order to erect a new civilization process."[39] He makes the individual intellectual responsible for understanding the two worlds of tradition and modernity through a process of re-thinking. Hajjarian utilizes the four mystical journeys that the seventeenth-century Iranian philosopher Mulla Sadra (d. 1642) had instituted and proposes a similar process for the new intellectuals in Iran.

In Sadra's philosophy an individual seeker of the truth has to seek the truth, but through a four-stage journey. The first stage is to elevate oneself from the masses to the truth (God). The second is to immerse oneself in the truth and comprehend the various dimensions of it. The third stage of the journey is a journey of return from the truth to the masses. And the final journey refers to immersing in the masses but armed with the truth. The journey is completed in the final stage and the seeker has completed his task by acting as a contributing member of humanity.

Hajjarian replaces the masses with tradition and the truth with modernity. As he writes, any given contemporary Iranian intellectual "has to prepare for four paths: journey from Tradition to Modernity; journey within Modernity; journey from Modernity to Tradition, and finally journey within Modernity with Tradition." This process can never happen unless instigated and stemmed from within. There is always internal dynamics and interaction, but there is a strong role for the tradition. There appears to be a break from the past, but in a reality there is a new form of continuity. "The agent-actors who are mature and responsible utilize outside sources without falling either into dependency or backwardness and thus, will capture the treasure of development."[40] Contemporary demands of public life have changed Iranians, and the mature population of Iran requires sophisticated and mature institutions, thereby completing the revolt of the masses in Iran.[41] The reform movement of the mid-1990s has become the voice of this revolt, and it was Hajjarian's thinking that shaped the strategy for reform in President Khatami's government.

*****

The dynamics of the debate in Iran, revealed in the samples provided here, indicate how the local is becoming global and the global becoming local as the terms of debate transfer from reactive, apologetic, modernist, and defensive into sober rethinking, renovation, deconstruction, reconstruction, indigenous tradition, and globalization. Hyper-globalizers and hyper-traditionalists have no use for such slow, gradual, inclusive, and accommodating but non-efficient ways. But in the long run, it is this method that holds enormous promise. To manage change without sacrificing valuable aspects of tradition, and to guard the tradition without losing opportunities for innovation or change, constitute the paradoxical path of displaying sensitivity toward both tradition and modernity, the particular and universal, and the local and global. The irony is that launching such an ambitious project in the short run would deepen modernism and traditionalism – the excessive forms of modernity and tradition. This is exactly what is happening in Iran at this moment. The society appears to have never been so entrapped into traditionalism, superstitions, localism, and parochial ways, and yet it is enveloped in hedonism, extreme individualism, fetishism of market, and Hollywoodism. At the same time, these extreme conditions have given rise to serious questions; thus it seems that there has never been so much serious soul-searching and questioning of hitherto considered sacred and obvious facts. The globalization process has facilitated and sharpened the process enormously. In the long run, Iran may provide a successful case of the empowerment of a marginal Third World region to become an active player in the globalized world, while enhancing the cultural particularity of its local tradition.

12

Globalization: The Search for a Christian Standpoint

Fernando Franco S.J.

Why have you thrown this challenge, god?
Solve this riddle of mine;
Enter my shoes, know in your own self:
An outcaste, what rights do I enjoy?
Says Chokha, this low born human body
Every one drives away[1]

Introduction

Grounded in an Indian context, this chapter grapples with a hermeneutic conundrum: how to find a Christian standpoint from whence to offer a Christian critique of globalization. I share with many others the fearful concern that our seminars on globalization tend to end in a draw: there are positives and negatives, the phenomenon is too complex, and hence no conclusive stance can be taken. In the context of globalization, I am also reminded of the biblical warning that obduracy may obscure our vision; that we may listen without understanding and look without seeing (Mt 13:10-17). I believe that this blindness is not the subject matter of theology alone but has, in addition, a certain social relevance in our time. I dare say that the biblical insistence on the need to scrutinize the signs of the times is a way of acknowledging that the failure to see has something to do with our self-interest.

The main argument developed in this chapter may be stated as follows. The hermeneutical method to yield a Christian standpoint needs to be located among those who have been variously described as the wretched of the earth, the subalterns, the victims of history, the poor people, and the multitude (*ochlos*) of the Synoptic gospels. In the aggrieved voice of the dalit poet-saint Chokhamela addressing his god (quoted in the epigraph at the beginning), we can find the way only if we understand his plight – the plight of the victim. To achieve that understanding we have to enter his shoes and know his pain in ourselves. I hope to show that, from this perspective, the potential promised by globalization looks unreal, while the temporary setbacks, as the defenders of globalization call them, have been devastating.

A term used frequently in this chapter is subaltern. I use the expression synonymously with a constellation of terms like poor and victim. The term subaltern has by now had a long pedigree in Indian sociology.[2] It was coined to describe the non-official, non-elite actors in the making of colonial history. Subaltern communities mean social groups that played a part in the history of daily life and survival in India, but who were never written about and never spoken of in official and known historical accounts. I use, therefore, subaltern and victim to refer to an unofficial, unacknowledged, and often illegal and unwanted mass of human beings who exist at the margins of society and who, like Jesus, die a seemingly dishonourable death.

Certain experiences have gently nudged me in this direction. One in particular that has accompanied me for many years and nurtured my commitment to the dalit struggle is the awareness of a difference that emerged in the course of exchanges with colleagues and peers in India. Whenever I sat with non-dalits to discuss issues such as poverty, rural development, or even the possibility of a revolution from below, the atmosphere of the debate was always distended and free. The mood subtly changed when one brought to the table issues like caste and gender. Talk about dalit oppression would invite a cold stare from a Marxist. Well-intentioned academics would quickly, too quickly for my taste, point out that the processes of sanskritization – that is, adopting upper-caste behavioural patterns – and westernization were actually driving away the spectre of caste. In some training sessions with reputable NGOs I had to repeatedly face the participants' resentment whenever I proposed a discussion on caste discrimination. This heightened sensitivity to the discussion of caste issues contrasts with their indifference towards the richness of dalit and adivasi culture. This unrecorded mass of people is often kept in the backyard, away from the public gaze, in an attempt to preserve the honour of family and country. I maintain that this attitude is not only a manifestation of gross insensitivity, but a bludgeoning of historical truth.[3]

The first three sections of the chapter lay the foundation for my understanding of the victim as the privileged standpoint from whence to look critically at globalization. Section 4 describes a few traits of globalization in a developing country like India, and section 5 attempts to look at the same phenomenon from the perspective of the dalits. The chapter closes with a few suggestions along which Catholic Social Thought (CST) may be developed from the perspective of the Crucified.

The Metaphor of *Lagaan*

The unwillingness, mentioned above, of mainstream forces to highlight the importance of the subaltern calls for a metaphor that unlocks its ability to speak and deal with history on its own terms. The importance given in recent years to the analysis of metaphors and narratives as revealing the deeper social dreams of a community leads us to search for a meaningful metaphor of the subaltern. We can locate it in the success of the Indian movie *Lagaan,* which was nominated for an Academy Award in 2001.[4]

The story of the film is set around 1893 during British colonial domination in the region of Awad, a princely state in what is today central India. An arrogant Englishman, Captain Russell, living with a small military detachment in a town surrounded by villages, is responsible for the interests of the Crown. The local ruler (*Raja*), who doubles also as a *zamindar* (large landlord), has to pay taxes (*lagaan*) to the Crown to remain a landholder – a *taluqdar* in more technical terms. A repeated failure of the monsoon drives the villagers, a heterogeneous mass of peasants, to plead with the landlord-raja for a tax waiver, while he is watching a cricket match being played by the British officials. However, the local landlord acknowledges his helplessness, and the peasants are left with no option but to approach the British representative and make the same plea to him. Captain Russell has overheard the comment of Bhuvan, a youth accompanying the protesters, describing the game of cricket as silly and childish, and he intervenes with supreme arrogance. To the astonished villagers, the captain accedes to their request with one condition: let the villagers defeat the Englishmen at a game of cricket! If they fail, the village must pay double the amount of pending taxes in the whole province; if they win, the tax will be waived. The challenge is taken up by a group of villagers led by the handsome Bhuvan, and the process of building a cricket team out of an interreligious and inter-caste collection of peasants starts in earnest. The English sister of Captain Russell gives the rag-tag group its first lesson in the white-man's most typical game. A cricket team made up of a Muslim, an untouchable, a handicapped person, a Sikh ex-army man, and an assorted number of village peasants under the motivating leadership of a down-to-earth young farmer (Bhuvan) defeats the English team in a memorable match.

The popular success of this Bollywood[5] film attests to the widespread resonance of the metaphor in India. Interpretations[6] of the film have been varied, and in presenting my own here I keep in mind the particular point of view of this chapter. In the specific context of India's independence, the subalterns were neither pro-British (as, for example, the landlords and trading classes were) nor anti-British (as were those involved in the official nationalist movement represented by the Congress). The fact is that the subalterns suffered from both defenders and enemies of the British Raj. From my point of view, the subalterns are important because they represent the unheard voices, the unwritten grammar of those pronouncements lying at the margins of the dominant political discourse. In the film, the bunch of peasants led by Bhuvan follows a shrewd, though not very glorious, strategy. They do not organize an insurrection against Russell, attack the weak raja, or lynch the corrupt village merchant; instead they stand together. Among the members of the victorious cricket team are social and gender discrepancies visible to all, but it is clear that more important than old grudges and resentments is a territorial need to survive by building alliances through kinship ties. Alliances, even with an English woman, are welcome when survival is at stake. Surviving is what they have done for centuries and what they will continue to do.

The metaphor of defeating the English has a universal appeal in India. The fact that a group of subalterns learned to play an unfamiliar game and thrashed the English team is something new. It is undoubtedly a departure from old nationalistic odes that liberally apportioned the responsibility for generating national pride to a small high-caste, high-class, and generally male elite. For once, the subaltern is not only shown, but shown as heroic – a necessary reminder to us of their unstated claim to pass sentence on the ongoing historical process of globalization.

The Sign of Jonah as a Hermeneutical Standpoint

Let me return from the narrative of the victorious subaltern to the crucial importance of hermeneutics – of finding the right standpoint for viewing globalization. To approach this issue I want to delve deeper into the mystery of the subaltern that takes the specific form of a victim, and find a biblical echo in the Christian tradition of the Crucified.

Modern social anthropology has paid special attention to the ethnographic study of violence and suffering.[7] More specifically it has analyzed, on the one hand, the whole assemblage of human problems resulting from the exercise of political, economic, and institutional power over people. On the other hand, it has analyzed the human responses to these issues as they are influenced by the same forms of institutional power. The victims of social violence, according to modern social anthropology, embody at least two aspects of suffering: first its uselessness and absurdity and, second, its differentiated assessment when it is experienced by the victor and when it is suffered by the loser. The absurdity of inflicted pain is epitomized in the accumulated suffering of the victims of the Holocaust, the Bhopal gas tragedy, apartheid, and the adivasis displaced by the Narmada river project. The list of victims is endless. What has become more worrisome is, in the words of Veena Das, the untranslatability of pain and suffering.[8] The suffering of a victorious army or of a conquering superpower is the right price to be paid for the defence of freedom and democracy. The quantification of this victorious suffering seems to be necessary to buttress our faith in these fundamental values. In tragic contrast, the Iraqi children that died of malnutrition before the war and the degraded lives of the mass of internally displaced adivasis are, at best, sacrifices humanity must make for embracing the globalizing logic of the market.

In short, I am drawing attention, first, to the rise of social suffering in the world and, second, to the evoked distinction separating shamelessly these two forms of human suffering. This is the view of the victor as distinct from that of the victim, so that the pain of the one cannot be translated into the suffering of the other. Needless to say, from the standpoint of hermeneutics, the difference between these two types of pain is crucial: the suffering caused by the powerful to those considered as its own and on its side is always a transparent and meaningful sign. The suffering of the subaltern, on whom suffering is imposed, remains always dispensable, like an unrecognized and undecipherable sign.

In this context of suffering I want to look at the biblical tradition and, show, if possible, the relationship between the inability to see the sign and the scandal of the Crucified. Proximity to Jesus is not a sufficient condition to recognize him. The Pharisees watched him feeding four thousand ordinary peasants, and they witnessed his compassion for the crowd. But they still went on to ask him for a sign (Mt 15:32). Skilled as they were at reading natural signs, Jesus reproaches their inability and unwillingness to interpret the signs of the times, and adds, "An evil and adulterous generation asks for a sign, but no sign will be given to it except the sign of Jonah" (Mt 16:4).

I would like to state that the key signifier, the pivotal hermeneutic requirement to see and recognize Jesus, is related to the sign of Jonah – that is, to Jesus' death (and resurrection). It is only when one can recognize Jesus as the victim, as the crucified subaltern who is raised by God, that meaning and salvation become possible. We may conclude that blindness lies in the unwillingness to look at the Gospel message from the standpoint of the Cross – from the viewpoint of a servant executed between two robbers on the margins[9] of the holy city. In the terms of this chapter, the failure to look at globalization from the standpoint of the crucified, the subaltern,[10] or the victim may lead us to partial or total blindness. I claim that to discover the meaning of globalization from a Christian perspective, we need to position ourselves near his death as a subaltern – with the subalterns among whom and with whom he died. We need to enter into the victim's pain, as Chokhamela reminds us.

To summarize: this particular hermeneutic first takes cognizance of the Crucified as a symbol of this large mass of unrecognized and seemingly useless suffering; second, it chooses to highlight the role of the subaltern and the victim as the locus of historical meaning. I am aware of the link with a tradition that has seen the suffering of the Crucified in highly expiatory terms or which has looked at suffering as a disciplining practice. This is not the standpoint of this chapter. The hermeneutic value of the victim is rooted in its power to unlock the full meaning of history: as a hermeneutic not of passivity but of active redemption and as the code that unveils the dominating practices of the modern state.

Having set up the broad characteristics of the hermeneutical standpoint posited in this chapter, let me turn to the issue of globalization. I attempt to look at this process from below in two different ways; that is, from the perspective of a so-called developing country like India, and from the standpoint of one subaltern Indian group – the dalits.

Characterizing the Process of Globalization in India

In my attempt to shift the standpoint for evaluating globalization towards the subaltern, I start by presenting a view of globalization from an Indian perspective. At this point, a brief history of the period that preceded the advent of globalization in India may be useful. The attempt to describe 44 years (1947–1991) of India's political and economic history may appear audacious. The truth is, however, that after 1991, the debates about the comparative advantages of pre- and post-liberalization policies have been so prolific as to greatly facilitate the work of producing a thumbnail sketch of the period.

In an illuminating essay, Deepak Nayyar[11] characterizes the political economy of India in terms of the contradictions emerging between the promise of political equity (one person, one vote) and the frustrations of those excluded by economic inequality. One may say that until 1966 the economic promise of equality, even though it never matched the political offer, was at least kept alive: efforts were made to accommodate interests and to initiate profound reforms. These years, filled with Nehru's vision of modern India, witnessed a political consensus achieved at two levels.[12] At one level, the process of industrialization was equated with the principle of development for all. At the political level, the Congress party, a composite of contradictory interests, served as a sort of political laboratory where political deals were struck before the conflict could spill over to the open battlefield of society. The problem was that the "accommodation of the poor, who were the ruled...was long on words and short of substance."[13]

From 1966 to the middle of the 1980s, tensions in the process of accommodation reached a number of critical points. From the economic side, we may note the metamorphosis of the middle castes into powerful regional landowning classes, the bottlenecks in the industrialization process, and the failure of the developmental agenda to provide basic minimums in food, health, and education. These factors generated a widespread discontent among dalits, tribals, and backward castes. At the political level, the Congress started going into a slow decline and this was accompanied by its increasing inability to broker a political consensus of opposing interests.

Not by chance, the landscape began to change dramatically around the mid-1980s. By this time, the contradictions between economic and political equality had become unbearable. The example of sustained economic growth in China and East Asia convinced domestic capitalists of the need to throw off the fetters imposed by the politics of accommodation. From 1985 onwards, Rajiv Gandhi initiated a number of liberal, but ill-conceived, economic policies that led to the accumulation of unsustainable levels of foreign debt and to the financial crisis of 1991. Promises of political equality, however, percolated through all social layers and brought to the political scene a number of popular groups of backward castes,[14] dalits, and adivasis. The reverse side of this popular politics was the re-emergence of the Bharatiya Janta Party that embodied the interests of a high-caste professional class in its discourse of hardcore nationalism.

Let me pick up again the thread of my argument. I have chosen to characterize the post-1991 period of Indian globalization by a set of seemingly unrelated traits that may, I hope, serve to describe its subaltern flavour.

Globalization, firstly, will always be remembered, not as a blissful transition to a higher stage in the life of humanity, but as a time of traumatic political and economic change. The old economic and political framework lay broken, its remnants scattered to the winds. The reasons for this complete *bouleversement* are not difficult to fathom. Economic liberalization embodied in the New Economic Policy (NEP) had began to run its course on the waters of a strong cultural nationalism.

From an economic point of view, the NEP initiated the dismantling of the licence raj – the complex bureaucratic system of controls and privileges that had dominated all spheres of Indian economic life since independence. The failure of the state to develop the economy was exaggerated for obvious reasons. In the public eye, this process of liberalization was characterized by opening the economy to foreign capital and by opening the state sector to private entrepreneurs. As indicated earlier, the NEP also wrought the demise of the Nehruvian approach to economics and politics. Under the Congress governments at the centre, the state had been made the guarantor of development and of social well-being. This function of the state began to disappear slowly as some primary services started to be handed over to private entrepreneurs. From a political point of view, the sense that a profound and irreversible change had taken place was due not only to the death of Nehruvian humanism, but to the substitution of a layered and, to some extent, ordered Indian identity by a set of fragments "suspicious and resentful of each other, unwilling or unable to speak the other's language."[15]

The second trait characterizing this new era of globalization is the realization that the process of modernity, as proclaimed by the defenders of neo-liberalism, has not been univocal and linear. Fault lines have appeared all over its course. The Nehruvian concept of modernity and progress worked on the assumption, shared by many intellectuals, that the development of a secular state and of a modern economy – both based on a scientific temper – would do away with caste and religious obscurantism. Precisely the opposite seems to have happened, deeply upsetting the dreams of a generation of liberals, secularists, and activists. Let me comment more specifically on the failure of these two prophecies about the doom of caste and religion.

Take the case of caste. Gandhi assumed that a return to the idyllic conditions of the village, moral pressure, and example would destroy caste. For his part, Nehru believed that unleashing the process of industrialization in India would dissolve the old social ties and substitute class relations.[16] Caste identities, rather than disappearing, have become more important in the attempt by disadvantaged groups to gain the economic and political benefits available to them through the policy of positive discrimination. The process of strengthening caste identities operates at the level of those whose identities are in question, and at the level of those who promote them. As regards the first group of dalits and backward castes, they have learned to define their political strategies along caste lines. The second group, comprising politicians of various hues, have perfected the skill of securing vote banks along caste lines.[17]

Take next the case of religion. Rather than disappearing, religion has proved to be the source of much pain and turmoil. The destruction of the mosque in Ayodhya, the carnage of Godhra, and the subsequent killing of Muslims in Gujarat have all been perpetrated in the name of cultural nationalism. This holds a version of Hinduism (Hindutva) as the trump-card to forge a political unity among the contradictory interests of Hindu society. This strategy is not very different from the principle of accommodative politics followed by the Congress party in the early years after independence. The intensity and the pervasiveness of the violence against Muslims seems to subvert the conclusions of some scholars who had attributed differences in Hindu-Muslim violence to the existence of some "institutionalized peace systems."[18] I am not the only one to detect in this and similar positions a certain naïveté and a disturbing, blind refusal to name the agents of this violence.[19] It is difficult to imagine that this practice of silencing concrete and culpable agency is emerging from the standpoint of the victim.

Let me sum up the argument of this section. The first impression is that globalization in India has been quite messy. Under the Indian brand-name of liberalization, it has produced two remarkable effects: the consolidation of the powerful and the fragmentation of the weak. The combination of Hindutva and liberalizing economic policies has consolidated and legitimized the aspirations of upper (and middle) class and caste interests. The same process has resulted in the impoverishment of a large mass of people and its fragmentation along religious, caste, and ethnic lines. Let me complete now the double shift in perspective I mentioned earlier, and look at globalization in India from the perspective of a subaltern group, the dalits.

Interpreting Globalization from Below

How does a subaltern group like the dalits look at this messy process of globalization in India? While striving to answer this question, I hope to show that, viewed from the perspective of the dalits, the policies of the state and of its supporting elite – committed to the process of globalization – appear as a final desperate attempt to weaken, dismember, and discard the subaltern. An interpretation of globalization in India from the perspective of the subaltern is likely to gravitate around two negative visions of the state. The first is a passive state that retreats from its obligations, leaving the social field to a rapacious set of private entrepreneurs; the second is an active state that advances and asserts its political power to crush the subaltern identity in imperial fashion. For more detailed analysis, I take up two examples of this latter attitude of the state: the insistence on keeping caste away from the public discourse and its relentless attack on conversion.

Neo-liberalism has brought in its wake a considerable retreat by the state from its social obligations. This has affected dalits, tribals, and other backward castes in at least two reinforcing ways. First, as the size of the public sector diminishes, the number of jobs under the purview of positive discrimination falls. Second, as health, education, and sanitary services – including water distribution – are privatized, the access of subalterns to these services becomes more and more limited. Their anger and frustration when they compare the rising living standards of the affluent with their daily struggle to secure employment in a much-segmented market, and reasonable education and health services, are mounting steadily.[20] Even those subalterns who have made it to the middle class feel that the future of their children is in jeopardy.

Neo-liberalism has also been accompanied by the advance of the state to crush the subaltern identity. I select for special analysis two phenomena: the willingness to erase caste from the public and political domains, and the insistent condemnation of the act of conversion. In a lucid article, Pandian[21] has emphasized the way in which upper castes silenced the discourse of caste during colonial times – a practice they continue even now. Pandian notes that while writing an autobiography, an upper caste person talks of caste by other means, whereas dalits, having to contend daily with the word and the reality of caste, talk about it in its own terms. He also remarks that Brahmin custom gets encoded as Indian tradition, and this definition of Indian culture is always exclusive of the subaltern.

Of far-reaching significance is Pandian's partial critique of Partha Chatterji's famous distinction between the material and spiritual realms marked off by anti-colonial nationalism.[22] He agrees that by marking off the cultural and spiritual areas from the material dimension, nationalism succeeded in exercising agency in the cultural domain vis-à-vis the colonial domination of the material realm. But Pandian goes further to suggest that under a similar scheme of things, nationalism failed to enter, understand, break, and dominate the spiritual and cultural universe of the subaltern. Putting it differently: by setting brahminical culture in opposition to the culture of the colonizers, nationalism necessarily implied the downsizing or de-recognition of dalit and subaltern cultures. It is to this phenomenon of an apparent erasure, a complicit silence, that I referred at the beginning of this paper. This is important, not only from the point of view of justice, but also from a hermeneutic point of view. It is a telling example of looking and not seeing, hearing and not listening.

There is a need, however, to move from silence to subtler forms of identity obliteration. The insistence by the nationalist discourse that the entire issue of caste was to be located within the sphere of the cultural, meant that it could not be brought into the public sphere of political life. The victory of Gandhi over Ambedkar and the Pune Pact follow the same script: the caste discourse of Ambedkar not only had to be entirely subordinated to Gandhi's higher nationalistic goal, but Ambedkar could not represent all Indians at the London Round-Table conference. The physical separation imposed by caste rules was equated, as Pandian remarks, with hygienic principles. Talking about caste in public, therefore, becomes, unhygienic, non-modern, and unbecoming of a person who prides herself on having stepped over to the side of modernity.

Pandian further argues that M.N. Srinivas' analysis of modernity and caste with the help of the processes of sanskritization and westernization repeats the pre-independence nationalist obsession of not only keeping caste outside the pale of modernity, but assuming deep down brahminic superiority. Sanskritization is the only channel open for lower castes if they want to move towards modernity. It is like saying that aping the whites is the road followed by blacks in this modernity. Westernization, we may remind ourselves, is a vehicle that only upper castes have taken to modernize themselves. In Srinivas' list of eminent Indians who have moved along the westernization path, the names of Babasaheb Ambedkar and Periyar E.V. Ramasamy Naicker are conspicuous by their absence.

In the face of this consistent strategy to obliterate dalit identity while retaining its discriminatory elements, I feel uneasy with the plea of Ramachandra Guha[23] for intellectual equilibrium. He positions himself within the liberal Indian tradition – that is, in the middle of the road between the extreme right of Hindutva and the extreme left, which is further subdivided into the old Marxist left and the new left anchored in the axis of caste. Then he bemoans the excessive ideological weight of the two extreme positions and the flight of old liberals to both sides of the spectrum. Although Guha's call to moderation, scientific balance, and middle-of-the-road commonsense is persuasive and enticing, I am left with the eerie feeling that it might, in the end, be one more attempt to drive caste identities from the public discourse.

So far, I have insisted on describing certain indirect ways of pushing caste out of public sight. The state, both colonial and nationalist, has from time to time played a role in crushing subaltern identities. As an example, I would like to recall briefly the story of a bahujan (literally majority) community:[24] the sweepers of New Delhi. In a meticulously researched book, Vijay Prashad[25] unveils the community's painful pilgrimage from being marginal farmers and agricultural labourers in Punjab to becoming sweepers by caste in Delhi; from worshiping dalit and bahujan deities to becoming Hindu devotees of Valmiki; and from being proud defenders of their own leadership to accepting non-dalit patronage. The colonial system helped them to fit into the bottom of a rigid and inhuman caste system. But to ensure the efficient disposal of human waste in Delhi, the clash between Ambedkar and Gandhi convinced militant Hindus and Gandhian organizations to anchor this community within an acceptable Hindu fold. By installing the figure of Valmiki as the guru (if not the god) of their community, they destroyed the old elements of Muslim culture (burial, songs, and names). And they made a conscious effort to attribute their low social status to the fact that they had become the slaves of Muslim rulers. As the author ironically remarks, the followers of Gandhi concentrated their efforts to uplift the community by changing the shape of the broom or re-designing more efficient toilets. Gandhi´s notion of *varnashram* (caste system) would not tolerate the possibility that they could be trained for other jobs.

Let me end this section by touching on the highly controversial theme of conversion. Attacks against past conversions have come from many different quarters. For some the act of conversion is tantamount to cultural invasion and genocide. For others it is a fraudulent way of increasing institutional power. My interest at this moment is not theological but sociological and ultimately hermeneutical. As I have argued elsewhere, conversion is a complex process that must be "viewed in the light of two sets of dichotomies: spiritual-material on the one hand, and individual-social on the other."[26] Conversion, and more concretely the movement of dalit groups to Christianity, cannot be analyzed from a purely material and individual standpoint.[27]

My opposition to those blank condemnations of conversion stems, however, from the fact that conversion is evaluated and judged without asking those converted for their opinion. It is as if the converted subaltern has neither the right nor the human maturity to decide for herself. During the last ten years, a strong body of opinion has come from Christian subaltern circles that has fiercely contested the position of Hindutva and other progressive Christian theologians. I am not proposing here a naïve defence of conversion, much less on purely theological grounds. I am aware of proselytizing practices that commit the same sin of disregarding the dignity of the poor. Notwithstanding these corrections, I do feel that the time has come to proclaim loudly the right of subaltern individuals and groups to look for dignity. I find inspiration and courage in the response written by Rudi Heredia to another stigmatizer of past conversions.

> Perhaps it is time now for the converted to speak from the point of view of their own civil rights and the freedoms that they can legitimately claim, not just freedom from religious oppression, but also from hunger and disease, from violence and pogroms, but also freedom for fellowship and fraternity, for development and pursuit of happiness.[28]

CST from the Standpoint of the Victim

In attempting to suggest new avenues for CST to deal with the process of globalization, I start by proposing a repositioning of CST along the lines of the argument developed so far. As a community witnessing to the Crucified Lord, the Church must stand on the side of the victim and her suffering. From this position, one may expect that the increasing mass of human suffering due to political, social, and economic reasons would be denounced more forcefully. It also follows that new issues need to be part of the CST, and, finally, that a greater openness must be shown by the Church to the possibility of collaborating with forces that are in the process of creating an alternative paradigm. Let me develop some of these points in more detail.

The Church must go beyond showing a vague "global vision of attention...to the poorest and the weakest,"[29] and position herself clearly and unambiguously on their side. This will result in a consistent and forceful denunciation of the concrete and identifiable forces that stand, for example, in the way of achieving food security for all, of attaining the Millennium Development Goals, and of substituting higher levels of social security outlays for large chunks of defence expenditure.

In the past, CST has successfully defended the dignity of labour and vigorously denounced the attempts to curtail its freedom of association. Notwithstanding the importance this position had in defending the victims of the industrial revolution, it appears totally powerless to offer a critique and an alternative to globalization. Of greater importance, however, is the need to shift the focus of CST from the family to modern nation-states, international economic organisms (such as the World Trade Organization) operating outside the control of the UN, and multinational corporations. The time has come for CST to deal with the issue of unequal distribution and uncontrolled use of power (economic, military, and political) in the world. We need to evolve an ethical understanding of power that includes outlining the mechanism to effectively control its abuse at the international level. The Church must unambiguously state what the Christian principles of good governance are today. The hidden, faceless, and unaccountable power of states, corporations, security apparatuses, and the military business has produced innumerable victims, and that has marked these bodies with the signs of suffering.

I am particularly concerned that the efforts by the present UN Secretary General, Kofi A. Annan, to call a conference for democratizing the UN and endowing it with executive powers may ultimately be thwarted. The same political structure working against these efforts has systematically avoided international treaties and has not yet recognized the powers of an international court. Vague calls to an internationally ordered solidarity are not enough at this moment. What the victims expect is a serious pronouncement on the absolute need to have an independent international institution capable, on the one hand, of restraining any abuse of power and, on the other, of imposing sanctions on those nation-states that are not fulfilling their promises of financial and technical help.

The laudable CST emphasis on the dignity of the person must be complemented by a resolute defence of the dignity of collectivities and states. I am referring, for example, to the manner in which poorer, smaller, and less developed nation-states are silenced, manipulated at many international forums, and finally dumped into the dustbin of history.

CST and the Church may finally have the historical role of decisively promoting the diversity of the fragments and dissolving their differences. The greatest tragedy brought about by this process of globalization is the fragmentation of the victims. I may conclude that, from the side of the victim, globalization stands culpable and condemned. It has increased the number and the intensity of the victims' suffering, and it has succeeded in finding subtler means to mask their faces and muffle their voices.

13

Notes on the Public Dimension of a Humanizing Globalization

Arturo Sosa S.J.

This chapter is an attempt to put in order some of the ideas that emerged from our reading and discussions during the International Seminar on "Present Crisis, Future Hope: Globalization and Catholic Social Teaching."[1] I do not pretend, in consequence, to provide a Latin-American vision of the globalization process. Latin America is noted for its cultural diversity and the variety of its social systems. As in the rest of the world, a huge range of views on globalization exists – some are complementary while others are contradictory and even incompatible. To offer a Latin American vision is, therefore, impossible – unless one takes the risk of simplifying such diverse situations and, thus, sacrificing their richness.

As a result, this chapter only aims to share the vision of a Latin American, trained in political science, committed by vocation to Catholic Social Thought (CST), who has lived in only one country of the continent – Venezuela – with its geographical, historical, and political peculiarities. The literary style of this chapter permits freedom to write from the author's own perspective – which includes elements from the academic world, from political discourse, and from the theological and spiritual dimensions that permeate my life. One of the best lessons that comes from contact with the Latin-American world of ordinary people and their experience of God is precisely the greatest richness to be found in the dialogue among human beings that comes from their own identity, with all the dimensions that shape it. In the same way, comments will be offered on Latin America as a whole in an attempt to profit as much as possible from its experience, with the limitations noted above. Additionally, I have the honest intention of provoking necessary discussion, both from the perspective of CST and of political science, for the future of Venezuela, the US, and the world.

This chapter will not discuss the concept of globalization, for which many and very rich elements can already be found in this collection. For the reflections shared here, it is necessary to underline the complex nature of the globalization process. Additionally, I will note the lack of synchrony with which it is experienced by each of the different societies and cultures making up the continent and, in addition, by the different components in each of these societies and cultures.

Globalization is a process that characterizes the present change of epoch in human history. To describe it as a process means globalization is not a finished product but a phenomenon that is still developing. As such, it is not only open to novelty and change; its very nature is to produce novelty and change as it develops. To recognize globalization as complex emphasizes that we cannot lose sight of the number and quality of aspects that shape human life, people, cultures, societies, institutions, and so forth that are caught up in so-called globalization. It also recognizes the impossibility of tackling globalization from only one perspective in an effort to describe and explain it.

From the viewpoint of this chapter, the tension between local and global is not a dilemma and does not oblige us to opt for one or the other. On the contrary, they are complementary as dimensions inherent in human life in any society formed by free individuals who shape history.

As the title suggests, the chapter concentrates on the public and political dimension of the complex globalization process and from a perspective associated with the faith that considers globalization to be one of the contributions to the humanization of history.[2] The public dimension stems from the social character of human nature; that is, the impossibility of considering a human being as a complete individual since that individual needs a relationship with other human beings to become fully a person.[3] The public dimension is, therefore, constituted by the complex network of relations that form to produce common life among human beings and in virtue of which the ends of society are decided. This is the space for citizenship – the place where that essential dimension of a complete human being that allows him to be called a citizen is developed. It is, therefore, closely linked to the exciting theme of the common good, one of the key themes in CST. Additionally, politics are constituted by social relations set up to define common objectives and specific ways of bringing them into reality. This is the area of conflict and the exercise of power.

To choose such an approach for this chapter presumes that a humanizing globalization is only possible if one takes into account, in all its importance, the public dimension of human life and its history. This is the opposite of strong currents of contemporary thought that call for the suppression of politics as a step forward.[4] From the perspective of this chapter, the human or humanizing efficacy of globalization is indissolubly linked with the recognition of the public arena and the importance of the political activity of human beings as citizens.

1. Lessons from the Failure of Modernization in Latin America

Throughout the twentieth century, all the Latin American elites tried to convert their countries into industrialized and modern states. Around the program of modernization were concentrated the hopes of peoples whose basic maintenance came from mining activities and pre-modern agriculture. The modernizing program in Latin America was understood as moving from backward peasant societies to societies developed according to the capitalist model. Even socialists and communists accepted such a step as necessary to advance towards a supposed revolution. In this way, during the first half of the twentieth century, there was wide agreement in Latin America about the sort of society that needed to be built. Political confrontation was seen as something between the forces representing backwardness and those advocating progress, though there were different and even contradictory ways of understanding progress.

Positivism, in its Latin American variants,[5] became the most widespread ideological inspiration among the modernizing elites of Latin America, giving way later on to socialist, communist, social democrat, and social Christian tendencies. Democracy as a form of government was part of the modern aspirations, though some of the modernizing theories justified dictatorial governments as necessary and temporary instruments to obtain the minimum conditions for beginning the modernization process.[6] The frequent presence of the military in Latin American governments, including governments of the armed forces, was explained by this need to ensure the order needed for progress to occur. To this it should be added that, in many countries, the armed forces were the first modern public institutions to be formed.

After a hundred years, the balance is deficient. Clear signs of modernization can be found in all Latin American countries and in all spheres of society, especially in material infrastructures, policies of economic development, and the formation of public institutions. In varying degrees, peasant culture has given way to a modern urban culture, even in zones distant from the cities, without hiding the persistence of very backward living conditions in vast rural zones and the peripheries of modern cities.

Poverty continues to be a characteristic of life for most of the population of Latin America. Modernization has increased scandalously the gap between rich and poor, with little success in forming a numerous or consistent middle class. The existence of unjust social structures is the best indicator of the deficiencies in the modernization process promoted by the Latin American elites. To the ongoing ancient forms of violence, one has to add the appearance of new forms characteristic of modernity and postmodernity. After a hundred years, the experience of Latin American people is of a modernization that has failed.

At the same time, it must be said that Latin American people are full of life. In the midst of unjust structures, an immense social gap, inhuman conditions of poverty, and constant threats by different forms of violence, they live life to the full. And they live life to the full because the people of Latin America love life. This love of life in all its forms becomes the great motivating strength in a never-ending search for many and creative ways of producing life and being able to live it fully.

The love of life, characteristic of Latin American people, is closely linked to their experience of God. Both the greater part of pre-Hispanic religions and the Catholic religion spread by the missionaries who accompanied the Spanish and Portuguese conquests have been vehicles for an experience of God as creator of Life and bringer of strength to those who wish to live and communicate life. Tuning into the faith of the people makes it easier to understand the apparent contradictions for someone who ignores this dimension of the cultures and lives of Latin American people.

On the basis of this experience, I venture to suggest five great lessons from the modernization process lived by Latin America during the twentieth century.

- The model of modern society, characteristic of the developed West, is not always successful. In other words, what has been proposed as a model for modern development is not equally successful for all peoples and all nations. Latin American experience contradicts what is presented as a consensus in development theories both in the academic world and in international institutions, public and private, which promote development. These theories attribute the failure of modern development to deficiencies of peoples or governments incapable of applying them systematically. Normally, the model itself is neither examined nor questioned. On the contrary, there is an insistence on applying it, with small variations, again and again, and successive failures do not lead to questions about its practical or theoretical validity.

  From a Latin American perspective, we can affirm the need to formulate alternative models of human development that really lead to a substantial improvement in the quality of life for the huge majorities of people who have been excluded from the known development processes up until now. The experience of creating and reproducing life in the middle of the failure of these models shows that human history has neither ended nor closed; on the contrary, it is open to new methods of life, products of the characteristic freedom and creativity of persons and peoples.

- The majority of Latin American societies are experiencing the characteristics of postmodernity without having arrived at being completely modern. Rather, they know only too well the reverse, or dark, side of modernity – that is the enormous gaps of social inequality, endemic poverty, political instability, and violence. One of the characteristics of the globalized world is the simultaneous presence of processes with different characteristics in the same society. In the countries of Latin America there live together, with no solution for continuity, indigenous communities with a pre-Columbian life-style, traditional peasants, inhabitants of suburban zones, and industrial workers. To this mix can be added universities capable of competing with those of the developed world, transnational financial organizations, firms and public institutions with the latest technologies, and so forth. This lack of synchronism has been a characteristic of the modernization process for more than a century. And added to it now are the signs of a postmodernity, which are critical of a modernity that hasn't yet been sufficiently experienced.

Paradoxically the failure of modernization in Latin America allows the establishment of a positive link between the so-called postmodern epoch and pre-modern cultural roots. For living forms of pre-modern, modern, and postmodern relations to come together in the same societies allows an interesting relationship to be set up between the plural cultural roots of Latin American people with modern and postmodern relationships, both among themselves and with the rest of the world.

The European conquest of America in the sixteenth century was not a humanizing experience of globalization, although it presumed establishing relations among the American continent, Europe, and Asia. This was because it took place as a confrontation between the indigenous and European cultures. The result was that pre-Columbian forms of civilization disappeared or barely survived in those areas the Spanish-Portuguese domination could not occupy, or through crossbreeding between different races and cultures. The phenomenon of crossbreeding has been especially important in those Latin American areas where there was a forced immigration of African people as slaves. Crossbreeding, forcing the argument a little, could be considered a more human form of globalization since, from the mixture of different races and cultures, there emerged new forms of living among very different human groups that enriched each other mutually and resulted in new cultural expressions.

The surviving pre-modern elements – for example, the relationship with the Earth as mother – present in indigenous, peasant, and suburban cultures in Latin America find an easy link with the postmodern preoccupation with ecology and the preservation of the environment, so neglected by modernity. These elements, among others, contribute to the appearance of alternative models of sustainable development and overcoming poverty. Such models propose not only to preserve, but also to use and strengthen, the natural resources that are essential for the survival of the planet. At the same time, they safeguard the cultural resources created by humanity throughout history, which can become part of the wisdom necessary for a humanizing globalization.

The postmodern epoch is beginning to be seen as the age of information. What appears at first sight is the impressive development of communication media that permit a circulation of information unknown in any other age. Without question, this increase in the circulation of information has contributed to globalization. To make this contribution humanizing is the challenge. On one hand, access to the means of communication threatens to become a new factor in widening the social gap.[7] On the other hand, the contents that circulate in mass communication and the highways of information tend to be no more than a one-way message rather than an exchange of the riches present in the different cultures and geographic situations that make up humanity.

- Politically speaking, the greatest lack in Latin American societies is a deficiency in citizenship; this means the public sphere occupies second place in the life of people, firms, or social groups. This also explains the weaknesses of democratic institutions, in spite of being enshrined in beautiful constitutions and laws.

  Many suggestions have been made to explain this absence of commitment to citizenship among Latin American people. It is neither possible nor necessary to summarize them all in this chapter. For the arguments we have been presenting, it will be sufficient to note this fact as one of the important ingredients in the failure of the modernizing process, which, in turn, becomes one of the major challenges for a humanizing globalization.

  To become a citizen is a necessary condition to develop oneself as a person, forming part of a common or public sphere to achieve the common good in the different levels that make up social life from the local to the global.

- A narrow, though frequent, vision of modernization sees religious practice and expression – especially in its popular and collective forms – as part of the backwardness to be overcome. It relegates the religious dimension to the private sphere of each individual. Nevertheless, it is impossible to understand the love for life and creativity present in the daily existence of the poor, if one denies their experience of God. The experience of God in all its variety that is lived by the Latin American people teaches us at least two things.

  The first is that the privileged perspective to insert oneself in, know, and understand the world is from the poor and their commitment to life. The intellectual and practical challenge at this moment in Latin American history is to devise a theory from the real conditions in which the people are living. This theory must start from a reverse of the situation. That is, it must start not from the successful individual in a capitalist society, but from the poor people themselves as they are caught up in a modernizing process with their defects and failures, and their achievements and successes. The mere mention of such a proposal arouses, in most parts of the academic and political world, hidden and open smiles of scepticism or rejection because it is considered gullible and utopian. The most convenient, from the perspective of currently used theories, is to declare this proposal and those who support it out of order.

Nevertheless, sharing with ordinary people leads to the challenge of thinking from outside the established order as an alternative way of contributing effectively to a humanizing globalization. A humanizing globalization can only be conceived from below – from the reverse side of history (the unsuccessful, according to the dominant ideology) – and from building a public domain at all levels: local, national, regional, and international, becoming worldwide.

The second lesson is that a prayerful reading of the Word of God (the Bible) is the privileged method to find meaning in life and a way to follow in contributing effectively to the struggle for social justice – an essential ingredient for a humanizing globalization. Human life without meaning is inconceivable. The experience of the Latin American people confirms the relation between religious expression and a life with meaning. For the Christian and Catholic majority of the people of the subcontinent, hearing the Word of God is a unique moment in their religious experience. It is a way of giving meaning to a life, which is in many aspects inhuman, from an active hope in the humanization of global conditions. The relationship with God, through prayer and listening to his Word, is a key factor in the personalization of each individual. For the poor it is often the most important moment in a process of feeling and becoming persons, and it can be the definitive drive to recognize others as human beings and brothers, seeing differences as themselves a source of richness. The individual converted into a person and, therefore, a brother or sister, is also a citizen committed to achieve just and peaceful social relations.

What is called a prayerful reading of the Bible in the basic communities of Latin America is a simple method of putting a person in contact with the reality they live. It connects with possibilities for a more human future in this same reality, in so far as one relates to other people and forms a community that shares the faith and holds out prospects for a better life. Normally, this leads people to participate in social organizations aiming to change the structures of this reality by slowly embracing its complexity.

- The Catholic Church was an important actor in the modernization processes of Latin America, including the training of leading elites. Reviewing her role from a religious aspect, the Church should ask herself sincerely if she is adequately nourishing these religious roots of the people and their sacramental expressions in rural life as in the urban and suburban cultures that come from modernization.

To contribute authentically to a humanizing globalization means taking seriously what Pope John Paul II constantly called "new evangelization"

– that is, to convert the complex process of globalization into a new phase of the humanization of history into Good News, especially for the poor. This is the mission, meaning, and reason for existence of the Catholic Church and for CST.

The experience of God among the mainly poor Latin American people has been a source of life in adverse conditions of poverty, political and cultural domination, the failure to recognize their human rights, and uncertainty with regard to the future. To tune into this experience is to be transformed by it and support it so that it grows and becomes part of the humanizing current in history, giving hope for all.

2. Politics, Conflict, and Humanizing Globalization

The public sphere is an essential part of a process of humanizing globalization, which is enriched by diversity, and this is why it is committed to preserving what exists and promoting newness – the result of human creativity. The public, civic, and political dimension of human history also finds its basis in religious experience. That is, it is related to:

- Faith, since God lives in the midst of his people[8] in society – publicly – not only within each person. The relationship with God leads to the creation of a public space and of a feeling as members of the people, or citizens. The house of God, in the midst of the people, is the public space par excellence.[9] Only when this space is occupied is the life of the people possible; only if this step is taken towards the public domain can the people be formed. For this reason, when we affirm that human beings – humanity – are created in the image and likeness of God,[10] we are saying that cultures, social structures, politics, or other groupings are expressions of the very richness of God and his sacrament. These are factors that build his house – the house of the people.

- Justice, resulting from a distribution of goods produced by the shared efforts of all, which guarantee a dignified life for every human being and make peace possible. Justice and peace are characteristics of God's kingdom and a paradigm of the public space. They are the horizon towards which are directed relationships between persons that make up peoples and peoples who form the world (*oecumene*). Justice and peace are the mature fruit of love, the original source of life's meaning to which we are called.[11]

The public sphere is the result of the complex gamut of relations between human beings, peoples, nations, their institutions, and so forth through which the course of history is traced. These are the relations that decide the long-term, medium, and short-term objectives of each of the levels in which they exist. Even more, these are the relations that decide the way to achieve agreed objectives or, in other words, the path along which one reaches the shared horizon revealing the vision of humanity's future.

In this perspective, it becomes clear that the public sphere is the space for conflict and power. Conflict is an inevitable part of the human reality that we call politics. Conflict comes from tension between those wishing to direct society along one path or another – a particular pattern of advance – and those who resist because they feel their interests are threatened or do not coincide with the current model or way of realizing their interests. As a result, politics is the activity through which power is exercised in the search to resolve conflicts arising on the journey towards the goal of an agreed future. To contribute to the humanization of history requires overcoming prejudices regarding political activity and the exercise of power that are frequently associated with religious or moral convictions that consider both political activity and the exercise of power as dirty.

Citizens are the actors in the public sphere of human life. To become a citizen is to overcome the barrier of individuality as the exclusive centre of life and definition of objectives and interests. The political tradition of the ancient Greeks described as idiots those occupying themselves exclusively with their own house: that is, those individuals whose actions are motivated solely by their own good and that of their family and who are incapable of recognizing others, their legitimate interests, and the common domain. Citizens, on the other hand, are those for whom common aims and a preoccupation for the houses of all (public domain) are motivating factors in their actions. Citizens have their own interests as individuals and members of various groups and associations. But they are aware that they cannot achieve their own objectives or safeguard their interests by prescinding from common objectives and the interests of other members of society. Both from an individualist and altruistic perspective, human life becomes impossible without taking others into account.

Conflict is normally understood as a discrepancy or incompatibility between the interests of some actors with those of others. The public domain is, therefore, the setting up of relations that enable all the actors to realize their interests to the greatest possible degree. The only way to do this is to identify common interests that are accepted by all and in the function of which, once assured, margins can be set up to pursue partial interests.[12]

At this point, it is easy to see the importance of the concept of the common good that forms part of the philosophical and theological tradition of CST. The development of this tradition will enable active participation in setting up a socio-political horizon common to the whole of humanity and inspiring efforts to bring it about in the future.

The initiative of the Earth Charter is a good example of an effort in this direction as far as it permits all to identify some common objectives and, at the same time, leaves each nation or group free to decide the best means for achieving them. The common horizon contains the advances of human history that have not yet become realities for all peoples: human rights; care of the earth; sexual equality; authentic cultural, religious, and intellectual pluralism; active democracy; security for all; and so forth. At each level – local, national, regional, and international – it is necessary to become aware of the distance that separates it from the agreed horizon and design an adequate strategy for advancing towards this as efficiently as possible.

Recognition of the diversity of legitimate interests and the inevitability of conflict in seeking their realization leads us to reflect on political power. To process antagonistic interests capable of generating conflict in a political system requires setting up relationships of power. The correlation of forces between the social actors making up society is what will define the image of common interests at each moment of the historical process. Power is another name for what we have described as political relations: that is, those for which social objectives are identified and ways of putting them into the effect decided. Power is, therefore, not a thing to be possessed, accumulated, sold, or bought. Nor is it force in the physical sense of the word and still less violence. Power is the total of social relations through which civil society takes its decisions.

Power is often associated with its instruments (the state, armed forces, trade unions, political parties, and so forth) or the offices that symbolize relationships of power (president, governor, commander, and so forth). However, it is necessary to go beyond this view to properly understand the importance of the social distribution of power. The humanization of social relations – local or global – is directly related to the distribution of power. The more power is concentrated, the less human are relations. The concentration of power is the main mechanism for exclusion in society's life. The distribution of power is the best guarantee that the process of taking political decisions includes social justice. As a result, humanization requires the sharing of power and the empowerment of all peoples.

Democracy is the political regime that has succeeded throughout history in most efficiently managing conflicts arising in complex and plural societies. Democracy is understood as a way to take public decisions through the participation of all concerned in dialogue and negotiation. It renounces the use of force and war[13] as means to impose political decisions.

Among the conditions for dialogue are:

- The recognition of every person, all peoples, and all cultures as social actors invited to take part in the process of taking decisions.

- The recovery of the value of the word through which persons and peoples commit themselves. The renunciation of violence and force makes the human word the privileged instrument of political action. It must, therefore, be a word that commits whoever pronounces it; it is capable of creating different situations to the extent that, spoken and heard, it can produce a change in initial positions and open a space to new positions.

Politically speaking, to dialogue is to negotiate. It is a question of taking decisions between those with diverging interests, so it is not enough to listen to and recognize the initial positions of each of these involved. To arrive at a decision means that the common point of arrival is different from the setting-out point of each. A common decision is possible because those involved are able to change their positions and yield, at least in part, their interests to arrive at a position that is the best possible for each and good for all, within the limits of the issue at stake.

Democracy also requires free access to complete information on political issues as an indispensable condition for taking part in political decisions. Free access to information means transparency on the part of institutions and public entities as well as respect for confidentiality. Freedom of expression and information, without which democracy is impossible, is nevertheless a very sensitive area of common life. Its exercise requires civic maturity and unrestricted acceptance of the ethical principles of political life. This is another area in which the contribution of CST can direct the globalization process towards what is fully human.

Closely linked to freedom of expression and information as essential dimensions of democracy is the role of the mass media. In freedom of expression and information the immense advantages of power converge to receive information and make it available in every corner of society. The media have a priceless contribution to transparency in public affairs and a huge capacity to manipulate by slanting information or deforming it by the way it is presented, interpreted, and so forth. The commitment of those administering or using the mass media to the principles of political ethics is not enough; it is also necessary to develop and demand fulfillment of a special code of ethics for the use of the information media.[14]

Accountability is another characteristic of a democratic system that contributes to the humanization of local and global relations. Accountability is a need for both those who exercise public office and each citizen. Those who hold public office are obliged to accountability with the greatest possible transparency. This is true not only for those who are elected to a particular office but every citizen with any responsibility for serving the community. At the same time, citizens have an obligation to demand accounting from public officers. Taking part in political life includes keeping a watch on the efficiency of institutions created to help achieve the common good.

Democracy is practised by citizens – persons conscious of and organized for it. It needs a political subject – a people. The word "people" has many meanings. In the present context, it is equivalent to civil society or, what is the same, to citizens organized to look after public affairs. The variety of public affairs to be cared for, and the concerns and capabilities of the citizens, give rise to a great diversity of organizations that participate in public life. The diversity, extension, and capacity to call many "citizens" are indicators of the democratic quality of a determined society. The strengthening of democracy begins, therefore, by a systematic and prolonged effort to promote citizenship as a condition for members of Latin American societies until they form an organized people; this becomes the conscious subject of public life and a guarantee of democratic procedures.

A necessary task to contribute effectively to the democratization of Latin American countries is an ambitious program for civic education. To become a citizen and make up an organized people requires important cultural changes so that they really become the solid basis of a responsible and shared public life. It is not enough to set up laws and channels for sharing and information to create a democratic society. Social and political participation costs a lot in human terms. For the majority of people, this is not a spontaneous attitude. It is necessary to motivate and educate them so that this participation becomes a cultural acquisition and a habit of life.

The civic fabric or civil society, product of a culture involved in public affairs, normally needs specifically political organizations; we ordinarily know these as political parties that are concerned in canalizing actions in the domain of the state and the government, promoting alternatives, and so forth. A political organization (party) normally needs an ideology to carry out its task, that is, a systematic body of ideas that explains the model of society, political regime, and government it proposes. It also needs a plan to make this model feasible, including a government program for the different state agencies. And, finally, it needs a qualified team of people capable of carrying it out once the party is in government and an organization to communicate with society and its citizens to convince them of its proposals and obtain their support through voting.

An increase in citizenship and democracy, then, becomes one of the principal criteria for evaluating a humanizing globalization.

3. The Role of the People of God

This essay cannot dodge the question about the role of the Catholic Church that, in the Second Vatican Council, defined itself as the people of God in the humanization of the globalization process at this moment of history.

Allusion was previously made to evangelization as the reason for the Catholic Church's existence and the meaning of its role in history. To evangelize – to announce the good news in all corners of the earth – is to bring to life the incarnation of Jesus of Nazareth, poor among the poor. To allow oneself to be led by the Holy Spirit – to live Christian spirituality – is to bring conversion to the poor; this is to bring the historical face of God made man in the poor man Jesus of Nazareth. To convert oneself to the poor is a call to every baptized person and to the Catholic Church as a community of followers of Jesus Christ. It begins by taking as one's own the perspective of the poor so as to know and analyze the society in which they live. To be able to see, perceive, and evaluate what happens from the eyes of the poor permits one to live the principal signs of the presence of God's kingdom in history: the good news is announced to the poor and they evangelize us.[15] To own this vision makes it possible to come close to the poor as a brother or sister, as well as to recognize their cultures and religious expressions that are born from this nearness to God – the friend of the poor. The Catholic Church has to follow the same kenotic process as Jesus did in his life.[16]

To keep alive the tradition of the risen Jesus as the solid basis for hope in a more just and human future for all is another contribution of the people of God to the process of globalization. A look at today's world can produce a sense of despair. We see the poverty of the majority of human beings, the growing social gap within nations and among them, and ongoing armed conflicts whose most numerous victims are innocent civilians. There is also the limited application of human rights, the weakness of democracies, the effects of industrialization on nature, and so forth. For thousands of millions of human beings a better future is only a dream. To be witnesses of hope, living and announcing it in words and deeds, is an inescapable commitment for the followers of Jesus Christ. In addition to a theology of hope, CST faces the challenge of proposing social and political actions that will become signs of hope for the poor of the earth.

There is a series of humanizing tendencies in today's world to which the people of God can contribute spontaneously by being in tune with Christ's gospel. The spreading of human rights, the struggle for equality between sexes, and the defence of nature through the incorporation of ecology in local and global decisions are a few important examples.

Directly linked to the development of CST and the actions it could inspire would be:

- A conscious and systematic drive towards the politicization of individuals and societies where it is present. This is no more than a consistent commitment to the expansion of citizenship as a direct consequence of seeing the human being as being bound by the Gospel values of brotherhood and solidarity. Both values remain pure abstractions as long as they are not converted into a deliberate acceptance of the political dimension of every person and an effort to build structures guaranteeing social justice for all the inhabitants of the planet.

- At the same time, to accept the challenge of offering a serious contribution to the complex process of building alternative social and political models that would lead to more just and humane relations and structures. In the letter to the Ephesians,[17] Paul invites the Church to make known God's comprehensive wisdom and the incalculable riches of Jesus Christ to the sovereignties and powers – to those who take the decisions that affect the common domain and people. To offer viable alternatives to world order is not a simple task, nor is it one from which the Church can prescind if it is to remain faithful to the Gospel.

For the Church to carry out its humanizing role in the globalization process, it needs a profound transformation. Almost 40 years afterwards, the Church has not fully absorbed the teaching of Vatican II precisely because of internal tensions that have given rise to resistance against the Vatican II decisions. To become people of God, as defined by Vatican II, continues to be a challenge for the institutional Church with its strong tendency towards clerical domination. The ongoing conversion of the heart of those responsible – the baptized – and of the ecclesiatical structures themselves are unfinished tasks on which it is necessary to continue insisting. The renewal of spiritual life within the Catholic Church is a necessary condition for making discernment the means of assuring the guidance of the Holy Spirit in the thoughts and actions of Christ's followers, united in an ecclesial community.

The fruits of the Catholic Church's conversion into a people of God serving the humanization of world history can be seen through some references to CST, among which I venture to mention the following:

- An increase of pluralism within the Church itself. The tension between unity and diversity normal in a body that brings together people of every race, culture, and condition will always be present in the Church's life. The Church's history shows periods in which unity has tended towards uniformity in discipline, rites, language, and philosophical and theological thought. In other periods, the unity of faith has expressed itself in a diversity of forms considered one of the greatest of the Church's riches. The people of God will be a humanizing ferment of globalization to the extent they succeed in accepting this pluralism that enables the seed of God's kingdom to be born in the very diversity of human cultures and places their unity in the Spirit.

- A Church wishing to contribute to democracy in public life, both in the local life of countries as in the needed new world order, discovering its own form of internal democracy. The Catholic Church is not exactly the same as a civil society or nation and, for this reason, does not have to adopt institutions and forms of government suitable for countries.[18] Yet it is still called, in faithfulness to its Gospel mission, to produce in its own structures forms of sharing in church decisions that contribute to a civic life.

- Interreligious dialogue is another indication of how much believers can contribute to the humanization of history. If all war is inhuman, wars that allege religious motives are the very denial of a relationship with a God whom all recognize, in some form, as the author of life and love. If those who find meaning in their lives through faith and a relationship with God are unable to recognize each other and enter into meaningful dialogue, how can they pretend to contribute to the reconciliation of human beings between themselves? The Catholic Church has made significant moves in dialogue with other Christian churches and religious confessions. However, much still remains to be done.

- Following the prophetic tradition of the Old Testament and the prophetic action of Jesus Christ, the Catholic Church is called to play a prophetic role. This is important at this moment of world history when globalization could mean a qualitative leap in history's humanization or a period of domination by a few over the majority of humanity. To pronounce the saving word of God – to make it echo with clarity as did the prophets in all ages – is a constitutive part of the mission of God's people and an indication of faithfulness to this mission.[19]

Globalization offers itself, then, as an opportunity to make this world more human to the extent that the public sphere is present. This means that people, converted into citizens of the world, are those who decide its direction. CST has a mission and a challenge of considerable importance in this process.

14

Globalization Viewed from Central America and the Caribbean

Michael Campbell-Johnston S.J.

Introduction: The Setting

The lands around and within the Caribbean Sea are made up mainly of the Central American republics to the west; the English- or French-speaking islands of the Lesser Antilles to the east; and the English-, French-, and Spanish-speaking islands of the Greater Antilles to the north. Admittedly, Colombia and Venezuela have long Caribbean seaboards to the south, but both are continental countries more properly belonging to South America. Mexico, too, has a Carribean seaboard but it is insignificant in comparison to its frontage on the Gulf of Mexico. However, the three ex-colonial Guyanas, geographically out of the region, are nevertheless bound to it by culture and history, and they can perhaps best be described as Caribbean islands surrounded on three sides by land. This is the area with which the present chapter is concerned.

The countries belonging to the region share a number of common characteristics. They are, on the whole, small in comparison with other countries in the hemisphere – the islands of the Lesser Antilles being miniscule by world standards. It is, therefore, essential for them to group together in entities such as the Caribbean Community Secretariat (CARICOM) or the Central American Free Trade Area to defend their interests and have any voice at all at a regional level. Coupled with this is a shared fear of mega-groupings such as the Free Trade Area of the Americas in which the US alone would be responsible for some 79 per cent of gross production. Because of geographical position, many of the countries have tourist industries that sometimes constitute their main source of income. However, they are often largely foreign owned and, thus, escape national control. To control and develop national resources in other areas, in addition to the tourist industry, to benefit the local population is a major and permanent concern for governments of small countries. Linked to this is the appalling brain drain of professional and trained people, especially the young, to wealthier countries outside the region.

In light of this situation, an indiscriminate globalization appears as a major threat. Countries within the region share a concern, voiced by so many, about the distribution of wealth and the seeming failure to take any measures to correct it. As James Wolfensohn of the World Bank recently put it: "In our world of 6 billion people, one billion own 80 per cent of global GDP, while another billion struggle to survive on less than a dollar a day. This is a world out of balance."[1] And where the wealthy countries could act, they resolutely refuse to do so. Wolfensohn went on to contrast the paltry sums that the rich countries spend on aid – $56 billion or just 0.22 per cent of their GDP – with the massive $300 billion given in subsidies to farmers in rich countries and the even more outrageous $600 billion spent on defence.[2] As a result of this, "For many countries the 1990s were a decade of despair. Some 54 countries are poorer now than in 1990. In 21 countries a larger proportion of people is going hungry. In fourteen, more children are dying before the age of five. In twelve countries, primary school enrollments are shrinking. In 34, life expectancy has fallen."[3] This is why the Archbishop of Tegucigalpa, Cardinal Oscar Rodriguez, stated recently that for him, the weapons of mass destruction are poverty, corruption, and social injustice.[4] The massive net transfer of money and other resources from a poor Third World to a wealthy First World is both intolerable and scandalously shameful. As long as it persists, there can be little hope for a peaceful, let alone non-violent, future.

What, if anything, can be done? The most depressing fact is that the experts know perfectly well what needs to be done. In 2000, the UN Millennium Declaration was signed by the largest gathering of world leaders ever held, committing them to work together for advancing development and reducing poverty by 2015 or earlier. Each of the eight goals that were adopted contained specific targets for achievement. Yet the world is already falling short and few, if any, of the targets are likely to be met. What is lacking is neither expertise nor finance but political will. What is needed is an alternative vision of development to counter the neo-liberal approach through market primacy and trade liberalization that violates essential human values. It is here that Catholic social thought has a key role to play. Globalization cannot be reversed, but it can be modified and redirected towards what has been called a globalization of solidarity. This chapter looks at two attempts to suggest this in the region of Central America and the Caribbean.

1. A Civilization of Poverty

The first is based on a concept developed in his later writings by Ignacio Ellacuría, a Jesuit philosopher and theologian who spent most of his working life in the Central American University (UCA) in El Salvador and was its Rector for his last ten years. It was there that, on November 16, 1989, he was assassinated along with five Jesuit colleagues, their housekeeper, and her 15-year-old daughter. He first broached the topic of "a civilization of poverty" in an article in *Concilium*[5] and then again while describing what he felt should be the mission of the Society of Jesus.[6] He gave the fullest development to this proposal in one of the last articles he wrote.[7] Arguing that both prophecy and utopia, if held in conjunction, can become – especially in an explicitly Christian perspective – forces for renewal and liberation, he applies them to the precise geo-socio-temporal reality of Latin America. He sees the ideal of the kingdom of God as a Christian utopia that needs to be historicized by individuals, social groups, and countries through prophetic declaration and action.

Perhaps the clearest description of what Ellacuría understood by a "civilization of poverty" is contained in the first article. He describes "a civilization of poverty where poverty will no longer be the lack of what is basic and necessary due to the action in history of groups or social classes or of countries or groups of countries, but a universal state of things in which the satisfaction of basic necessities is guaranteed together with the freedom of personal choices and a climate of personal and community creativity permitting the appearance of new forms of life and culture, new relations with nature, with other people, with oneself and with God."[8]

Such a vision presupposes a rejection of the state of dependency typical of so many poor countries as well as of a capitalist system that holds them there. The external debt problem is clear evidence of the former, responsible for a world formed by injustice to be the patent and verifiable negation of the kingdom of God. The present capitalist system is dismissed not only because its application produces pitiless exploitation of both people and raw materials, but because it is vitiated within itself. As Ellacuría writes, there is

> an almost irresistible pull towards a profound dehumanization as an intrinsic part of the real dynamics of the capitalist system: abusive and/or superficial and alienating ways of seeking one's own security and happiness by means of private accumulation, of consumption, and of entertainment. The fundamental dynamic of selling one's own goods to another at the highest price possible and buying the other's at the lowest price possible, along with the dynamic of imposing one's own cultural norms so as to make others dependent, clearly shows the inhumanity of the system, constructed more on the principle of homo homini lupus than on the principle of a possible and desirable universal solidarity. Predatory ferocity becomes the fundamental dynamic, and generous solidarity remains reduced to curing incidentally and superficially the wounds of the poor caused by the depredation.[9]

Another reason for rejecting the capitalist system is that it cannot be universalized. Ellacuría argues for some sort of levelling process – what the Bolsheviks used to call *uravnilovka* in the early days of the revolution – since the planet does not, nor ever will, have sufficient resources for everyone to live like Europeans or North Americans. As Mahatma Gandhi said, when asked if newly independent India would now attain British standards of living: "It took Britain half the resources of this planet to achieve its prosperity. How many planets do you think a country like India will require?" But if the behaviour and even the ideal of a few cannot become the behaviour and reality of the greater part of humanity, that behaviour and that ideal cannot be said to be moral or even human. This is all the more true if the enjoyment of a few is at the cost of depriving the rest. For Ellacuría, the universalization is not only impossible but also undesirable, since it is based on a lifestyle characterized by greed and self-gratification. Abundance and consumerism are goals that cannot and should not be offered for universal application.

The principle of universalization must be a valid condition for any global project. Any world order that generates a constantly greater number of people in poverty, can only be maintained by force and by the threat of humanity's total destruction through increasing ecological destruction and nuclear annihilation, and generates no ideals of qualitative growth is totally unacceptable. A world order favourable for a few and unfavourable for most is something that dehumanizes and de-Christianizes each person and humanity as a whole. But universalization does not mean uniformity nor, as Ellacuría insists, still less uniformity that is imposed from a powerful centre on an amorphous and subordinated periphery. He is quite clear that the universalization envisaged must result from a preferential option for the poor, since the preferential option for the rich and powerful has brought more ill than good to humanity.

In this prophetic march towards an utopia that can be historically universalized, those whom Ellacuría calls the "poor-with-spirit" have a determining role to play that is qualitatively new and fundamentally Christian. Total rejection of the past is neither possible nor desirable, but the Gospel calls us to be "born anew" (John 3:3) so that "all might have life and have it more abundantly" (John 10:10). This calls for a permanent conversion and liberation process that includes not only "liberation-from" but also "liberation-for" and "liberation-towards." A new human being is thus fashioned whose values are radically different, especially with regard to wealth and poverty. This liberation cannot consist of passing from poverty to wealth by making oneself rich because of the poverty of others. It consists, rather, in surmounting poverty through solidarity. It rejects the civilization of wealth and capital that Ellacuría describes as one that, in the final analysis, "proposes the private accumulation of the greatest possible capital on the part of individuals, groups, multinationals, states or groups of states as the fundamental basis of development, and individuals' or families' possessive accumulation of the most possible wealth as the fundamental basis for their own security and for the possibility of ever growing consumption as the basis of their own happiness."[10]

The civilization of poverty, on the other hand, is based on diametrically opposed principles. "Founded on a materialist humanism transformed by Christian light and inspiration, it rejects the accumulation of capital as the energizer of history and the possession-enjoyment of wealth as principle of humanization, and it makes the universal satisfying of basic needs the principle of development, and the growth of shared solidarity the foundation of humanization."[11] Ellacuría insists that, in spite of the call for a "civilization of poverty," he is not proposing universal pauperization as an ideal of life. On the contrary, he is calling for a poverty that can enable all to have access to some material and cultural goods that would make for a truly human life. The basic needs to be satisfied include proper nourishment, minimal housing, basic health care, primary education, and sufficient employment.

But these are only first steps. With the satisfying of basic needs institutionally assured as the primary phase of a liberation process, people would be free to be what they want to be, provided that what is wanted not become a new mechanism of domination. For the poverty envisaged "is what makes room for the spirit, which now will not be choked by the desire to have more than the other, by the concupiscent desire to have all kinds of superfluities when most of humanity lacks what is necessary. Thus the gospel spirit will be lived out more easily, according to which it is not necessary to have much in order to be much; on the contrary, there is a limit at which having is opposed to being."[12]

In such a society work takes on its full human value, having as its principle object not the production of capital but the perfecting of the human being. Clearly, a society not structured by the laws of capital but giving priority to the dynamism of humanizing work would be shaped in a very different way from the present one because the shaping principle is totally different. For example, the benefits of nature and all the natural resources for production, use, and enjoyment would no longer be privately appropriated by any individual person, group, or nation. The question arises as to which of the two great economic arrangements available today, capitalist or socialist, is more fitting to attain this ideal. Ellacuría has little problem in dismissing both as inadequate. "Capitalist systems in Latin America have been unable to satisfy the basic needs of the greater part of the population, they have created bitter inequalities between the few who have much and the many who have little, they have led to a gigantic foreign debt imposed on human beings who in no way enjoyed or received benefit from the loans, they have often produced deep economic crises, and they have promoted an immoral culture of consumption and of easy profit."[13] But neither is socialism, as it has been practised in Latin America, satisfactory; for Ellacuría, though, its ideals come closer than the capitalist to the utopian demands of the kingdom.

What Ellacuría proposes is not a third way between liberalism and collectivism in the economic area or between liberal democracy and social democracy in the political. He quotes with approval Pope John Paul's "On Social Concern," which states that the Church's social teaching is not a third way, not even as an ideal solution.[14] What is, however, possible would be a two-way opening up of each of the systems that "could be evidence not only of the insufficiency of each but also of a possible leap forward to a now scarcely recognizable new political system."[15] Whether this can be achieved through reformist rather than revolutionary change is a moot question in Latin America. Ellacuría is clear that the real question is not if a revolution is needed, but what sort of revolution is needed and how to bring it about. It must come out of a genuine liberation process that should be not merely political but fundamentally social and undertaken from a preferential option for the mass of the people. This requires a profound transformation in people according to the values and ideals already noted. It is a task not only for current Catholic social thought but also a cry for reform in the Church itself. Attempts to date have not measured up to these criteria and have, in some cases, made the Church worldly and capitalist more than they have made the structures and behaviour of the world Christian and evangelical.

Ellacuría concludes his arguments for a civilization of poverty by calling for a new cultural order and a "new heaven." Culture must be truly liberating – the generator of real freedom. It must be orientated towards persons, communities, peoples, and nations who are constructing their own self-being in an effort of creation and not only of acceptance. And above all, it must be a culture for the majority and not just the elite.

"The creation of a new heaven supposes achieving a new presence of God among humans that will let the old Babylon be transformed into a new Jerusalem."[16] It is basically an opening to the Spirit of Christ for, as St Paul says, "When everything is subjected to him, then the Son himself will be subject in his turn to the One who subjected all things to him, so that God may be all in all." (1 Cor 15:28) This will require profound change on the part of the Church as an institution. It will need to be permanently open and attentive to the newness and the universality of the Spirit that breaks the fossilized routine of the past and the limits of a restricted self-conception. For, as Ellacuría concludes, "the utopian exercise of prophecy can lead it to become – in a genuine conversion – a church of the poor that really can be the heaven of a new earth where a civilization of poverty becomes dominant and where humans are not only intentionally and spiritually poor, but really and materially so, that is, detached from what is superfluous and from the constraining dynamisms of individual monopolizing and collective accumulation."[17]

Is this pie in the sky, an idealist's dream, or an unrealizable utopia, however much historicized by prophetic action? It may well seem so, but two considerations should be borne in mind. There can be no doubt that the civilization proposed is much more in accordance with the ideals of the Gospel than the existing one. Jesus Christ came to build a new kingdom and the Church he founded should always remain open to this challenge. Recent developments in Catholic social thought have pointed to specific ways that might give entrance to such a new world.

What is required now is the further development of that teaching and, above all, its bold implementation by a Church not afraid of losing positions of power and influence in a corrupt and flawed world. The crucified people of Latin America and the Third World in general are calling all to a conversion whose first step is to look at the world through their eyes and begin to understand it in a different way. With them we must accept the fact that there is no viable solution along present lines of development and that, therefore, we must open ourselves to the need for a fundamental change of direction that will be as difficult as it is costly. Is it too late? Some analysts argue that we have already lost control. Half of the one hundred largest economies of the world are not countries but multinational corporations under the control of no one but themselves. Try to pin them down in one place and, like jellyfish, they will ooze into another in the relentless search for maximum profits. The challenge is truly tremendous and awesome. The only alternative, however, seems to be to try and face it before it really is too late.

A second consideration is that a civilization for poverty is calling for new attitudes towards wealth and possessions that will only be possible to achieve through a radical change in lifestyles. It would be naive to believe that any redistribution of the world's current wealth and resources is either economically or politically possible. But at least it should be possible to put in place measures that can halt the transfer of wealth from the poor to the rich – to reverse current flows before they drown us all. For, as Gandhi is believed to have said: "God has provided for the needs of the world, but he has not provided for its greeds." Is it too idealistic to believe that many young people today, looking for meaning in what is to them an often meaningless world, would accept the challenge that new lifestyles can be more rewarding, more diverse, and more exciting than those in which they are trapped today? The root of the challenge is a spiritual one. But are not many young people today looking for a new spirituality to make sense of their lives? Will the institutional churches, with all their weight of historical conditioning and conservative practice, find sufficient adaptability to meet these needs? Perhaps the next section of this chapter will provide some answers to these questions.

2. Globalization and New Evangelization

Globalization and New Evangelization in Latin America and the Caribbean is the title of a book recently published by CELAM that records a four-year effort of serious, in-depth reflection on the two key issues facing the region.[18] An effort was made from the outset to engage as many of CELAM's collaborators as possible in the discussions: experts, executive secretaries, and advisors of each department as well as bishops and the lay people participating in the various conferences convened by CELAM. The document's objective is threefold, with each aspect corresponding to a chapter:

1. To analyze the phenomenon of globalization and its effects on society.

2. To discern, in the light of faith, the epochal change through which we are living.

3. To provide new perspectives on the new evangelization in Latin America and the Caribbean.

We will be more concerned with the final chapter that attempts to identify some of the challenges to, and opportunities for, Catholic social thought that are offered by patterns of globalization experienced in the region.

But, first of all, what are we talking about? CELAM proposes the following definition: "By globalization we understand a recent and accelerated phenomenon of rapid changes, mainly characterized by closer integration among countries and peoples of the world, which has upset the old systems of economics and labor, trade and international finance, communications and culture around the globe. The causes of this phenomenon include advances in technology, especially computer science, telematics, the network of worldwide connections (satellites and the 'Internet') and the free market, political decision-making and centres of power. Globalization is part of an authentic 'change of epoch.'"[19]

This globalization shows itself in all dimensions of our human existence. We find it in:

- greater worldwide production and wealth, although its distribution is increasingly inequitable;
- greater independence and exchange among the nations of the world, although this is asymmetrical;
- greater knowledge and dominion over nature, although this favours small hegemonic elites and, in most cases, degrades ecosystems;
- greater, better, and more rapid intercontinental communication, the conquest of space and the atom, although with no real benefit for the great majority of people who lack access to the real-time information network;
- the fight against disease and natural disasters, although enormous inequalities still place the most vulnerable people at a disadvantage;
- progress, as well as setbacks, in culture and art, but with unequal distribution of benefits and a deterioration of culture;
- greater insistence on universal human rights, although in this new epoch we still do not see clearly an appropriate foundation of values and ethical principles;
- a few changes in patterns of hygiene and nutrition.

From the preceding it is clear that, for some people, globalization has meant life and creativity, and progress and fulfillment; for the great majority it signifies selfishness and frustration, and exclusion and death. Hence the challenge now is to humanize globalization and globalize solidarity.[20] As Pope John Paul stated; "Globalization is not, a priori, either good or evil. It will be what people make of it."[21]

In a globalization so flawed that it seeks efficiency and economic success at any cost, one of the principal contributions Christians can make is remembering that the element of gratuity is essential for humanity. As CELAM says: "That which is most human cannot be bought or sold; it has value, but no price. Friendship, a smile, joy, fidelity, love, life and death are received and given as a gift. So, too, art and poetry, contemplation, esthetics and beauty are part of a human dimension that lies in the realm of the gratuitous."[22] Christianity is, in its essence, a religion of gratuity. God loves the poor and the outcasts unconditionally. Faith in

Latin America should be seen not only from a perspective of poverty, oppression, and injustice, but also from one of humanity, simplicity, solidarity, and joy.

Another challenge is recovering the meaning of life. When material goods become the end that determine people's existence, a wasteland of emptiness and lack of meaning is created that tends to be filled with drugs, sex, violence, and work that bewilders instead of humanizes. The popular religiosity of the original peoples of Latin America and the strength of their Christianity today make them important guides in the search for a transcendence that our world so urgently needs. They are also called to live and construct their surroundings in solidarity and in open relationship with other believers and members of society. This will involve taking a stand against the excessive individualism that so often leads to the breakdown of the family, community, and other ethnic or social groups. A genuine ethic of globalization is needed to guarantee a humanizing process similar to the ideals and principles of Christianity.

The task that faces Christians is expressed as follows:

> Properly understood and guided, globalization could provide sufficient food and a dignified life for all the planet's inhabitants. It would be capable of a healthy transfer of technology that would make it possible to destroy the scandalous differences that currently exist among peoples. For globalization to bear fruit, however, it must be diverted from its current neo-liberal, economicist path and guided towards the building up of all society. It is a challenge for Christians to show that beyond the profit motive and unbridled competition among individuals and countries in a deregulated market, the common values of collaboration, exchange, solidarity and responsibility can be developed. Only in this way will globalization cease to crush the weak and to be a threat, and become an immense opportunity for all humanity.[23]

This is where the social teaching of the Church has a key role to play. It does not oppose market economics, but it does require that human beings and their relationships with others be the central focus. It also requires that their dignity and freedom be respected, that goods be used for the benefit of all, and that the legitimate right to property, healthy competition, and solidarity be respected. Therefore, it rejects indiscriminate consumption, lack of concern for those who are marginalized, and lack of respect for the environment. It considers that any model supporting these values is unrealistic, unstable, and immoral. And it is clear that a culture based on having and enjoying, more than on being, destroys people and fosters lifestyles that are contrary to freedom, justice, and the welfare of those who are poorest.

But Christian social teaching is not in itself enough, unless it leads to a genuine change in basic attitudes. The attitudes singled out are a capacity for critical discernment that enables one to identify God's presence and will in the ambiguity of history and, more important, a willingness to demonstrate this presence by giving witness to it. For "if the task of evangelization is not supported by witness or by living what we preach, it is nothing more than empty, deceptive rhetoric."[24] A ministry of incarnation is necessary for a church that mediates salvation. This will include not only becoming inculturated, but valuing and respecting pluralistic societies and being open to change. We will need to learn from others and discern together in a spirit of humility.

What are the specific elements of witness Christians are called on to give? The study mentions six in particular. First, though united in catholicity, we act locally in the community and society where we live. Second, in a world that worships profit, we offer God as a gratuity. In words similar to those of Ellacuría, the document claims that "detachment, selflessness, unconditional devotion to the noblest causes of humanity – in a word, poverty of spirit – are the language of witness that the world needs today."[25] Third, to a society saturated with horizontal communication by cybernetic media, we show that prayerful encounter with the Trinity is the highest form of communication. Fourth, in a society that marginalizes the poor, we renew our option for them without fear or prejudice. Fifth, in a globalized world insensitive to signs of death, we declare ourselves defenders of life, rejecting cases where economic help given for the advancement of peoples is made conditional on programs of contraception, sterilization, and procured abortion. And sixth, a strong Christian witness is required in situations of ecological crisis, problems of peace, and contempt for the fundamental human rights of so many people, especially children.

This will require a new spirituality, aware that God is able to reveal himself with new faces that demand unprecedented responses. It will be a spirituality of mission, of communion, and of *diakonia* and solidarity. The call to the Church itself is to redefine its presence and its service in a global world – a task that needs discernment as well as bold experimentation. Some of the problems that have to be faced include ministry to small communities, new forms of family co-existence, popular religiosity, a loss of Christian identity, and new roles for the laity. Pastoral creativity will be vital since the Church cannot rely on the same models that were created in a different historical context.

The study ends with what it calls a "Decalogue for Action," which sets out not only an agenda for Christian social teaching but also for specific action on the part of Christian communities at local, regional, and national levels. The first need is to develop a worldwide ethic capable of providing a foundation for a society based on the common good. This, in turn, implies action leading directly to the inclusion of the excluded – the two-thirds of humanity orphaned by the current process of globalization. Another need is the remaking of a social fabric that is often fragmented or broken and resulting in isolation. Not only must the family, the first school of communion and participation, be strengthened, but also many other associations and social groups at various levels. Also important is the fostering of a culture of hospitality, since this will strengthen the gratuity emphasized above. Here special attention should be paid to migrants and the role of women in society. There must be a deliberate and intensive dialogue with the sciences, with cultures, and with other religions and faiths. The diverse forms of modern communication must be made more democratic and opened up to all. Connected with this is the need for globalization from the grassroots – the strengthening of community organizations and projects so that governments are motivated to decentralize power and structures to ensure a greater participation by the poor and excluded.

Movements towards integration in various regions of Latin America should be supported with the proviso that they bring equal benefits to all. Emphasis must be placed on improving and extending educational resources at all levels since, in a globalized world, knowledge is a key to entry. Finally, it is also the task of the Church to encourage civil society's search for a new concept of development that considers the human person its beginning and its end.

This is a massive task by any measure. But the document ends on a word of hope. The negative phenomena of globalization urgently demand "the presence of a community that has the prophetic courage to proclaim 'Be not afraid', because hope is something that belongs by right to Latin America."[26] If Christians can measure up to the challenges and tasks outlined above, they and their churches will become salt of the earth and light for the world as it advances towards globalization.

Conclusion: Monseñor Romero

I wish to conclude these reflections by referring to one of the truly great sons of the region who showed by his words and example what can be achieved in the struggle for justice and for the poor. Monseñor Oscar Romero, Archbishop of San Salvador, was assassinated on March 24, 1980, while offering Mass in the chapel of the Divine Providence hospital where he lived. The day before in his cathedral he had made a strong appeal to the ranks in the army and police forces to listen to their consciences and stop obeying immoral commands from their officers to torture and kill fellow Salvadorans. He was murdered, as the UN Truth Commission clearly established after the end of the civil war, by death squads controlled by Major Roberto D'Aubuisson who later became President of the National Assembly and founder of ARENA, the current ruling political party in the country.

Romero's greatness and relevance to the theme of this book lie in two facts. First of all, he himself was wholly committed to the cause of the poor and the building of a more just society in El Salvador. He fully identified with the call of the Latin American Bishops at Medellin for "the conversion of the whole church to a preferential option for the poor with a view to their integral liberation."[27] It was a call he once described as "the subversive witness of the Beatitudes which have turned everything upside down."[28] He saw quite clearly where the root of the problem lay. "I will not tire of declaring that if we really want an effective end to the violence, we must remove the violence that lies at the root of all violence: structural violence, social injustice, the exclusion of citizens from the management of the country, repression. All this is what constitutes the primal cause, from which the rest flows naturally."[29] Hence, he concluded, it is the duty of the Church and all its members "to know the mechanisms that generate poverty, to struggle for a more just world, to support the workers and the peasants in their claims and in their right to organize, and to be close to the people."[30]

Secondly, Romero was able to inspire a similar dedication in others, especially the young. He, himself, made a public vow of fidelity to the people: "I want to assure you – and I ask your prayers to be faithful to this promise – that I will not abandon my people but together with them I will run all the risks that my ministry demands."[31] And he called on the whole Church, including its wealthy members, to do the same. "I am glad, brothers and sisters, that our church is persecuted precisely for its preferential option for the poor and for trying to become incarnate in the interests of the poor and for saying to all the people, to rulers, to the rich and powerful, if you do not concern yourselves for the poverty of our people as though they were your own family, you will not be able to save society."[32]

Many took up this challenge and many young people offered their lives for it. I believe it is just as relevant and just as needed in today's globalized world. Romero did not mince words: "It is inconceivable to call oneself a Christian without making, like Christ, a preferential option for the poor."[33] And again: "A Christian who defends unjust situations, is no longer a Christian."[34] Or: "The wealthy person who kneels before his money, even though he goes to Mass, is an idolater and not a Christian."[35] And finally a warning: "It is a caricature of love to cover over with alms what is lacking in justice, to patch over with an appearance of benevolence when social justice is missing."[36]

May Romero's word and example continue to inspire others to work for a more just model of globalization in which the poor and excluded will find their rightful place.

15

Globalization and Africa: A Grassroots Analysis with an Emphasis on Culture

Peter Henriot S.J.

Globalization as a process has often been accused of homogenizing culture. It is also frequently alleged that globalization leaves much of Africa marginalized. The cultures of Africa are not congenial to a neo-liberal project for the world economy. We need, then, to pay attention to cultural analysis and its role in economic development. Analysts concerned with the impact of globalization in Africa will need to turn to a new emphasis on culture. Is it possible to do good social analysis without doing serious cultural analysis? This is the way I would phrase a very practical question that has arisen for me in many years of experience of working with popular movements for change in the US and, over the past decade, in Africa – most specifically in Zambia.

This practical question is related directly to the important issues raised by Georges De Schrivjer in his book, *The Paradigm Shift in Third World Theologies of Liberation: From Socio-Economic Analysis to Cultural Analysis: Assessment and Status of the Question.*[1] De Schrivjer traces the shift to culture in both the writings of Latin American liberation theologians and in the nuancing of the evangelization and liberation themes enunciated at the Medellin (1968), Puebla (1979), and Santo Domingo (1992) conferences.

From my own experience, I find the most interesting question De Schrivjer raises is at the end of his essay about the significance of the shift to culture in the activities of new social movements. He asks:

> Could it be that the discourse about unjust structures has been, in a sense, too abstract? Is not the cultural emphasis, especially when shouldered by the new social movements, a fresh way of tackling structural questions, a way that is more understandable to common people?[2]

Involvement with movements of what De Schrivjer calls common people – grassroot communities – has sharpened my own appreciation of the cultural emphasis. I, therefore, want to focus my attention on the role and use of cultural analysis in movements that involve local efforts for justice and peace, development, ecology, women's concerns, and religious inculturation. My intention will be to demonstrate how cultural analysis has both the potential and the reality of making a significant contribution to liberation in Africa.

But before moving into my own examination of analysis of the cultural emphasis at the grassroots level in Africa, let me describe what I mean by culture. I find particularly helpful a description of culture expressed in poetic form by a young Zambian Jesuit friend of mine.

African Culture

African culture: tell us, who are you?

I am the pattern of values and meanings
expressed through images and symbols.

I am the dance, and the song, and the drum.
I am the food and the manner of eating it.
I am the dress and the way of dressing.
I am the art in all its forms.
I am the music.
I am the ceremonies and the rituals.

Oh, let me tell you, if I were to tell you
everything about myself,
you would not have enough paper and ink
to describe me.
For I am life, the way of life.
And one can understand life well by living it.

I want to add, though, that
I am identity.
A person is what he or she is because of me.
It is I who gives meaning to life.
Those who do not possess me are doomed.
Faceless, a nameless shadow.
Like a dead piece of wood floating on a river,
tossed about aimlessly, without a destination,
following the rhythm of waves.

I am unity.
I gather people.
Bring them close to each other.
Give them a sense of belonging,

a reason to live, a reason to die.
A common vision of the world,
a similar destiny,
for life cannot be lived in isolation.

I am not the only culture that exists.
There are many others, uncountable,
like the cattle of the Ila and the Tonga people.
I have met most of these cultures.
For me the first meeting
has not been very pleasant.
I was looked down upon,
nearly all my qualities spat on.

"If you want to merit the name culture,"
so I was told,
"reshape, redefine, better still, abandon,
what makes you what you are,
and adopt our qualities."

I felt oppressed; it was very unfair, unjust.
I cried, but there was no one to help me.
I had no strength to fight back.
Unwillingly, I submitted.
But inside me, I kindled a flame of hope.
Someday, I said to myself,
I will be myself again.

Things are better now;
other cultures have started
slowly to recognise me.
They realise that I have something to offer.
I who was crippled have started to walk again.
My legs are still numb,
I have not been able to make great strides.
But I know that I will make them soon.

When the sun has risen,
no one can force it back to its rising place.

Joachim Pelekamoyo Nthawie S.J.[3]

I. A Shift in My Orientation

By way of introduction, I can be very specific in indicating the explicit expression of this shift to culture in my own involvement in programs of conscientization for faith and justice in the work for social change. Two moments accounted for this orientation in the decade preceeding my move to Africa.

A. Intellectual Moment

First, there was an intellectual moment. Here I acknowledge the insight and emphasis of my colleague for many years at the Center of Concern in Washington, DC – Joe Holland. Writing in the Preface of the revised and enlarged edition (1983) of the very popular book we co-authored in 1980, *Social Analysis: Linking Faith and Justice*, Holland emphasized: "It is this question of culture, and within it religion, which reveals, I believe, the most radical dimension of our social crisis."[4] Noting that our book focused primarily on economics and politics, he stated that there was a need to search for "a deeper cultural key" to understanding both the roots and the transformation of industrial capitalism.[5]

This intellectual search was not a denial that culture arises from and is shaped by the surrounding economic and political context, for culture cannot be understood except as embodied in such a context. "Culture is never an angelic spirit floating above society."[6] On the other hand, Holland emphasized, culture is not the prisoner of its context, nor does it merely reflect economic drives and political forces and provide only an ideological justification for social structures. "Certainly culture often functions in the mode of legitimation, but it can also be the point of critique and creativity."[7]

Holland applied his cultural analysis in a variety of ways, especially developing Gibson Winter's discussion of "root metaphors" that shape civilizations.[8] This would have implications, Holland felt, for the strategies developed to bring about social change.

In the context of social movements of left and right in the US, Holland offered a critique of the left's failure to take seriously the deep cultural symbols of the people, leaving these symbols to fall into the manipulating hands of the right. Examples of such symbols were flag, faith, and family (nation, religion, and kinship). He felt that the left in the US had not adequately grasped the creative role of these collective symbols in the process of social change and had let them become culturally conservative reinforcements of a status quo of exclusion and oppression.[9]

This intellectual appreciation of the importance of paying attention to culture meant that the Center of Concern's workshops on social analysis always took seriously the cultural dimensions of situations. In the practical methodology offered in the 1983 edition of *Social Analysis*, I suggested that the following question should be asked when analyzing the important influences on a particular situation: "What are the major *cultural* structures which determine how society organizes *meaning*? E.g., religion; symbols, myths, dreams; art, music, folk-lore; lifestyle, traditions."[10] Right from the outset, therefore, the element of cultural analysis was to be considered essential in the approaches that the Center of Concern took in promoting social analysis.

B. Experiential Moment

Second, there occurred an experiential moment that both gave impetus to the intellectual insight and also reinforced my understanding of it. This was the experience of attempting grassroots programs of social analysis in the Philippines and in Africa. In 1980, I spent a month giving a series of workshops in the Philippines, based on the first draft of the book written by Holland and me. The participants in the program were mostly groups of church workers and students. Just a few weeks before I arrived, the Philippines Bishops' Conference had issued an order that no more social analysis workshops were to be conducted under church auspices. This was certainly a challenge to the program prepared for my visit. I, therefore, conducted a month of social discernment workshops. In good Jesuit fashion, I was able to work with the same topics, but under different names!

Why had there been this reaction of the bishops of the Philippines to the approach of social analysis? I was told that they feared that the approach being taken in much of the work of social analysis was primarily Marxist-inspired, or at least strongly Marxist-influenced, and therefore played into the hands of communist movements. During the especially tense times of the early years of the Marcos dictatorship, charges that social analysis programs were Marxist or communist were dangerous charges. The officials of the Church felt they could take no chances.

Having only recently arrived, I was, of course, not competent to judge the validity of the charges. But in many of the analytical approaches that I experienced being used in the Philippines (and elsewhere) at that time, I did find a disconcerting over-emphasis upon purely economic factors in explaining the constitution and dynamics of the local society. I recall asking a young student participating in one of my workshops about the cultural background to one problem that we were studying, something relating to family influences in politics. He dismissed the question with the sentiment that all such influences were simply economic and had no basis in popular culture. After all, culture was only a determined supra-structure and not a dynamic element on its own in shaping society. An older woman in the group smiled and commented that the student must have forgotten his upbringing, ignored the stories and songs he would have heard at home, and swallowed too easily a foreign-imported explanation of reality. The culture of family relationships in the Philippines was too real, too strong, to be dismissed with a simple economic explanation.

Whatever the relevance of my question about culture and politics, and the ensuing discussion about economic influences, I began to realize that a social analysis that ignored cultural dimensions was not too helpful in explaining the Filipino reality or, for that matter, any other social reality. Having lived for a year in Latin America in the mid-1970s, I knew the power of popular religiosity to shape perspectives and inspire actions. Moreover, I appreciated the faith of the small Christian communities and the vision of the theology of liberation. I saw that these elements in society and in the Church were also present, in varying degrees, in the Philippines. I realized that only a cultural analysis could get at the underlying dynamics shaping social movements in such settings.

This experience of the necessity of cultural analysis (certainly not replacing socio-economic analysis or supplementing it, but actually deepening it) was reinforced during another month's tour of workshops on social analysis – this time in Africa. I came to Zambia and Zimbabwe in 1982 for programs with church workers, students, laity leadership, and members of religious congregations (many of them expatriates). What struck me – and would, of course, strike me more forcefully when I came back to Africa a few years later to become a full-time resident and not simply a visitor – was that culture was not simply the content of analysis but also the context and the method. What do I mean?

As will be developed further in this chapter when I review my recent work with social movements in Africa, the content of good social analysis must include the cultural traditions, structures, events, history, personalities, and so forth of the people and their society. In Africa I experienced that these cultural elements deserve treatment on their own right, not as mere supra-structures based on economic foundations. But I also learned in the workshops in Zambia and Zimbabwe in 1982 that culture was the context and the method of good analysis in the sense that the analytical framework was more than an intellectual exercise or rational explication of the reality being examined. The framework itself was influenced by song, drama, art, story-telling, and religious celebration – all significant cultural elements. This necessarily meant that a cultural methodology had to be employed: artistic expression of the social reality had to be given equal weight with reasoned dissection.

II. Analysis Within the Pastoral Circle

These two moments just described have influenced my own understanding of the importance of a shift to culture and shaped my practical approach to social analysis. While I might be reluctant to give the intellectual and experiential moments shaping my own orientation the label of a paradigm shift, I do see the importance of what De Schrijver refers to as a "change or complementarity in method."[11] Cultural sciences are, indeed, as essential as socio-economic approaches in understanding the reality we confront.

A. Approaches and Aims

How and where one situates the task of social analysis is, of course, very relevant to our discussion here, as is the motivation for undertaking the project. I see three possible approaches to analysis:

> A pastoral tool for use at the grassroots, for example with local development groups, justice and peace committees, student groups, small Christian communities, and so forth. Here the aim of the analysis is to organize a local and immediate response to some pressing social issue. For example, a group might be involved in dealing with the problems of voter apathy, wages paid to domestic workers, or provision of services by a local council.

An academic tool for a research project carried out on a large topic, with or without the aim of any action to be taken or any response to be made. Such analysis is often carried out by professional social scientists associated with academic institutions that do field research through on-site visits but do not actually live in the midst of the reality being analyzed. For example, a research team might study the transition to multi-party democracies in Africa, the increasing growth of Islam, or the macro-economic consequences of privatization.

An organizational tool for studying major issues affecting institutions and societies at national or international levels, with the aim of providing guidelines for possible large-scale activities. UN studies, government reports, and church surveys would be examples of this approach. For example, analysts might look at the global impact of neo-liberal economics, the root causes of the rising numbers of refugees, or the process and progress of inculturation in the African context.

Although I personally have been engaged in many analysis projects utilizing the approaches of the academic and organizational tools, my primary work in recent years has been with the pastoral tool. That is, my engagement is with local popular movements and my focus is on moving toward some response to a pressing problem. For this reason, the social analysis I am most engaged with now has been located within the Pastoral Circle.

B. Moments of Interpretation

The Pastoral Circle is the name Holland and I used in our book, *Social Analysis*, to describe a methodological approach that emphasizes the relationship between reflection and action.[12] The approach relates to what authors like Paulo Friere refer to as praxis (reflection based on experience, and experience based on reflection) or liberation theologians such as Juan Luis Segundo call the hermeneutic circle (new questions raised to older explanations because of contact with new situations). The place of social analysis within the Circle can be seen by noting the four moments of interpretation that arise out of basic questioning of a reality.

- **Contact**: What is happening here? This is the moment of gathering data through insertion in the reality and touching it by gathering objective observations and subjective feelings.

- **Analysis**: Why is it happening? This is the moment of explanation through analysis of the reality, and of probing the causes, connections, and consequences of the reality. Again and again, the question "why?" is asked.

- **Reflection**: How do we evaluate it? This is the moment of discerning the meaning of the reality in light of our values, faith perspectives, community norms, and so forth.

- **Response**: How do we respond to it? This is the moment of action through planning, deciding, and evaluating in order to effect change in the reality.

As an aside at this point, the important role that culture plays can be seen not only in analysis but also in the other three moments of the Pastoral Circle. Thus, subjective feelings are powerfully revealed in story-telling, values are uncovered through the traditional wisdom of proverbs, and customs of respect and deference influence certain styles of response.

The reason for emphasizing that the social analysis is always set within the Pastoral Circle is to stress that it is done in vital contact with reality (not abstracted or purely academic), amid explicit value reflections (not value-free or non-committal), and oriented towards action (not speculative or non-pragmatic). The analysis as a pastoral tool is not conducted on its own. Its location within the Pastoral Circle marks the method and the operation of the analysis that is undertaken and the result and outcome that is desired.

III. Culture and Popular Movements

My own understanding of the importance of cultural analysis in Africa, particularly among some popular movements, comes from my participation in various local programs, mostly associated with development and justice and peace groups. In the examples that follow, I will note how the emphasis on culture provides the movements with deeper insights than would be available if only socio-economic analysis were considered.

A. Culture and Development

Surely one of the most damaging consequences of the Western-inspired developmentalism – over-emphasis on economic growth models – propagated in the poor countries of the South has been to downplay culture as a major shaper of societal relationships and progress. Frequently, culture was not even seen by outsiders; it was ignored or not recognized as a significant reality to be dealt with. The World Bank and other major Western development agencies rarely included an anthropologist on their planning teams. When acknowledged, culture was more often than not seen as a hindrance to economic development – as a backward influence that had to be overcome if true progress was to be achieved within a given society. Ways had to be found to bypass local cultural influences if certain externally sponsored development projects were to be successful.

Examples of the effects of this mentality abound in the stories told about failed development projects. For instance, the outside development worker arrives in a village and finds the women spending hours each day around a communal water standpipe, waiting for their turn to draw water in buckets and carry it back home. The worker – usually a man – estimates the economic inefficiencies of time lost in such activity and decides that the women need water pipes brought directly into their houses, or huts, so that they will not need to gather at the village centre to draw water. He leaves the village satisfied with progress when each house has its own tap. He returns to visit some months later, only to be disappointed to find the village unity destroyed and an alarming rise in family problems – marriage break-ups, difficulties with children, and so forth. What he had failed to take into account in his economic analysis of water-gathering were the cultural advantages of providing space and time for women to share important local news, discuss mutual problems, and offer each other practical advice and commitments to help.

To counter this narrow economic focus, a development education program (DEP) approach is being used in many parts of Africa. The approach I am familiar with in Zambia uses the *Training for Transformation* manuals based upon Paulo Friere's methodology of conscientization.[13] It emphasizes participation by the local communities in identifying projects, planning and deciding, engaging in action, and evaluation. For example, the DEP team that I was part of as a field worker in the Diocese of Monze, 1989-1990, would not go into a village to do something for the people but would empower the people to do something for themselves. Integral, participative, self-reliant, and sustainable were the key words we used to describe our approach.

I remember one workshop in a village where we asked the people to talk about the cultural traditions that they found positive, or helpful, and negative, or restraining, in the efforts being made to achieve the integral, participative, self-reliant, and sustainable development they wanted in their area. (One obvious challenge was to put all these nice English words into ciTonga, the local language!) This stimulated a lively conversation where positive elements of sharing and solidarity were recalled as central to community development, and traditions of care for widows and orphans were seen as instilling social responsibilities in the whole village. But negative elements were also noted, such as the exclusion of women and young people from decision-making processes, and the influence of witchcraft on the spread of fears and suspicions. The analysis that we did in that workshop enabled us to reinforce the positive elements in our training programs and try to reduce the impact of the negative elements.

Another example of cultural analysis that opened up new economic understandings for me was a look at the role of extended families. The extended family system in Africa is a significant cultural pattern that has a very large impact on development. The family should not be, and in Africa is not, seen simply as an economic unit – a mode of production and reproduction. A whole complex set of relationships of meanings, values, expectations, norms, and so forth are central to the life and activity of families. In other words, culture plays a significant role.

An example of this significance can be seen in the organization and operation of what Goran Hyden has called the "economy of affection."[14] Looking particularly at Eastern Africa, he has explored the economic relations that arise when the extended family operates in a subsistence environment. The economy of affection does not of itself involve fond emotions, but "denotes a network of support, communications and interaction among structurally defined groups connected by blood, kin, community and other affinities, for example, religion."[15]

Certain economic decisions are made precisely to preserve – both for individuals and for the community – the "safety net" of the extended family. There are also, of course, corresponding political and social decisions, affecting who makes decisions, what levels of social interchanges take place, and so forth. Some decisions that go against the logic of the economy of capitalism or the economy of socialism are very congruent with the economy of affection. For instance, disposition of property is neither a private affair (capitalistic) nor a matter of state management (socialistic). Property exchanges are viewed as good or bad in light of their impact on strengthening or weakening the extended family. Here culture and economy come very close together.

On two occasions, I found some activity very difficult to appreciate until a cultural analysis opened up the picture for me. First, the diocesan development program for which I worked ran a two-year course in carpentry for youth chosen by their local villages. At the conclusion of the course, the young carpenter would have saved enough money to purchase a set of tools with which, once back in the village, he could earn a good living. But visiting the village six months later, I was disappointed to find the would-be carpenter sitting idle, having sold off his tools to get money for his nephew's school fees and for funeral expenses for a recently deceased relative in the village. Within a capitalist or socialist economic structure, the young carpenter would be judged to have sacrificed his future. But within the economy of affection, he had, in fact, guaranteed his future. This was because whenever difficult times might come, as surely they would, he had maintained both in symbolic gestures and in real life the bonds of affection. Second, a young friend of mine lost his very good job because of some fraudulent actions involving small amounts of money. When I asked him why he had taken such a great risk, he answered that pressures from the extended family for assistance were simply too strong to resist if he hoped to remain in the good graces of that family.[16]

B. Culture and Environmental Concerns

At the time of the UN Conference on Environment and Development (1992), the DEP focused attention on some of Zambia's serious ecological challenges such as deforestation, pollution, and poaching. As part of an effort to strengthen community responses by recovering traditional sources of ecological respect, I was involved with a program of cultural analysis of attitudes toward natural environment. In a workshop setting, we asked participants to recall stories, myths, proverbs, taboos, and so forth that spoke of their relationships to nature. Many creation myths were recounted, as well as many instructions on appropriate or inappropriate attitudes and actions toward nature.

Analyzing this data, we discovered grounds for the validity, indeed the necessity, of these traditional instructions. The analytical process of continually asking the question "why" uncovered important reasons. Elders in the workshop were able to explain to younger members some of these reasons by reflecting on their significance in the light of current concerns about the environment. For instance:

Certain trees were not to be cut down since they were considered sacred. In fact, the trees grew over water sources such as springs, both marking them and sustaining them.

The local chief would determine each year where wild fruit could be picked, because by tradition all the fruits belonged to him. This allowed for a wise pattern of crop rotation, conserving fragile plant life.

No one was allowed to hunt for game alone but only in a designated village group, lest the spirits of the animals would attack him. Such a custom assured that all the wild animals killed did in fact benefit the whole village.

There were cultural taboos against urinating or defecating close to huts in a village; if persons violated these taboos, evil spirits would fall upon them. Thus, basic sanitary hygiene was promoted to keep the locality clean and healthy.

This process of analysis should not be viewed strictly as a "demythologizing" of culture, but rather as a recognition of the wisdom and strength of the culture. Cultural analysis, done largely through storytelling, uncovered many profound reasons for the traditional wisdom. And in a setting that used the Pastoral Circle, this analytical process could lead to more effective responses to meeting ecological concerns.

Another example of cultural analysis that has implications for environmental concerns is the work promoted by a network of scholars from both Third World and First World settings who are interested so-called indigenous knowledge (IK). In epistemological terms, IK is contrasted with Western scientific knowledge in that it is knowledge based more on the belief and customs of local communities than on the empirical data and logical deductions of formal scientific methodology. Especially in dealing with issues of the environment, it is important to pay attention to IK, indeed, more so than in the past. Focus on culture, then, is central to IK considerations about sustainable development, agriculture, local participation, and so forth.

C. Culture and Women

As is true in many places today, the status and role of women in society (and in the Church) is a critically important issue – not just for women but also for men and for the whole of a well-ordered society. But equality of women and men is often viewed by many in Africa – both women and men – as a strictly Western idea and not in line with African culture. It is certainly true that women hold a subservient role and, in many circumstances, are mistreated, exploited, and underdeveloped. For instance, there are alarming statistics about the decline in enrolment of girls in schools. With the imposition of school fees as a result of the IMF-imposed austerity programs of structural adjustment, parents tend to see the best investment to be in boys who one day will get a job. The cultural expectation is that girls will only get married.

By and large, women work much harder than men – longer hours, double jobs (an outside workplace and work at home). Expectations that this is normal are deep in the culture. I commented once to a Zambian man that I was surprised and disturbed to see a very pregnant woman walking along the road with a small baby on her back, another child clutching her right hand, one piece of luggage on her head, and another in her left hand. Meanwhile her husband walked leisurely behind her carrying only a walking stick. I was told – with an almost straight face! – that the man was protecting his wife from any lions they might encounter. The fact that there had been no lions in this particular region for decades did not distract from the cultural imperative that men do not carry their wife's luggage in public, let alone look after children.

A particularly disturbing phenomenon present among many tribes in Zambia, and elsewhere in Africa, is the property grabbing or stripping inflicted upon widows after the death of their husband. The husband's family descends upon the home of the sister-in-law, and takes away everything, even basic necessities like cooking utensils or school books for the children. This is done in the name of the cultural tradition of inheritance whereby the widow, children, and all possessions belong to the husband's family. Civil legislation now makes it possible to draw up wills to protect the widow and children, but implementation of this protection is often extremely difficult for reasons of ignorance, expense, or fear of retaliation (witchcraft).

Local justice and peace groups in Zambia, along with development groups, have taken up the issue of women's rights. They have found that a particularly helpful approach is to do a cultural analysis looking at the deeper reasons for discrimination against women. Often the causes of this discrimination today are distortions of past efforts at protection. For example, the explanation of looking out for the lions may have been valid at one time – an instance of the orderly division of labour. More interesting and relevant is the recognition that the tradition of inheritance assured that the widow and children were, in fact, looked after by the husband's family. Care was taken that the woman was not left isolated on her own, subject to economic and social hardships. But the practice today of stripping – prevalent and intensified in harsh economic situations and circumstances of weakened cultural respect – is the opposite of protection!

By asking the question "why?" again and again, other insights are gained from cultural analysis of women's status and role in society today. These insights contribute to the promotion of greater justice for the whole of society.

D. Culture and Church

The issue of inculturation is too large for this short chapter to take up. But this challenge for the task of evangelization by the Church in Africa does indeed relate to the local use of cultural analysis that I have been discussing here. The central theme of the African Synod (1994) was inculturation.[17] An inculturated faith is one that is authentically Christian and genuinely African. It is a faith wherein one feels at home – not only in liturgical expression but also in credal symbols, theological categories, authority legitimation, instructional procedures, canonical legislation, and so forth.

Two analytical points seem to me to be very important in going about the process of inculturation. These points are analytical in the sense of going deeper into issues and their causes, connections, and consequences. And both points lend themselves to discussions at grass-root levels. For at least the past 20 years, the pastoral strategy of the Church in East Africa has been to build up the small Christian communities (SCCs) – the church in the neighbourhood.[18] Within these SCCs, a cultural analysis of local situations can occur that facilitates both deeper understanding of the faith and more authentic inculturation of its basics.

The first point to note is the necessity of critical analysis of even the most basic faith expressions offered by non-African Christianity and cultural expressions esteemed by Africans. This means asking the why question again and again. When this is done in a group discussion process among ordinary Christians, some very interesting observations come out. One recognition that usually occurs is that much of what we take for granted as being essentials or the way things are done are simply an accepted cultural way of doing things in Europe, North America, or Africa. They are unrelated to any Gospel imperative or essential truth of our faith.

I recall an early experience in Zambia that illustrates this. I was puzzled that people remained sitting during the Gospel reading at Mass. Why did they fail to show respect by standing, the kind of respectful gesture I had grown up with in my own country? A Zambian told me that in their culture, respect was shown by taking a lower place when an elder or important person was speaking. One did not show respect by standing but by sitting. I came to appreciate that the value of respect is expressed in different ways in different cultures. This is a very simple lesson, but one with profound consequences in efforts to inculturate the faith.

Moreover, the analytical questioning process must also be brought to bear on elements of African Traditional Religion that need to be explained and evaluated in the light of shared community norms. For example, cultural analysis needs to examine the proverbs, myths, dreams, visions, and so forth that express the religious wisdom of the people. During one workshop with community development workers, we explored the significance of traditional rain shrine ceremonies and the lessons that could be learned for today's experience of droughts and subsequent famine among the people.

A second point is the need to recognize that inculturation and liberation must go hand-in-hand. Jean-Marc Ela has frequently called attention to the fact that commitment to an inculturation that does not include genuine liberation can be only antiquarianism – an escapist fascination with folklore.

> A church that seeks to say something to today's African cannot content itself with an authentically African liturgy, catechetics, and theology. The modes of expression of the faith have sense and meaning only if the

> church is deeply involved in the battles being waged by human beings against conditions that stifle their human liberty. The participation of the church in these battles, then, becomes the necessary condition for any liturgy, any catechesis, any theology in Africa. It is in the vital experience of the communities and of their striving for life, liberty, and justice, that any reference to Jesus and his mission—a mission of the liberation of the oppressed—will find genuine sense and meaning.[19]

But liberation in Africa must address not only politico-socio-economic realities that are oppressive and unjust. It must also address the cultural oppression that is the historic legacy of colonialism and the contemporary consequence of globalization. Western media pervades local settings with foreign values of individualism, consumerism, sexual licence, and so forth. Foreign imports are often considered of greater value than local products, both in material goods and as cultural expressions. Several African scholars have spoken of anthropological poverty as the most serious impoverishment experienced on the continent. This is the depersonalization of the African, a result of racist interpretations of psychology, religion, and history. Cultural analysis opens up this reality and enables the Church to more effectively engage in a truly liberating evangelization.

IV. Conclusion: Relevance to African Liberation Theology

To repeat the point made at the beginning of this chapter, my intention has been to demonstrate how cultural analysis has both the potential and the reality of making a significant contribution to the liberation of Africa today. I have tried to do this by describing how cultural analysis is used in many of the social movements that involve people at the local level in the process of change. Speaking from my own experience with some of these movements of justice and peace, development, ecology, women's concerns, and inculturation with the Church, I believe that several conclusions can be drawn.

> Cultural considerations can never be absent from any good analysis of the African situation. Despite the influence of the dominant neo-liberal economic environment with the consequent prominence of the culture of the market, an environment fostered by the structural adjustment programs spreading across the continent, deep cultural realities still exist and are influential.
>
> Cultural considerations affect not only the content of good analysis in Africa but also the methodology. Socio-economic analysis relies heavily on social science methodologies of questionnaires, comparative studies, computer examinations, and so forth. While, of course, not ignoring these aids to understanding, cultural analysis also uses storytelling, drama, art, music, proverbs, and so forth to go deeper into the realities being studied.

> Cultural considerations are particularly relevant and important when participating in social movements that are directed toward change at the local level. This does not mean ignoring structural issues of a more economic or political character, but supplementing analysis of these with an emphasis on culture that speaks more to people at the grassroots.

Finally, it is appropriate to let theologians draw conclusions about the implications of all this for African liberation theology. But it should certainly be obvious that in a church that takes seriously the agenda of the African Synod, grassroots analysis will necessarily put an emphasis on culture that will shape the integral evangelization task of the coming years. And central to that evangelization, of course, will be the project of liberation.

16

Global Governance, the State, and Multinational Corporations

John A. Coleman S.J.

Three important partial lacunae, or bits of unfinished business, remain in our discussions so far in this volume about globalization and Catholic Social Thought (CST): global governance, the enduring essential role for strong and effective states, and the new forms of multinational corporations. Each one also points to lacunae for CST itself, since CST remains quite jejune in its treatment of these three units. All three units – international government organizations, states, and multinational corporations – will need to function well and communicate with the other units, if what we envision is a humane globalization. Each topic – although not entirely missing elsewhere in the essays – needs a slightly more developed presentation. Because each of these three themes is truly a vast subject, I must limit myself to some pointed remarks about why they are important to the issues of globalization and how they might connect back to CST.

I. Global Governance

The term being used is important: governance, not government. We need to think in new ways about governing, ways that are not synonymous with states and intergovernmental organizations (IGOs) – the main governance terms found in CST. We should start thinking about new and flexible, if still somewhat amorphous, governing units that are called regimes and global policy networks. Clearly, a number of groups, such as The Commission on Global Governance, have recognized the existence of crucial gaps in global governance. A major gap exists in jurisdictional bodies; some examples are an international criminal court and a civil society forum at the UN. Another important gap is in participatory mechanisms to protect against rule by technocrats who can run IGOs without any input from non-governmental sources. A third crucial gap is the lack of incentives to protect against the infamous free-rider problem. For example, this occurs when states or non-governmental organizations (NGOs), including multinational corporations, benefit from global governance but do not share its costs or, for private gains, elude global regulatory codes with impunity and without sanctions.

Some fairly straightforward intuitive notions can help guide our thinking about global governance. One is that truly global problems need truly global solutions that are workable and effective. A second intuition is that no one really wants some super-global world government that would be open to the abuse of power and undermine subsidiarity. A third is that there can be little genuine continued growth and economic development without a strong institutional infrastructure. It has become clearer that without some new global governance structures, globalization risks leading to quite severe policy failures and social decay.

A fourth intuition is that there are multiple actors – such as states, NGOs, multinational corporations, churches, lawyers, and citizens' groups – with legitimate stakeholder interests in global governance schemes. All legitimate stakeholders must have input into global governance. A fifth intuitive notion is that debates about global governance look both to designing new institutions and formulating new rules of the game. A sixth is that, for the foreseeable future, nation states will continue to demand to play key roles in intergovernmental units such as the World Trade Organization (WTO) and The Basle Accord on Banking that, among other things, stipulate a minimal lending capacity for bank lending across countries. Finally, as any introductory Political Science class would demonstrate, governance at any level raises ethically fraught issues of who rules, in whose interests, by what mechanisms, and for what purposes. Governance that lacks legitimacy or permits a gross democratic deficit forfeits consensus or compliance. Debates about the current state of globalization frequently fix on just these questions of who rules and in whose interests.

Let us begin with a discussion of IGOs where states, as such, generally remain the major voting members, although some IGOs, such as the World Bank, contain specific provisions that bring NGOs into crucial policy formulation. Some IGOs contain clear adjudication mechanisms and can apply sanctions to offending states, as, for example, the WTO and the International Monetary Fund (IMF); they have a mechanism for resolving disputes. Other IGOs must depend almost entirely on persuasion and consensus. The International Labor Organization (ILO), for example, since its founding in 1919, has devised important codes for workers and has fought child labour and championed safe working conditions. But it lacks effective sanctions or enforcement mechanisms. *Global Governance*, the document written for the European Bishops, calls for a new UN Environmental Organization, related in its scope to the WTO and the ILO.[1] Clearly, the interests of labour and the environment have less clout in current international governance organizations than do financial and business interests, raising both a legitimacy and an integration issue.

Our Global Neighborhood, the essentially liberal internationalist proposal of the Commission on Global Governance, is more ambitious in its proposals for reorganization of global governance. It asks for a global taxation scheme to finance the work of IGOs and to further development aid to poorer countries. This proposal for a global tax to finance development becomes all the more pressing since the levels of foreign aid from developed to developing countries have dropped precipitously in the last decade, leading some cynics to claim that development has become the first casualty of globalization. Some have championed the so-called Tobin Tax – named after the Nobel Economic laureate, James Tobin, who first proposed it – on international currency and financial transfers across borders. This would serve both as a way of raising revenue for global campaigns of IGOs and as a brake on financial volatility that eludes the capacity of even large central banks – such as the Bank of England or the Federal Reserve Board – to monitor or regulate. Many reputable economists, however, question how practicable and enforceable a Tobin Tax could be. They doubt it could work and also question its negative impact on the free flow of investments, so key to the globalization project.[2]

But clearly, some elements of what German Chancellor Helmut Schmitt once called casino capitalism – trading on future commodities, interest rates, derivatives, or currency fluctuations – stand in need of restraint and regulation. Just as clearly, some viable means of raising revenues for global governance – beyond the present strategy of financial support through often reluctant states – need to be addressed and implemented. Without adequate money, the high-sounding development goals to reduce poverty and increase education and health standards around the world will remain only ideals and fantasies.

Our Global Neighborhood pleads for a standing UN peace force and for an Economic Security Council at the UN (cognate to but without the veto rights of the Great Powers, as found in the Security Council). It asks for UN authority over the global commons (space, Antarctica, and the oceans) and for a new quasi-parliamentary body of civil society – a sort of second chamber of representatives of global NGOs – to counterbalance the UN General Assembly, which is only made up of states. In 1995, *Our Global Neighborhood* endorsed the creation of a new International Criminal Court that became a reality in 1998 and also called for a special UN unit to permit direct access for citizens' petitions to bypass the mediation of their own home governments. Somewhat similar global governance measures have recently been presented to the Club of Rome.[3]

Regimes

Yet these proposals of *Our Global Neighborhood* seem, at times, both overly idealistic and still old-fashioned, because the document does not adequately talk about regimes and global policy networks. Neither does it sufficiently address bureaucratic inertia and distancing from the grassroots that is often endemic in many IGOs, or the way corruption in Third World states has fraudulently siphoned off foreign aid. Such corruption partially explains the fall-off in foreign aid.

Regimes embody sufficient functional powers, delegated to them by states through multilateral agreements, for limited purposes to regulate, coordinate, or implement global rules. Thus, most states' shipping laws are really written by the

International Maritime Organization (IMO) in London and air safety laws are set in Montreal by the International Civil Aviation Organization. Food standards are hashed out in Rome by the Food and Agricultural Organization (FAO) and intellectual property disputes are adjudicated in Geneva by a sub-unit of the WTO. When we look at effective global regimes (for example, the International Postal Union) we make a number of discoveries. (1) Some are purely state-centred and controlled through a standing IGO, such as the WTO, or through multilateral treaties. (2) Some regimes, such as the World Bank, are state-centred but with specific provisions for private sector access, input, and voice. (3) Some, such as the Basle Committee on Banking Regulations and Supervisory Practices, involve public-private partnerships between, for example, IGOs and banks. (4) Other regimes, such as the Internet Corporation for Assigned Names, are purely private regimes in the public interest.

No government or IGO directly regulates the Internet. Similarly, bond-rating agencies – such as Standard and Poor, the International Accounting Standards Committee, the Global Water Partnership, the International Committee on Standards – are neither states nor, strictly speaking, IGOs. A private diamond cartel self-regulates the mining of diamonds and the International Chemical Association drew up its own codes to regulate chemical pollution. International scientific and medical societies also function as regimes that frequently set international standards.

What one looks for in international regimes is efficiency, accountability, transparency, participatory access for legitimate stakeholders, and the removal of corruption, both from governments and multinational corporations. One seeks effective coordination and a kind of socialization of global actors to a quasi-constitution of rules about issues such as aviation, banking, the environment, the postal union, anti-personnel landmines, and so forth. Note that these salient themes – accountability, transparency, corruption, and regimes that are neither states nor IGOs – are not really articulated anywhere in current CST. CST does not address the remit of various units of global governance nor the ethics needed to guide their regimes. In that sense, for all its vaunted call for an international common good, the CST tradition has remained much too vague and moralistic when it comes to the guiding criteria it brings to thinking through global governance.

Global Policy Networks

The other new unit in globalization thinking is that amorphous thing called a global policy network – a kind of flexible public-private and frequently time-bound concatenation of NGOs, IGOs, and multinational corporations. Kofi Annan, the Secretary General of the UN, observed their emergence and vital importance for global governance in the following terms: "The United Nations once dealt only with governments. By now we know that peace and prosperity cannot be achieved without partnership involving governments, international organizations, the business community and civil society." The Secretary General expands on this point: "Formal institutional arrangements may often lack the scope, speed and informational capacity to keep up with the rapidly changing global agenda. Mobilizing the skills and the resources of diverse global actors, therefore, may increasingly involve forming loose and temporary global policy networks that cut across national, international and disciplinary lines."[4]

Global policy networks are difficult to define or type. They bring together both diverse countries and diverse sectors of activity. Often they have shown ingenuity in their use of information technologies. In terms of global governance, networks place new issues on the global agenda and raise issues that have been neglected or treaties that are not being implemented. They help to facilitate a truly public discourse on such issues. Global policy networks can facilitate the negotiating and setting of global standards – for example, for financial regulation, regulations to catch and monitor money laundering, or environmental management. Global policy networks are natural mechanisms for gathering and disseminating knowledge. They can serve, at times, as innovative implementation mechanisms by which IGOs outsource pieces of the implementation of their policy to the global policy network. They close the participatory gap in global governance.

Many of us, of course, are aware of some important global policy networks. These include the International Campaign to Ban Landmines, winner of a Nobel Prize for Peace, which could bypass the UN – where the issue of landmines came to a stalemate because of the intransigence of the US – and bring about a new regime, anchored in a multilateral treaty.[5] There are already more than a hundred functioning global policy networks. Some examples are the World Commission on Dams – which unites IGOs such as the World Bank, corporations, governments, and environmental NGOs; the International Coalition to Stop the Use of Child Soldiers; and Transparency International, which focuses on exposing and reforming corruption in governments and corporations. These are less than regimes but more than just the civil society organizations that Appleby limns for us in his chapter.

More and more, the trajectory of global governance has been following the logic of networks. Functionally specific and defined, such networks avoid bureaucratic inertia and bring together diverse sectors of society. They would seem to serve the purposes of subsidiarity. Too often we think of subsidiarity as a kind of vertical subsidiarity – going from local to regional to national to intergovernmental governance. But there is also a kind of horizontal subsidiarity that looks to a leaner form of governance – one that bypasses top-heavy bureaucracy and coordinates the many stake-holders into governance units that respect both the local and the legitimate stakeholders. If a coordinating global network can do the job, why introduce a more cumbersome bureaucratic IGO? The important thing is that the unit is no bigger than necessary to get the global job done.[6]

To become more effective and credible in globalization debates, CST needs to give more attention to the question of global governance. This includes its institutional forms, the ethical criteria brought to judge those institutions, and the arenas – such as, for example, raising revenues or citizens' access to IGOs – where governance needs to be expanded or reformed. CST needs, I suggest, to introduce two new essential concepts about governance units that are at present totally lacking in its vocabulary: regimes and global policy networks. Only then will its sometimes lofty, yet often vague, talk about a global common good gain some deeper bite and purchase.

II. States

Strong and viable states still matter. Few things so endanger a humane globalization than weak, failed, or corrupt states; Hehir raises the issue of failed states in his chapter in this volume. These states become festering breeding grounds for crime, money laundering, drug cartels, terrorism, the arms trade, violence, and human rights violations. Strong nations can still thwart sensible moves to regulate the negative aspects of globalization. Thus, the US and China have refused to abide by the Kyoto protocols to reduce greenhouse gas emissions over a set time period. Indeed, the unilateralism of the strong powers can derail the necessary arrangements for a more ethical globalization. I suspect this will not be in effect in long run since unilateralism is not really a very viable option in the age of globalization, as the debacle of US unilateral actions in Iraq has shown.

Only a kind of cooperative multilateralism – in the interest of most states – and some transfer of a limited piece of sovereignty by states will allow a humane global order. Conversely, a strong government – even in a state like Malaysia that is not a superpower – could successfully resist even such a powerful instrument of global governance as the IMF. During the Asian financial crisis of the late 1990s, Malaysia wisely refused the bidding of the IMF; Malaysia withstood the crisis better than its neighbours and bounced back faster.

As Dirk Messner ably states: "Workable supranational regulatory systems are based on functioning national institutions. No viable global governance can come about without strong and effective states."[7] Richard Falk echoes that sentiment: "Nationalism remains the most popular force on the planet. Peoples without a state generally feel unrepresented or at least inadequately represented. Such peoples often claim a right of self-determination, including the right to form their own independent state. The territorial state in the wake of the collapse of empires, is the only political form that exerts authority in a way that is fully acknowledged on the global level."[8]

States remain central in IGOs – although, in an organization such as the IMF, some states are more equal than others. States remain the preeminent domain for democratic governance. The hope lingers everywhere that, when hard pressed, states will listen to their citizens. Most global NGOs are located and anchored in developed countries. Often, their actions – for example, on human rights and environmental issues – are criticized in developing nations as a kind of Western imperialism. The true success of such global NGOs comes when they can link up with NGOs from more local Southern tier nations on issues such as human rights, de-forestation, and so forth, and then press their own states for action. What Tip O'Neill, the former US House Majority Leader, once said remains true, even in an age of globalization: in the end, all politics is local. IGOs or outside states can never, on their own, revive a failed state, remove corruption in state governments, or provide the social capital necessary to build a viable state. These must come from forces operating within the state.[9]

In point of fact, most of the successful so-called civil society campaigns in global governance have involved some crucial action by states. The successful landmine treaty would never have occurred without the key role played by Canada and its foreign minister, Lloyd Axworthy. The campaign against the Multilateral Investment Agreement, which would have globally deregulated all foreign investment, only really achieved a breakthrough – despite very strong NGO support for the campaign around the world – when France withdrew its support for the agreement. The NGOs in Brazil who asked for the publication of their country-specific plan imposed by the IMF – against IMF policy to keep country-specific plans from public scrutiny beyond the financial technocrats in a country – could only have succeeded with the support of the Brazilian Congress. As Daphné Josselin and William Wallace write: "Global campaigning is unlikely to bring positive results unless at least some state actors (and preferably those in the West) endorse the agenda of the NGOs."[10]

To be sure, international NGOs often skirt recalcitrant states and go directly to global civil society or to IGOs to create a boomerang effect back home. Some examples are the campaigns against China's use of prison labour and Myanmar's abuses of human rights and its permission for timber companies to invade its rain forest. Even here, however, the ultimate aim is to bring about a responsive state. Moreover, there is a danger that the NGOs, which Appleby rightly champions in his chapter in this volume, may actually sometimes undercut the necessary strength of states by going too soon to international action to boycott, shame, or pressure states. They risk bypassing state-centred civil society NGOs in the Third World that, in the long run, must monitor and implement progress on human rights, environmental protection, and so forth in their home locales.

Wolfgang Reinecke states the equation correctly: " For the foreseeable future governments will remain the core constituent elements of global governance. Governing the global economy without governments is not an option. Yet for global governance to succeed, governments will have to enlist the active cooperation of non-state actors."[11] Stated in other terms, the creation of strong democratic states is an essential building block for a more democratic global order. Or, in Catholic terms, subsidiarity means that, even under conditions of globalization, we must continue to work assiduously for viable and effective states.

III. Multinational Corporations

A journalist writing in the *Manchester Guardian* claimed that "corporations have never been more powerful, yet less regulated, never more pampered by government yet less questioned, never more needed to take social responsibility, yet never more secretive. To whom will these fabulously self-motivated, self-interested supranational bodies be accountable?"[12] There is no question that corporations can be extensively powerful. Moreover, corporations have, in some ways, mutated their organizational logic in the era of globalization. One third of all the international trade in our world takes place as intra-firm trade – Ford Germany to Ford US, for example. Indeed, much of the US deficit flows from intra-firm trade between US corporations and their foreign affiliates. There are currently some 45,000 multinational corporations – most of their headquarters are located in the developed, industrial world – with more than 280,000 foreign affiliates worldwide. Globalization has shifted the organizational logic of companies. They engage in more mergers and acquisitions. Frequently, they enter into secure inter-firm alliances to defray research and development costs or they outsource intermediate inputs.

Notoriously, parts of a Japanese auto may have components made in France and the US and an American auto may have fewer made-in-US components than an auto made in Japan. International outsourcing and multiple affiliates help the multinational corporation insulate the company from risks, as well as exchange rate fluctuations and unwanted regulations. Thus, if country X engages in an embargo of its products to country Y, the headquarters of a company in country X – making arms, pharmaceuticals, or autos – can simply transfer the contracts to an affiliate to avoid the regulation. The new multinational business organization makes regulation of industry or its taxation by any one country more difficult to achieve. Indeed, many multinationals are the prototypes of the free-rider as they frequently profit from governmental research and development money, often elude the payment of taxes, and benefit from state policies of corporate welfare. That is why the multinational corporation in itself – and in its successful forms of new inter-firm strategic alliances – is, organizationally, very different from the free enterprise entrepreneurial unit described by John Paul II in his social encyclical, *Centesimus Annus*.[13] CST does not currently have a coherent treatment of multinational corporations as they have evolved under globalization. Ford Motor Company's economy is larger than that of Saudi Arabia; Phillip Morris' is larger than that of New Zealand; and IBM's – even though it has recently fallen on some hard times – is still larger than that of the Philippines.

But there is also no question that a humane globalization will never occur without the cooperation of multinational organizations. In 1999, the UN proposed a Global Compact with multinationals, based on nine crucial principles of fair enterprise for corporate behaviour in global contexts. These nine crucial principles included avoidance of child labour, respect for the human rights of workers, and a guarantee of labour safety. The Global Compact remains a purely voluntary, largely self-regulated code. One must question whether corporations, on their own, will protect public goods – this flies, after all, in the face of the logic of the market – or will build into their true market price the so-called externality costs, for example, in environmental pollution. Nevertheless, corporations, under the prod of both persuasion and pressure, have shown some responsibility and taken some initiatives in cooperation. They have worked, for example, with the World Commission on Dams – which tries to protect the environment from excessive erosion by unnecessarily large dams – and with the forest industry on ecological and conservation issues.

One reason corporations do so well in being generally efficient and cost effective is that their remit remains very narrow – to make a profit for shareholders – and they are allowed to bracket and pass on to governments or consumers side social costs of their actions. Only when they are, unwontedly, forced to conceive their enterprise in larger social terms, will corporations become good global citizens. Multinationals need effective monitoring.

NGOs have successfully engaged in consumer boycotts – the boycott of Nestlé's products because of its marketing of infant formulas in Third-World countries is the most memorable. They have exposed corporate misconduct of the highest order – examples are Shell Oil's use of private militias who killed private citizens, Shell's other violations of human rights in Nigeria, and Coca-Cola's similar behaviour in Colombia. NGOs sometimes engage in counter-advertising to expose corporate misdoings, such as Nike's resort to sweatshops in Asia. They appeal to shareholder activism at board meetings. They spearhead movements for socially responsible investment. Still other NGOs – for example, the Forestry Stewardship Council – engage corporations and use a special logo to show that lumber has not come from Burmese, Malaysian, or Brazilian rain forests. Because multinational corporations engage forcefully to have effect on governmental policies and pay huge sums in lobbying at national capitals, their political activity also needs careful monitoring, regulation, and exposure.

But multinationals have also engaged in good citizenship behaviour. They have collaborated in fostering global codes of ethics. McDonald's and the Environmental Defense Fund, for example, worked collaboratively to get rid of, and find a more sustainable substitute for, the environmentally polluting polystyrene containers that were used for hamburgers. Some corporations in defined niches, such as the International Chemical Industry, have engaged in self-regulation – often as a ploy to avoid more stringent regulation by governments. Self-regulated business codes often remain notoriously weak and represent more rhetoric than reality, but going from no codes to self-regulated ones can be a genuine, if modest, achievement.[14] Other corporations have joined the Coalition for Environmentally Responsible Economies around a code, called the Valdez Principles, that commits the corporation to "minimize release of pollutants, conserve non-renewable resources, use sustainable energy sources, use environmental commitments in naming nominees to the board of directors."[15] For its part, the International Chamber of Commerce has endorsed cogent principles for environmental sustainability.

Clearly, there are, as yet, no effective global regulations against monopolies and cartels on the world market; monopoly laws still only apply within nations. Some inter-firm alliances verge on cartels. The terms of trade ought to be truly free and fair. No less clearly, consumers need to remain both vigilant of abuses yet supportive of corporate behaviour that respects human rights, the environment, and labour standards. A broader consumer education and movement seems desirable to prepare consumers for misleading advertisements and to demand a more transparent labeling of the contents of products. We also need a more vigorous concern about the pervasive role of corporations in setting agendas in politics or in dominating regulatory agencies. David Korten may go too far, but he suggests that corporations, as such, be kept from any direct political lobbying or involvement.[16] By almost any standards, the disproportionate sway of corporations and moneyed interests over politics seems excessive and dangerous to democratic principles.

Peter Newell writes, "Codes of conduct to govern multi-national corporations are of little use unless they are backed by large scale consumer pressure to enforce them."[17] Because corporations have sometimes shown themselves to be good global citizens and have, on occasion, voluntarily subscribed to ethical principles for a more humane economy, we cannot simply demonize them. They provide jobs and create wealth. They find ways, through the market, to maximize efficiencies and bring out new products. They will be indispensable actors in discovering and marketing more environmentally friendly energy sources. The Sullivan principles, applied to apartheid in South Africa by corporations, gave leverage to those resisting a racist regime. The challenge for those interested in a global common good remains: how to turn paper gains to grassroots enactment; how to engage corporations in the public interest.

Some years ago I was part of a project at the Center for Ethics and Public Policy at the Graduate Theological Union in Berkeley to entice banks to genuinely factor the social impacts of their lending policies into their financial equations. This had some real effect on the Wells Fargo Bank. That bank and other corporations underwent an ethical training period in social responsibility for its executives. The multinational corporation, like globalization, is not, per se, good or bad. But it needs some codes of conduct with more teeth and monitoring, some regulations concerning monopolies and cartels, and new moves toward socially responsible investment. The political impact of the multinational corporation may need curtailing. One of the things global policy networks have demonstrated is that corporations are most likely to exhibit socially exemplary behaviours when they take part in tri-sectoral alliances – such as among NGOs, IGOs and states, and corporations – to address global issues and policies.

CST, for its part, should pay more attention to a careful description of the new organizational forms of the multinational corporation – to both strengths and weaknesses. In the end, CST's analysis of globalization will call for more careful attention to the three crucial agents in globalization and their interrelations: intergovernmental organizations, regimes and policy networks; states; and multinational corporations.

In reference to the content of CST writing: where is the political line? Is there one?

17

Personal Comments, Reflections, and Hopes

William F. Ryan S.J.

While it is rooted in the teachings of the Old Testament prophets and of Jesus, Catholic Social Thought (CST) is usually dated from Pope Leo XIII in the 1890s. Later popes, Vatican Council II, and local bishops have added to it. Our seminar explored the relevance of this teaching for the 21st century. In this chapter I will dwell briefly on a few major themes covered by our authors. These include: What is globalization? What is CST today? Can globalization and CST be related and, if so, how? Can CST influence the future processes of globalization? My treatment will be personal, evocative, and highly selective. I make no pretence of commenting on all the riches of opinion shared by the authors of earlier chapters.

Globalization

Our authors and the other participants in our seminar were unanimous that a satisfactory definition of globalization cannot be given at this time. Rather, they chose to use it as a helpful umbrella concept, like sustainable development. This may be just as well, when we find political philosophers of the stature of John Ralston Saul stating categorically in a recent issue of *Harper's* magazine that globalization is already dead. After reviewing the short-time fate of such grand economic theories as communism and Keynesianism, Saul wrote: "Our own Globalization, with its technocratic and technological determinism and market ideology, had thirty years. And now it, too, is dead."[1]

Our authors saw globalization as a multidimensional concept with great potential for sharing information and knowledge and for building solidarity and community at all levels of society. However, in current usage, globalization has come to be identified almost exclusively with its economic dimension and even with one specific economic theory. In this usage, they would agree, I believe, with Ralston Saul that globalization is a return to 1929 laissez-faire marketism newly wrapped in modern technology that includes the Internet. Our group did not accept the processes of economic globalization as inevitable or predetermined, but rather saw these processes as human constructions that can be changed by human decisions and ingenuity. They did not discuss an end date for economic globalization. Instead, they foresaw that with its strong growth bias it would sooner or later confront natural limits, whether ecological or human.

Only Joe Holland – in his long-term, cosmological vision – saw globalization, with its dominant mechanical metaphor, as already dying and giving way to a return to localization and local cultures and pluralism. This is consonant with Karl Polanyi's remedy of re-imbedding people's work in their social relations, to which Gregory Baum refers. It is a view also remotely consonant with that of Ralston Saul, who, since 1995, sees a growing disillusionment with economic globalization and a sharp return to various forms of nationalism and tribalism in many instances. Witness the most recent impasse at the World Trade Organization meeting at Cancun, where a new group of poor countries – led by China, India, and Brazil – finally mounted some countervailing bargaining power against the persistent control strategies of the rich countries.

The judgment of *Foreign Policy's* Global Index is modest. The authors suggest that the discussion has now moved from whether globalization will come to a screeching halt to whether the positive aspects of global integration can be harnessed to offset the negative ones.[2] For them, interconnective technology is the gas pedal and economics and politics the brake for globalization. For future momentum, they are counting more on technology than on foreign trade and investment.[3]

My personal view is that it is becoming clearer each day that global democratic, corporate free-market capitalism is as utopian, as unrealizable a situation as was global democratic communism or socialism. The human and environmental costs are simply too high.[4] For others at our symposium, their overarching concern about globalization was its close association with massive human poverty and environmental destruction. There seems to be little evidence to suggest, in spite of considerable public rhetoric, that either massive poverty or environmental destruction – the major concerns of our authors – will be off the world agenda in the foreseeable future. Even if security-conscious nation states reclaim more of their governing role from powerful transnational corporations, the latter show few signs of changing their individualistic, greed-driven, and global way of doing business.

Catholic Social Thought

Our authors are unanimous in their conviction that CST is relevant and has a high potential for challenging and even offering human healing to this globalized economic system that is generating so much poverty and environmental destruction. They are dismayed, however, at how little of that potential is presently being deployed by the Church. They also see clearly how that teaching needs to be updated and rooted more adequately in the context of today's world.

Our authors raise no challenge to the core principles of CST. These include the human dignity of every person created in the divine image, and the social nature of humans that roots the virtue of solidarity. Others are the principle of subsidiarity that balances power between the individual and the collective and insists that people participate democratically in decision-making at all levels of society and, finally, the preferential option for the poor that should mark all Christian thought and action. The challenge, as always, is to find the right balance between the individual and social nature of humans in whatever they do and to build bridges between them in the global context. For the Church today, it seems that kind of thinking and acting will be carried out more and more with other civil society groupings and not, as in the past, by seeking special access or privilege from the state.

Indeed, the task of CST is to be seen as a search for balance on multiple levels and in multiple contexts between the extremes of spiritualism and fundamentalism, between historical consciousness and tradition, and between the individual and the collective. A balance is also needed between reading the signs of the times and advancing natural law, between ecological holism and scientific reductionism, between a "Mr. Fix-it" hubris and respect for nature's rhythms, between realism and idealism, and, finally, between the prophetic and the political. CST is always trying to find more human middle positions, institutions, and practices between these extremes, or trying to bridge them in tension with various umbrella formulae such as redemptive natural law.

Major Concerns, Tensions, and Proposals

At our symposium, CST was discussed within the common vision of Vatican II's *Gaudium et spes* (The Church in the Modern World). It proclaims that "the joys and hopes, the griefs and anxieties of men and women of this age, especially those who are poor or in any way afflicted, are the joys and the hopes, the griefs and anxieties of the followers of Christ. That is why Christians cherish a deep feeling of solidarity with the human race and its history."[5] This concrete vision was made still clearer in the statement *Justice in the World* by the 1971 Synod of Bishops. It said: "Action on behalf of justice and participation in the transformation of the world fully appear to us as a constitutive dimension of the preaching of the Gospel, or, in other words, of the Church's mission for the redemption of the human race and its liberation from every oppressive situation."[6]

This vision of CST rejects the earlier separation between the supernatural and the natural that fostered a division for Catholics between their spiritual life and their work life and, inevitably, between clergy and laity. CST not only rejects such dualism but forcefully insists on the basic faith awareness of the constant presence and action of the divine in all creation – in both humans and nature. This vision roots most of the discussion, insights, and proposals of our authors. I will discuss some of them here.

A major concern championed by Mary Evelyn Tucker and others is for a more integrated and better-articulated place for the environment in CST. As is clear from the Appendix to her article, formal papal references and statements about the environment have increased in number since 1972, with Pope John Paul II calling urgently for "a true education in [environmental] responsibility [that] entails a genuine conversion in ways of thought and behaviour..."[7] He recognizes that the environmental crisis is a moral crisis and thus sees the urgent need for ecological conversion and ecumenical and interreligious dialogue and cooperation.

All seminar participants agreed with this development – some more strongly than others. Personally, I believe that the environment can no longer be simply listed or given more space in CST. Its urgency calls for a recasting of social teaching from a cosmological point of view in which a biblical, scientific, and historical framework becomes the framework for CST. From its genesis in the industrial revolution, CST has focused on European issues and today on the global economy gradually integrating such issues as environment, war, and peace into the global economy. But the earth's ecological systems cannot be integrated into one of its subsystems – that is, the economy. The environment is, itself, the comprehensive framework for all creation. In fact, as we are discovering today, our growth-biased market economy is already hitting against external limits such as clean water, fresh air, and non-renewable resources, leaving most economists and many scientists in a state of denial. With good reason, some environmental scientists are turning to world religions, their scriptures, and their traditions for new interpretations, visions, and motivation for what they now see as the original and ongoing unfolding of the universe.

This is, first of all, a challenge for theologians and experts in CST. I believe the elements of such an interpretative statement can be found in the late David Toolan's book *At Home in the Cosmos.*[8] His is a visionary synthesis of science and theology. He shows how Christ-centred, incarnational faith provides a most appropriate setting for contemporary scientific cosmology.

There appeared to be some tension in our seminar between those who see the world through the eyes of the poor in their present economic situation and those who would see the world more holistically and apparently more contemplatively. Some seem to fear that an ecological approach is deterministic, so that when extended to humans it would see suffering, for example, as inevitable; and we know very well that it will be the poorest who suffer most. Indeed, social activists are resisting a similar determinism in the present neo-liberal economic ideology. I believe several factors are at play here. The most important is a lack of adequate language on the part of the environmentalists, whose language can at times seem quite detached from the poor. I also believe that, now that water, air, and soil/land are becoming central concerns for both environmentalists and social justice activists, their ideas and concerns will overlap more and more and require urgent, even prophetic, cooperation and action.

Another factor is that many social activists – because they are daily forced to work concretely in the dominant reductionist economic paradigm to better the present situation of the poor – may not have acquired the ability to see the world as a whole. They may not be able to see that environmental problems cannot be solved within the limited market or societal framework of the agents that caused these problems. However, environmental and social activists will both quickly agree that an action – such as the privatization of water – does not bring clean water to the poor or solve the growing shortage of clean water in the world.

Another factor at play here is the concern of environmentalists that humans need to learn to live more gracefully with the basic rhythms of nature, rather than always try to control them. The social activists are struggling to change a social practice, a law, or an institution. They must work with passion and so cannot be fully detached. They have to recognize and confront power. Yet, as Christians, they cannot accept the Mr. Fix-it hubris of our technological elite who act as if they can and will ultimately control both nature and all human constructions. I believe that looking at the world holistically with the eyes of faith will foster a more contemplative stance. This will recognize more clearly the gifts, the limits, and the basic rhythms of nature; one can still struggle on behalf of the poor while rejecting the control complex that dulls freedom and creative imagination.

Finally, there is the matter of cosmogenesis – the scientific story of how the universe began and continues to unfold – which does not sit easily with everyone. I believe this hesitation is somewhat related to concerns about Darwin's theory of evolution and present questions about the centrality of humans in the universe. Personally, I believe there is also, at times, an older view lurking here that God is not in evolution and that humans are not fully part of evolution. But God as God has been and is in evolution – creating, sustaining, and letting God's creation freely evolve through billions of years. And in Jesus, God is incarnate and still God. Our God is not afraid of *kenosis,* of self-giving and self-emptying.

On this point, I find John F. Haught's book, *God After Darwin: A Theology of Evolution,*[9] both helpful and challenging. He explains how God can co-exist with violence in evolution as evidence of God exercising self-restraint with nature and with humans. He writes: "A world truly loved by God must have room to wander about, experimenting with various possibilities. Love allows the universe to remain unfinished for now. If God had completed creation in such a way that the world was frozen into a deadness with no future, it would have been an exercise of God's being rather than an independent creation. Evolution, therefore, seems to me to be essential to a world truly loved by God."[10]

This vision is consonant with that of Teilhard de Chardin in *The Divine Milieu.*[11] Teilhard, the mystic and scientific visionary, sees God present and vividly active in all evolving creation. Humans remain special, for it is they who alone bring the wonder of God's action in creation into consciousness and so can love and make decisions freely in it. These considerations may help to reduce present or potential tensions between social and environmental activists who really complement and overlap one another in their concerns and struggles. However, this Chardinian vision – that sees history as whole but neither linear nor determined, being led freely by Christ to its fulfillment in the kingdom of God – may not satisfy those, like Gregory Baum, who have a darker, more Augustinian and more piecemeal, vision of history and the role of the Church therein.

Globalization and Reading the Signs of the Times

Johan Verstraeten has given us a central, stimulating and hope-filled challenge in his chapter. I quote his rich comprehensive conclusion before commenting on it:

> CST is a living tradition of practice and thought that has legitimacy on its own, but also has the potential to become an inspiring voice in the great debates of our time. The Church serves the world not by sticking to a univocal reiteration of principles, but by developing a social ethic. This ethic is based on discernment and reading the gospels as source of moral imagination capable of moving people beyond the status quo, as the status quo is determined by narrow frameworks of interpretation. Drawing on its narrative and metaphoric sources, the Church enables people to look at social, political, and economic realities with new eyes. Having access to a hermeneutical horizon that is different from the dominant interpretive frameworks of our time, and inspired by new root metaphors, it can contribute to transforming globalization into a process of humanization. Theological discernment as hermeneutic process is a necessary, but not a sufficient, condition. It has to be supplemented by a careful analysis mediated by social sciences, ethical reasoning, and a search for concrete solutions. This reflexive work has to be more than merely top-down thinking. It must be rooted in the sapiential experience of the victims of globalization and in the life of the Church as a concrete community of communities (synod of 1985) that takes into account the diversity of real life contexts.[12]

I am personally very much at home with his thesis in a more primitive form. In this regard, I am particularly influenced by three personal experiences: participating as a *peritus* or expert for the Canadian bishops at the Roman Synod in 1971 on *Justice in the World;* experimenting with reading the signs of the times at the Center of Concern in Washington during the 1970s; and participating in the Jesuits' difficult 32nd General Congregation, 1974–75, when they reached a consensus statement that henceforth their faith could not be separated from doing justice.[13]

At the 1971 Synod, Canadian Cardinal George Flahiff addressed the question of why CST has had such little impact. He stressed the need to relativize academic knowledge with experiential participatory knowledge, and the need to remain free from the slavery of any system or ideology. I quote him:

> If we are unable to break out of the system, or unable at least to remain clear-sighted within it, so as to judge it and if necessary to reject it, we have become mere cogs in the machine. Fidelity to the Gospel of Jesus Christ demands that His people rise above slavery to any system, for neither an ideology nor a system can ever adequately represent the Kingdom of God....

> I suggest that henceforth, our basic principle must be: only knowledge gained through participation is valid in this area of justice; true knowledge can be gained only through concern and solidarity. We must have recourse to the biblical notion of knowledge, experience shared with others.... Unless we are in solidarity with the people who are poor, marginal, or isolated we cannot even speak effectively about their problems. Theoretical knowledge is indispensable, but it is partial and limited; when it abstracts from lived concrete experience, it merely projects the present into the future.[14]

The Center of Concern under the leadership of Joe Holland and Peter Henriot SJ quickly adopted the methodology of the pastoral circle of experience, social analysis, and theological reflection marked by a preferential option for the poor that leads finally to action. It was an elementary reading of the signs of the times, largely motivated by a concern to relativize academic knowledge, especially economic knowledge. *Soundings*, published by the Center in 1974 as a tabloid, reported the findings of the Center's Task Force on Social Consciousness and Ignatian spirituality. In one article, "Mindsets and New Horizons for Discernment," I puzzled over why many good, knowledgeable, and prayerful people do not perceive the sin and evil that is embedded in many of our institutions, laws, and social policies. They are, instead, content with feeding or clothing the poor people they know.[15] They seem oblivious to the need for new eyes and spiritual freedom to escape the slavery of current ideologies and systems.

As I was leaving the Center of Concern in 1978, we had set up a year-long seminar on "Reading the Signs of the Times." Unfortunately, the excellent work done by theologians such as Joe Komonchak, Tom Clarke, John Coleman, and others was not published. I discuss personal experience here because I do believe that some reading of the signs of the times is evident in the preparation of CST statements over the years. However, one cannot help but wonder whether there has not, at times, been a disjuncture between the mindset and rhetoric of the drafters and their spiritual freedom.

I was frankly astonished at the discernment experience of the 250 Jesuit participants at the 32nd General Congregation. First, we decided that the group was too large to make decisions by discernment. Then, in the course of 13 weeks, under the angry watchful eye of Pope Paul VI who had told us he did not like our attitude, we painfully and freely did discern and reach consensus that our faith henceforth had to be linked irrevocably with our doing of justice. At that point I realized how difficult it is for individuals and a group to achieve the spiritual freedom necessary to do the prayerful social discernment necessary to read the signs of the times.

Cardinal Maurice Roy, President of the Pontifical Commission for Justice and Peace, in his *Reflections on the 10th Anniversary of* Pacem in Terris *of Pope John XXIII,* made a remarkable and confident statement. He said that the methodology of reading the signs of the times and discerning history is now completed – on both experiential and theoretical levels – by Paul VI's *Octogesima Adveniens* (1971).[16]

That completion is seen primarily in a caution that the interpretation of this reading can legitimately lead to different attitudes and different readings among believers. Additionally, the temptation to pseudo-prophetism and neoclericalism must be removed by exercising this reading in the Christian community, but remaining open to scientists and people of good will. He calls it a "dialogue with the world."

It is remarkable that this clearly authoritative guideline for using this new instrument for reading the signs of the times does not appear to have had any significant sequel. Nor does it appear to have been widely used, at least not under the conditions set forth by Paul VI and Cardinal Roy. The Center of Concern's 1979 seminar seemed to conclude that its methodology was simply too demanding in its integration of social sciences with theology and spirituality.

I believe we are particularly blessed in Johan Verstraeten's renewed approach to a reading of the signs of times, especially with his more developed use of biblical and other metaphors. He gives our faith new eyes to break open our slavery to the dominant individualistic economic and cultural paradigm of the day – indeed, to give us the necessary humility and spiritual freedom to believe in, to imagine, and to develop utopian alternatives. An additional timely metaphor here may be to see poverty, war, and AIDS as weapons of mass destruction that cannot easily be hidden from the eyes of the world. My chief concern is the need to develop and integrate into Johan's excellent presentation the essential underlying spirituality of deep prayerful gratitude, and to foster the spiritual freedom, inner peace, and detachment that permit one to see things new with the eyes of faith. The fact that Johan's faculty of theology at the University of Leuven hosted a conference of experienced specialists in September 2004 on scrutinizing the signs of the times is further encouragement that this conversation will continue and its implications for the future of CST become clearer.

Other Concerns in Harmony with Reading the Signs of the Times

Several of the articles mentioned the concern that CST should be considered an up-down rather than a down-up process as it has usually been seen in the past. This is important even though the key experiences and ideas in CST from the time of Leo XIII have always been rooted in local community experiences and ideas, reflected on by drafting experts, and finalized by the popes.

Another concern is that the Church be open to constant dialogue, not only within itself but also with other faiths and all people of good will. In fact, CST in the future should be the result of a visible, open, sustained process of dialogue with the whole Church, wherein the lengthy process of arriving at a statement on a particular issue would be seen as more important than the final statement itself. The result would still be an authoritative statement, even if not infallible, since trust in the constant presence and action of the Spirit in the Church and in the world is more important than a statement on any social justice issue in a changing world.

We have to admit that up to the present most adult lay persons have had little sense of CST other than of its basic biblical and philosophical principles. Few professionals have understood its often pompous language and positions that seldom seemed to depend on authorities other than its own. Most bishops and priests seem to feel inadequate or fearful to preach CST from the pulpit, feeling their own inadequacy in the Church's social teaching and not wanting to cause division or misunderstanding among parishioners. This situation must obviously change if CST is to have a future.

CST also needs more local relevance and concrete context in an age of globalization. Already in 1971, Pope Paul VI foresaw that local experiences and cultures were becoming so different one from another that it was hardly possible to continue to make universal statements in CST that had application for the whole Church and the whole world. This concern has even more application as globalizing processes threaten to homogenize local values, cultures, and practices. We are more aware than 50 years ago that unless local people are themselves the agents and accept the ownership of their progress, development projects will continue to fail no matter how much money is thrown at them. This is surely even more true for CST. Unless it is rooted in people's own experiences, neither outside expertise nor authority will make it succeed. An area of special concern here, not discussed by our seminar, is how under economic globalization minority ethnic elites profit disproportionally from newly created wealth – a recipe for increased political instability and violence.

Another recurring theme was that the Church, and more specifically CST, lacks a formal theology of power. Some felt that the dominance in CST of natural law – with its rational solutions without direct reference to the forces of evil and sin in individuals, institutions, and societies – led in the past to excessive optimism about the possibility of arriving at social harmony. The thinking seemed to be that if we could find a solution to end class warfare between employers and employees through worker associations or even guild-like corporatism, we would not have to deal directly with power. Alternately, church leaders put much more confidence in the benevolence of the powerful elite than they did in the power of workers and ordinary people to achieve change. In *Centesimus Annus*, Pope John Paul II marvels at his discovery that the protest power of the Solidarity movement – a people's movement – could itself bring about change.

CST still does not deal adequately with the awesome, often invisible and unaccountable power of business corporations – especially transnational corporations, media, and financial interests – that are today the most powerful shapers of global society and the lives of all peoples. Our seminar looked at this matter only in passing. CST is forthright concerning the abuses of the neo-liberal trinity of the Washington consensus – privatization, investment, and trade – but fails to come to grips with the octopus-like structures by which powerful enterprises reach into every country, every government, and, increasingly, every home on earth. Even after the monstrous revelations of the Enron scandal, governments continue to be pressed to privatize public services; private ownership now is reaching disastrously into human survival areas such as clean water.

Some, such as Ralston Saul, believe that after the September 11, 2001, disaster and its tragic fallout around the world – which only governments could handle – corporate CEOs are beginning to return to their proper role as servants rather than masters. In this view, governments and nations are rediscovering and exercising roles that only a few years ago they were all too willing to give to private corporations for the sake of unproven, but greater, efficiency. But there is little evidence that corporations are willing to abdicate their disproportionate political power. This is not the place to develop the thesis that I believe should be adopted by CST – namely, that business corporations should be stripped of their political power. A corporation should have no more power than an individual private citizen in democratically shaping public policy. Until CST tackles this problem of big business interests dominating politics, its call to empower local and poor people to play a fuller role in democratic society will surely fall on deaf ears.

CST must also address much more firmly the social responsibilities of stockholders, who have come to view investments almost like slot machines. Many take only casual interest in the product, service, or means of production that generate their profits. Often they pay CEOs salaries that are hundreds of times those of their workers. In other words, the juridical and moral framework within which capitalist enterprise may be considered moral has to be spelled out more clearly and regulated vigorously, without apology. Additionally, the right to work, job security, and the necessary role of unions in the economy have to be updated in sound legislation based on the basic principle that, in a democratic society, people come before profits. Workers and managers should be recognized as genuine stakeholders in an enterprise, and their contribution considered more crucial to its future than that of short-term shareholders.

In recent years, financial operations have far outrun the dollar value of total production in the world. This greatly increased the elements of risk, instability, and speculation in the money and investment markets. Yet the pope and bishops are almost silent about the blatant social justice abuses evident in these operations. The fact that Michael Camdessus, former head of the International Monetary Fund (IMF), was recently named a member of the Pontifical Council on Justice in Peace did not seem to change that situation noticeably. In technical and complex areas, such as finance, CST must regularly engage the assistance of thoroughly knowledgeable experts who view corporate social responsibilities seriously.

Another area of concern that is not sufficiently discussed in our seminar nor in the papers contributed to this volume is the matter of global governance. Today this is centred in the UN and its many satellite organizations, including the United Nations Conference on Trade and Development (UNCTAD), the World Health Organization, the United Nations Development Program (UNDP) and the World Court. Though these agencies have contributed greatly to human well-being around the world, the system still has glaring deficiencies. It is especially striking that the three most powerful economic agencies – the World Bank, the IMF, and the World Trade Organization (WTO) – remain effectively outside the UN system, which is where poorer countries have a more effective voice and vote. Besides, these three powerful international agencies are effectively subject to US veto. Yet under their watch, poor countries – especially in Africa – continue to become failed states, usually overwhelmed by debt repayments on loans or trade agreements mostly organized under the tutelage of these agencies.

Poorer countries are being forbidden use of the very instruments of protection that enabled rich countries to develop in earlier years. Rich countries are removing from poor countries the very ladders they themselves used to become rich. Nor is it encouraging to watch them blatantly break the very rules and conditions of trade they have imposed on poorer countries, especially in regard to trade in food, textiles, drugs, natural resources, and so forth. In this area of trade, it is discouraging to find that richer countries still collect half as much in tariffs from poor countries as they give them in aid.

Jim Hug argues that CST holds that, to be morally binding, contracts must be agreed on freely and not under pressure or compulsion. This prophetic dimension of CST surely needs better articulation and visibility in our times. Perhaps John Kenneth Galbraith's concept of countervailing powers needs to be invoked here as a method for poorer countries to increase their bargaining power to protect their own threatened economic, political, and cultural interests.

At the recent WTO meeting at Cancun, the larger poor countries of India, China, and Brazil gave leadership to a new G20 of poor countries to reject more favourable rules for rich countries in the areas of foreign investments and intellectual properties in poor countries.

Ideally, within an updated UN structure, the economic rights and security of poor countries should be effectively protected by the Economic Social Council (ESC) to be structured on the pattern of the present Security Council, which itself needs to give countries like India and Japan full membership. The ESC should, however, have a more representative membership than the G7. It should be a global forum with jurisdiction to provide effective leadership in the economic, social, and environmental fields. This was one of the strong recommendations made by the Report of the Commission on Global Governance, entitled *Our Global Neigbourhood*, which reviewed the arrangements for governance of global society.[17] The main challenge of this prestigious commission was to mobilize political will for multilateral action, a task in which it obviously has not been very successful. I believe this is a crucial area in which CST should become articulate and prophetic. In fact, Pope John Paul called for a strong update and reforms to the UN system in his annual New Year's message in 2004.[18]

Our individual authors and the seminar paid much attention to the rapid development of non-profit non-governmental organizations (NGOs) or civil society organizations (CSOs). Lisa Cahill looks to them to become strong and representative enough to undergird an effective global common good, foreseen in CST. At our seminar, Scott Appleby saw the Catholic Church giving up political privileges and, along with other religious organizations, joining with these NGOs to present a common front on poverty and environmental issues. The implications are far-reaching for CST, both in its articulation and its concrete action. It means that to be effective the Church's actions must be owned not only by the hierarchy but also, and especially, by its full membership. For this to happen CST has to be, and be seen to be, largely the product of lay Catholics actively building up the kingdom of God in the world through whatever their daily labours may be.

This striking change will come about only with great difficulty on the part of both clergy and laity. For example, at the Synod on the Vocations of the Laity in 1987, some Canadian bishop delegates made a minor attempt to insist on a fuller role for lay involvement in the preparation of CST statements. Their effort was interpreted by the synod secretariat as simply a concern by these bishops for better treatment of women in the Church. In general, the lay Catholic mindset, which long fostered separation of faith and prayer life from work life, still has a strong hold on many Catholics. It has to be dispelled before the practice of reading the signs of the times can gain a strong hold among ordinary Catholics.

Another difficulty is the exaggerated fear many bishops still have that Catholics and Catholic organizations will take positions or work with groups holding positions that are contrary to some Catholic teaching or practice. Some years ago the Canadian bishops were publicly split about whether the Canadian Catholic Organization for Development and Peace, Catholic women, and even bishops could support and join a women's march on behalf of the poor. Many of those supporting the march had a solid record of helping the poor, especially poor women, but some were not against abortion. The concept of a holistic or seamless life ethic that is concerned about human life for its duration and under all circumstances does not come easily.

At times, an imperfect law or public policy will be seen to be better than no law or no public policy on crucial public social issues. In this context, Pope John Paul II's constant appeal for dialogue across differences of all kinds, as the beginning of finding a solution to most social problems, is very insightful and promising. It should permit Catholics to make necessary compromises in the public forum to facilitate the achievement of laws or public policies that reflect CST only imperfectly or only lead ambiguously in the direction of its guidance. In this regard, the new Global Social Forum that emerged from Catholic inspiration in Brazil is surely a sign of hope.

It is also a positive sign that Catholics and Catholic groups from around the world are among the organizers and participants in the huge assemblies – earlier at Porto Alegre and more recently at Mumbai in India. Of the 130,000 participants in this latter assembly, about 30,000 were dalits, the poorest and most excluded of India's poor. The attendance of the poorest in this very open forum will surely mark its future development significantly. These experiences indicate that, to be effective as an NGO in the public forum, the Church has to be present visibly as a communion of all its members, and not only as representatives of the bishops and pope.

Can and does CST positively influence and shape global society today? This is one final dimension of CST on which I would like to reflect briefly. It was implicit in all our chapters but not directly addressed. Our authors all work hard at making CST an instrument of social evangelization better adapted and more suited to our times. However, the more basic question still stands: can and does religion have significant influence in the public forum to shape society? The thesis long held by sociologists – that religion would wither away – is now moot after the evident recent widespread revival of religious influence and, especially, after the shocking events in New York on September 11, 2001.

Nevertheless, I believe that Harvey Cox's negative review of John Paul's upbeat *Centesimus Annus* in 1991 echoed the views about CST held by many observers, including many Catholics, even after Vatican II with its strong challenge to Catholics to be the Church in the modern world. Cox, writing in *New York Newsday* shortly after the appearance of the encyclical, scornfully dismissed John Paul's claims of great influence for CST. Cox wrote: "Unfortunately, his years in Rome have not sharpened Karol Woytyla's pen. He succeeds in being pretentious, provincial and pedestrian at the same time.... But let us be more generous. What is exhausted is not the Pope but the social encyclical genre itself, with its improbable claims to universal validity and its consequent temptation to resort to bland truths.... My hope is that *Centesimus annus* marks not only the 100th anniversary of papal social teaching but the end of that chapter in Christian history."[19] I suspect that Cox was more vexed with the triumphal self-sufficient genre of the social encylicals and their poor English translations than he was grounded in empirical evidence about whether CST has had societal influence. Can and does CST positively influence and shape global society today? For me, such influence is clear to those with eyes to see. I mention only a few historical cases with which I am personally familiar, but they could be multiplied all over the world.

Until the Quiet Revolution in the Canadian province of Quebec, the Catholic bishops and clergy were judged to have, and to have had, substantial influence in public social affairs. For example, at the turn of the twentieth century, the Quebec bishops – disillusioned because so-called neutral American trade unions lacked respect for Quebec's distinct linguistic, cultural, and religious values – decided to found what came to be called, in 1921, La Confédération des travailleurs catholiques du Canada. Initially scorned as company unions, over the years these unions have won significant labour legislation in Quebec. By the time of the famous Asbestos Strike in 1949, they were almost 100,000 strong and were fast becoming the most aggressive and influential unions in Quebec. They shed their Catholic name but not their Catholic ideology. The Canadian National Trade Unions continued to be among the most radical in North America.[20]

Several years later, my doctoral thesis in economics at Harvard University that was later published in 1966 under the title *The Clergy and Economic Growth in Quebec (1896–1914)*,[21] examined economic development. I was able to establish, contrary to common English Canadian bias, that the Church's role in Quebec's economic development was, on balance, positive, without being either decisive or determining. I did find that it was difficult to discern whether clergy acted here more out of French nationalist, cultural, and linguistic motivation than in fidelity to CST.

I believe this finding is still relevant today at the international level, and this conclusion is supported by my recent research in cooperation with the International Development Reseach Centre in Ottawa. I concluded that the large failure rate of development projects in poor countries is related to the stubborn refusal of many Western development experts to take into account the cultural and spiritual values and beliefs of the local people involved.[22] A more recent example of CST in action is the role of religion in the Velvet Revolution in Eastern Europe. It began with the stubborn, faith-based Solidarity movement in Poland in its successful confrontation with its Communist government, which had the open encouragement of Pope John Paul II. Some observers have expressed surprise that Samuel Huntington, author of *The Clash of Civilizations,* has pointed out that the Catholic Church was the strongest institutional force in the latter part of the twentieth century that favoured democracy throughout the world.[23]

Sociologist Jose Casanova of the New School for Social Research, in his book *Public Religion in the Modern World,* includes case studies from Spain, Poland, Brazil, USA, and significant happenings from other countries such as Iran. He documents "the fact that religious traditions throughout the world are refusing to accept the marginal and privileged role which theories of modernity as well as theories of secularization had reserved for them."[24] In several countries, Casanova was tracing the impact that John XXIII's *Pacem in terris* (Peace on Earth) encyclical, with its strong articulation of human rights, had in several European and Latin America countries. He believes that the narrow secular view that sees religion as dying or withering away is itself now dead. In a final, rather cocky, paragraph of his book Casanova plays the prophet, writing:

> Western modernity is at a crossroads. If it does not enter into a creative dialogue with the other, with those traditions which are challenging its identity, modernity will most likely triumph. But it may end up being devoured by the inflexible, inhuman logic of its own creations. It would be profoundly ironic if, after all the beatings it has received from modernity, religion could somehow unintentionally help modernity to save itself.[25]

A far bigger concern for CST today is that most Catholics, especially the laity, remain largely untouched by it, both in their faith and daily work lives. The Center of Concern published a book in 1985 entitled *Catholic Social Teaching: Our Best Kept Secret.*[26] Here, I believe I cannot do better than summarize the insightful response of Richard McCormick SJ to this general lack of a lively Catholic awareness of CST and its urgent call for personal social responsibility and effective action. He explains it by ignorance, inadequacy, and apathy. Ignorance has its root in the separatist or dualistic mentality mentioned earlier that puts a disconnect between life and afterlife, and between practice and piety. The intellectual root of a socially dormant conscience is individualism that reduces social responsibility to one-on-one relationships. Separatism and individualism lead to other components of socially dormant conscience and inadequacy, which works for poverty programs but doesn't question the institutions that create poverty and apathy, and that leave people with a sense of hopelessness and powerlessness.

McCormick proposes three antidotes for such ignorance. One is feeling right; this comes from having deeper roots than cerebral analysis in feelings of passionate moral outrage. The second is thinking right; this comes from correcting the two errors of separatism and individualism with the help of liberation theology, which sees the Church and the Christian community as a continuation of Christ's own liberating presence among us. Her task is to work for liberation from enslavement, in all its personal, structural, and institutional forms. The third antidote is acting right, and this comes from using power, corporate persuasiveness, public opinion, and political pressure to change unjust structures. In this area, there are no certain formulae, other than participating in a flexible and patient manner and hoping against hope.[27]

It would be easy to list dozens of Catholic organizations that tackle the action side of McCormick's recommendations. However, it appears they often do so without spending enough time reading the signs of the times with gratitude and freedom and, thus, rooting their action in the mystery of Christ building the kingdom of heaven among us. Pedro Arrupe SJ, former Jesuit superior general, points out the crucial importance in our work for justice of learning how to relativize specialized knowledge, technologies, and ideologies. I quote him: "Put it this way. They are tools, imperfect tools. And it is the Christian ethos, the Christian vision of values, that must use these tools while submitting them to judgment and relativizing their tendency to make absolutes of themselves. Relativizing them, putting them in their place, as it were, with full realization that the Christian ethos cannot possibly construct a new world without their assistance."[28]

What is clearly lacking among Catholic laity, in most parts of the world, is adequate adult formation in the social dimensions of their faith. We need papal and episcopal social statements prepared in dialogue, not only with the laity but also with believers from other faiths. But, even more, we need to learn from the experience of the earlier Catholic Action movement that put so much importance on social faith formation for young people entering professional life. CST needs to be articulated in easily understandable language. It needs to be preached regularly in every parish. However, I believe church leaders should put the highest priority in fostering the creation of small prayer and social-faith groupings of lay adults, such as the base communities in Brazil and elsewhere. Without such an ongoing adult lay formation in their faith, potential and actual lay Catholic leaders will continue to be handicapped in finding Christ in their professional activity. And today, these small groups can be mutually inspired and challenged by relating regularly to believers of other faiths.

A distinguished friend of mine, Claude Ryan, died in February 2004. He was a Quebec francophone Catholic who was successively a leader in the Catholic Action movement, editor and publisher of the daily newpaper *Le Devoir*, and leader and cabinet member in the Quebec Liberal Party, serving in several portfolios. In his last years, before dying of stomach cancer, he lectured at McGill University in Montreal on CST. He received a state funeral attended by thousands, including political leaders from across Canada. For a week his story and memory filled the media which took up the popular acclaim in calling him "the conscience of Quebec" and, at times, "the pope of Quebec." He had achieved this respect and admiration by his solid reflective political editorials, which had come to be must-read for many political leaders. In his last testimony, read at the funeral, Claude attributed much of what he was able to do in life to his early Catholic formation and later Catholic Action formation. I believe we can take hope from Claude's life and incentive to provide for the adult faith formation required of lay Catholics who are now being challenged to read the signs of times in their own daily secular experience with the eyes and skill of mature faith.

I conclude with a few hope-filled signs of our own times:

1) Pope John Paul II's constant insistence on the necessity for dialogue across difference, especially interreligious dialogue, will, I believe, prove a very fruitful dynamism for developing the adult social faith formation required to read the signs of the times in the future.

2) A sign of great hope is the active participation of Catholics and Catholic organizations in the Global Social Forums. At its recent assembly in Mumbai, more than 130,000 participated from round the world – about 30,000 of them were dalits, India's poorest of the poor. I was encouraged to learn that 1,300 Jesuits participated, the Indian Jesuits bringing with them dalits with whom they work daily. While these assemblies have still to discover a specific focus, they are already a very open public workshop helping people across differences that divide them to imagine alternative possible futures. The inclusion of the poorest into this open forum will surely significantly mark the future forums.

3) Hope also springs from the growing dialogue among world religions, but particularly between Catholicism and Islam, the two largest and most rapidly growing religions in the world. The presence of Farhang Rajaee among our authors is especially telling, with his current story of how Iranian Muslim thinkers are searching to blend Islamic tradition creatively with contemporary thinking.

4) And, finally, hope comes from the fact that faith-based NGOs are beginning to make common cause with other NGOs because of the considerable overlap in their critique of globalization processes. Remarkably, the International Forum on Globalization, which represents a wide spectrum of NGOs, in its recent report entitled *Alternatives to Economic Globalization: A Better World Is Possible,* without using religious language adopts core principles that echo CST to undergird their own mission. Namely, it affirms the inviolable dignity of every human, solidarity within the human

family and all creation, subsidiarity in decision-making, and seeing and acting on issues from the point of view of the poor and marginalized.[29]

A personal reflection by Martin Khor of the Third World Network, highlighted in this report, is particularly insightful and helpful. He challenges readers to work for that possible better world by working in a clear-eyed way in two conflicting paradigms, or mindsets, at the same time. In the first, which many may see as tinkering, one works within the system for fairer trade, fairer economic and environmental relations, and a better deal for the poor. In the second paradigm, the present corporate economic system is seen as incompatible with long-time survival; it will inevitably blow up as its exaggerated economic growth rates clash with nature's ecological limits. Khor urges the personnel of civil society NGOs to work pragmatically in the first paradigm's short-term perspective to make things better for the poor and the environment. However, he himself emotionally lives and belongs in the second paradigm. He invites others to follow his example, in the hope that by living out of this vision they can foster the creation of new trade mechanisms, systems of prices, and so forth, that can serve as a transition into their "alternative better world."[30]

This idealistic pragmatic approach fits well, I believe, with the CST utopian vision of how we can realistically set about building what Pope John Paul called "a civilization of love." I believe that prayerful spiritual discernment can free us to see with new eyes and, therefore, be able to go beyond social analysis or desire for gain, and destroy in ourselves the false gods of slavish materialism and consumerism on which corporate neo-liberalism feasts today. In faith and hope, being free enough to see the world through the eyes of the poor means living and belonging in Khor's second paradigm. To advance in this direction, the Church will, of course, require fearless, faith-filled, imaginative, and charismatic leadership at all levels of the clergy, and especially among the laity.[31]

From this feast of thought, analysis, and spirituality that our authors have placed before us, one stark challenge recurs like a haunting bell; it is highlighted dramatically by Fernando Franco in his story of the dalits. The challenge is for the Church today to become the church of the poor – to be clearly on the side of the poor, not only in rhetoric and projects but in our whole way of being church. Thus far, with admirable exceptions, our church leadership and most Catholics have not dared to take this option. In the future, the Church will become the church of the poor, with the majority of Catholics living in poor countries. Can we hope that most Catholics will come to discover their true identity in the church of the poor and have a recreated CST to nourish them in that conviction? Could not such an unexpected conversion give a welcome boost to the present fragile millennium commitment by governments to eradicate extreme poverty and hunger by the year 2015?

Endnotes

Preface

1 Peter Henriot's chapter originally appeared in the volume *Liberation Theologies on Shifting Grounds: A Clash of Socio-Economic and Cultural Paradigms,* George de Schriver, ed. (Leuven: University of Louvain Press, 1998). It is reproduced here with the permission of that publisher. It has been slightly edited for this book.

2 Daly's book *Beyond Secrecy: The Untold Story of Canada and the Second Vatican Council* was published in 2003 by Novalis.

Chapter 1

1 Anthony Giddens, "Runaway World: The Reith Lectures Revisited," Lecture One, Nov. 10, 1999, at www.lse.global.

2 Robert Keohane, "Governance in a Partially Globalized World" in David Held and Anthony McGrew, eds., *Governing Globalization: Power, Authority and Global Governance* (Malden, MA: Blackwell, 2002).

3 Roland Robertson, *Globalization: Social Theory and Global Culture* (London: Sage Publications, 1992).

4 David Korten, *When Corporations Rule the World* (San Francisco: Berret Koehler Publishers Inc., 2001), 3.

5 Zygmunt Bauman, *Globalization: The Human Consequences* (New York: Columbia University Press, 1998), 123.

6 www:worldsocialforum.org/English/Charter of Principles

7 Thomas Friedman, *The Lexus and the Olive Tree* (New York: Anchor Books, 1999), ix.

8 Richard Falk, *Predatory Globalization* (Malden, MA: Blackwell, 1999), 217.

9 Cf. Chapter 9, "Reconstructing World Order: Towards Cosmopolitan Social Democracy," in David Held and Anthony McGrew, *Globalization/Anti-Globalization* (Malden, MA: Blackwell, 2002), 118–136.

10 Dirk Messner, "World Society: Structure and Trends" in Paul Kennedy, Dirk

Messner and Franz Nuscheler, *Global Trends and Global Governance* (London: Pluto Press, 2002), 39.

11 Leslie Gelb, "Who Won the Cold War?" *New York Times* Aug. 20, 1992, p. A27, citing Marshal Nikolai Ogavor: "In the US, small children—even before they begin school—play with computers. Here we don't even have computers in every office of the Defense Ministry and for reasons you know well, we cannot make computers widely available in our society."

12 Roland Robertson, "Anti-Global Religion" in Mark Juergensmeyer, ed., *Global Religions: An Introduction* (New York: Oxford University Press, 2003), 145.

13 Cf. chapter 4, "Environmental Advocacy Networks" in Margaret Keck and Katheryn Sikkink, *Activists Beyond Borders: Advocacy Networks in International Politics* (Ithica, NY: Cornell University Press, 1998).

14 Paul Kennedy, "Global Challenges at the Beginning of the 21st Century" in Kennedy et al., *Global Trends and Global Governance,* 16.

15 Pierre Hamel, "Introduction" in Pierre Hamel et al., eds., *Globalization and Social Movements* (New York: Palgrave, 2001), 3–4.

16 William Reinecke, et al., *Critical Choices: The UN, Networks and the Future of Global Governance* (Ottawa: International Development Research Centre, 2000), xvi.

17 Held and McGrew, *Globalization/Anti-Globalization,* 1.

18 William Reineke, *Global Public Policy: Governing Without Governance?* (Washington, DC: Brookings Institute Press, 1998), 5.

19 Franz Nuscheler, "Global Governance, Development and Peace" in Paul Kennedy, et al., *Global Trends and Global Governance*. Cf. also Samuel Huntington, "The Lonely Superpower," *Foreign Affairs* vol. 78(2), 1999:35–49.

20 Cf. Msgr. Frank Dewane, "Theological Response to Globalization and the Role of the Church" June 5, 2002, available at www: comece.org.

21 *Centesimus Annus,* no. 26.

22 David Hollenbach, *Claims in Conflict: Retrieving and Renewing the Human Rights Tradition* (New York: Paulist Press, 1979).

23 Alasdair MacIntyre, *Dependent Rational Animals: Why Humans Need the Virtues* (Chicago: Open Court Press, 1999).

24 David Hollenbach, *The Common Good and Christian Ethics* (New York: Cambridge University Press, 2002).

25 I treat of subsidiarity at more length in my chapter, "A Limited State and a Vigorous Society: Christianity and Civil Society" in Nancy Rosenblum and Robert Post, eds., *Civil Society and Government* (Princeton, NJ: Princeton University Press, 2002).

26 For a careful Kantian argument to 'imperfect' obligations to help others who

do not have strict rights to one's help cf. Onora O'Neil, *Bounds of Justice* (New York: Cambridge University Press, 2000), 65–80.

27 Donal Dorr, *Option for the Poor: A Hundred Years of Vatican Social Teaching* (Maryknoll, NY: Orbis, 1983).

28 For a classic statement of integral humanism cf. Jacques Maritain, *Integral Humanism* (New York: Scribner, 1968).

29 David Ryall, "The Catholic Church as a Transnational Actor" in Daphné Josselin and William Wallace, eds., *Non-State Actors in World Politics* (London: Palgrave, 2001), 46.

30 For the Jubilee 2000 movement cf. Paula Grenier, "Jubilee 2000: Laying the Foundations for a Global Movement" in John Clark, ed., *Globalizing Civic Engagement* (Sterling, VA: Earthcan, 2003).

31 These statistics for global Catholicism are from Brian Froehle and Mary Gautier, *Global Catholicism: Portrait of a World Church* (Maryknoll, NY: Orbis, 2003).

32 Cf. Dewane, "Theological Response to Globalization and the Role of the Church," 2.

33 Cf. Daniel Levine and David Stohl, "Bridging the Gap Between Empowerment and Power in Latin America," in Suzanne Hoeber Rudolph and James Piscatori, eds., *Trans-National Religion and Fading States* (Boulder, CO: Westview, 1997).

34 These six themes for a humane globalization are found in Patricia Mische and Melissa Merkling, eds., *Toward a Global Civilization: The Contribution of Religions* (New York: Peter Lang, 2001).

35 "Global Governance: Our Responsibility to Make Globalization an Opportunity for All", available at www.comece.org.

36 Hans Kung, *A Global Ethic for Global Politics and Economics* (New York: Oxford University Press, 1998).

37 *Our Global Neighborhood*, available at the website of the Commission on Global Governance.

38 Address of John Paul II to the Pontifical Academy of Social Sciences, April, 2001 on www.vatican.va.

39 John Paul II, "Message for the Celebration of the World Day of Peace" 2000 on www. vatican.va.

40 Jose Casanova, "Religion, the New Millennium and Globalization," *Sociology of Religion* 2001 vol. 62(4):315–441 at 433.

41 cf. Diarmuid Martin, "Globalization in the Social Teaching of the Church" in Louis Sabourin et al., eds., *The Social Dimensions of Globalization* (Vatican: Pontifical Academy of the Social Sciences, 2000), 82–93.

42 Dewane, "Theological Response to Globalization," 2, 5.

43 For a claim of a blindness of secular social science thought to a role of religion in globalization cf. Richard Falk, *Religion and Humane Global Governance* (New York: Palgrave, 2001).

44 John Clark, "Civil Society and Trans-National Action" in Clark, ed., *Globalizing Civic Engagement,* 8.

45 For the unique role of flexible global networks for effective action and advocacy cf. Keck and Sikkink, *Activists Beyond Borders.*

46 Casanova, "Religion, the New Millennium and Globalization," 430–31.

47 Frank Lechner, "Religious Rejections of Globalization and Their Directions," paper presented to the annual meeting of the Association for the Sociology of Religion, 2002.

48 Richard Falk, "The Religious Foundations of Global Governance" in Mischle and Merkling, *Toward a Global Civilization: The Contribution of Religions,* 52.

49 Ibid., 54.

Chapter 2

1 According to Anthony Giddens, it is precisely the resistance against the discursive or economic arrangements of the globalists that produces more insistence on identity, nationality, and fundamentalism. These are expressions of an unavoidable distrust in the imposition from above of a Western monoculture.

2 It is perfectly possible to write an article on how the ethical principles of Catholic Social Thought can be applied to the problem of globalization. This is however not the intention of this article. A good example of such an analysis is *Global Governance: Our Responsibility to Make Globalization an Opportunity for All. A Report to the Bishops of COMECE* (Commission of the Bishops' Conferences of the European Community), Brussels, COMECE, 2001.

3 *Gaudium et spes*, no. 4.

4 For a reflection on this problem see Johan De Tavernier, *Eschatology and Social Ethics*, in Joseph A. Selling, *Personalist Morals: Essays in Honor of Professor Louis Janssens* (B.E.T.L. LXXXIII) (Leuven, Peeters/University Press, 1988), 279–300.

5 Cf. Ronald A. Heifetz, *Leadership Without Easy Answers* (Cambridge, MA: The Belknap Press of Harvard University Press, 1994), 24.

6 For a more extensive approach of the relation between reading the bible and Catholic Social Thought, see Johan Verstraeten, *Catholic Social Thought as Living Tradition*, in J. Boswell, F. McHugh, J. Verstraeten, eds., *Catholic Social Thought: Twilight or Renaissance?* (BETL, CLVII) (Leuven, Peeters/University Press, 2000), 239–248.

7 My interpretation of Ricoeur is mainly influenced by Alain Thomasset, *Paul Ricoeur: Une poétique de la morale* (B.E.T.L. CXXIV) (Leuven, Peeters/University

Press, 1996).

8 Karen Lebacqz, as quoted from her book *The Three 'R's of Justice* (Oxford, 1986), in Duncan B. Forrester, *Beliefs, Values and Policies: Conviction Politics in a Secular Age* (Oxford: Clarendon Press, 1989), 29.

9 Mary Elsbernd, Reimund Bieringer, *When Love Is Not Enough: A Theo-Ethic of Justice* (Collegeville, MN: The Liturgical Press, 2002), 156, note 20.

10 Ibid., 155.

11 Biblical stories do not simply tell us something about the past. They open a new world of meaning and make semantic and practical innovation possible. Particularly, the metaphors play a crucial role here. They not only function on the denominational level of words, but also as *predicative metaphors:* they function on a level of predication in the broader context of sentence or text. As such, biblical narratives function as metaphors. Together with extravagant and eccentric elements, they create a metaphoric tension between everyday life and the extravagant world of the narrative Cf. Paul Ricoeur, "Word, Polysemy, Metaphor," in M.J. Valdez, ed., *A Ricoeur Reader: Reflection and Imagination* (New York: Harverster/Wheatsheaf, 1991, 79.

The metaphors awaken human energies, generate a world of meaning and open new vistas of human possibilities. Metaphors make a deeper understanding of reality possible, by producing an emotional shock "by an intentional misuse of language," an impertinent addition to "normal" understandings, or, to put it in the words of Ricoeur, by a "kinship where ordinary vision does not perceive any relationship" or by a "new predicative pertinence … a *pertinence within impertinence."* (Paul Ricoeur, The Function of Fiction in Shaping Reality, in Valdez, *A Ricoeur Reader,* 125 and 127.) They are based on a *calculated error* which brings together things that do not go together and by means of this apparent misunderstanding it causes a new, hitherto unnoticed, relation of meaning to spring up between the terms that previous systems of classification had ignored or not allowed." (See J. Verstraeten, "Rethinking Catholic Social Thought as Tradition, in J.S. Boswell, F.P. McHugh and J. Verstraeten, eds., Catholic Social Thought: Twilight or Renaissance? Leuven: Peeters/University Press, 2000, 72–73.)

12 E.R. MacCormac, *Metaphor and Myth in Science and Religion* (Durham, NC: Duke University Press, 1976), 84–85.

13 Ibid., 84–85.

14 Ibid., 84–85.

15 Ibid., 94–95.

16 David Hollenbach, "A Communitarian Reconstruction of Human Rights," in R. Bruce Douglass and David Hollenbach, eds., *Catholicism and Liberalism: Contributions to American Public Philosophy* (Cambridge, Cambridge University Press, 1994), 127–150.

17 Henri Nouwen, as quoted by Theodore.J. Koontz, "Christian Nonviolence: An Interpretation," in Thomas Nardin, ed., *The Ethics of War and Peace* (Princeton: Princeton University Press, 1996), 178–179.

18 Henri Nouwen, "Letting Go of All Things: Prayer as Action" in *A Matter of Faith: A Study Guide for Churches on the Nuclear Arms Race.* Compiled and edited by the staff of *Sojourners* magazine. Washington, DC: Sojourners, 1981, 87.

19 Theodore Weber, *Theological Symbols of International Order, Journal of Church and State*, 29 (1987)1, 79–99.

20 Ibid., 98.

21 In this context one can understand fundamentalism, not as a revival of pre-modern thinking, but as something which is related to globalization. As Anthony Giddens puts it: "Fundamentalism is a child of globalization, which it both responds to and utilizes … [it] isn't just the antithesis of globalizing modernity but poses questions to it. The most basic one is this: can we live in a world where nothing is sacred?" (Anthony Giddens, *Runaway World: How Globalisation Is Reshaping Our Lives* (London, Profile Books, 1999), 50.

22 This is not only implicitly the case in Lynn White, "The Historical Roots of Our Ecological Crisis," in *Science* 155 (1967), 1203-1207, but particularly in contentions based on this article and leading to the thesis that the disappearance of the Jewish and Christian religions is the basic solution of the ecological problem (cf. Ton Lemaire in Holland and the new-right philosopher Alain De Benoist in France who pleads for a new pagan Europe without Christian religion).

23 This materialist interpretation is certainly not only Marxist but also typical for a neo-liberal interpretation of globalization ("spreading capitalism will lead to spreading more individual freedom and democracy").

24 Pierre Teilhard de Chardin, *Hymne de l'Univers* (Paris: Éditions du Seuil, 1961), 17.

25 Ibid., 18.

26 Ibid., 18.

27 Ibid., 19.

28 The original French text is as follows: "Dans la nouvelle humanité qui s'engendre aujourd'hui, le Verbe a prolongé l'acte sans fin de sa naissance; et, par la vertu de son immersion au sein du Monde, les grandes eaux de la Matière, sans un frisson, se sont chargées de vie. Rien n'a frémi, (en apparence), sous l'ineffable transformation. Et cependant, mystérieusement et réellement, au contacte de la substantielle Parole, l'univers, immense Hostie, est devenu chair. Toute matière est désormais incarnée, mon Dieu, par votre incarnation." Ibid., 23.

29 Pierre Teilhard de Chardin, *The Divine Milieu: An Essay on the Interior Life*, trans. Bernard Wall (New York: Harper & Row, 1960), 35.

30 Justice et Paix France, *Maîtriser la mondialisation* (Paris: Editions Bayard, Centurion/Cerf/Fleurus-Mame, 1999).

31 Ibid., 49.

32 Ibid., 52.

33 For a clear distinction between fundamentalism and extremism, see Scott Appleby, *The Ambivalence of the Sacred: Religion, Violence, and Reconciliation, Religion* (Carnegie Commission on Preventing Deadly Conflict) Lanham/Boulder/New York/Oxford: Rowman & Littlefield, 2000), 1–21. For an explanation of the link between globalization and fundamentalism, see Anthony Giddens, *Runaway World*.

34 A clear example of an ideological use of just war thinking is Michael Novak, "An Argument that War Against Iraq Is Just," in *Origins*, 32 52003:36. Symptomatic is what he writes on p. 597, referring to Thomas Aquinas and Augustine. Making a mix of the quite different approaches of both theologians he states that in their view just war does not begin with a presumption against violence. This is precisely the contrary of what Thomas Aquinas writes. Thomas raises the question 'Ut bellum semper sit peccatum' and he treats his question on war (IIaIIae qu. 40) in the context of a series of sins against love!

34 Cf. Horowitz as quoted in Frank.J. Barret, David.L. Cooperrider, "Generative Metaphor Intervention: A New Approach for Working with Systems Divided by Conflict and Caught in Defensive Perception," *The Journal of Applied Behavioral Science*, 26 (1990), 2, 221: "The active denial of the world to allay the threat of anxiety, takes many forms, including avoided associations (…) dimming of attention, constricted thought, memory failure, disavowal and blocking through fantasy.

35 Dennis P. McCann, *Umpire or Batsman: Is It Cricket to Be Both*? in *Journal of Business Ethics*, 5 (1986):445–451.

36 Ibid., 156.

37 Ibid., 49.

38 Klaus Demmer, *Naturrecht und Offenbarung*, in Marianne Heimbach-Steins, Andreas Lienkamp und Joachim Wiemeyer (Hrsg.), *Brennpunkt Sozialethik. Theorien, Aufgaben, Methoden* (Freiburg/Basel/Wien: Herder, 1995), 42.

39 *Redemptor hominis,* as quoted in *Centesimus annus,* 53.

40 James Wolfensohn, as quoted in Benjamin R. Barber, *Jihad versus McWorld: Terrorism's Challenge to Democracy*, second rev. ed. (New York: Ballantine Books, 2001), xxviii.

Chapter 3

1 Francesca Polletta, *Freedom Is an Endless Meeting: Democracy in American Social Movements* (Chicago and London: University of Chicago Press, 2000).

2 Bob Chodos and Jamie Swift, *Faith and Freedom: The Life and Times of Bill Ryan, S.J.* (Ottawa: Novalis, Saint Paul University, 2002); as cited in Michael Campbell-Johnson, S.J., "Review of *Faith and Freedom: The Life and Times of Bill Ryan, S.J.," Promotio Justitiae* 79 (2003/3):38.

3 Ibid., 38.

4 STI-II.90, a. 4.

5 Robert J. Schreiter, *The New Catholicity: Theology between the Global and the Local* (Maryknoll, NY: Orbis, 1997), 4–10.

6 John A. Coleman, "Retrieving or Re-Inventing Social Catholicism," in J.S. Boswell, F.P. McHugh, J. Verstraeten, eds., *Catholic Social Thought: Twilight or Renaissance?* (Leuven: Leuven University Press, 2000), 283–86.

7 See, for example, Margaret E. Keck and Kathryn Sikkink, *Activists Beyond Borders: Advocacy Networks in International Politics* (Ithaca and London: Cornell University Press, 1998); Richard Falk, *Law in an Emerging Global Village: A Post-Westphalian Perspective* (Ardsley, NY: Transnational Publishers, 1998); Anne-Marie Slaughter, "Everyday Global Governance," *Daedalus*, Winter 2003, 83-90; and, on a slightly more pessimistic but not despairing note, Stanley Hoffman, "World Governance Beyond Utopia," *Daedalus*, Winter 2003, 27–35.

8 John S. Boswell, "Solidarity, Justice, and Power Sharing: Patterns and Policies," in J.S. Boswell, F.P. McHugh, J. Verstraeten, eds., *Catholic Social Thought: Twilight or Renaissance?* (Leuven: Leuven University Press, 2000), 103-04; Francis P. McHugh, "Muddle or Middle-Level? A Place for Natural Law in Catholic Social Thought," in *Catholic Social Thought: Twilight or Renaissance?*, 51.

9 See Charles E. Curran, *Catholic Social Teaching, 1891–present: A Historical, Theological and Ethical Analysis* (Washington, D.C: Georgetown University Press, 2002), 188–98. Curran believes the Catholic philosophy of justice is underdeveloped.

10 David Hollenbach S.J., *The Common Good and Christian Ethics* (New York: Cambridge University Press, 2002), 13.

11 Schreiter, *The New Catholicity,* 43.

12 Hollenbach, *The Common Good,* 152–159. Hollenbach also accentuates the importance of "intellectual solidarity."

13 Schreiter, *The New Catholicity,* 40–42.

14 Nira Yuval-Davis, "Women, Ethnicity and Empowerment," in Ann Oakley and Juliet Mitchell, *Who's Afraid of Feminism? Seeing through the Backlash* (New York: The New Press, 1977); see also Hilary Charlesworth and Christine Chinkin, *The Boundaries of International Law: A Feminist Analysis* (Manchester, UK: Manchester University Press, 2000), 51.

15 Martha C. Nussbaum, *Women and Human Development: The Capabilities Approach* (New York and Cambridge: Cambridge University Press, 2000), 78-80.

16 Immanuel Wallerstein, "The Inter-state Structure of the Modern World System," in Steve Smith, Ken Booth, and Maysia Zalewski, eds., *International Positivism and Beyond* (New York: Cambridge University Press, 1996), 87, 106; as cited in Falk, *Law in an Emerging Global Village*, 30.

17 Richard Falk, *Predatory Globalization: A Critique* (Malden, MA: Polity Press, 1999), 59–60.

18 Falk, *Emerging Global Village*, 29. Hugo Grotius was the seventeenth-century Dutch father of international law.

19 Ibid., 27–28.

20 Ibid., 206.

21 Keck and Sikkink, *Activists Beyond Borders*, 2.

22 Charlesworth and Chinkin, *The Boundaries of International Law*, 20.

23 Hollenbach, *The Common Good*, 102.

24 In *Mater et Magistra*, nos. 33–34, John XXIII contrasts the original formulation of the principle of subsidiarity in *Quadragesimo Anno* with his own on this score. For a discussion, see Curran, *Catholic Social Teaching,* 141–44.

25 See John XXIII, *Pacem in terris*, nos. 135–45.

26 Boswell, "Solidarity, Justice, and Power-Sharing," 106–07.

27 Reinhold Niebuhr, *Man's Nature and His Communities* (New York: Charles Scribner's Sons, 1965), 24. Niebuhr is quoting *The Times Literary Supplement*.

28 Johan Verstraeten, "Re-thinking Catholic Social Thought as Tradition," in *Catholic Social Thought*, 64–68, 71–74.

29 Schreiter, *The New Catholicity*, 16.

30 In an address to theologians, Richard Falk hopes for "the re-emergence of religion as a world-political force" that is ecumenical and prophetic ("Religion and Globalization," 2002–2003 Boston Theological Institute Opening Lecture, *Bulletin of the Boston Theological Institute* 2, 2).

31 Boswell, "Solidarity, Justice and Power Sharing," 106.

32 Charles E. Curran, Kenneth R. Himes, and Thomas A. Shannon, "Commentary on *Sollicitudo Rei Socialis,*" in Kenneth R. Himes, ed., *Commentary on Catholic Social Teaching* (Washington, DC: Georgetown University Press, forthcoming), 31 ff. in manuscript. In his first encyclical, Pius XII mentioned neglect of "the law of solidarity" (*Summi pontificatus*, no. 35).

33 Margaret A. Farley, *Compassionate Respect: A Feminist Approach to Medical Ethics and Other Questions* (New York/Mahwah: Paulist Press, 2002), 19.

34 For an example, see David Barnard, "In the High Court of South Africa, Case No. 4138/98: The Global Politics of Access to Low-Cost AIDS Drugs in Poor Countries," *Kennedy Institute of Ethics Journal*, no. 2 (2002) 159–174; and Lisa Sowle Cahill, "Biotech and Justice: Catching Up with the Real World Order," *Hastings Center Report* 33/4, September-October 2003, 34–44.

35 Schreiter, *The New Catholicity*, 27.

36 Boswell, "Solidarity, Justice, and Power Sharing," 95.

37 Ibid., 97.

38 Schreiter, *The New Catholicity*, 112–113.

39 Ibid., 108-110. A task of "proposals" could also be added after critique in order better to represent the role of systematic and constructive theological scholarship, which interfaces with the other tasks, but is not their equivalent.

40 Ibid., 110.

41 J. H. Oldham and W.A. Visser't Hooft, *Church, Community and State, Volume I: The Church and Its Function in Society* (London: George Allen and Unwin, 1937).

42 John C. Bennett, *Christian Ethics and Social Policy* (New York: Scribner's Sons, 1956).

43 Charles Villa-Vicencio, *A Theology of Reconstruction: Nation-Building and Human Rights* (Cambridge and New York: Cambridge University Press, 1992).

44 Schreiter, *The New Catholicity*, 112.

45 Wendy Tyndale, "National Forum of Fish Workers: a spiritually inspired movement for alternative development," paper prepared for the World Faiths Development Dialogue, 5, available at www.wfdd.org.uk/programmes/case_studies/fishworkers.

46 Ibid., 9.

Chapter 4

1 Published for the United Nations Development Programme (New York: Oxford University Press, 2003), 2 Available online at http://hdr.undp.org/reports/global/2003/.

2 New York: Oxford University Press, 1995, 6. Available on line at http://hdr.undp.org/reports/global/1995/en/.

3 Tenth Anniversary Edition. United States Catholic Conference, 1997, especially #170, 252, 260.

Chapter 5

1 No single volume history of Catholic teaching on war and peace exists; sources which provide accounts of the tradition include: R.H. Bainton, *Christian Attitudes Toward War and Peace* (New York: Abington Press, 1960): F.H. Russell, *The Just War in the Middle Ages* (London: Cambridge University Press, 1977); J.T. Johnson, *Just War Tradition and the Restraint of War* (Princeton, NJ: Princeton University Press, 1981).

2 I have tried to chart this course of development in two essays: "The Just-War Ethic and Catholic Theology: Dynamics of Continuity and Change," in T.A. Shannon, ed., *War or Peace? The Search for New Answers* (Maryknoll, NY: Orbis, 1980), 15–39;

"Catholic Teaching on War and Peace: The Decade 1978–89," in C. Curran, ed., *Moral Theology: Challenges for the Future* (New York: Paulist Press, 1990), 355–384.

3 V. Yzermans, ed., *Major Addresses of Pius XII*, vol. II (St. Paul: North Central Publishing Co., 1961).

4 Cf. commentary of J.C. Murray, S.J., "The Pattern for Peace and the Papal Peace Program" and "The Judicial Organization of the International Community" in L.J. Hooper, ed., *Bridging the Sacred and the Secular: Selected Writings of John Courtney Murray, S.J.,* (Washington, DC: Georgetown University Press, 1994), 6–27, 28–41.

5 J.C. Murray, *We Hold These Truths: Catholic Reflections on the American Proposition* (New York: Sheed and Ward, 1960), 249–273.

6 Cf. D.J. O'Brien and T.A. Shannon, eds., *Catholic Social Thought: The Documentary Heritage* (Maryknoll, NY: Orbis, 1992), 82–128, 129–162.

7 *Pacem in Terris,* nos. 136–138.

8 Cf. National Conference of Catholic Bishops, *The Challenge of Peace: God's Promise and Our Response* (Washington, DC: United States Catholic Conference, 1983).

9 *Gaudium et Spes*, no. 78.

10 Paul VI, *Populorum Progressio*.

11 The growing significance of international economics in world politics was reflected early in R.O. Keohane and J.S. Nye, *Power and Interdependence: World Politics in Transition* (Boston: Little Brown, 1977); more recently in International Monetary Fund, *Globalization: Challenges and Opportunities* (Washington, DC: IMF, 1997).

12 C.F. Heinz, in *Catholic Teaching on War and Peace*.

13 Essentially, the Pope asserted the right and duty of states to use force in certain circumstances; he seldom drew specific conclusions.

14 John Paul II, *Centesimus Annus*, no. 10.

15 For examples of this literature, cf, C. Krauthammer, "The Unipolar Moment," *Foreign Affairs* 70 (1991); J.S. Nye, "What New World Order?" *Foreign Affairs* 71 (1996):83–96; J.L. Gaddis, "Toward the Post–Cold War World," *Foreign Affairs* 70 (1991):102–122.

16 Cf. citations in note 11 above; also Keohane and Nye, "Power and Interdependence Revisited," *International Organization* 41 (1987).

17 IMF, *Globalization: Challenges and Opportunities*.

18 Gaddis, "Toward the Post–Cold War World."

19 John Paul II, *Sollicitudo Rei Socialis* and *Centesimus Annus*.

20 J.B. Hehir, "The Moral Measurement of War: A Tradition of Change and Continuity," in J.D. Carlson and E.O. Owens, eds., *The Sacred and the Sovereign:*

Religion and International Politics (Washington, DC: Georgetown University Press, 2003), 47–63.

21 The history of this challenge is set forth in McGeorge Bundy, *Danger and Survival: Choices About the Bomb in the First Fifty Years* (New York: Random House, 1988).

22 The definitive treatment of nonintervention is found in J. Vincent, *Nonintervention and International Order* (Princeton, NJ: Princeton University Press, 1974). A sense of recent history is found in A. Roberts, "From San Francisco to Sarajevo: The United Nations and the Use of Force," *Survival* (Winter 1995–96):29–51; "Law and the Use of Force After Iraq," *Survival* (Summer 2003):31–56.

23 C. Cuicherd, "International Law and War in Kosovo," *Survival* 41 (1999):19–34; also Roberts, "Law and the Use of Force."

24 Cf. the valuable review by K. Himes, "Intervention, Just War and U.S. National Security," *Theological Studies* 65 (2004):143–157.

25Cf. Roberts, "Law and the Use of Force"; also *Pew Forum on Religion and Public Life Discussion: Just War Tradition and the New Terrorism*; G. Weigel, "The Just War Tradition After September 11"; *Logos* 5 (Summer 2002):13–44.

Chapter 6

1 *Our Common Future: The World Commission on Environment and Development*. Oxford: Oxford University Press, 1987, 8.

2 See *Science*, May 2003.

3 Catholic theologians have devoted significant attention to the environment. In particular, Diane Bergant, Leonardo Boff, Anne Clifford, Heather Eaton, Denis Edwards, Matthew Fox (now Episcopal), John Hart, Brennan Hill, Christine Firer Hinze, John Haught, Elizabeth Johnson, Paul Knitter, Daniel Maguire, Sean McDonough, Rosemary Radford Ruether, Stephen Scharper, and David Toolan.

Chapter 7

1 The first of this two-book series is Joe Holland, *Modern Catholic Social Teaching: The Popes Confront the Industrial Age 1740–1958* (New York: Paulist Press, 2003). The second book will address "Postmodern Catholic Social Teaching" from 1958 to 2000.

2 A fine summary of many critical analyses of the deep crisis of the "neo-liberal" corporate-dominated capitalist globalization, see John Cavanagh et al., *Alternatives to Economic Globalization [A Better World is Possible]: A Report of the International Forum on Globalization* (San Francisco: Barrett-Koehler Publishers, 2002). See also various analyses available from the World Social Forum at www.wsf.org.

3 For more on my interpretation of global capitalism, see Joe Holland, *The*

Three Stages of Modern Industrial Capitalism and the Birth of the Postmodern Electronic-Ecological Era (electronic book, 2003), available by email upon request from JoeHollandOffice@aol.com.

4 On the successive historical-societal roles of speech, handwriting, mechanical printing, and now electronics, see Joe Holland, *The Postmodern Electronic-Ecological Era: Religious Myth, Sexual Symbol, and Technological Design* (Washington DC: The Warwick Institute, 1992), now available only in electronic form by e-mail request from JoeHollandOffice@aol.com.

5 For a helpful summary of the ecologically scientific revision of economic theory already underway, see Robert Costanza, et al., *An Introduction to Ecological Economics* (Boca Raton, FL: International Society for Ecological Economics, 1997).

6 For more academic deconstructionism as the subjective ideology of late-modern global capitalism on its expressive side, see the rich study of Fredrick Jameson, *Postmodernism, or the Cultural Logic of Late Capitalism* (Durham, North Carolina: Duke University Press, 1991). By "postmodernism," Jameson means deconstructionism. On the origins of deconstructive postmodernism as a literary movement in Peru, and on its subsequent evolution and spread, see Perry Anderson, *The Origins of Postmodernity* (London: New Left Books, 1998).

7 See Charlene Spretnak, *States of Grace: The Recovery of Meaning in the Postmodern Age* (New York: HarperCollins Publishers, 1993) and Charlene Spretnak, *The Resurgence of the Real: Body, Nature, and Place in a Hypermodern World* (New York: Routledge, 1999).

8 See various volumes edited by David Ray Griffith and others in the SUNY Press Series on Constructive Postmodernism.

9 See, for example, Bruce B. Lawrence, *Defenders of God: The Fundamentalist Revolt against the Modern Age* (Columbia, SC: University of South Carolina Press, 1995).

10 On the new ecological paradigm, see Thomas Berry, *The Great Work: Our Way into the Future* (New York: Bell Tower, 1999); Thomas Berry & Brian Swimme, *The Universe Story: From the Primordial Flaring Forth to the Ecozoic Era – A Celebration of the Unfolding of the Cosmos* (San Francisco: Harper-Collins, 1992); and Fritjof Capra, *The Turning Point: Science, Society, and the Rising Culture* (New York: Bantam, 1983), as well as his *The Web of Life: A New Scientific Understanding of Living Systems* (New York: Doubleday, 1996). On the Catholic theological side, see Drew Christiansen S.J. and Walter Grazer, *"And God Saw That It Was Good": Catholic Theology and the Environment* (Washington DC: United States Catholic Conference, 1996). For another Catholic but ecumenically inclusive perspective, see Brennan R. Hill, *Christian Faith and the Environment: Making Vital Connections* (Maryknoll, NY: Orbis Books, 1998). For a mainline Protestant perspective, see Larry L. Rasmussen, *Earth Community, Earth Ethics* (Maryknoll, NY: Orbis, 1997). For eco-feminist perspectives, see Charlene Spretnak, *States of Grace: The Recovery of Meaning in the Postmodern Age* (New York: HarperCollins Publishers, 1993); Charlene Spretnak, *The Resurgence of the Real: Body, Nature, and Place in a Hypermodern World* (Routledge, 1999);

and Sallie McFague, *Metaphorical Theology: Models of God in Religious Language* (Philadelphia: Fortress Press, 1993).

11 For the work of Sean McDonaugh, see his three books: *To Care for the Earth: A Call to a New Theology* (Santa Fe, NM: Bear, 1986, 1987); *The Greening of the Church* (Maryknoll, NY: Orbis Books, 1990); and *Passion for the Earth* (Maryknoll, NY: Orbis Books, 1994).

12 See Michael J. Schuck, *The Social Teachings of the Papal Encyclicals, 1740–1989* (Washington, DC: Georgetown University Press, 1991).

13 See the earlier reference to Schuck's work, above.

14 For example, research in the sociology of religion indicates that at least those Christian streams that understand ordained leadership in lay form increasingly succeed at evangelization. See Donald E. Miller, *Reinventing American Protestantism* (University of California Press, 1999). The implications also seem to be global. Thus, in the case of Brazil, though Catholic evangelization has been present for half a millennium and Pentecostal evangelization has been present for scarcely half a century, there are now in Brazil twice as many Pentecostal ministers as Catholic priests. See Harvey Cox, *Fire from Heaven: The Rise of Pentecostal Spirituality and the Reshaping of Religion in the Twenty-First Century* (New York: Perseus Publishing, 1995).

15 See Donald L. Gelpi, SJ, *The Divine Mother: A Trinitarian Image of God* (New York: University of America Press, 1984).

16 John Paul II, *Evangelium Vitae*.

Chapter 8

1 See John A. Hall, ed., *Civil Society: Theory, History, Comparison* (Cambridge, UK: Polity Press, 1995), 81, 251, 32, 304.

2 Ashutosh Varshney, *Ethnic Conflict and Civic Life: Hindus and Muslims in India* (New Haven and London: Yale University Press, 2002).

3 Address to the Pontifical Academy of Social Sciences, April 27, 2001, 2.

4 Dani Rodrik, *Has Globalization Gone Too Far?* (Washington, DC: Institute for International Economics, 1997), 70–71.

5 Jorge Castañeda, "Mexico's Circle of Misery," *Foreign Affairs* 75, no. 4 (July/August 1996):95.

6 Ibid., 95.

7 Ernest Gellner, in Hall, *Civil Society: Theory, History, Comparison,* 42.

8 John Keane, *Global Civil Society?* (Cambridge: Cambridge University Press, 2003), 8. Italics in original.

9 Ibid., 11. Italics added.

10 Ibid., 12.

11 Ibid., 13–14.

12 Ibid., 16. Italics in original.

13 Ibid., 19.

14 Jackie Smith has underscored the transnational salience and "spine" of such movements by cataloguing the "industries"—the new initiatives, resources, forms of organization they have spawned in the realm of human rights, the environment, conflict resolution and peacemaking, development and ethnic self-determination. Jackie Smith, "Characteristics of the Modern Transnational Social Movement Sector," in Jackie Smith, Charles Chatfield, and Ron Pagnucco, eds., *Transnational Social Movements and Global Politics: Solidarity Beyond the State* (Syracuse, NY: Syracuse University Press, 1997), 47.

15 Louis Kriesberg, "Social Movements and Global Transformation," in Smith, Chatfield, and Pagnucco, eds., *Transnational Social Movements and Global Politics*.

16 Keane, *Global Civil Society?*, 59.

17 Ibid., 61-62.

18 Jeffrey C. Alexander, *Real Civil Societies: Dilemmas of Institutionalization* (London, 1998), 7.

19 For these and other examples see Loramy Conradi Gerstbauer, "Having Faith in NGOs? A Comparative Study of Faith-Based and Secular NGOs Engaged in International Peacemaking," unpublished Ph.D. dissertation, University of Notre Dame, 2001.

20 For a more detailed account, see R. Scott Appleby, *The Ambivalence of the Sacred: Religion, Violence and Reconciliation* (Rowman & Littlefield, 2000), chapter 4.

21 Helmut Anheier, ed., *Global Civil Society 2001* (Cambridge, UK: Cambridge University Press, 2001).

Chapter 9

1 Gregory Baum, "After September 11: The Dialogue of Religions," *The Ecumenist* 39(summer 2002):8–11.

2 "A Declaration of American Catholics on the War against Terrorism," *The Ecumenist* 39(spring 2002):4–6.

3 Address of the Holy Father to members of the John Paul II Center in Washington, DC, on November 2, 2001.

4 See www.holyseemission.org/ 15oct 2001.html

5 See the Appendix, 155.

6 Samuel Huntington, *The Clash of Civilizations and the Remaking of the World*

Order (New York: Simon & Schuster, 1996); Gregory Baum, "The Clash of Civilizations or their Reconciliation?" *The Ecumenist* 39(spring 2002):12–17.

7 Joe Feuerherd, "Christian opposition to attack on Iraq is widespread, but not universal," *The National Catholic Reporter*, February 7, 2003.

8 In a statement of Sept. 25, 2001, the Canadian bishops ask all citizens to refrain from expressing anger at any particular people or religion. They write, "We reaffirm the respect that we hold toward Islam and its adherents, and we deeply deplore all crimes of hate directed toward Arab people."

9 Scott Appleby, *The Ambivalence of the Sacred* (Lanham, MD: Rowman & Littlefield Publishers, 2000).

10 Mohammed Abu-Nimer, *Nonviolence and Peace-Building in Islam: Theory and Practice* (Gainsville, FL: University Press of Florida, 2003).

11 Eknath Easwaram, *Non-violent Soldier of Islam* (Tomalis, CA: Nilgiri Press, 1984, 1999).

12 Marc Gopin, *Between Eden and Armageddon: The Future of World Religions, Violence and Peace* (New York: Oxford University Press, 2000) and *Holy War, Holy Peace* (New York: Oxford University Press, 2002).

13 Paul Knitter, Chandra Muzaffar, eds., *Subverting Greed: Religious Perspectives on the Global Economy* (Maryknoll, NY: Orbis, 2002).

14 Paul Knitter, *One Earth, Many Religions* (Maryknoll, NY: Orbis, 1995).

15 See Chandra Muzaffar, "Roundtable on Religion and Globalization," *The Ecumenist*, 40(summer 2003):15–16. He is the author of *Globalization: The Perspectives and Experiences of the Religious Traditions of Asia Pacific* and *Politics for Asia: A Buddhist-Muslim Dialogue*, both published by the International Movement for a Just Peace in 1998 and 1999 respectively.

16 Hans Küng, *A Global Ethics for Global Politics and Economics* (New York: Oxford University Press, 1998).

17 The Forum of Religion and Ecology: http://environment.harvard.edu/religion.

18 *Nostra aetate* [The Declaration of the Church's Relation to Non-Christian Religions], no. 4.

19 Bernard M. Daly, *Beyond Secrecy: The Untold Story of Canada and the Second Vatican Council* (Ottawa: Novalis, 2003), 64–66.

20 "Violence en héritage: réflexions pastorales sur la violence conjugale," l'Assemblée des évêques du Québec (1989). See also *l'Église canadienne*, 24(1991):295–298.

21 Pamela Brubaker, "The Ecumenical Decade of the Churches in Solidarity with Women," *The Ecumenist* 36(Aug.–Sept. 1999):1-3.

22 Gregory Baum, "Bulletin: The Apostolic Letter *Mulieris dignitatem,*" *Concilium* 206(6/1989):144–149.

23 April 15, 2003, Letter to the Federal Justice Minister Martin Cauchon regarding Bill C-25).

24 E.F. Sheridan SJ, ed., *Do Justice: The Social Teaching of the Canadian Catholic Bishops* (Montreal: Éditions Paulines, 1987), 411–434, 412.

25 Karl Polanyi, *The Great Transformation* (Boston: Beacon Press, 1944). See Gregory Baum, *Karl Polanyi: On Ethics and Economics* (Montreal: McGill-Queen's University Press, 1996).

26 See Eric Shragge and Jean-Marc Fontan, *Social Economy: International Debates and Perspectives* (Montreal: Black Rose Books, 2000). In Quebec, the entire review *Économie et solidarité* deals with issues related to the social economy.

27 Address of Pope John Paul II to the peace meeting for religious leaders, January 24, 2002, Assisi.

28 Address of Pope John Paul II at the meeting with Muslim leaders at the Great Mosque of Damascus, May 6, 2001.

29 Address of Pope John Paul II to the members of an interreligious delegation from Indonesia, Rome, February 20, 2003.

30 See Daniel Kendall and Gerald O'Collins, eds., *In Many and Diverse Ways: In Honor of Jacques Dupuis* (Maryknoll, NY: Orbis Books, 2003), especially Hans Waldenfells, SJ, "Ecclesia in Asia," 194–208.

31 Gregory Baum, "The Theology of Cardinal Ratzinger: A Response to *Dominus Iesus,*" *The Ecumenist* 37(fall 2000):1–3, 2.

32 Gregory Baum, "An Extraordinary Ecclesiastical Event," *The Ecumenist* 37(fall 2000):16–18.

33 See *Religiosa: Indonesian Journal on Religious Harmony*, 1,1 (August 1995)

34 Juergen Moltmann, *God in Creation* (San Francisco: Harper & Row, 1985), 87–88.

35 John Paul II, *Crossing the Threshold of Hope* (New York: Alfred A. Knopf, 1994), 64.

Chapter 10

1 Wendy Tyndale, "National Forum of Fishworkers: A Spiritually Inspired Movement for Alternative Development," www.wfdd.org.uk/programmes/case_studies/fishworkers

2 www.wfdd.org.uk/programmes/case_studies/awakatan_eng.pdf

3 Speech to the UNDP in 1997: Kamla Chowdhry, *The Sarvodaya Shramadan Movement in Sri Lanka,* Paranape, Makarand, ed. Dharma and Development, Samvad Idea Foundation, New Delhi, 2005.

4 "Study of the organisation and functioning of a development association: The case of Sarkan Zoumountsi in Yaoundé, Cameroon," www.wfdd.org.uk/programmes/case_studies/SarkanZoumountsi

5 Wendy Tyndale, "National Forum of Fishworkers: A Spiritually Inspired Movement for Alternative Development," www.wfdd.org.uk/programmes/case_studies/fishworkers

6 Jane Rasbach and Pracha Hutanuwatra, "Engaged Buddhism," www.wfdd.org.uk/programmes/case_studies/engbuddhism.pdf

7 Jonathan Sacks, *The Dignity of Difference* (New York: Continuum, 2003), 82.

8 Etienne Zikra, "Tokombéré: A Project for Human Promotion Founded on Faith," www.wfdd.org.uk/programmes,case_studies/Tokombere

9 Deepa Naryan, *Voices of the Poor: Can Anyone Hear Us?* Washington, DC: World Bank, 2000, 64.

10 K.R. Usha, "Vivekananda Girijana Kalyana Kendra (VGKK)," www.wfdd.org.uk/programmes/case_studies/VGKK

11 World Faiths Development Dialogue, The provision of services for poor people: A contribution to WDR 2004, 2003 www.wfdd.org.uk/programmes/wdr/wfddwdr2005,pdf.9

12 Hans Küng, ed., *Yes to a Global Ethic* (Norwich, UK: SCM Press, 1995).

Chapter 11

1 Peter Beyer, *Religion and Globalization* (London: Sage Publications, 1994), 174.

2 Asghar Schirazi, *Islamic Development Policy: The Agrarian Question in Iran.* Translated from the German by P.J. Ziess-Lawrence (Boulder, CO: Lynne Reiner, 1993), 76.

3 Interview with the author in Tehran, 1983.

4 Jean Bethke Elshtain, *Democracy on Trial* (Concord, ON: Anansi, 1993), 133.

5 In a recent book in Persian, I have elaborated on these four elements and how they shape the flowing river of Iranian identity. See Farhang Rajaee, *Moshkeleye Hoviate Iranian Emruz* (The Problematic of Contemporary Iranian Identity) (Tehran: Nashre Ney, 2004).

6 A technical notion in international law, originally utilized by the Greeks, *androlepsia* was used whenever a group who felt wronged would capture the citizens of the place that has committed the wrong and hold them for ransom or for judicial

condemnation to pay compensation.

7 Schirazi, *Islamic Development Policy,* 82.

8 Ibn Khaldun, *The Muqaddimah: An Introduction to History*, translated from the Arabic by Franz Rosenthal (New York: Pantheon Books, 1958), vol. 1, 65.

9 Omid Safi, ed., *Progressive Muslims: On Justice, Gender and Pluralism* (Oxford: Oneworld Publications Ltd., 2003).

10 Farhang Rajaee, "A Thermidor of Islamic Yuppies? Conflict and Compromise in Iran's Politics," *The Middle East Journal*. Vol. 53, no. 2, Spring 1999:217–231.

11 Mohammed Mojtahed Shabestari, *Naqdi bar Quera'at Rasmi as Din: Bohranya, Chaleshha, Rahhallia* (A Critique of the Official Reading of Religion: Crisis, Challenges and Solutions) (Tehran: Entesharat-e-Tarh-e No 2002), 7.

12 Ibid., 11.

13 Ibid., 15–18.

14 Mohammed Mojtahed Shabestari, *Iman va Azadi* (Faith and Freedom) (Tehran: Entessharat-e-Tarh-e No, 2000), 33.

15 Ibid., 122–124.

16 Shabestari, *A Critique*, 334.

17 Shabestari, *Faith and Freedom,* 38.

18 Mohammed Mojtahed Shabestari, *Hermanotik, Ketab, va sonat* (Hermeneutic, The Scripture and Tradition) (Tehran: Entesharat-e-Tarh-e No, 1978), 202–203.

19 Ibid., 161.

20 Shabestari, *Naqdi bar* (A Critique), 335.

21 Abolkarim Soroush, "Qabz-o Bast dar Mizan Naqd-o Bahs" ("Contraction and Expansion at the Level of Criticism and Discussion"), *Keyan*, vol. 1, no. 2 (1991):5–13.

22 Abdolkarim Soroush, "Ma'na va Mabny-e Seckolarizm" (Meaning and Foundation of Secularism), *Keyan* no. 26 (1993):13.

23 Ibid., 11.

24 Abdolkarim Soroush, *Razdani, Roshanfekri va Dindari* (Knowing the Secrets, Intellectualism and Religiosity) (Tehran: Sertat, 1998), 146.

25 Cited from Fahrang Rajaee, "Islam and Modernity: The Reconstruction of an Alternative Shi'ite Islamic Worldview in Iran" in Martin Marty and Scott Appleby, eds., *Fundamentalism and Society: Reclaiming the Sciences, the Family and Education* (Chicago: University of Chicago Press, 1993), 114. Soroush first introduced this idea in a set of articles in a cultural monthly called *Keyhnan Farhangi* in 1988–90 but it became the most debated issue in the 1990s, forcing Soroush to elaborate on his point in a volume

of more than 600 pages and even the Council of Foreign Relations to commission a study of it: Valla Vakili, *Debating Religion and Politics in Iran: The Political Thought of Abdolkarim Soroush* (New York: Council on Foreign Religions, 1997).

26 Abdolkarim Soroush, *Farbatar az Ideology* (Broader than Ideology) (Tehran: Sertat, 1996), 130.

27 Ibid., 155.

28 Abdolkarim Soroush, *Tafaroj Son'* (A Journey to the World of Technology) (Tehran: Sertat, 1994), 250.

29 Ibid., 244.

30 Ibid., 239.

31 Saeed Hajarian, *Az Shehed Qodsi ta Shahed Bazari: Orfi Shodan Din dar Sepehr Siyassat* (From the Sacred Witness to the Profane Witness: Secularization of Religion in the Political Sphere) (Tehran: Entesharat-eTarh-e No, 2001), 102–104.

32 Ibid., 10.

33 Saeed Hajarian, *Jamhuriyat: Afsunsedaei az Qodrat* (Republicanism, Disenchanting of Power) (Tehran: Tarh-e No, 2000), 47.

34 Ibid., 48.

35 Ibid., 50.

36 Ibid., 190.

37 Hajarian, *From the Sacred Witness*, 199

38 Ibid., 201.

39 Ibid., 201.

40 Ibid., 202.

41 Hajarian, *Republicanism*, 372–373.

Chapter 12

1 *On the Threshold," Songs of Chokhamela,* trans. Rohini Mokashi-Punekar (The Book Review Literary Trust: New Delhi, 2000), 14. Chokhamela was a fourteenth-century untouchable saint-poet who belonged to the *varkari* tradition of Maharashtra. These poems, the first expression of dalit poetry, express poignantly a peculiar dichotomy: the awareness of living at the margin, and God's need and love for him.

2 Ranajit Guha, "On Some Aspects of the Historiography of Colonial India" in *Subaltern Studies I: Writings on South Asian History and Society,* Ranajit Guha, ed. (Delhi: Oxford University Press, 1982). Partha Chatterjee, "The Nation and Its Peasants" in *Mapping Subaltern Studies and the Postcolonial,* Vinayak Chaturvedi, ed. (New York: Verso, 2000). Rosalind O'Hanlon, "Recovering the Subject: Subaltern

Studies and Histories of Resistance in Colonial South Asia," *Modern Asian Studies,* Vol. 22, no. 1, 1988.

3 I have dealt with various forms of this attitude in the past. Fernando Franco and Suguna Ramanathan, "The Recovery of Religious Meaning," *Textual Practice*, Vol. 5, no. 2, Summer 1991:183–94. Suguna Ramanathan and Fernando Franco, "Universality and Identity," *The Way*, Vol. 34, no 1, Jan 1994:17–27.

4 The movie was produced by film star Aamir Khan, won the Audience Award at the 2001 Locarno film festival, and catapulted to fame in the English-dominated film world with its nomination in the Best Foreign Film category for the 2001 Academy Awards.

5 The term "Bollywood" derives from the juxtaposition of parts from two words: *Bo*mbay and Ho*llywood*, and is used the describe the flourishing Indian (Hindi) film industry located in Bombay which has been as astute as its counterpart in the US to adapt to the changing needs of the Indian public.

6 Chandrima Chakraborty, "Subaltern Studies, Bollywood and *Lagaan,*" *Economic and Political Weekly,* Vol. 38, no. 19, May 12, 2003:1879–1883. Boria Majumdar, "Politics of Leisure in Colonial India, 'Lagaan' – Invocation of a Lost History," *Economic and Political Weekly,* Vol. 36, no. 35, September 1, 2001:3399–404. Nissim Mannathukkaren, "Subalterns, Cricket and the Nation: The Silences of Lagaan", *Economic and Political Weekly,* Vol. 36, no. 49, December 8, 2001:4580–88.

7 Veena Das, Arthur Kleinman, Mamphela Ramphele, Pamela Reynolds et al., *Violence and Subjectivity*_(Berkeley: University of California Press, 2000). Arthur Kleinman, Veena Das, and Margaret Lock, eds., *Social Suffering* (Berkeley, University of California Press, 1997).

8 Veena Das, "Violence and Translation." http://www.ssrc.org/sept11/essays/das.htm

9 The term is used to highlight the political connotation of what happens at the margins of society or rather at the margins of the state, as being not only replicating forms of state domination but determining the role of the state. For a comprehensive discussion see Veena Das, Deborah Poole, *Anthropology in the Margins of the State* (Sar, 2004).

10 The term "subaltern" refers to the Indian historical school that has delved into the narratives of persons, communities, and events which were rarely taken into consideration in dominant historical scholarship. Though highly contested, this new perspective has been defended by Sumit Sarkar, Ranajit Guha, Veena Das, and others.

11 "Economic Development and Political Democracy. Interaction of Economics and Politics in Independent India," *Economic and Political Weekly,* Vol. 33, no. 49, December 5, 1998:3121–131.

12 I have discussed this point in greater detail in "Active Capitalism: The Rise of India's Rural Elites," Ambrose Pinto, ed., *Resisting the Status Quo: Transforming Society* (New Delhi: Indian Social Institute Publications, 2000), 87–130.

13 Ibid., 3124.

14 Unlike the case of scheduled castes (dalits), the Constitution does not provide an official list of those "jatis" or social groups characterized as backward. This work has been delegated to the various States and hence one observes little agreement on the criteria to define backwardness, and a shift of the issue of "identity politics" to the regional arena of the States.

15 Sunil Khilnani, *The Idea of India* (New Delhi: Penguin, 1999), 193.

16 Ibid., 74.

17 To give an example drawn from my own experience: If the Congress in Gujarat leans towards the *Vankars*, a concrete Scheduled Caste (SC) group (*jati)*, the BJP will systematically woo the *Chamars* or *Rohits,* the other substantial SC group among dalits.

18 I refer to the work of Ashutosh Varshney and Steven Wilkinson, *Hindu-Muslim Riots 1960–93: New Findings, Possible Remedies* (New Delhi: Rajiv Gandhi Institute for Contemporary Studies, 1996).

19 Paul R. Brass writes: "The simplistic character [of Varshney's arguments] arises from the unsophisticated belief that the development of intercommunal linkages between communal groups can really prevent riots…his arguments…fail to identify clearly and precisely the principal actors, agents, and institutions that are responsible for the perpetration of communal violence and the uses to which such violence is put" (3037). "India, Myron Wiener and the Political Science of Development," *Economic and Political Weekly*, July 20, 2002, Vol. 37, no. 18:1735–1741.

20 This has been extensively noticed in the study based on 56 in-depth interviews of dalits in Gujarat. Fernando Franco, Jyotsna Macwan, Suguna Ramanathan, *Journeys to Freedom: Dalit Narratives,* (Calcutta: Samya, 2004).

21 M.S.S. Pandian, "One Step Outside Modernity. Caste Identity Politics and Public Sphere," *Economic and Political Weekly,* May 4, 2002, Vol. 37, no. 18:1735–1741.

22 Anti-colonial nationalism, according to Partha Chatterjee, cordons off the domain of culture or spirituality as "its own domain of sovereignty within colonial society well before it begins its political battle with the imperial power." Partha Chatterjee, *The Nation and Its Fragments: Colonial and Postcolonial Histories* (Delhi: Oxford University Press, 1995, 1993), 7.

23 "The Absent Liberal. An Essay on Politics and Intellectual Life," *Economic and Political Weekly*, December 15, 2001, Vol. 36, no. 50,:4663–70.

24 The term "bahujan" literally means a group of people forming the majority of the population. It has been coined by various subaltern leaders trying to convey the idea that the subalterns are a majority in India.

25 *Untouchable Freedom: A Social History of a Dalit Community* (New Delhi: Oxford University Press, 2000).

26 Fernando Franco, Suguna Ramanathan, Savar V. Sherry Chand, "Tribals: The Politics of Identity Construction," *Indian Social Science Review*, Vol. 3, no. 1, 2001:145–174, p. 103.

27 In a nuanced study of Christian conversions in Goa, Rowena Robinson suggests that the analysis of conversion must be located within particular social and historical contexts. Rowena Robinson, *Conversion, Continuity and Change: Lived Christianity in Southern Goa* (Delhi: Sage Publication, 1998).

28 "Relevance of Conversion," *Economic and Political Weekly,* Vol. 38, no. 9, March 1, 2003:850 and 915.

29 Intervention of the Holy See at the 32nd session of the FAO Conference (Rome, 29 November–10 December 2003).http://www.vatican.va/news_services/bulletin/news/14084.php?index=14084&po date_05.12.2003&lang=en

Chapter 13

1 Called by the Jesuit Centre for Social Faith and Justice and held in Guelph, Ontario, Canada from the 25th to the 28th of September, 2003.

2 This perspective makes explicit reference to the works of Pierre Teilhard de Chardin SJ.

3 From the *zoon politikon* of Aristotle to the personalist theories of the twentieth century, Western culture has debated this theme, also present in other cultures.

4 Part of this way of thinking and acting is grouped under the title "anti-political."

5 "Posivitism" refers to the sociological trend started by Auguste Comte. Under this name there came into being in Latin America an extensive current of thought and action, linked to various fields of knowledge and with a huge impact on society.

6 Positivism is clear on this point of affirming "order" as the first condition for "progress," thus justifying those governments which impose order by force, including restricting public freedom, so as to neutralize forces disturbing this order.

7 Figures on access to the use of computers and cyberspace between developed and poor countries are simply incredible. Within developing countries the differences are even greater, dangerously widening differences between social strata.

8 The image in the prologue to the fourth Gospel – "The Word was made flesh and lived (pitched its tent) among us" (Jn 1:14) – expresses well this idea of God's presence in the midst of his people; it is also found in many Old Testament passages, such as the following: "I have always led a wanderer's life in a tent. In all my journeying with the whole people of Israel..." (2 Sam 7:6b, 7a).

9 The prophet Haggai (1:1-11), on returning from exile, accuses the Israelites of their lack of citizenship because they are concerned only with their own houses, the private domain, and not with the common house (which is the House of God), the public domain. As a result, their efforts to lead a dignified life are useless.

10 Gen 1:26-27.

11 In the words of Latin-American theology: God, Creator of Life, shines in many ways through the experience of peoples. Faith in Him is the basis for hope in the shared horizon of a world where justice and peace live together.

12 Common interests fundamentally include a way of defining them and bringing them to reality. In other words, an important part of common interests are the "rules of the game" produced among all and observed by all, as well as the institutions charged with watching over their fulfillment.

13 The theme of war represents a challenge to Catholic thought, social as well as philosophical and theological. It has been too easy to stay with the opinions of past centuries to find some justification for the use of war as a political instrument. The development of human awareness and the radical nature of the Gospel rather invite the thought that all war is inhuman. The humanization of history will lead to a commitment for global relations without war.

14 Literature on this theme is extensive, as well as the diversity of opinions on the role of mass media and the freedom of expression and information. Here all that is intended is to recall the need to keep it present in the development of Catholic thought on democracy and globalization.

15 See Mt 11:2-6.

16 Philippians 2:1-12.

17 "Ut innotescant multiformis sapientia Dei." Eph 3:10.

18 This criterion is equally valid for the "importation" of republican, democratic, or monarchical models. If the Church is not a democratic, parliamentary, or socialist republic, neither is it an absolute or constitutional monarchy. The Church is not the reign of God either in its method of government or in its eschatological reality. Its challenge is to incarnate the method of government which Jesus of Nazareth himself sketched in Mk 10:41-45.

19 The Gospel also has much to tell us about this prophetic dimension of the Church's pastoral mission. Among other things, there is no excuse for neglecting people's needs and continuing to teach, preaching the salvation that comes from God. (See, for example, Mk 6:30-34.)

Chapter 14

1 James Wolfensohn at Annual Meeting of the World Bank Group and the International Monetary Fund in Durban, September 2003, quoted by Kevin Rafferty in "The world is out of balance" in *The Tablet*, 4 October 2003, 4.

2 Ibid., 4.

3 *Human Development Report 2003,* UNDP, 2.

4 In a BBC World Programme Radio Interview, 2 November 2003.

5 See "El reino de Dios y el paro en el tercer mundo," *Concilium*, 180 (1982):588–596.

6 See "Misión actual de la Compañía de Jesús," in *Revista Latinoamericana de Teología*, 29 (1983):115–126.

7 See "Utopía y profetismo desde América Latina," in *Revista Latinoamericana de Teología*, 17 (1989):141–184. For English version used here, see "Utopia and Prophecy in Latin America" in *Towards a Society that Serves Its People*, edited by John Hassett & Hugh Lacey (Washington, DC: Georgetown University Press, 1991), 44–88.

8 "El Reino de Dios," 595.

9 "Utopia & Prophecy," 54–55.

10 Ibid., 73.

11 Ibid., 74.

12 "Misión actual," 119.

13 "Utopia & Prophecy," 77.

14 See *Solicitudo Rei Socialis*, 1987, no. 41.

15 "Utopia & Prophecy," 81.

16 Ibid., 85.

17 "Utopia & Prophecy," 87.

18 *Globalization and New Evangelization in Latin America and the Caribbean* (Bogotá: CELAM, 2003).

19 Ibid., 11–12.

20 See "Address to the members of the Ethics and Economics Foundation," Pope John Paul II, 17 May 2001, no. 4.

21 "Address to the Pontifical Academy of Social Sciences," Pope John Paul II, 27 April 2001, no. 2.

22 *Globalization*, 122–123.

23 Ibid., 128–129.

24 Ibid., 155.

25 Ibid., 168.

26 Ibid., 207.

27 *Puebla: La evangelización en el presente y en el futuro de América Latina* (Mexico: UCA Editores, 1985), 233: #1134.

28 *Homilias*, Vol. IV, San Salvador, 1981, 226.

29 *Homilias*, Vol. VII, San Salvador, 1988, 294.

30 Ibid., 153.

31 Ibid., 432.

32 Ibid., 79.

33 Ibid., 236.

34 Ibid., 262.

35 Ibid., 426.

36 *Homilias*, Vol VI, San Salvador, 1981, 276.

Chapter 15

1 Leuven, Belgium: University of Louvain Press, 1998.

2 Ibid., 82.

3 This poem was composed during a grassroots workshop exploring culture and development. The Ila and the Tonga are two tribes in the southern part of Zambia, well-known for their prowess in cattle-rearing. The poem was first published in the *Bulletin of the Jesuit Centre for Theological Reflection* (No. 14, October 1992):13–14.

4 Joe Holland and Peter Henriot, S.J., *Social Analysis: Linking Faith and Justice*, Revised and Enlarged Edition (Maryknoll NY: Orbis Books, and Washington DC: Center of Concern, 1983), xii.

5 Ibid., xiii.

6 Ibid., xiii.

7 Ibid., xiii.

8 Ibid., xvi–xvii.

9 See Joe Holland, *Flag, Faith and Family: Rooting the American Left in Everyday Symbols* (Chicago: New Patriotic Alliance, 1979).

10 *Social Analysis*, 99.

11 *Paradigm Shift*, 31.

12 See *Social Analysis*, 7–9.

13 See Anne Hope and Sally Timmel, *Training for Transformation: A Handbook for Community Workers.* Revised edition; three volumes (Gweru, Zimbabwe: Mambo Press, 1995).

14 See Goran Hyden, *No Shortcuts to Progress: African Development Management in Perspective* (London: Heinemann, 1983), 8–16.

15 Ibid., 8.

16 One of the most significant efforts at utilizing cultural analysis to deepen the

understanding of the successes and failures of development is found in the work of Thierry Verhelst, *No Life Without Roots: Culture and Development*, translated by Bob Cumming (London: Zed Books, 1990). Verhelst has organized a group of scholars from around the world, "The South-North Network Cultures and Development," that is involved in research, training, community organizing and advocacy, and publishes a bilingual journal three times a year, *Cultures and Development: Quid Pro Quo*. One significant collaborator in this effort, a pioneer in the effort to bring cultural concerns to the forefront of development, is Denis Goulet of the University of Notre Dame. See his The Cruel Choice (New York: Atheneum, 1971).

17 An excellent overview of the Synod preparations, event, and conclusions can be found in the essays presented in Africa Faith and Justice Network, *The African Synod: Documents, Reflections, Perspectives* (Maryknoll, NY: Orbis, 1995). This volume also contains the Apostolic Exhortation of John Paul II, *Ecclesia in Africa*, 1995.

18 See Rodrigo Mejia S.J., *The Church in the Neighbourhood* (Nairobi: Daughters of St. Paul, 1990).

19 Jean-Marc Ela, *African Cry*. Translated by Robert R. Barr (Maryknoll, NY: Orbis, 1986), 132.

Chapter 16

1 "Global Governance: Our Responsibility to Make Globalization an Opportunity for All," available at www.comece.org.

2 For the Tobin tax and an NGO (The Association for the Taxation of Financial Transactions for the Aid of Citizens – ATTAC) that promotes it, cf. Diego Muro, "Campaign for a Robin Hood Tax for Foreign Exchange Markets" in John Clark, ed., *Globalizing Civic Engagement* (Sterling, VA: Earthcan, 2003).

3 *Our Global Neighborhood*, available on the web site of the Commission on Global Governance. Cf. also Yehzkel Dror, *The Capacity to Govern: A Report to the Club of Rome* (Portland, OR: F.Cass, 2001).

4 Kofi Annan as cited in Wolfgang Reinecke et al., *Critical Choices: The United Nations, Networks and the Future of Global Goverance* (Ottawa: International Development Research Centre, 2000), xviii–xix.

5 Matthew Scott, "Danger Landmines: NGO-Government Collaboration in the Ottawa Process," chapter 9 in Michael Edwards and John Gaventa, eds., *Global Citizen Action* (Boulder, CO: Lynne Reinner Publishers, 2001).

6 For a useful parsing of vertical and horizontal subsidiarity cf. Wolfgang Reinecke, *Global Public Policy: Governing Without Government?* (Washington, DC: The Brookings Institute, 1998), 89–90.

7 Dirk Messner, "Global Challenges for the 21st Century," in Paul Kennedy, Dirk Messner and Franz Nuscheler, *Global Trends and Global Governance* (London: Pluto Press, 2002), 37.

8 Richard Falk, *Religion and Humane Global Governance* (New York: Palgrave, 2001), 72.

9 This was a point forcefully made by the 2003 Nobel Peace Laureate, Shirin Ebadi, in her lecture "Islam, Democracy and Human Rights" at the University of California, Santa Barbara, May 17, 2004.

10 Daphné Josselin and William Wallace, "Non-State Actors in World Politics: The Lessons," in Daphné Josselin and William Wallace, eds., *Non-State Actors in World Politics* (London: Palgrave, 2001), 257.

11 Reinecke, *Global Public Policy,* 219. The idea of a boomerang effect from global civic society back to states can be found in Margaret Keck and Katheryn Sikkink, *Activists Beyond Borders: Advocacy Networks in International Politics* (Ithica, NY: Cornell University Press, 1998).

12 John Vidal, *Manchester Guardian,* April 23, 1999, 23.

13 For an argument that multinational corporations have a different organizational logic and form than their earlier national corporation types cf. Reinecke, *Global Public Policy,* 11–51.

14 Close monitoring of a self-regulated apparel compact by the Los Angeles garment industry to avoid buying from sweatshops did show improvement on this behaviour, even under a self-regulated regime.

15 Michael Edwards and John Gaventa, eds., *Global Citizen Action*, 10.

16 David Korten, *When Corporations Rule the World* (San Francisco: Berret Koehler Publishers, 2001), 266–269.

17 Peter Newell, "Campaigning for Corporate Change: Global Citizen Action on the Environment" in Edwards and Gaventa, eds., *Global Citizen Action*, 194.

Chapter 17

1 John Raston Saul, "The Collapse of Globalism – And the Rebirth of Nationalism," *Harper's,* March 24, 2003, 33.

2 See *The Fourth Annual Kearney/Foreign Policy Global Index,* entitled, "Measuring Globalization, Economic Reversals, Forward Momentum," *Foreign Policy,* March/April 2004, 68.

3 Ibid., 68.

4 For further development of this thinking, see John Gray, "The True Limits of Globalization," *Ethics Perspective,* no. 4, September, 2002:191–197.

5 The Church in the Modern World, no. 1.

6 Justice in the World, no. 6.

7 Cf. Appendix, under II, 4.

8 David Toolan, *At Home in the Cosmos* (Maryknoll, NY: Orbis, 2000).

9 John F. Haught, *God After Darwin: A Theology of Evolution* (Boulder, CO: Westview Press, 2000).

10 John F. Haught, "Evolution is essential to a world loved by God," *Prairie Messenger,* May 10, 2000.

11 Pierre Teilhard de Chardin S.J., *The Divine Milieu* (New York: Harper & Row Publishers, 1960).

12 See p. 40 of this book.

13 Decree Four "Our Mission Today: The Service of Faith and the Promotion of Justice," in *Documents of the 31st and 32nd General Congregatons of the Society of Jesus.* 411–438.

14 George B. Cardinal Flahiff, "Christian Formation for Justice," Presentation to the Synod of Bishops, Rome, October 20, 1971. In E.F. Sheridan S.J., ed., *Do Justice: The Social Teachinga of the Canadians Bishops* (Sherbrooke, QC: Editions Paulines, 1987), 218.

15 William F. Ryan S.J. "Mindsets and New Horizons for Discernment," *Soundings.* Findings of the Center of Concern's Task Force on Social Consciousness and Ignatian Spirituality (Washington, DC: Center of Concern, 1974), 4–6.

16 Maurice Cardinal Roy, *Reflections on the 10th Anniversary of* Pacem in Terris, April 11, 1973.

17 *Our Global Neighbourhood: Report of the Commission on Global Governance* (Oxford: Oxford University Press, 1995.)

18 Pope John Paul II, "An Ever Timely Commitment: Teaching Peace," World Day of Peace, January 1, 2004.

19 Harvey Cox, *New York Newsday*, June 11, 1991. Cited in Daniel P. Moynahan, "Social Justice in the Next Century," *America,* September 14, 1991, 133.

20 Cf. William F. Ryan SJ, "An Experiment in Catholic Syndicalism – A Brief History of the Origins, Growth and Ideological Evolution of the Canadian and Catholic Confederation of Labour" (Unpublished master's thesis, St Louis University, 1953).

21 William F. Ryan S.J., *The Clergy and Economic Growth in Quebec (1896–1914)* (Quebec: Les presses de l'Université Laval, 1966).

22 William F. Ryan S.J., *Spirituality, Culture and Economic Development: Opening a Dialogue* (Ottawa: The International Development Research Centre, 1995).

23 Cf. Charles E. Curran, in his Preface to Roger Aubert, *Catholic Social Teaching: A Historical Perspective,* David Boileau, ed. (Milwaukee: Marquette University Press, 2003).

24 Jose Casanova, *Public Religions in the Modern World* (Chicago University Press, 1994), 234.

25 Ibid., 234.

26 Peter Henriot, Edward J. DeBerri, Michael J, Schulteis, *Catholic Social Teaching: Our Best Kept Secret* (Maryknoll, NY: Orbis, 1985).

27 Cited in Roger Aubert, *Catholic Social Teaching*, 278–279.

28 Pedro Arrupe SJ, "Men for Others." Talk given in Valencia, July 31, 1979.

29 John Cavanagh and Jerry Manders, co-chairs, *Alternatives to Economic Globalization,* A Report of the International Forum on Globalization (San Francisco: Berrett-Koehler Publishers, 2002).

30 Ibid.

31 For more on the ecclesiology that this involves, see Paul Lakeland, "A Theology of the Laity is an Ecclesiology," *The Ecumenist*, winter 2004:1–6.

Bibliography

Africa Faith and Justice Network. *The African Synod: Documents, Reflections, Perspectives.* Maryknoll, NY: Orbis, 1995.

Agnivesh, Swami. *Religion, Spirituality and Social Action: New Agenda for Humanity.* New Delhi: Hope India Publications, 2001.

Alternatives to Economic Globalization: A Report of the International Forum on Globalization. San Francisco: Berrett-Koehler, 2002.

Anderson, Sarah, ed. *Views from the South: The Effects of Globalization and the WTO on Third-World Countries.* Milford, CT: Food First Books, 2000.

Anheier, Helmut, ed. *Global Civil Society 2001.* Cambridge, UK: Cambridge University Press, 2001.

Another World Is Possible: Popular Alternatives to Globalization at the World Social Forum. New York: Zed Books, 2003.

Appleby, R. Scott. *The Ambivalence of the Sacred: Religion, Violence and Reconstruction.* Lanham, MD: Rowman and Littlefield, 2000.

Aubert, Roger. *Catholic Social Teaching: A Historical Perspective*. Milwaukee: Marquette University Press, 2003.

Baum, Gregory. "The Clash of Civilizations or Their Reconciliation?" *The Ecumenist* 39 (spring 2002):12–17.

Bauman, Zygmunt. *Globalization: The Human Consequences.* New York: Columbia University Press, 1998.

Barber, Bernard. *Jihad versus McWorld: Terrorism's Challenge to Democracy*, second rev. ed. New York: Ballantine Books, 2001.

Berry, Thomas and Brian Swimme. *The Universe Story: From the Primordial Flaring Forth to the Ecozoic Era – A Celebration of the Unfolding of the Cosmos.* San Francisco: Harper-Collins, 1992.

Beyer, Peter. *Religion and Globalization.* London: Sage Publications, 1994.

Boswell, John, Francis McHugh and Johan Verstraeten, eds. *Catholic Social Thought: Twighlight or Renaissance?* Leuven, Belgium: Peeters/ University Press, 2000.

Broswimmer, Franz. *Ecocide: A Short History of Mass Extinction of Species.* London: Pluto Press, 2002.

Casanova, Jose. *Public Religion in the Modern World.* Chicago: Chicago University Press, 1994.

Catechism of the Catholic Church, second ed. Vatican City: Libreria Editrice Vaticana, 1997.

Cavanagh, John and Jerry Manders, eds. *Alternatives to Economic Globalization: A Better World Is Possible.* Report of the International Forum on Globalization. San Francisco: Berrett-Koehler Publishers, 2002.

Chaturvedi, Vinayak, ed. *Mapping Subaltern Studies and the Postcolonial.* New York: Verso, 2000.

Christiansen, Drew, S.J. and Walter Grazer, eds. *And God Saw that It Was Good.* Washington, DC: United States Catholic Conference, 1996.

Chryssavgis, John, ed. *Cosmic Grace and Humble Prayer: The Ecological Vision of the Green Patriarch, Bartholomew.* Grand Rapids, MI: Eerdmans, 2003.

Clark, John, ed. *Globalizing Civic Engagement.* Sterling, VA: Earthcan, 2003.

Commission on Global Governance. *Our Global Neighbourhood.* Oxford: Oxford University Press, 1995.

Curran, Charles E. *Catholic Social Teaching, 1891–Present: A Historical, Theological and Ethical Analysis.* Washington, DC: Georgetown University Press, 2002.

de Chardin, Teilhard. *The Divine Milieu.* New York: Harper & Row, 1960.

de Schrijver, Georges. *Liberation Theologies on Shifting Grounds: A Clash of Socio-Economic and Cultural Paradigms.* Leuven, Belgium: Peeters, Louvain University Press, 1998.

DeBerri, Edward P. and James E. Hug, with Peter J. Henriot and Michael J. Schultheis. *Catholic Social Teaching: Our Best Kept Secret,* fourth revised and expanded version. Maryknoll, NY: Orbis; Washington, DC: Center of Concern, 2003.

Dorr, Donal. *Option for the Poor: A Hundred Years of Vatican Social Teaching.* Maryknoll, NY: Orbis, 1983.

Elsbernd, Mary and Reimund Bieringer. *When Love Is Not Enough: A Theo-Ethic of Justice.* Collegeville, MN: The Liturgical Press, 2002.

Elshtain, Jean Bethke. *Democracy on Trial.* Concord, ON: Anansi, 1993.

Falk, Richard. *Law in an Emerging Global Village: A Post-Westphalian Perspective.* Ardsley, NY: Transnational Publishers, 1998.

———. *Predatory Globalization.* Malden, MA: Blackwell Publishers, 1999.

———. *Religion and Humane Global Governance.* New York: Palgrave, 2001.

Franco, Fernando, Jyotsna Macwan, and Suguna Ramanathan. *Journeys to Freedom: Dalit Narratives.* Calcutta: Samya, 2004.

Friedman, Thomas. *The Lexus and the Olive Tree.* New York: Anchor Books, 1999.

Giddens, Anthony. *Runaway World: How Globalization Is Reshaping Our Lives.* London: Profile Books, 1999.

Global Governance: Our Responsibility to Make Globalization an Opportunity to All. A Report to the Bishops of COMECE (Commission of the Bishops' Conferences of the European Community). Brussels: COMECE, 2001.

Goulet, Denis. *Development Ethics: A Guide to Theory and Practice.* New York and London: Apex Press & Zed Books, 1995.

Harper, Sharon, ed. *The Lab, the Temple and the Market: Reflections at the Intersection of Science, Religion and Development.* Ottawa: IDRC/CDRI & Bloomfield, CT: Kumarian Press, 2000.

Harvard website for the Forum on Religion and Ecology:www.environment.harvard.edu/religion

Haught, John F. *Deeper than Darwin: The Prospect for Religion in an Age of Evolution.* Boulder, CO: Westview Press, 2003.

———. *God After Darwin: A Theology of Evolution.* Boulder, CO: Westview Press, 2000.

Held, David and Anthony McGrew. *Globalization/Anti-Globalization.* Malden, MA: Blackwell Publishers, 2002.

Held, David and Anthony McGrew, eds. *Governing Globalization: Power, Authority and Global Governance.* Malden, MA.: Blackwell Publishers, 2002.

Hessel, Dieter and Rosemary Radford Ruether, Eds. *Christianity and Ecology: Seeking the Well-Being of Earth and Humans.* Cambridge: Harvard Center for the Study of World Religions, 1999.

Hoeber Rudolph, Suzanne and James Piscatori, eds. *Transnational Religion and Fading States*. Boulder, CO: Westview, 1997.

Holland, Joe. *Modern Catholic Social Teaching: The Popes Confront the Industrial Age 1740–1958.* New York: Paulist Press, 2003.

Holland, Joe and Peter Henriot S.J. *Social Analysis: Linking Faith and Justice.* Revised and enlarged edition. Maryknoll, NY: Orbis, 1983.

Hyden, Goran. *No Shortcuts to Progress: African Development Management in Perspective.* London: Heinemann, 1983.

Hollenbach, David S.J. *The Common Good and Christian Ethics.* New York: Cambridge University Press, 2002.

Huntington, Samuel. *The Clash of Civilizations and the Remaking of the World Order*. New York: Simon and Schuster, 1996.

Ibn Khaldun. *The Muqaddimah: An Introduction to History.* Translated from the Arabic by Franz Rosenthal. New York: Pantheon Books, 1958, vol. 1.

Johnston, Douglas and Cynthia Sampson, eds. *Religion: The Missing Dimension of Statecraft.* New York: Oxford University Press, 1994.

Josselin, Daphne and William Wallace, eds. *Non-State Actors in World Politics.* London: Palgrave, 2001.

Juergensmeyer, Mark, ed. *Global Religion*. New York: Oxford University Press, 2003.

Kaldor, Mary. *Global Civil Society: An Answer to War.* Malden, MA: Blackwell Publishers, 2003.

Keck, Margaret and Kathryn Sikkink. *Activists Beyond Borders: Advocacy Networks in International Politics.* Ithaca, NY: Cornell University Press, 1988.

Keenan, Marjorie, ed. *From Stockholm to Johannesburg: A Historical Overview of the Concern of the Holy See for the Environment 1972–2002.* Vatican City: Pontifical Council for Justice and Peace, 2002.

Keene, John. *Global Civil Society?* Cambridge, UK: Cambridge University Press, 2003.

Kennedy, Paul, Dirk Messner and Franz Nuscheler. *Global Trends and Global Governance.* London: Pluto Press, 2002.

Kilnani, Sunil. *The Idea of India*. New Delhi: Penguin, 1999.

Kleinman, Arthur, Veena Das, and Margaret Lock, eds. *Social Suffering.* Berkeley, CA: University of California Press, 1997.

Knitter, Paul. *One Earth: Many Religions*. Maryknoll, NY: Orbis, 1995.

Knitter, Paul and Chandra Muzaffar, eds. *Subverting Greed: Religious Perspectives on the Global Economy.* Maryknoll, NY: Orbis, 2002.

Korten, David. *When Corporations Rule the World.* San Francisco: Berrett-Koehler Publishers, 2001.

Küng, Hans. *A Global Ethics for Global Politics and Economics*. New York: Oxford University Press, 1998.

Loy, David. *The Great Awakening: A Buddhist Social Theory.* Somerville, MA: Wisdom Publications, 2003.

Nussbaum, Martha C. *Women and Human Development: The Capabilities Approach*. New York: Cambridge University Press, 2000.

Prasad, Vijay. *Untouchable Freedom. A Social History of a Dalit Community*. New Delhi: Oxford University Press, 2000.

Rajaee, Farhang. "A Thermidor of Islamic Yuppies? Conflict and Compromise in Iran's Politics," *The Middle East Journal,* vol. 53, no. 2 (Spring 1999):217–231.

———. "Islam and Modernity: The Reconstruction of an Alternative Shi'ite Worldview in Iran" in Martin Marty and Scott Appleby, eds. *Fundamentalism and Society: Reclaiming the Sciences, the Family and Education.* Chicago: University of Chicago Press, 1993.

Reinecke, William. *Global Public Policy: Governing Without Governance.* Washington, DC: Brookings Institute Press, 1998.

Reinecke, William, et al. *Critical Choices: The U.N., Networks and the Future of Global Governance.* Ottawa: International Development Research Centre, 2000.

Robertson, Roland. *Globalization: Social Theory and Global Culture.* London: Sage Publications, 2001.

Rodrik, Dani. *Has Globalization Gone Too Far?* Washington, DC: Institute for International Economics, 1997.

Ryan, William F. *Spirituality, Culture and Economic Development: Opening a Dialogue.* Ottawa: The International Development Research Centre, 1995.

———. *The Clergy and Economic Growth in Quebec (1896–1914).* Quebec: Les presses de l'Université Laval, 1966.

Sacks, Jonathon. *The Dignity of Difference.* New York: Continuum, 2003.

Safi, Omid, ed. *Progressive Muslims: On Justice, Gender and Pluralism.* Oxford: Oneworld Publications Ltd., 2003.

Schirazi, Asghar. *Islamic Development Policy: The Agrarian Question in Iran.* Translated from the German by P.J. Ziess-Lawrence. Boulder, CO: Lynne Reiner, 1993.

Schreiter, Robert. *The New Catholicity: Theology Between the Global and the Local.* Maryknoll, NY: Orbis, 1997.

Schuck, Michael J. *The Social Teachings of the Papal Encyclicals, 1740–1989.* Washington, DC: Georgetown University Press, 1991.

Sheridan, E.F. *Do Justice: The Social Teaching of the Canadian Bishops.* Sherbrooke, QC: Éditions Paulines, 1987.

Sivaraksa, Sulak. *Global Healing: Essays and Interviews on Structural Violence, Social Development and Spiritual Transformation.* Bangkok: Thai Inter-Religious Commission for Development, Sathirakoses-Nagapradipa Foundation, 1999.

Sobrino, Jon. *Christ the Liberator: A View from the Victims.* Maryknoll, NY: Orbis, 2001.

Sobrino, Jon and Juan Pico. *Theology of Christian Solidarity.* Maryknoll, NY: Orbis, 1983.

Sobrino, Jon and Felix Wilfred, eds. *Globalization and Its Victims.* London: SCM Press, 2001.

Spretnak, Charlene. *The Resurgence of the Real: Body, Nature, and Place in a Hypermodern World.* New York: Routledge, 1999.

Toolan, David. *At Home in the Cosmos.* Maryknoll, NY: Orbis, 2000.

Tucker, Evelyn. *Worldly Wonder: Religions Enter Their Ecological Phase.* Chicago and La Salle, IL: Open Court, 2003.

Vakili, Valla. *Debating Religion and Politics in Iran: The Political Thought of Abdolkarim Sorush.* New York: Council on Foreign Relations, 1997.

Contributors

R. Scott Appleby is Professor of History at the University of Notre Dame, where he also serves as the John M. Reagan Jr. Director of the Joan B. Kroc Institute for International Peace Studies. From 1993 to 2002 Appleby directed Notre Dame's Cushwa Center for the Study of American Catholicism. From 1988 to 1993 he was, with Martin E. Marty, the co-director of the Fundamentalism Project, an international public policy study conducted by the American Academy of Arts and Sciences which eventuated in five volumes, a number of which Appleby edited. His most recent book is *The Ambivalence of the Sacred: Religion, Violence and Reconciliation* (Rowman and Littlefield, 2000).

Gregory Baum is professor emeritus at McGill University's (Montreal) Faculty of Religious Studies. During the Vatican Council II, Baum was a peritus at the Secretariat of Christian Unity. He served for twenty years as a member of the board of directors of *Concilium* and for forty years edited *The Ecumenist.* He presently serves on the editorial committee of the French-Canadian Jesuit monthly, *Relations*. Baum has written several books dealing with Catholic social teaching. His most recent book is *Amazing Church: A Catholic Theologian Remembers a Half-Century of Change* (Ottawa: Novalis, 2005).

Lisa Sowle Cahill is J. Donald Monan S.J. Professor at Boston College where she is the Director of Graduate Programs in Theology. She is a past president of the Catholic Theological Society of America (1992–93) and of the Society of Christian Ethics (1997–98). She has served on the editorial boards of *Concilium, Journal of Religious Ethics, Horizons* and *Journal of Law and Religion*. Her most recent book (of many) is *Family: A Christian Social Perspective* (Philadelphia: Fortress Press, 2000).

Michael Campbell-Johnston S.J. is presently a parish priest and Director of Besant House in Barbados. He was the founder and director of the Guyana Institute for Social Research and Action in Guyana and editor of the quarterly publication *GISRA*. He served as a lecturer in economics at the University of Guyana. He has also served as the Director of the Social Secretariat for the Society of Jesus in Rome (1975–1984) and was Director of the Jesuit Refugee Service of Central America and Mexico and El Salvador. He served as Provincial of the

British Province of the Society of Jesus and as Director of the Jesuit Development Service in El Salvador.

John A. Coleman S.J. is the Charles Casassa Professor of Social Justice at Loyola Marymount University, Los Angeles. Coleman received his Ph.D in sociology from the University of California, Berkeley. Coleman served for seventeen years as an editor and a member of the foundation of *Concilium*. Among his seventeen edited or authored books are *One Hundred Years of Catholic Social Teaching* (Maryknoll, NY: Orbis, 1991). Coleman regularly teaches courses on Catholic Social Teaching (about which he has frequently written) and a course on globalization, ethics, and religion. Coleman has been a visiting faculty at the University of Chicago, Louvain University, Princeton, and the University of California, Santa Barbara. In 2005 Coleman will hold the Thomas More Chair at the University of Western Australia, Perth.

Fernando Franco S.J., originally from Spain, has spent decades working in India where he received a Ph.D. in Economics from Bombay University and taught Macroeconomics and Development Economics at St. Xavier's College, Ahmedabad. Franco worked extensively in training programs for dalit and tribal community organizers. His most recent books are *Pain and Awakening* (New Delhi: Indian Social Institute, 2002) and *Journeys to Freedom* (Calcutta: Stree, 2004), which deals with the ways, including conversion, dalits escape from caste discrimination. Franco is, at present, the Secretary for Social Justice at the Jesuit Curia at Rome.

J. Bryan Hehir is presently director of Catholic Charities, Boston, and Secretary for Public Policy in the cabinet of the Archbishop of Boston. Previously, he was President of Catholic Charities USA and directed the Office of International Affairs and the Department of Social and Political Affairs at the United States Catholic Conference where Hehir played a key role in the drafting of the American bishops' pastoral, *The Challenge of Peace*. Hehir has served as the Dean of the Divinity School at Harvard University and as the Joseph P. Kennedy Professor of Ethics at the School of Foreign Service, Georgetown University. Hehir's numerous publications include essays on the just war, the role of religion in world politics, and Catholic social teaching.

Peter Henriot S.J. holds a Ph.D. in Political Science from the University of Chicago. His main interests have been in the political economy of development. He was for many years a staff member at and then the director of the Center of Concern, Washington, D.C. Since 1989 Henriot has worked in Zambia where is the director of the Jesuit Center for Theological Reflection, Lusaka and serves as a consultant for justice, peace, and development with the Zambia Catholic Bishops' Conference. Henriot has written extensively in the areas of social analysis, development, and the Church's social teaching.

Joe Holland holds a Ph.D in Theology from the University of Chicago with a specialization in social ethics. He has been a Fulbright Scholar at the Catholic University of Santiago in Chile and currently is a Professor of Philosophy at Saint Thomas University in Miami, Florida. Holland is also the President of the United States federation of *Pax Romana* and serves as a permanent visiting Professor at the Andean University of Peru in Puno. Holland was for fifteen years a scholar-activist at the Center of Concern in Washington, D.C. where he co-authored the book *Social Analysis: Linking Faith and Justice* (Maryknoll, NY: Orbis, 1983). He has written hundreds of articles on issues of spirituality, work, social analysis, and Catholic social teaching. His most recent book is *Modern Catholic Social Teaching: 1740–1958: The Popes Confront the Industrial Age* (Maryknoll, NY: Orbis, 2004).

James E. Hug S.J. holds a Ph.D in Christian Ethics from the University of Chicago. Hug taught at the Jesuit School of Theology, Chicago and was a fellow at the Woodstock Center at Georgetown University. In 1985 he joined the Washington-based Center of Concern of which he has been the President/ Executive Director since 1989. Hug organized an international conference on Social Responsibility in the Age of Globalization to celebrate the twenty-fifth anniversary of the Center of Concern. Hug serves on the board of the International Jesuit Network for Development and of CIDSR (Coopération Internationale pour le Développement et la Solidarité). Among his books are *Tracing the Spirit: Communities, Social Action and Theological Reflection* (Mahwah, NJ: Paulist, 1983), and the revised edition of *Catholic Social Teaching: Our Best Kept Secret* (Maryknoll, NY: Orbis, 2003).

Farhang Rajaee is an Associate Professor of Political Science and Humanities at Carleton University in Canada. He holds a Ph.D. in foreign affairs from the University of Virginia. His research specializes in political theory and international relations with an emphasis on non-Western traditions, particularly modern Islamic Political Thought. He taught in Iran from 1986 to 1996. He has been a fellow at St. Anthony's College, Oxford University, and at the Zentrum Moderner Orient in Berlin. His most recent book is *Globalization on Trial* (Ottawa: International Development Research Centre, 2000).

William F. Ryan S.J. holds a Ph.D. in economics from Harvard University. He is the founding director of the Center of Concern, Washington, D.C., and has served as the Jesuit Provincial of the English Canadian province and general secretary of the Canadian Conference of Catholic Bishops. Ryan is presently the Coordinator of the Jesuit Centre for Social Faith and Justice (Ottawa office) and has recently served as a Special Advisor to the International Development Research Centre, Ottawa where he directed a study on the relationship between science, development, and religion. His most recent book is *The Lab, The Temple and the Market: Expanding the Conversation* (Ottawa: International Development Research Centre, 2000). A book about his life, *Faith and Freedom: The Life* *and Times of Bill Ryan S.J.,* has been published by Bob Chodos and Jamie Swift (Ottawa: Novalis, 2000).

Arturo Sosa S.J. is a political scientist who has most recently finished a seven-year term as the Jesuit Provincial of Venezuela. Previously, he had served as the Vice Chancellor of the Jesuit University in Caracas, where he taught political science and the history of Venezuela. For ten years Sosa served as the editor of the journal *SIC*. Sosa has published over ten books and was recently frequently interviewed about the political situation in Venezuela and the call for a referendum to remove President Chavez (cf. his two articles, "Del Choque de Trenes al Programma Minimo" and "Conyunturo Venezolano," in *America Latina en Movimiento* 2002).

Mary Evelyn Tucker is professor of religion at Bucknell University in Pennsylvania. She received her Ph.D. from Columbia University in history of religions, specializing in Confucianism in Japan, where she has lived for several years. With her husband, John Grim, Tucker directed a series of ten conferences on World Religions and Ecology at the Center for the Study of World Religions at Harvard Divinity School from 1996-1998, which have eventuated in ten volumes published by Harvard University Press. She is the author of *Worldly Wonder: Religions Enter Their Ecological Phase* (Chicago: Open Court Press, 2003) and co-editor (with Tu Weiming) of *Confucian Spirituality* (New York: Crossroad, 2003). With John Grim, Tucker edited a special issue of *Daedalus* on "Religion and Ecology: Can the Climate Change?" (Fall, 2001); they coordinate the ongoing Forum on Religion and Ecology.

Wendy Tyndale has an MA in Spanish and French and a B.Phil from St. Andrews University in Scotland and has lived extensively abroad in Chile, India, Peru, Germany, and Guatemala. She has worked for Amnesty International and the Latin America Department of Christian Aid. From 1998 to 2001, Tyndale coordinated World Faiths Development Dialogue, an interreligious dialogue between people from different religious traditions and the World Bank on poverty and development. Since 2001, she has been a researcher for World Faiths Development Dialogue. She has written widely on case studies on development and religion.

Johan Verstraeten is Professor of Theological Ethics at the University of Louvain, Leuven, Belgium. He has been the director of the Center for Ethics at that university and also has served as the director and chair of the European Ethics Network. Verstraeten's Ph.D. dissertation at Leuven was *Between Powerless Moralism and Amoral Power: The Ethics of Justified Defense.* He co-edited the volume *Catholic Social Thought: Twilight or Renaissance?* (Leuven: Peeters/ Leuven University Press, 2000). Verstraeten has been an advisor to the Belgium Bishops' Conference on issues of society, globalization, and ethics.

Index